TITO SANTANA: DON'T CALL ME CHICO

TITO SANTANA & KENNY CASANOVA

TITO SANTANA: DON'T CALL ME CHICO

Copyright © 2019 by Walking on Hot Waffles Publishers
in conjunction with Kenny Casanova & WOHW.com

ISBN: 978-1-941356-09-8

Printed in the USA

CREDITS:

Written by Tito Santana & Kenny Casanova
Editor Brandi Mankiewicz
Published by WOHW Publishing
Cover art by Jay Kay

WARNING:

© All rights reserved. No part of this book may be reproduced or transmitted in any form or by any means whatsoever without express written permission from the author, except in the case of brief quotations embodied in critical articles and reviews. Please refer all pertinent questions to the author. Failure to do so could result in a figure-four leg lock, or a Flying Burrito.

All people in this publication were very important people in Tito Santana's life at one time or another. Therefore, we have tried to best recreate events, locations and conversations from Tito's memories of them, but in some cases, minor details have changed due to the effects of many years of steel chair shots to the head. In order to maintain anonymity, Tito has also changed the names of a few individuals, places, identifying characteristics, and details - such as physical properties, occupations and locations. Although the author and publisher have made every effort to ensure that the information in this book was correct at press time, the author and publisher do not assume and hereby disclaim any liability to any party for any loss, damage, or disruption caused by errors or omissions, whether such errors or omissions result from negligence, accident, or any other cause.

TABLE OF CONTENTS

CHAPTER ZERO 3
CHAPTER 1 – Kid Stuff 10
CHAPTER 2 – College 30
CHAPTER 3 – Training & Florida 44
CHAPTER 4 – Atlanta 70
CHAPTER 5 – Charlotte 87
CHAPTER 6 – All Japan 100
CHAPTER 7 – Texas 115
CHAPTER 8 – WWWF 125
CHAPTER 9 – New Japan 144
CHAPTER 10 – AWA 149
CHAPTER 11 – Making Connections 163
CHAPTER 12 – Screwed By Ole Again 168
CHAPTER 13 – Back In The WWF 176
CHAPTER 14 – Intercontinental Champion 186
CHAPTER 15 – Greg Valentine 200
CHAPTER 16 – WrestleMania I & II 216
CHAPTER 17 – Fame 257
CHAPTER 18 – Strike Force 286
CHAPTER 19 – El Matador 308
CHAPTER 20 – Taking The Heat 333
CHAPTER 21 – More Road Stories 354
CHAPTER 22 – ECW 367
CHAPTER 23 – AWF 375
CHAPTER 24 – Return to WWF 382
CHAPTER 25 – Semi-Retirement 392

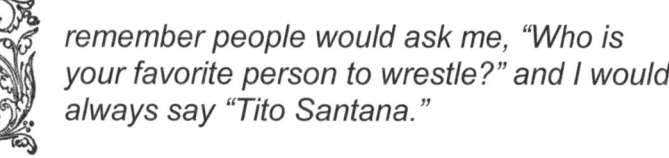remember people would ask me, "Who is your favorite person to wrestle?" and I would always say "Tito Santana."

For some reason, Tito's style and my own blended perfectly. Tito knew me. He really knew how I needed to work, and he was just so wonderful. He and I had matches together where the announcer would say "10 minutes gone" and we hadn't even touched each other. And yet, the people had been up and out of their seats probably three times.

Tito would allow me to be me in the ring, and his timing was always just phenomenal. And when it was his time, he trusted me to be there for him and knew I would give it to him, because you got to give the babyface their due. You know? You got to let them beat you up at some point so you can be a coward.

–Jesse Ventura

CHAPTER ZERO

"Attention!"

I didn't really know what to do, because I hadn't really taught at this level before. I had somewhere in the area of 20 students, all at the absolute lowest level.

In the past, I did one-on-one type teaching stuff for Vince, like traveling around with The Warlord to show him the ropes. But this kind of teaching to a group was different. This type of training had to be much more structured and organized than whatever I had ever done in the past. Even though I thought I was prepared, it seemed like nobody in the room was listening, nor even cared who I was.

"Attention!" I repeated.

Twenty heads continued to ignore me in unison.

"I said ... ATTENTION!"

Okay, yes, it sounded like I was stealing Slaughter's catchphrase, but didn't figure I would get called out on any sort of gimmick infringement on the account of how young they were.

I looked around the gym. Some of them were wrestling around on the mat, others were jumping up and down like crazy, working up some high levels of cardio. They were all doing their own thing.

They did not seem too nervous that there was a new sheriff in town. If anybody was nervous, it was me.

The mainstream population is so fragmented with interests today. They are used to being hit from everywhere with content that tries to compete for their attention. I assumed I was going to have to work even harder. I figured there was no way that my past, or my fame, or whatever, was going to help me win them over. Even if they had seen a picture that somebody Googled, or maybe heard who I was from a relative, I figured that none of that was going to matter. I was going to really have to earn their respect by showing how knowledgeable I was and not by whatever name factor I was bringing to the table.

I looked down at the notes on my clipboard and nervously realized that I had one last resort hanging around my neck so I used it.

TWEET!!! TWEEEEEETTT!!!

I blew the whistle.

The twenty-something students all stopped like deer in headlights.

Wow. That actually worked.

The group realized I meant business and need to talk to them about business stuff before we started.

One ran toward me. Then another sheep saw and followed. Then another. After that, the whole herd came running and fell into place, finally giving me an opportunity to speak.

"So, I know that a lot of you have had other people in here trying to show you the way in the past, but now it is my turn. And I think if you give me a chance and listen to me, I can help you become successful in the future."

Some nodded at my words. I felt like I finally was getting their attention.

I thought back to the old days of when I was training in the Florida territory. What our trainers did back then was start by running us rough. This included tiring us out every single day from the very first minute. Before we did any of the "cool stuff," they would hit us hard with exercise to see who had what it took. I figured that was exactly what I needed to do. Where them out and conquer.

"What we are going to do today before we get into anything else is to focus on our fitness. In order to move on to bigger and better things down the road, we must make sure that our bodies are healthy and able to bring us down these paths. So, therefore, we will not be doing anything on the mats or anything else today inside these walls," I said to many faces of disappointment.

I finally felt like I had them in the palm of my hand.

"Do you want to do well? In order for the doors of opportunity to open up for us in the future, we will have to be able to motivate ourselves to reach out and open those doors for ourselves when nobody else will do it for us. And today, we will start with those doors right over there and get to work."

They heard what I had to say. I hit them with the same type of motivational speech that Hiro Matsuda hit me and guys like Hulk Hogan with back when we walked into his gym back in the early 70s. I figured if this worked for us, it would work for them.

I had them. At this moment, I looked over their faces and saw them trying to imagine their futures.

"Are you ready?"

The group nodded.

"Okay then. We will start with running. Everybody get into a line. And when I open the doors, we will go. And you won't stop until I blow the whistle. Okay?"

They agreed.

I opened the doors. Daylight hit the floor on our gym. If I had known the sun would have come in as it did, I probably would have worked that into my promo before this. But regardless, it had finally begun.

They all jogged out in a line. They stayed organized for about 30 seconds, but then started to scramble. They didn't care about the old timer being brought in to teach them how to do things "like we did in the olden days." They were all running still, but spilling out of the line and eventually were all over the place.

I blew the whistle ... and they just kept on going.

"Stop!" I said, blowing the whistle again. "STOP!!!"

Nobody listened.

Disrespect maybe? Or was it just an age thing?

The twenty-plus students were swarming all over the place. In the distance, I could see a handful of them actually trying to climb the fence to make a break for it.

Oh my god, this is bullshit.

Now, to be clear, these weren't wrestling students that I could just go over and stretch for being assholes. I had to figure out what to do with these preschoolers, and what to do fast!

I surveyed the situation. The ones closest to me were not an immediate threat as far as losing anyone was concerned. So I huddled over them to go after the others in the distance. In doing so, I tripped and fell over a few of them and we all went down like dominos. They all had a good laugh for a second but went right back into swarm mode.

I blew the whistle again. About five of the students got into a line formation and started running in circles. I shook my head. One of the preschoolers was almost at the top of the fence and I knew that would really be trouble. Borrowing from my old football days, I sprinted to the far end of the school's property. I grabbed him just as he was about to pass over the top and tucked him under my arm.

Pass interception!

Then I looked to my right, about a half a football field away. Another little boy was trying to do the same thing. I ran to him as fast as I could. I pulled him down and tucked him under my other arm.

Both of them, of course, were laughing their asses off.

Those little bastards!

Running out of breath towards the gym, I gathered two more of them up and pushed them back through my bullshit "doors of opportunity."

"Stay in here!" I said as I returned to gather the rest of the herd.

One by one, looking like a deleted scene out of *Kindergarten Cop*, I grabbed kids and scooped them up the best that I could. I was holding one under my arm, and another by the back of his shirt. Finally, I got to the last one. It was a little girl, all by herself, standing in the middle of the yard.

"Ok, I need you to get in the gym," I pointed.

She shook her head.

"I need you to go now!"

She shook her head again and then started to pick at her clothing.

That is when I realized she had shit her pants.

When I finally convinced her to follow me back over to the school, I remembered back to the day when my wife was trying to convince me to become a teacher in the first place.

"It's very easy," she said. "One you get the hang of it, you will love it. Weekends and summers off for you to go off to gigs. It will be a piece of cake."

A piece of cake? Yeah, right.

Back in the gym, I did a head count the best I could, then stuck my head out in the hallway and found a hall monitor.

"Can you watch these kids a second, I need to grab the school nurse. One had an, um, accident in here."

The monitor laughed, but obliged.

While running frantically down the hall to find the school nurse who could clean the girl up with an industrial-sized pooper scooper in a hazmat outfit, I ran by the Principal's office and stopped.

There is the culprit.

I was assigned to be a gym teacher at Bound Brook Elementary Bound Brook, New Jersey. My job was to teach to third, fourth, fifth and sixth graders. Not preschoolers!

For my first three weeks as a middle school gym teacher, everything was going just fine. Everything was fine that is until the principal decided to throw a curve ball at me; he gave me an extra class to teach of all little kids.

It turned out exactly as I thought it would… *terrible!*

"How are things going, Mr. Solis?"

"I blow my whistle, and the kids just keep on running," I said. "I am sorry, but I just am not trained to be a pre-k teacher."

"No problem," she said, smiling. "We can give you the training."

She walked out of her office and had me follow.

"I am afraid that the only way I'm going to be able to teach those kids is if I just keep them locked up in the gym."

She listened, but kept walking. When we got back to the gymnasium, she opened the doors. She walked through the battlefield and ignored all the chaos and opened a closet.

The principal turned, counted heads, and then grabbed something from behind the doors. When she returned, she tossed a big pile of hula-hoops in the center of the gym. The kids came running.

One by one, the kids picked up the plastic tubing in amazement and started spinning and spinning and spinning.

In less than 30 seconds, order was completely restored. She laughed. She looked like a world champion who had just successfully defended her title.

On her way out the door, she reached down for little miss poopy pants and disappeared down the hall.

Without really looking at me or saying a word, she turned and walked out of there like her shit didn't stink (even the one kid's had started to.)

"How did she do that?" I asked one of the preschoolers who was spinning away on the hulahoop like it was the greatest invention in the world.

He shrugged. He didn't answer my question and kept right on spinning… (right along with my head, that is.)

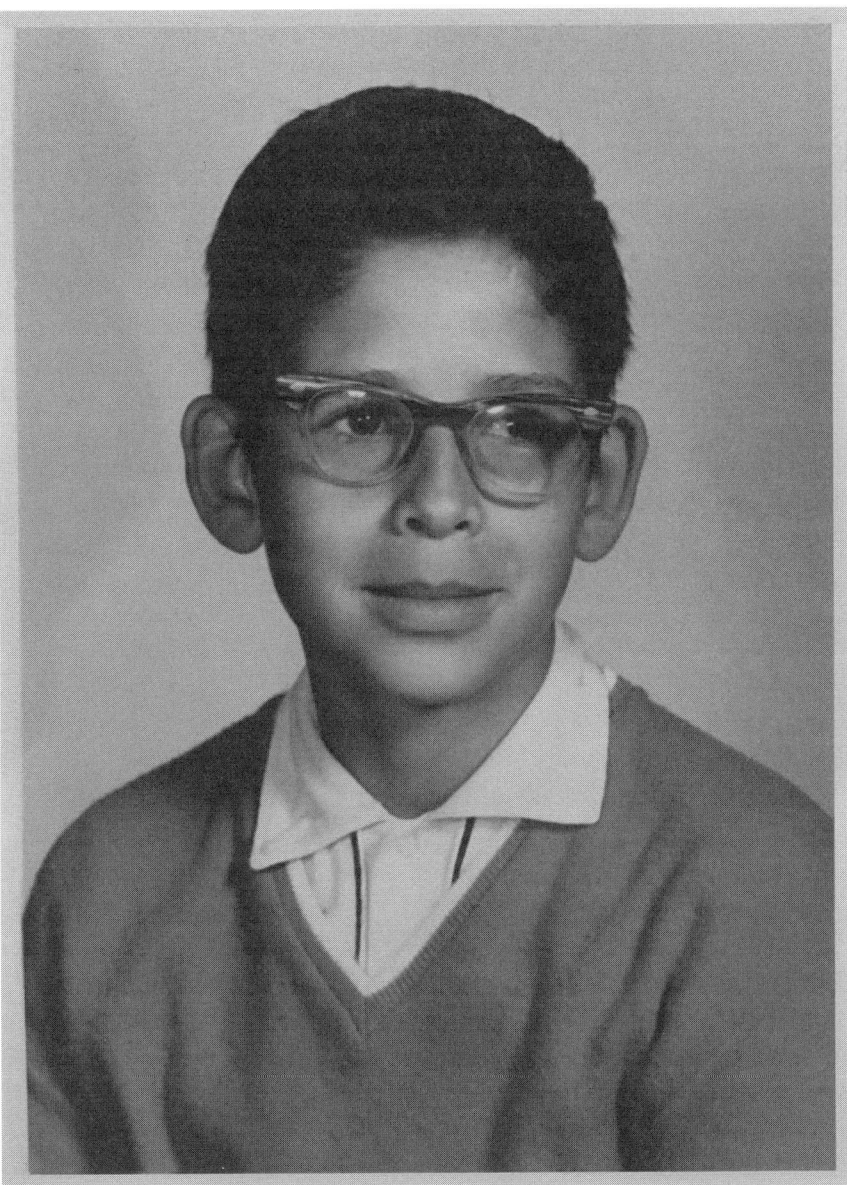

CHAPTER 1 - KID STUFF

In 1953, I was born in a small city called Mission, Texas, which is about 250 miles south of San Antonio and probably 75 miles west of the Gulf of Mexico. The city is at the southern tip of the state, about five miles away from the Mexican Border along the Rio Grande Valley. In this tropical area, about 90 percent of the people there were Mexican. Farming is the main industry in Mission. Since 1921, they have advertised themselves as being the "Home of the Ruby Red Grapefruit" due to the vast amounts of that fruit being commonly grown in the area.

My parents were migrant farm workers, like most everyone in Mission. They got married when my mother (Juanita Cavazos Solis) was 30 years old, and my father (Merced Solis) was 31. It's funny because my mom's family was pretty well off, her parents owned an entire block of houses in Mission that they rented out, while my dad came from a family of poor farm laborers.

My dad was a farmer. Like many people who come from a farming family, he wanted a big family so that he could put everyone out to work in the fields. Therefore, I had three sisters, Viola, Belia and Dalia, and one brother, Roberto. Unfortunately, our dear sister Dalia was born with cystic fibrosis and died very young.

We didn't have a lot, but that was all we knew. We lived in a small two-bedroom house that was given to us by my grandparents. My brother and I shared a wobbly bed with our dad, and my two sisters shared another one on its last legs with my mom. For most of my childhood, I never lived in a house that had running water, but my mom had pride and kept our house immaculate. She was always busy ironing our clothes and fixing us three home-cooked meals a day.

My mother was the oldest of sixteen kids, herself. Because of this, she knew how to bring order to chaos. In our house, she was always the glue that held us together. She was very strict while my siblings and I were growing up, and made sure we didn't veer off course too much. She was never shy about speaking her mind and was straightforward

CHAPTER 1 – Kid Stuff

and to the point. However, as much as she ruled with an iron fist, she also was very loving. I remember us kissing her often as a child and comparing all our love to that of little parakeets, like the ones my grandmother kept as pets. (I mean, *look at me*. What's not to love?)

Actually, I wasn't always the perfect model son for her to raise. In fifth grade, I started hanging around with a group of kids that mom didn't like. They were destructive and swore a lot. They were pretty much known as the "bad kids" around the neighborhood. I refused to quit spending time with them. I guess I have a history of hanging out with heels.

"Were you with those boys again, Nuné?" she asked me one day when I came home. She was getting dinner together and I couldn't see her face but knew she was angry.

"…"

"That's it," she warned, finally having enough. "You think I am playing around with you but I am not." She stopped what she was doing. She turned around and slammed some dishes down so hard I thought they were going to break.

"What mama?"

"I told you before," she said. "If I saw you with them again, I was going to have to do something to split you guys up and that's just what I'm going to do."

"They aren't so bad," I argued. "What do you mean?"

"I know you didn't see me, but I saw you today with them, and it's already too late. I called a reform school and enrolled you."

"You what?"

Oh no! Reform school; prison for kids!

She grabbed me by my hand and went over to the boy's bedroom. She pulled out a large suitcase and threw it on the bed.

"Now, Nuné, I hate to do this, but pack up your stuff and let's get going." At that, my mother took a stack of my clothing and threw it on the bed. "Better finish up because you are getting picked up before supper." I was crying a little so she started packing that old suitcase for me. Once it was full, she led me out to the stoop and made me sit and wait for whoever was coming.

I sat out on the stairs in silence. A few kids walked by that I knew from down the way. They didn't say anything and ran off. They knew I was in some kind of trouble.

The hour or so I spent waiting, seemed like days, weeks, months even. I was sweating like crazy every time a car drove near the house.

Is this it? Are they coming for me?

A car pulled up. It was somewhat official looking and my heart was pounding.

"I'm a goner."

But then, the car kept going.

It started getting dark. When no one showed up, my mom finally came and looked through the old screen door.

"They must have gotten lost," she said. "Well, I guess you are lucky. Might as well go to bed." She said it so calmly that I believed her. Looking back on this now, I think maybe she figured I learned my lesson. She handed me a sandwich and I was off to my room.

Needless to say, the next day I saw soe of the riff raff that my mom didn't like. I was nervous but knew I had to talk to them one more time to cut things off. "I'm sorry but I'm not allowed to hang out with you anymore."

They looked up at me puzzled. "Huh?" one said.

"Bye," I said and I took off running. After that, I eventually found new friends who met my mother's approval.

Speaking of running, if you are wondering where I got my athletic genes from, it was mostly my father. He was a big man with broad shoulders, about 6'1" and 220 pounds. He was, I guess, a very handsome man whose family came right over to America from Spain. He had a light complexion and always wore a Stetson cowboy hat & cowboy boots. He had "the look."

Unlike my mom who was always there for us, my dad wasn't around much even when we were young, especially if it was a weekend. When he wasn't working, he liked his time off.

CHAPTER 1 – Kid Stuff

My dad wasn't really a drinker, but he liked to frequent the local cantinas. He really liked to dance and socialize with women. He also liked playing pool at the local pool halls.

Quite often, he would come home from a hard day's work. My mother would have plans for the evening, but my father usually had something different in mind.

"Merced," she would say, "Are we still on for dinner?"

"Dinner?" he would repeat. "Oh, yes dinner. I have to finish up some work, but yes, after that. Dinner of course."

"Dinner it is!" She'd say and kiss him on the cheek.

"Make sure everybody gets cleaned up good and ready to go, and I'll be back in a little bit," he would say, rushing out the door.

So we would wait a little bit, then a little bit longer. A little bit became a long time and dinner would never come.

This happened a lot. He would tell the family that he was taking us out for dinner. We would get all dressed up nice and await his return, but then it just wouldn't happen. Sometimes, he wouldn't return until early the next morning.

The next morning, the door would creak open. My poor mom would pull him outside to confront him, as to not upset us. However, we had thin walls. Out in the yard, she would scream and shout after being let down, but he would just sit there and take it. We only really heard her voice.

My father would never speak up. In fact, he pretty much didn't speak at all. He never admitted to anything she accused him of; instead, he would respond with silence. It was just his way.

Late one Friday afternoon, I think my mother had finally learned. My father hadn't come back to the house yet with his empty promises and my mother was already loading us into the car, driving us off for a nice dinner *without him*.

"Where is dad?" my brother Roberto asked from the back seat.

"He's like never here on the weekends anymore," Belia added.

"He's just got some kind of business to do," I remember mom explaining to us being as protective as she could be.

"But how?" Roberto asked. "Where does he go?"

"Some Fridays," she explained, "He just parks his truck at the Mexican border, takes a cab across and does his business."

"When is he coming back?" Belia asked.

"Don't worry. He will be back soon. Now, let's not worry about that and have us a good supper."

He didn't return until Monday morning.

Despite his overly "social" lifestyle, however, my father was still a good provider for his family. He took good care of us and there was always money and there was always food on the table. However, there just is no doubt about it that he was a horrible husband to my mother.

MIGRANT WORK

Like most of the other migrant kids at our school, we would miss the first six weeks and the last six weeks of the school year because of work. That is when we would all be out working the fields for harvesting and the families depended on this time as the majority of their incomes sometimes for the year.

The school system had a built-in afterschool program made to help us catch up. It was like a fast track tutoring thing that would go on throughout the year constantly. If they didn't make this accommodation for migrating students, we would have been left in the scholastic dust, so to speak. These special migrant family catch-up programs were important because, for families like us, this is how we got promoted from grade to grade each year despite missing so much class time.

The thing about it is, not only was the school part hard but so was the work. Migrating means moving. This meant we were always on the go. Our work helped make us very disciplined as kids, but the whole thing was very carnie like in nature, always setting up shop in a new town, doing what had to be done, then moving on to the next one... *just like wrestling.*

(ABOVE) Me picking tomatoes Oct '66. (BELOW) My father and his crew.

The harvesting routine for my family was always the same; first, we went to Milford, Illinois to pick asparagus; from there we moved to Wisconsin or Michigan to pick cherries or strawberries. Then next, in early September, we would move to Indiana to pick tomatoes and we stayed there until the about the middle of October or until the frost ruined the tomato crop. During the Christmas holidays, we would pick oranges, grapefruits or carrots. When March came around, we would pick onions after school and on weekends.

The first time I can remember, it was the middle of April. My siblings and I got pulled out of school. We were very excited as we packed into our brand new blue and white 1956 Chevy Bel Air, which my dad had purchased new off the lot after a lot of hard work. As we got ready for the road trip, my grandparents who lived next door came by and slid mom $20 to help pay for food for us kids. It was our first trip as a family. Little did I know that traveling would become a way of life for the rest of our life and that our summer vacations from school would always be spent working.

That was the very first trip I can remember taking as a migrant worker. I was six. We were excited. The kids and I pictured that we were going to a beautiful splendid place with fun and laughter. We talked about what we thought we would see together in the back of that car, whispering back and forth for what seemed like an eternity.

"I bet they have a playground... and a Ferris Wheel!"

"A Ferris Wheel?!" my brother laughed.

After two days on the road, we finally pulled up to a farm in the middle of nowhere in Milton, Illinois.

"Here we are," my dad said, popping the trunk as we began to collect our things. And that is when we set up in our new mysterious home ... *some cheap aluminum shed next to a dairy farm that looked like what it smelled like.*

COW MANURE

When we went inside the barracks that first time, I remember looking at my brother. He wrinkled his face and pinched his nose. "Uggghhh!!!" he laughed.

CHAPTER 1 – Kid Stuff

I'll never forget the nasty smell of the cow manure thick in the air. The stink almost burned my nostrils.

The rooms in the migrant worker quarters were small with no inside facilities at all. The bathrooms and all where outside in a different place. Inside, we had just an aluminum wall separating us from our neighbors on both sides.

Sadly, there was no Ferris Wheel, but our heads were spinning from the smell. On the bright side, we did each have our own bed, and the room came fully-equipped with a small gas stove and a small refrigerator.

As we unpacked our belongings and started to make do with what we had, my mother went right to work like she had done it probably a hundred times before.

I watched from my new cot as my mother started laying fresh mouse traps in the corners.

At seven o'clock sharp the next morning, we began our first day at the farm. We opened the door and went outside right alongside another 150 other migrant workers. We went over to a long shelving rack and found baskets.

I actually get my own basket!

"Wooo!" Roberto yelled as we followed the line of workers. Not knowing what we were all really in for, my brothers and sisters and I were actually excited about working with our parents.

When we got out into the field, I looked around at the new sights. For as far as I could see it was just soil, with long rows of leafy green. My dad disappeared for a minute then rushed back. Then he went ahead of us, rustling around inside one the long lines of crop for the perfect specimen.

"Here," he said, as he held out the treasure he found; a *stalk of asparagus*. He went on to give us our instructions. "I just talked to the boss," he told us. "This is the size we want you to put in the baskets. Any questions?"

"Yes. Just one," I asked. *"What is that?!"*

My dad laughed. "Asparagus."

"*As-pair-ah-guss*," I repeated. "Never heard of that before. People eat this?"

Asparagus was new to us. The vegetable grew from the ground up, and we would break it off, leaving behind a couple of inches. The smaller asparagus were left behind for future picking.

"Alright, *Nuné*," my mother said. "Now you know."

"Yes, mom," I said.

My mother always called me by my nickname, "*Nuné*," which, by the way, means "Junior" in Spanish.

"*Nuné*," she said to me smiling a little. "You come with me and help me fill my basket. Belia, you go with your dad."

"Okay," I replied. I started walking right behind her along the long rows in a sing-song fashion, pointing at the crop. "Asparagus. Asparagus. Asparagus."

Mom glanced at me, then quickly upward and shook her head. "May the good Lord help us!"

After that first day, I think my mother would always say that Lord line every time we went out to the fields.

My dad and mom were not slave drivers at all. They were very nice to us and realized that we were just kids. They didn't expect too much and mostly just let us work at our own pace. Anything we accomplished at was extra.

"We will work for an hour and then we can stop and eat breakfast, okay?" It was an achievable goal that kept us working without much complaining.

After some work, we would head back to the cabins. My mom would make breakfast at eight o'clock in the morning, then lunch around noon, and then a smaller meal/snack around four in the afternoon.

We always ate as a family, usually on the ground, with a big blanket laid out picnic-style. They were actually pretty happy times and we would laugh a lot. We did a lot of bonding, living so close together in foreign parts of the country.

After we finished eating, my dad would usually officially end the meal by saying, "Are we ready? Full stomach, happy heart, let's go back to work!"

After that third meal, we usually worked until six o'clock in the evening.

Every night, after we came back from work, we would have another meal in the living quarters.

"Okay children," she would say. "It's time to clean the dirt off of you so you will be fresh for the morning. After my mother finished feeding us, she'd heat up a big bucket of water and wash the dirt off all four of us kids before bed.

PREJUDICE

You are not born being prejudice. It is something you have to learn. If you put a black baby next to a white baby, they will just play together like there is not a difference in the world. The difference comes much later in life from hearing what people say around you.

There is so much to learn in life, especially when you grow up as a minority. Certain things can only be learned by experience and learning how things work for you in certain situations. With that being said, I was introduced to prejudice early on the hard way.

I knew that I was different from a lot of the folks from back around my real home. I had a lot of little different things that had to happen for me at school. For one, I wasn't there all the time. I think because of that, sometimes the other students who did not come from similar like families would look at me like I was different. This "look" is something I can't explain to someone who has never seen it before, only other than saying it felt like they saw you as being inferior. Sadly, I also sometimes would get the same second-rate citizen look from some of the teachers.

Sometimes when us farmer kids would leave, heading off to say the northern states to work as migrants, we would all group up to travel together in the back of a truck. I remember it almost felt like the "Cowboys and Indians" movies that we would see advertised. It felt like we were all crowding into a covered wagon to head off to a new frontier, off into the sunset, into the wild, wild west.

I sometimes felt special, until the next time I got the "look" again. Then, I was brought back down to reality.

I didn't hate what I was, or who I was. I just couldn't understand why some people would stare at us when we would stop to eat at a truck stop. I can't say I heard any laughter or snide remarks from onlookers, but the stares alone cut pretty deep. Whenever we stopped to have a meal somewhere on one of our many journeys, after I became aware of this "look," I started to actually look for it myself. Whenever I saw it, however, I didn't like it.

I wanted something better for all of us.

LITTLE ROMEO

My first real serious experience with prejudice did not come about because of race, but more so because of social class. Back at school as a tenth grader, I remember falling in love for the first time with someone who I thought at the time was the most beautiful girl in the world, Carmen.

Carmen was a pretty Mexican girl who came from a well-to-do family in our town, Mission. Her father was a very successful doctor and her mother worked at her family's business. One day, Carmen invited me over to her house in my sophomore year of high school. While I was waiting for her to get ready so we could go see a movie, I was shown in and over to a seat to sit on their nice sofa.

"Hello," an older man said.

"Hello," I replied.

"I am Carmen's grandfather," he said, smoothing back his well-groomed white beard.

"Pleased to meet you, sir," I said.

"So, where do you live?" he started with what seemed like a pretty innocent line of questioning. But even before I could complete my answer he would start the next question, and the next one,   and the next one. "Who is your father? ...Who is your mother? ...Where does your father work? What does he do in his free time? ...What kind of car?"

The pleasantries ended right away. It felt like the room darkened and out of the ceiling dropped one of those ugly naked lightbulbs on a string like you would see in a Dick Tracy comic book. I was right in the middle of an interrogation room.

It was very clear that I was being grilled for information and my own answers as a whole startled me.

After being questioned by her grandfather, wanting to know everything he could about my family right down to the type of soap we used... after drowning in his stream of questions, I tried to come up for some air to breathe.

Since I was poor and her family was well-off, I have to admit, I was embarrassed by what I found myself saying to his line of questioning. Even though I was honest about everything I said, I felt like I had failed the test.

We left anyhow, and I soon forgot about Detective Grandpa. We had a blast at the movies. I had saved up my lunch money to buy those tickets, and even enough for the popcorn to impress her. Being a romantic at heart, I remember looking over at her during the film and wondering if she would be with me forever. I wondered if she was my future wife, and if we would have a big family one day.

The next day at school, I thought about our date all morning and couldn't wait to see her again. When I went to lunch, I sat down hoping to see her. Then, like clockwork, there she was. I saw her in the lunch line. My heart pounded.

I anticipated her arrival, but after she got her tray, she did something really odd. She set up the spot for her meal a few tables away from me first, before walking my way.

"Hey, Carmen!" I said smiling ear to ear.
"Hey, Merced," she replied.
"I had fun last night at the movies," I said.
"I did, too," she said, "but I have some bad news."
"Oh?"
"I'm sorry, but my family just doesn't want us to see each other anymore."

That son-of-a-bitch.

And there it was. That was the first time I was made to feel less than someone else over something that I had absolutely no control over. It was then I first realized that, in the future, I needed to take control of these situations and not allow others to hold me back from things that I wanted.

Yes, I was forbidden to date Carmen.

But that didn't stop me... we still dated for over two years behind her parents' backs! ¡Arriba!

SPORTS

Throughout high school, I would experience even more discrimination, of sorts. I was called "Mexican" in a derogatory sense by some of my white "friends." These comments bothered me at first, but eventually (even though I shouldn't have had to) I learned how to tell which comments were harmless and which ones were meant to hurt me.

One time at lunch, I was carrying my tray of food as I walked by a line of some kids who looked different than I did. One of them said something under his breath that I couldn't really understand, but I did hear something about me being a "Mexican." Again, I didn't hear exactly what he was saying about me, but I didn't need to. His little circle around him laughed at the words.

Something snapped. I never did anything wrong to anyone and didn't understand why people had to look at me as something less than what they were. I had had enough.

I sat my tray down on the table behind me, walked right up to the guy and punched him dead in the face.

I got into a few fights because of the name-calling. I had a short temper in high school. I knew I needed to grow out of that before I became an adult where I could really get in trouble for things, but didn't let that stop me at the time!

These early issues with prejudices and discrimination helped shape me into the person and professional I would eventually become. They made me strong. I also later learned valuable life-lessons in sports and a rule that helped me view the world differently; *Picking your battles is huge.*

I learned that sometimes it was better to overlook stupid and petty treatment from some people and find a way to fit in. This kind of tolerance was sometimes tough, but something that I found could really be worth considering. Getting into fist fights was going to get me nowhere fast.

In eighth grade, I first met my future football coach, a guy who would help discipline me into becoming something better. Louis Sanchez was a big man who had been an All-American catcher on the University of Texas baseball team.

One day in the middle of gym class, he called me into his office while the rest of the kids were playing around.

"How'd you like to try out for football?" he asked me.

"Me?"

"Yeah, you," he laughed. "You're great, and I think would do great on the team. I see a lot of potential in you."

I was speechless and caught completely by surprise. I was flattered, but I knew nothing about organized football.

CHAPTER 1 – Kid Stuff

Immediately, my preconditioned mind wandered and went somewhere that only a certain group of people can probably relate to and appreciate here. Football seemed cool and I really wanted to do it, but I thought I just couldn't. The reason for this was because there would be money involved which I knew I didn't have.

See, I saw the uniforms, and the pads, and the helmets. I thought a player had to pay for all his own gear, and I knew that my mom wouldn't go for that. We worked too hard for our money to spend it on a "luxury item" like football equipment. This money filter I had caused by growing up in a poor family also brings on a weird feeling of low self-esteem.

I also knew some of the other guys had already been playing for two years and were significantly more experienced than me. I immediately started thinking that the other players were huge and muscular, and was intimidated by them. Surely they had to be better than me.

"I'll have to ask my mother," I said, looking for an excuse not to look poor. "I don't think she will go for it. In fact, I think she would be totally against it, Coach."

"Tell your mother I will even drive you home after practice," Coach added, trying to sweeten the pot.

"I don't know," I said.

"Well, at least ask her," he said. "You can let me know tomorrow what she says."

That night, I wanted to ask my mother but figured I already knew what the answer would be, so I didn't.

I hadn't even bothered to ask Mom because I was also psyching myself out and becoming too scared to play.

The next day, I dreaded going to school. I knew Coach Sanchez was waiting for my answer, and I didn't want to look poor. My plan was just to avaoid him.

It was even worse than I expected. When I got there, the Coach was already waiting by my lockers.

"And?"

"I'm sorry," I said, looking away. "My mother won't allow it." But I guess he knew from my expression that I was lying.

"Okay," he smiled. "Maybe you can reconsider playing the next year."

Later on that year, Coach Sanchez was holding basketball tryouts. Even though I had never played, I decided to try out for the team and figured a jersey and shorts wouldn't cost as much as football stuff. This time around I had a different incentive for playing basketball.

Our school had an after-school study program for migrant students that was sometimes just brutal. Supposedly, the program was designed to help us catch up for the weeks we missed, but as far as I was concerned, it almost felt like the migrant students were being singled out and punished. They always had us doing what seemed like extra work, even if we hadn't missed any school. I hated it. So me and my good friend Louis Ortega tried out for the basketball team hoping it would make us exempt from the migrant student study hall program.

"Hey coach," I said, approaching him one day after school. "I know football was no good, but what about basketball?"

"Sure! You can try out," Coach said, looking up surprised to see me from something he was reading at his cluttered desk. "But I just need to warn you first. I've got all my starters coming back. We were undefeated last year, so I can't really guarantee you anything."

"That's good enough for me. All I want is a chance."

The idea of playing basketball just sounded way better than sitting in the migrant worker class afer school, writing why George killed Lenny at the end of the book.

In the end, I made the cut, but poor Louis had to go back to study hall and write haikus.

Therefore, in the end, I'm honestly proud to say, my scholastic laziness is what brought about my athletic career. Hey, you have to start somewhere!

During my junior and senior years in high school, I played basketball and learned that the school provided the uniforms for football, so I finally took that up, too!

CHAPTER 1 – Kid Stuff

I really enjoyed my time becoming an athlete. I couldn't believe the strides that I had made both on the football field and the basketball court. Most of the players worked out all year and went to training camps in the summer. However, I did none of that because I still needed to work in the fields to support my family. However, I think that the work on the asparagus field kept me sharp for the football field if that makes sense. In a weird way, it was almost like Mr. Miyagi training from *The Karate Kid*.

I also think I can attribute some of my success in sports to having some kind of natural athletic ability.

I played football very well in my senior year, starting as a running back and strong safety. However, from a statistical standpoint, I did even better at basketball, averaging 27.9 points per game as a 6'2" center going up against guys who were two to six inches taller!

Come the end of high school, even though I did great on the court, my team had a losing season and it was difficult for me to attract any attention from the college basketball scouts. I only received one basketball scholarship offer from San Marcos.

We had a losing season in football, too, but I was still good enough to be recruited in football over basketball. Two schools, in this case, offered me football scholarships; West Texas State and again San Marcos. Seeing that football was the best opportunity for me to get a tuition-free education, I accepted the full-ride offer from West Texas.

By this point, stuff was getting bad at home. I guess I picked West Texas State, in part, because it was actually further from home than San Marcos was. By my senior year, my dad and mom were on the verge of divorce. He was just making life for her miserable and she had had enough.

My two sisters were older than I was, and they had the right idea. They had gotten married young, also likely just to get out of the house. Seeing football as my best option for a new life, I decided to try to leave the old one behind, as far behind as possible. So I saw West Texas, in the town of Canyon, as being my new destination and hopefully the light at the end of the tunnel.

Can you guess which is me? (HINT: I'm one of the guys wearing glasses.)

Myself and one of my sisters, Viola Solis, in Texas back in 1969.

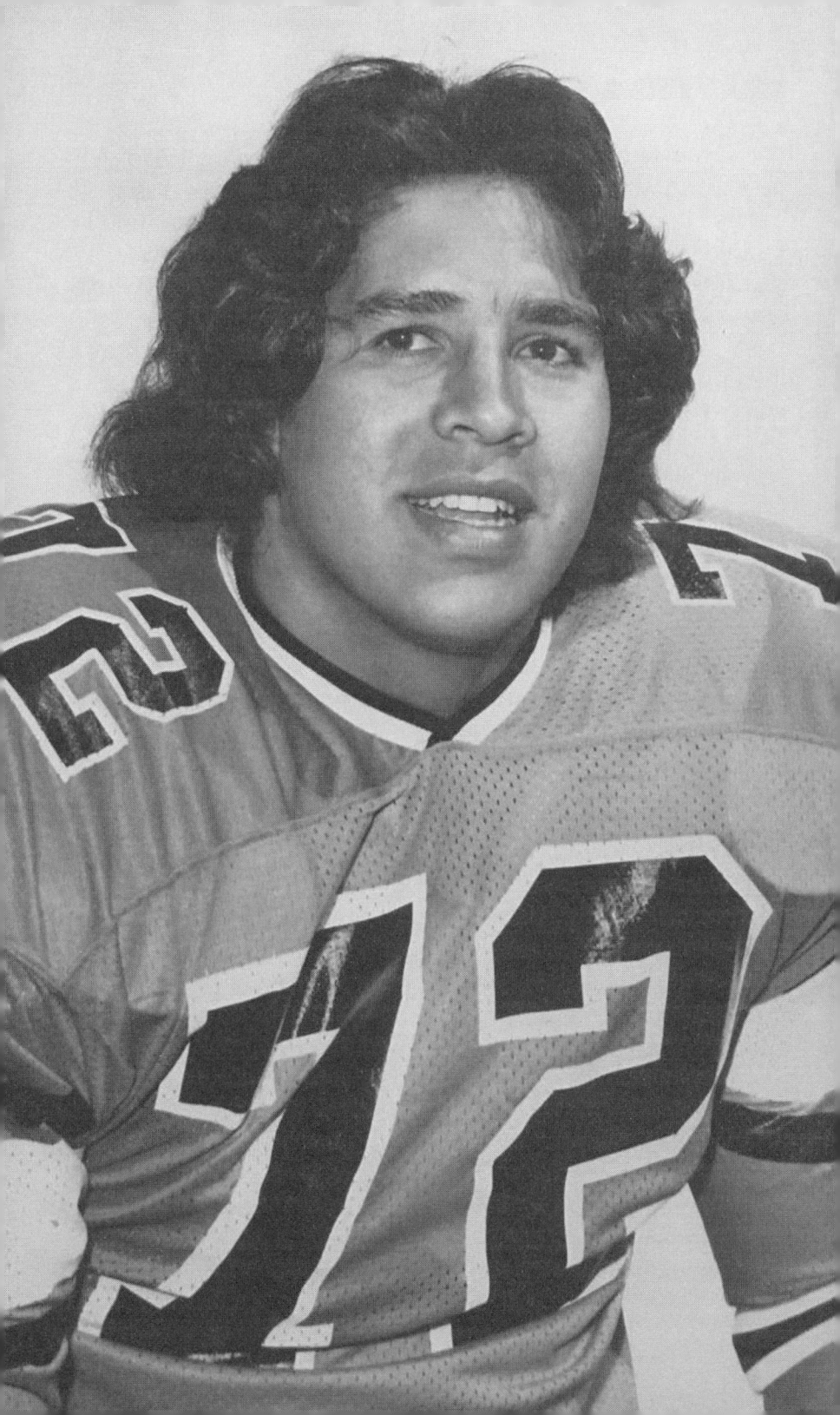

CHAPTER 2 - COLLEGE

When I started college in 1971, I was ready to go. A new world with new sights and new people to meet. West Texas University had around 6,600 students enrolled, and I figured none of them knew me. None of them knew my reputation of being one of the "poor kids," and it was a whole new fresh start for me.

West Texas, incidentally, was really better known for their business education program, but my major, of course, was physical education, and I was planning on owning it.

Unlike Mission, the city of Canyon was not very farm-friendly. The terrain itself was flat and almost desert like. The area was also notorious for sandstorms and tornadoes. It often got quite cold there, too. I didn't know why anyone would want to live there, but I kept my eyes focused on the goal; I was going to graduate and find success. I will say this, however. In my freshman year, I think I saw falling snow in person for the first time in my life. Even though I travelled a lot as a migrant worker, you never moved toward the snow in your loop, you always moved away from it.

College itself was a piece of cake for me. I had no problem making the adjustment, and soon I was getting the education that I always wanted, and it was all on their dime!

I loved playing football, so the biggest part of my "job" there was actually fun. All I had to do was play football and pass all of my classes. This was also something the coaches always made sure that we did as it was in their best interests. College was probably the best time of my life.

I still didn't have a lot of money. There were no real jobs in the area, so I just fell back on my conservative penny-pinching ways, but nobody ever knew it. I was getting by on the $250 I had saved up in the bank, plus the $15 a month I was given for laundry money as part of my scholarship. I was able to stretch that $15 a long way, which is probably why I did okay for myself in the early days of wrestling later on down the road. (I pretty much lived off of tuna out of the can when I first started my wrestling career.)

CHAPTER 2 – College

As far as the bills were concerned, with my scholarship, my room and board were all covered. I didn't have to pay for my room, and the cafeteria was always open. They only time I would be a little strapped for cash is when I wanted something else beyond necessities. I soon found that if I needed some extra spending cash, there was something I could do, even though it wasn't a traditional means of earning by any means.

I didn't join a strip club. I didn't sell drugs. I didn't break people's legs for the mafia, either. You want to talk about blood money?! I learned soon enough that I could make $10 extra a semester by donating a pint of my blood!

That first year, I was green by every sense of the word. I was pretty naive about the entire educational process as a freshman, and learned that I didn't have to go to every class and skipped many. Nobody ever explained it, and honestly, I never bothered to ask. Unlike high school where I had the same classes every day, I had no idea that there was no real attendance. Many of my teammates on the football team, therefore, didn't even bother to go to any of their classes. They just showed up for test days, and nobody seemed concerned like they did in high school. There wasn't an assistant principal or someone knocking down my door to tell me where I should be, so I blew off classes on day one.

At some point, however, I realized that there was a free education waiting for me at my feet. I just needed to show some initiative and bend over to pick it up. In a real "finding myself moment" I decided this opportunity could help make me better off than I was back in my days at home. It was a chance to break the cycle. I knew I needed to buckle down, despite what some of my teammates did.

By the middle of the first year at West Texas, I started attending every single class no matter what. I remember sitting down in classrooms for the first time where nobody recognized me, pretending that nothing was wrong and actually started learning stuff! Classroom stuff wasn't the only thing I learned. By going to class, I also learned that studying gave me a chance to mingle with pretty girls.

Ahhh, the pretty college girls. ¡*Arriba!*

ON THE FIELD

Let's back it up a little. The first day of football practice presented me with another first for me; *black teammates*. In Mission, I had been surrounded by mostly Latinos and Anglos my whole life and rarely if ever saw an African American. It wasn't until I arrived at West Texas that I had my first regular contact with black people. We got along well, just as I had done in high school when many of my teammates were white. It, of course, didn't matter to me.

Football practice started out pretty easy. We were weighed and measured, then we ran around the track for twelve minutes, so the coaches could see what kind of shape we were in. I had already been running for two weeks prior, so I did pretty well, coming in fifth out of sixty players.

After our run, we had a meeting to go over some of the plays that we would be working on that afternoon. During that first meeting, I found out I was going to play tight end on offense and linebacker on defense.

I wasn't really disappointed to learn that was fourth on the depth chart at tight end. At the time everyone around me looked pretty confident and I was worried I wouldn't get to play much anyhow. Once the afternoon practice began, I got a boost in confidence. I was watching some of my teammates, and I quickly realized I was better than I thought. I figured I was just as capable of competing for a starting position as the others were, even though I would be trying out for different positions than I had played in high school.

For me, I really wanted to play on defense because I enjoyed the physicality of the position, but I never got the chance. By the end of the first two weeks of practice, the coaches had determined that I would be a tight end, not a linebacker. Then, I had steadily moved up the depth chart, from fourth to third string. On the last day of two-a-days, I went head to head with the first string tight end and got the best of him. This impressed the coaches, big time.

After a lot of hard work and determination, as a freshman, I ended up winning the starting tight end position on the freshman team! That gave me a lot of confidence.

I really cool guy by the name of Ronnie Maknin was my freshman year coach. He was a very aggressive man and a great motivator who was always in top condition. The freshman team would scrimmage against the varsity team two or three times a week and we would always hold our own. This was a credit to Maknin's commitment to making us better, and his willingness to praise us when we did well. I did my best to make him proud and so did the entire team. That year, we won all four of our games and finished first in the conference!

My best friend at West Texas, Ed Alford, was from Harrisburg, Pennsylvania. We were both physical education majors and he was also on the team, at 6'2" and 260 pounds playing offensive tackle. Ed was a real happy-go-lucky guy, never in a bad mood, and there was not an ounce of prejudice in his body. We lived right next to each other in the athletic dorm and ended up being roommates by junior year.

Ed belonged to a fraternity called Lambda Chi Alpha. He occasional took me to the frat house to relax and play pool or other games. There was always a lot of beer and girls around, so it was a great way to socialize and to not have to spend any money. Eventually, I joined the fraternity myself out of default because I was there so much hanging with Ed. I absolutely loved every minute I spent with my new frat brothers.

Socially, I was finally starting to loosen up. I was meeting more and more people outside of football. But with all the other changes I was going through, I remained dedicated to my priorities; my education was number one, football was number two, and my social life was number three. In hindsight, this formula was good for me.

Staying focused on my studies, however, wasn't always easy to do because things weren't going well for my mom back in Mission.

During my sophomore year, I had just finished my finals and was ready for a much needed break. I went to visit my sister. When I arrived, my mother was there and she explained why she wasn't at home.

"He gave up on me," she said. It was very sad, but it was not really a surprise to me that it had happened. I guess my father could have walked out much earlier, but didn't. He at least seemed to wait for us kids to move out of the house.

Immediately after that, my father talked to my brother and me and asked us to forgive him. He simply said he did not love our mother anymore and had to go. (At the time, he was living with a lady who he ended up marrying later.)

I soon lost contact with my dad around 1973.

Now that I am a parent, I can see how difficult it is raising a family. I am grateful for the time our dad remained with our family, even if that time was less than ideal. I grew up believing he loved all of us. Now, I look back and think about how cramped we were in our little house. I can see why he felt the need to get out, but as a dad today, I cannot understand how a man would not want to be with his family on Christmas Eve, or even see his children's birthdays.

Although it wasn't surprising, the divorce still was heartbreaking for me. With him out of the picture, I think I went into some kind of mourning like you would a dead person. I felt more alone than ever living in north Texas, knowing he was no longer at home and that there wasn't a familiar home anymore there to return to.

After my father left, he was erased from our lives. My entire life from 1973 on with him was missed. I wouldn't really get back in touch with him until 1998. However, I still decided it was worth hunting him down and taking all three of my boys to meet him. When we met, we had a nice visit, and I'm glad we did it. I think it was important that my boys actually got to meet their grandfather.

Unfortunately, my father died shortly thereafter in a car accident. *Please, be a good father to you children.*

THANKSGIVING FALLOUT

My senior year at college, I experienced more heartbreak. I had been dating a white girl, Sandy, for about a year. She was a cheerleader, and I was just crazy about her.

CHAPTER 2 – College

Her parents were wealthy and lived about 15 miles from where we were in Canyon, in a little old town called Happy, Texas.

Since we had a big football game on Thanksgiving, I wasn't going to be able to go home to see my mother for dinner with the family. Sandy's father was a big football supporter, and as I good gesture he invited me over to have Thanksgiving dinner at his house. I thought that was super nice of him so I accepted his invitation.

The food was great. It was so nice to have a real dinner. Being a college student, I didn't get a lot of home cooked meals like that one. Coming from a poor family, huge meals like that rarely happened.

"Eat up, Merced!" her father said, seeing my plate was almost empty.

So "eat up" I did, I took another helping, and onother, and maybe another for the road!

Once we finished a feast that couldn't be beat, her father loosened his belt and laughed.

"How about some football?" he asked, pulling on one bond we had in common.

"Sounds good to me," I replied.

After dinner, we headed out to the living room to watch the Cowboys football game. At first, it was just me and Sandy's dad there, ready for some male bonding.

After maybe clearing the table and doing some dishes, Sandy joined us maybe twenty minutes or so later. Her father was sitting in the big reclining chair, and I was on the sofa. I was minding my oen business when she came over, hit my knee, and plopped right down on my lap.

Her old man's eyes were glued to the television, but when the commercials came, he looked over. He didn't like it, and I could tell something was up.

He looked like a bull ready to charge at us.

So, here is where things get a little weird. Sandy's parents had absolutely no idea that Sandy and I were dating. Her father thought I was just a friend from the team that Sandy as a cheerleader knew in passing and felt sorry for.

Now, I too was actually as surprised by her boldness as her father was! Even if he did know that we were dating, it would seem weird to put the moves on a boy in front of your dad. I don't know if she was being rebellious or what she was thinking, but once she knew it was bothering her him, she put her arm around me as if to make matters worse!

After I left, they had a big fight. "You are not allowed to see him anymore!" her father demanded.

"I'm not a little girl anymore!" Sandy replied during the power struggle.

I didn't find out about any of it until after the game on Saturday. Sandy came up to me after the game and told me that her father didn't want to see us together and that they were concerned about what the neighbors would think.

"Listen, I don't want to come in the way of your family," I said, reluctantly. "I really care about you, but I understand if you don't want to continue our relationship."

"No way. They need to start getting used to it."

Sandy decided to keep going out with me. (I guess I have this effect on women! ¡Arriba!) She continued having arguments with her parents about me so much so that she started to hate going home.

While she didn't outright propose to me, at one point she brought up the topic of eloping with me. I told her that it might be a good idea later on down the road, but I just couldn't afford to support a wife at that very moment, especially since we were both still in school.

"Well, how much money do you have in the bank?" she asked.

I told her.

I guess I had her fooled, too, just like everyone else. I was getting good at not looking so poor anymore.

Now, as Kanye West once said, "I'm not saying she's a gold digger," but soon after that, things clearly changed. Either Sandy's parents somehow suspiciously finally persuaded her to break up with me, or she saw poorness.

Sandy never told me the real reason why we were breaking up, but I've always suspected that it had something to do with the brand new Buick Regal she drove up to a game in one day.

Needless to say, I was crushed. It took me a long time to get over it. She was my first true love, and I never saw or heard from her again.

COLLEGE SUCCESS

Despite experiencing some failure at love, I continued to see success every year on the football field. I was named second team All-Missouri Valley Conference my junior year, then the first team for my senior year. I even made it into the record books after finishing second in receptions in a single season.

Still, however, I had some regrets. My sophomore year we finished co-champions with Tulsa University. We all had high hopes heading into my junior year, as we were picked to win the conference. But we ended the season with a disappointing 2-9 record. We also had a losing record my senior season. Playing on back-to-back losing seasons left a bad taste in my mouth and certainly didn't help my stock in the NFL draft.

I was happy, however, for another reason following my senior year; I got my degree in Physical Education with a minor in Spanish. On the bright side of things, while the sports thing didn't turn out as great as it could have, my number-one priority had become an overwhelming success!

Before the NFL draft, I had heard from my coaches that the Minnesota Vikings were real high on me. I thought they were going to draft me, but in the end, they didn't. I did, however, also hear from the Kansas City Chiefs and the Atlanta Falcons. They both made me decent offers to join their training camps and try out for their teams. As a tight end, I felt that the Chiefs offered me a better opportunity because of the players they currently had, so I accepted their offer.

I knew going in that I was a little slow for my position, and I was also told that technically I needed to be at least an inch taller. But I was determined to train hard and make the cut. That meant even more time in the gym.

I started my training regimen in May to be ready for rookie camp by mid-July. I got up every single morning at 7:30 a.m., rain or shine, and ran two miles. After that, I would go out to the field and run pass patterns for about an hour or so with the help of my friend Bull Delaney. On top of all that, I also hit the weights really hard five days a week.

I had never been so disciplined before, and it really made me feel good. My confidence was up and I felt that with all my hard work I could easily overcome my obstacles.

Two weeks before camp, I went out just like any morning. I finished up my run and headed over to the field for my pass patterns. As I was running a drill just as I had many times before, all of a sudden, I dropped.

POP!

I stepped in a hole and badly injured my ankle. I instantly knew something was wrong. It was on fire.

Our team trainer, Lynn Laird, iced my ankle for about a half an hour and wrapped it for me. Then, he sent me to our team doctor in Amarillo for an X-ray.

There, I learned that I had severely sprained my Achilles tendon.

The doctor gave me a cortisone shot in the ankle and told me there should be "no more training." I had to stay off it if it was going to get any better.

After being on crutches for a week, I returned for another cortisone shot. I was seeing Dr. Laird every day for therapy. My ankle was getting a little better, but it really had not improved enough to get back out on the field. I slowly but surely saw my dream of playing professional football coming to an end before my very eyes.

I returned for my third cortisone shot on the Saturday before I left to be looked at by their coaches. When I finally made it to Kansas City, I hadn't tested my tender ankle in about two weeks. I was worried to death about how it would hold up, to say the least.

On the morning of my first workout, I went in to see the Chiefs trainer. He was cool. He heard my story and

CHAPTER 2 – College

wrapped my ankle really good, almost like a cast, so I wouldn't show any signs of injury.

First, all of the players were being timed on a twelve minute run. I ran one and three-quarter miles, which actually was a good time. But when it came time for the 40 yard dash, I ran into some trouble. My fastest time was only 5.0 seconds, which really was not a good time for my position. My normal speed was usually 4.8, and I had even clocked in at 4.7 just days before the injury.

I had an inner conflict. With a slower time recorded, I first thought that maybe I should mention what had happened. But I also figured that I shouldn't complain about the injury, because that could be conceived as being a baby, and then I might lose my opportunity to prove myself altogether. In the end, I just kept my mouth shut and went back to work.

You can do it. You can do it.

We put on our pads in the afternoon for the next set of tests, and I put myself in the right mindset. I was ready for action.

Surprisingly enough, my ankle held up great. You would be surprised what a little positive thinking can really do for you.

In the end, they said that I was in better shape than 90 percent of the 150 players brought in! It didn't take me long to learn that I could soon be playing for the NFL!

Kansas City's number one draft pick that year was a tight-end from Kentucky, named Elmore Stephens. Two weeks into practice, I was actually playing in front of him and just behind their third-year player Gary Butler, who had come in late to camp. Kansas City's offensive coordinator, Bob Snelker, took a liking to me and he was very helpful. I had thought about asking to get timed again for that 40 yard dash, but I decided not to bring it up again because I was doing so well.

It was five minutes before the first game of our preseason.

"Get ready," one of the coaches said to me, as I was getting my gear situated.

"I'm ready," I said tying things up.

"No I mean **really** ready," he said.

"..."

"You are starting this game," he said, before turning and walking away, not waiting for any response. It was like a mic drop.

Just seconds before our first preseason game, and I was just being told that I was going to start.

I'll show them I'm ready.

I went on to start every preseason game after that, playing the whole first half. (Butler played the third, and Stephens on the last quarter.) Things were turning out great for me. The way I saw it, I was getting groomed to be the second-team tight end!

I hadn't thought of this, however. Because their number one guy Butler had suffered a preseason injury, I was being used as a substitute. As a result, the team continued to make trades for what they considered well-seasoned tight ends to start who were above me in talent. They brought in Billy Masters, an eight-year veteran from Denver, and Walter White a third-round pick that season from the Pittsburgh Steelers (not the guy from *Breaking Bad*.) The team was developing back-up plans.

Just before the start of the actual season, all the players were in the meeting room reviewing game footage from the previous week. We were watching the tape when one of the team trainers told me that our head coach, Paul Wiggin, wanted to see me in his office.

As I walked down the hall, it is accurate to say that I was crapping my pants. I was expecting the worst.

"Hello, Merced," he said, showing me to the chair in front of his desk. "I really want to tell you how great of a job you have been doing for us, which is why this is so hard for me to say."

I swallowed hard for the worst. I looked up at all the awards on the wall and immediately thought that I would never be a part of something like them.

CHAPTER 2 – College

"I'm sorry, Merced," he said. "We have come to the decision to let you go."

I was crushed and felt like crying.

"You really are a talented athlete and have a super great attitude, and I don't want our decision to stop you from continuing your football career."

"Can I just ask why?"

"Well, for one, you had a slow time on the 40-yard dash, and I guess we just felt uneasy about that you're your inexperience."

I wasn't mad. I knew he was trying to break it to me as easy as he could. I just sat there and listened without saying a word.

Shit. I should have insisted on being timed again on the 40-yard dash after my ankle healed!

"I understand," I said. "Thank you for the opportunity."

I left his office and went to the back of the locker room. As I undressed, the weight of it all hit me. The rest of the guys were in meetings, so nobody saw when I started crying. I had worked hard and to the very best of my ability, but I guess my best was just not enough.

I slowly got dressed and went outside to watch the guys practice in Arrowhead Stadium for the last time. I watched for about half an hour. I felt like a failure.

Feeling alone, I walked back to the hotel where we were staying, across the freeway from the stadium. I went up to my room to call my mom and give her the bad news.

As I waited for her to answer, I felt that I had let down a lot of people who were so proud of me. I guess I was looking for sympathy, too. I was a mess.

After I told her what had happened, I waited.

"Good," she said. "Now you can finally come home. I don't have to worry about you getting hurt anymore." Despite my mom's concern for my physical well-being, I still wanted to play football and remained determined to make that happen.

Soon after that, I went back to Canyon to meet with my tight ends coach at West Texas College, Jim Campbell, who had connections in the Canadian Football League. I figured that they might be just what I needed to get back to the NFL. He made a couple of phone calls and got me a tryout for the British Columbia Lions.

When I went up to British Columbia, they let me practice with the club for the remainder of the season. Then, I signed a contract for the 1976 season to play tight end.

The Kansas City Chiefs contacted me at the end of the 1975 season and wanted to sign me again as a free agent, but I turned them down. I figured I would play two or three seasons in Canada before trying out for the NFL again. But things don't always work out exactly the way you plan.

However, while I was doing the football thing, I ran into a guy named Tully Blanchard. Although I didn't know it at the time, he would be instrumental in finding me an answer for what life might look like after football.

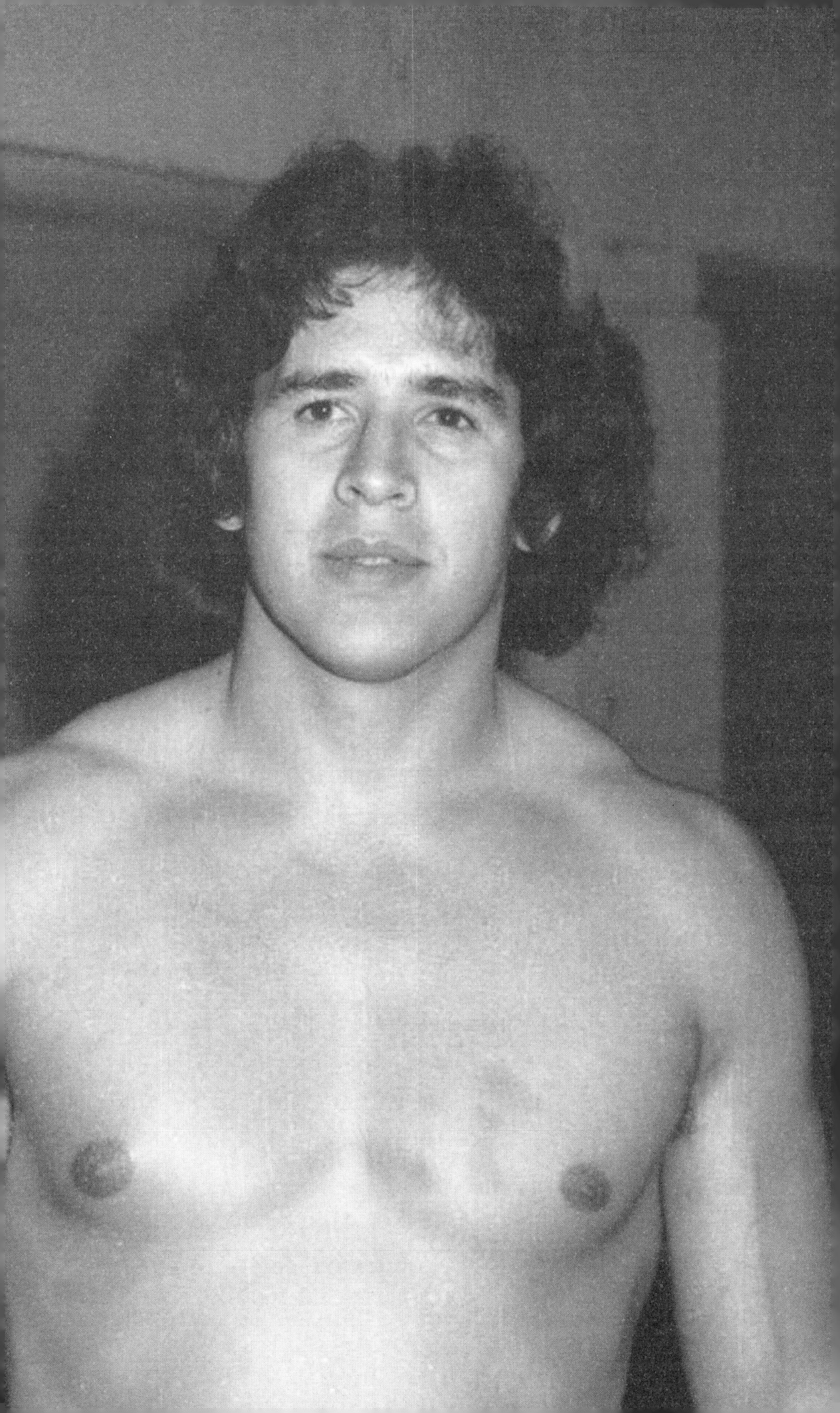

CHAPTER 3 – TRAINING & FLORIDA

I never wanted to be a pro wrestler, but while I was playing football, wrestling was already trying to intercept me.

One day, this guy who was the quarterback on the West Texas State football team during my junior year in 1974 approached me. His name was Tully Blanchard.

"Hey, man. You really should try out for wrestling."

"Wrestling?" I smiled. "No. That would never work.

"That's what my dad used to say," Tully said.

Then, Tully went on to tell me some stories about his father, Joe Blanchard, as a wrestler back in the day.

Tully's dad started his wrestling career playing his first three seasons for the Edmonton Eskimos in the Canadian Football League. Even playing in the Grey Cup of 1952. His teammates included some other guys who would eventually go on to become pro wrestling stars themselves, including guys like Gene Kiniski, Wilbur Snyder and Ted Tully. After Joe's last football season playing for the Calgary Stampeders in 1954, Joe went out for pro wrestling. He picked it up quickly and excelled. He made a lot of money.

Then, after a decent career as a wrestler, Joe kept going with the sport and began promoting wrestling in the Southern territory in Texas. The longevity interested me.

"See, if you play your cards right, you could do it a long, long time. That is, if you are any good," Tully said.

"You think?"

"Hell yeah. You are tall and decent-looking. You might find even more success in wrestling than you do in football."

"That sounds good, but I don't know."

"Now, my dad said there is a need now for a hero for Mexican fans," he said. "They don't really have many people to look up to, especially American ones with Latino heritage."

"I'll think about it," I said, but it all just seemed so out in left field. The offer was very random. I had no interest at all in a professional wrestling career at that time. I had my sights set on playing for the NFL, and really didn't take him seriously. However, I didn't forget his suggestion. I just filed it away as a potential backup plan in my mental Rolodex.

CHAPTER 3 – Training & Florida

A few years after our first conversation about me becoming a savior to the Mexican-American wrestling fans, something changed. I was cut by the Kansas City Chiefs. When I got the word, I sat there staring at a wall, not knowing what I was going to do next. I could go to British Columbia, but that was a little bit of a step backward. That is when I began to rethink the wrestling idea.

I called Tully who got me in touch with his father.

"From what Tully told me, he thinks you have the look," Joe Blanchard said. "If this is so, you could make like $90,000 a year in no time, and maybe become an idol for Mexican fans. There is a need for that in the market."

"I like the sound of that, but I think I have a little bit left to do in football first," I said. I don't know if I really believed that, or if I was honestly nervous about making the switch. So, I still resisted the call to wrestling. I guess I convinced myself that I still had a chance with football.

"Are you sure?"

"Yes. At least for now, that is," I told Tully's father. "I think that I want to play one more season in British Columbia and then possibly start training to be a wrestler after the 1976 football season."

"Well, Tully will be graduating from West Texas at around that time," he said. "He'll be starting his own wrestling career around then and you two can maybe try breaking in together then. Sound good?"

"Sounds god," I agreed, really just to end the talk. My only fear after that was the possibility of Joe following up with me in the future to make me make good on my plan.

Joe knew that I didn't know much about wrestling and that maybe his son could help me fill in the blanks. He did assure me that since I was a good athlete, I would probably pick up all the moves fast and be a quick learner of it.

The more I thought about it, the business end of the deal really sounded almost too good to be true. "$90,000 a year?" That sounded fine by me.

At the end of my 1976 season, I could see that the writing was on the wall.

"Okay, Tully," I said. "I am ready."

I finally decided to go ahead with wrestling, trusting my future to Joe, a guy who seemed to have done it all.

JOE BLANCHARD

Tully's dad was the man. He was a great athlete who played football and wrestled and did very well at both. In football back in the early 50s, he was an offensive lineman for the CFL Edmonton Eskimos with his teammates Wilbur Snyder and Gene Kiniski, who eventually helped break Joe into pro wrestling.

In 1953, Blanchard made his debut for Calgary's Stampede Wrestling. In Hawaii, he won the NWA Hawaiian Tag Team Championship with Lord James Blears and won the NWA Texas Heavyweight Championship in Texas.

Joe's experience helped him to excel behind the scenes. A few years after he helped me get into the sport, Joe would go on to build Southwest Championship Wrestling in San Antonio, where he would retire from active competition after 25 years to become a promoter. He would later go on to play a major role with AWA front office.

Joe eventually became a pretty good agent in a sport that had a lot of testosterone and egos. Joe told me the story once about having to deal with someone I would soon cross paths with, "Polish Power" Ivan Putski.

Putski was working a gimmick where he would do all kinds of feats of strength that went against the laws of nature, so Joe booked him against a wrestling bear.

The headline attraction for the main event was billed "The World's Strongest Man versus The World's Strongest Animal."

When they discussed the match some beforehand, Joe went over some comedy spots that he wanted Ivan to do, and end it in a 15-minute draw. However, Ivan had a different idea of how the match should go.

"Joe, I think I should beat the bear," he said. "Now, in case you didn't know, a lot of time in these "bear vs man" matches, you actually didn't know exactly what was going to happen. You just didn't have the control that you would have against a cooperating human.

For example, sometimes as a rib, guys would slap the bear's opponent on the ass with some honey or sugar water on the way out to the ring. The bear would smell it and go right after the wrestler's ass literally the whole match - and there was absolutely nothing the guy could do about it.

However, on this particular night, there was no ass-slapping. Ivan just felt it was best for him to get over on the bear and look good and get over more with the fans.

After expressing his feelings to Joe about the match, Joe just stopped and looked at him. "You can't beat the bear, man."

"Joe, serious, I am pretty sure that I can. I'm strong enough. I just need to get him off his feet."

"Well, yes, it is possible that you really could beat the bear, but think about it. Nobody wants to see the bear lose. It would make you a heel if you beat the bear!"

He was right, and Ivan knew it.

That's why Ivan and the bear went to a draw. Joe boked it this way to allow Ivan to save face but still do things Joe's way.

To say Joe knew wrestling well is an understatement.

ME THE REFEREE

Joe Blanchard gave me some basic instructions and started me as a ref for some matches in Texas, where I would continue to do some training as well.

My stint as a referee was a great idea. Learning every facet of the game gave me a bigger perspective of the whole picture. It was a way to teach me about the business but to also make a little money at the same time which I really needed by this point. This for me was huge.

Speaking of huge, I first met André the Giant at this time in 1976. I remember I was scheduled to be the ref for one of his matches in San Antonio, right before Christmas.

When I walked into the locker room, he was coming in right behind me. He was the biggest man I had ever seen in my whole life. His large size was due to excess secretion of pituitary growth hormone, a condition known as acromegaly. He stood at 7-foot-4. His hands were enormous; his pinky ring size was a size 15. His shoe size was a 22, and at this time, we think he weighed in around 500 pounds!

Before the bell rang that night, I remember being scared to death that I might mess up his match. He was just so big, I didn't know if I would be off my game trying to work around his sheer size.

The thing about it was… if André liked you, you knew it, and if he didn't like you, you also knew it by learning it **the hard way**. That night, I think I got on his good side and stayed there for the rest of his life, thank God!

André had very little privacy in his life, which I'm sure bothered him. Due to his size, he was an easy target for mean-spirited people who wanted to make fun of him. Many did so loudly and plainly so that he could hear their remarks. For years, he just took the insults. But eventually, he turned mean to anyone who bothered him.

For our relationship, I just tried to treat him like a normal person, and he appreciated that. To me, as the saying goes, he was a gentle giant. He took a liking to me right away, and was friendly, extending me offers to have drinks with him after matches.

Wrestling was his whole life. He also loved to play cribbage, a popular game with the wrestlers, and I would play with him every night in the dressing room or at the hotel during our vast periods of down time. We played so much cribbage that I sometimes didn't have time to properly stretch. I went straight from the cribbage game to the ring.

André the Giant was one of the biggest wrestling attractions of all time. It was unreal. Crowds of people would

CHAPTER 3 – Training & Florida   49

pile into small wrestling arenas with standing room only to see the big man in action. He knew that his life expectancy was much shorter than the rest of us, so I think that he decided he was just going to enjoy himself while he was here. André was always paid a huge amount of money but didn't think much about saving it for the future. He squandered most of it on food and booze, his two other passions (besides playing cards) that he really loved.

Excessive indulging became one of his trademarks. Drinking a hundred beers a night and a couple of boxes of wine wasn't uncommon. I remember sitting with him in a locker room one night where someone decided to count the empties. He consumed an astounding number of 158 beers in one sitting. Then, after he left, he went to the nearest restaurant and ordered almost everything on the menu.

Referee Danny Davis who was his handler for a time recalls his record for eating. "His portion would kill a normal man," he said. "One night, André wolfed down 16 steaks and 12 lobsters all in one sitting, washing it all down with numerous bottles of wine, a case of beer and a bottle of Jack Daniels. The bill was over a thousand dollars!"

TERRY FUNK

I spent about two months in Texas officiating matches against all kinds of people I didn't know. Then, by chance, I had an opportunity to referee a match for another huge wrestling legend, Terry Funk.

Now, Terry Funk was the NWA World Heavyweight Champion in 1977 when I was first breaking into wrestling. We already knew each other because coincidentally, Terry also attended West Texas State.

Terry took an interest with me because of our commonalities. He also remembered me because I had also spoken to him during some of our football practices, well before I had become interested in wrestling.

One night after the matches, Terry called me into the heel locker room. He knew that I was green, but I think he saw something in me and also took a liking to me like André. I walked into the dressing room and Terry gave me a big

TERRY FUNK   WEST TEXAS STATE UNIVERSITY

CHAPTER 3 – Training & Florida

hug. With our shared background serving to break the ice, I was ready to talk to Terry about my first few weeks as a referee.

"How are you doing, my boy! Have a seat and talk to me," he said, doing his best impersonation of promoter Jim Barnett, who owned Georgia Championship Wrestling. He grabbed his back as if he was in pain and added, "I've got to sit down."

I grabbed him a chair.

"I know some of the other boys are already talking highly of you, too. So, how do you like the wrestling business so far?"

"I love it," I said. "But honestly, I don't know how long I can stay in it."

"Why is that, kid?"

"I mean, I made some money from football, but I'm burning right through my savings chasing around the shows to ref. I know I am learning, but I just don't know if I can keep up this pace much longer."

"I see," he said, scratching his chin. He knew exactly where I was coming from. He had been there himself.

Honestly, I really wasn't sure if I could afford to stay involved much longer, financially. At this point, I was a long way from the $80,000 figure that Joe Blanchard had randomly quoted that I would be making.

Terry's cheerful expression faded and he said, "Do you want to stick with it?"

"Well, I am still learning a lot from Hiro Matsuda," I said, "but I haven't made any money yet. I was told after two weeks I would start getting matches and maybe making some money. Well, it's been two months and I haven't earned a single penny. I haven't even had a match yet. I guess they don't think I'm ready."

"So what are you thinking you might do?"

"If the wrestling doesn't work out, I may go back home soon and just prepare for another football season. They said the door is open for me to return to Canada to play for the British Columbia Lions."

"Do you not like wrestling?"

"Terry, I love the business, and I want to give it a shot again next year after the season is over in Canada. I honestly just can't afford to pay rent with no income."

"Wait a minute," he told me. "I am supposed to talk to Eddie tonight, okay?"

"Ok?"

"Well," Terry said, "don't do anything yet. Let me see if I can help. I'll talk to Eddie Graham for you."

Eddie Graham was the owner and promoter of Florida Championship Wrestling, right near I was training.

I told Terry that sounded fair and thanked him. The next morning I had a call from the secretary in the wrestling office. I had my first match scheduled that Saturday in Tampa.

Tully planted the seed in me to become a wrestler, but Terry is the one who really encouraged it to grow. That day he became my mentor, assuring me I would become a success. He was the real one who encouraged me to stick with it.

A few days later I was off to the Florida territory, but not to referee… *to actually wrestle.*

TRAINING

To say that I had absolutely no idea what I was getting into by taking up professional wrestling as a wrestler at this time would also an understatement. It really was a wakeup call.

My first day training, I walked into this beat up little warehouse of a place, with naked cinderblocks on the walls and dangling lightbulbs. It smelt like a combination of sweat and stale urine. That's right. No more NFL-quality training facilities for me. It looked like one of those shitty hole-in-the-wall gyms that Rocky Balboa would work out in, maybe meat hanging from a chain in the corner.

A typical training session began with reps of free squats and push-ups mixed with long-distance running. Then, after my tongue was hanging out of my head like a dog, I had to climb into the ring and wrestle one of the pros in front of a handful of new acquisitions.

CHAPTER 3 – Training & Florida

The head trainer was a man in his fifties named Hiro Matsuda.

Matsuda didn't say a word. He just motioned for me to take the center of the ring with him and pulled a little on my arm. I obliged. Then, in the blink of an eye, I was down on the mat. He had his legs wrapped around me, and I couldn't move. My arm was on fire.

After what felt like an eternity, he released the hold.

I got up and shook it off. I knew if I cowered or made myself immediately unavailable, that could be perceived as a weakness and I was not going to earn his respect. So I walked right over to him, all but actually saying, "Thank you, sir. May I have another?"

Submission holds. Painful submission holds!

He was in great physical condition and could really dish out the pain. But I had been coached by Joe Blanchard and knew the deal. I wasn't allowed to give up. I needed to do what was asked of me in order to potentially find success. He was a bit of a sadist. He liked to inflict pain. It was all a game to him, but one I had to play for a time if I was going to eventually win myself a spot with his blessing.

This means of trying to stretch me was a way of weeding out those who were non-deserving of the chance to become a professional wrestler and actually learn the ins and outs of the business. Back then, you couldn't just look online and find a wrestling school to go train at. It was a short list and very underground. One had to earn the right to be smartened up. If you couldn't make it through day one, they didn't want wrestling school dropouts going out into the public and exposing all the secrets. Therefore, everything really hurt.

Although I was really getting stretched on my first day of school, I was not about to quit.

Usually, the stretching was a means to weed out people who couldn't handle it. However, sometimes it was done to send a message that just because you think you are tough or athletic, *it doesn't mean you automatically can make the transition to professional wrestling*. A good example of this was another famous student of Matsuda, Hulk Hogan.

A few years after my initial training, Matsuda took on some more students to train at his tailor shop, right down the street from Briscos Body Shop in Tampa, Florida. After getting the lead from some of the wrestlers he had met at a bar, a very young and extremely jacked Terry Bollea showed up, ready for practice.

In the back of the shop, Terry walked in to find a decent-sized area where Matsuda had spread out some judo mats. Matsuda looked him up and down, sizing him up and he figured he knew his type; a muscle head who figured that he was getting into the sport no matter what merely based on his size. Matsuda decided to prove him wrong.

He called his new student over, but to Terry's surprise, no moves were to be taught on day one. Matsuda decided to check his wind.

"Sure, you have the size, but do you have the conditioning?"

"I think so," Terry said.

"Let's find out."

After this, he nailed Hulk with drill after drill after drill. Jumping jacks, burpies, squats… everything you could imagine for about three hours straight until he was almost ready to faint.

Terry was seeing stars when Matsuda was finally ready to go over some wrestling moves.

Thinking he needed to save face when they locked up, Terry took his trainer right down and just held him there.

This was probably a bad idea.

Matsuda laughed for a second, sitting there between Terry's monstrous legs. But then shook his head, jammed his elbow into his shin, and grabbed for his toe.

The giant's leg snapped right in half.

The man who would later become Hulk Hogan, one of the most popular wrestlers in the world couldn't even drive off the lot because he couldn't bend his foot even enough to step on the gas. He had to humble himself and call his dad to pick him up and tell him what had happened. His father was pissed.

To Terry's credit, he didn't give up. His friends at the gym (including Brutus Beefcake) all gave him some positive talk and encouragement. They convinced him to keep training hard to return to Matsuda. After 12 weeks of healing, Terry decided to finish what he started.

Once he got his cast off, he was right back over to Hiro Matsuda again. Matsuda respected this. This time, his hard work and dedication paid off in getting his face mashed into the canvass and only some chipped teeth.

This was the type of old school trainer Matsuda was. God, this is one time that I'm happy I wasn't big and jacked like Hogan was, nor confrontational by any means. I wasn't perceived to have a chip on my shoulder coming in, so nobody was there trying to knock it off.

I think things were a little different for me, as well because Matsuda saw me as being somewhat respectful. I also had a little in with Tully. Because of this, I was thankfully never really the target of his focus and managed to get through the majority of my training with no broken bones and keeping my charming smile.

Matsuda had a second trainer for this class. He was Bob Orton Senior, the grandfather of Randy Orton. Orton was the one who really taught me all the basics, starting right from scratch.

The wrestling training was tough and very physical. A few days in, I remember going home and looking at myself in the mirror naked. It seemed that huge portions of my body looked like a black and blue map of the world. I had big welts all over me.

I remember waking up one morning and felt like I had been hit by a train. I never imagined to become a professional wrestler would be so tough. After the first couple of training sessions, I had so much doubt. I wondered if I had really made the right decision after all.

Yes, professional wrestling has a reputation for being fake, but I learned quickly that you cannot fake gravity. I knew that the storylines were prepared and the winner was predetermined, but right away, I figured out that the wrestling was genuine. Because of this, it was easy to see why only a select few were tough enough to make it in the business.

Many of the guys I initially trained with were horrible. They had no business even trying out, but they wanted to become professional wrestlers, to live out a dream. Matsuda and Orton did not care who you were or what was going through your head. They did not take it easy on anyone. They made it tough so that the only way you would want to come back for your next workout was if you were serious enough and good enough to be a pro. To be given their seal of approval you really had to pay the price.

TAMPA

I was finally getting ready for the "Big Time."

Championship Wrestling From Florida (aka CWF) was the official name of the promotion where I was set to debut. Legendary announcer Gordon Solie was the voice of the show. He really was a legend.

CWF's weekly television matches were taped at the Tampa Sportatorium, a nice intimate outlet that held about a hundred fans, mostly in a bleacher-type seating. Like most of the televised wrestling of the time, Florida was using the studio approach for its tapings, rather than to set up at live events. It was tight, so it made it seem like there were actually more people there than there were. The packed atmosphere and the fact that the fans were seated right on top of the action added a unique element to the show. If a fan made noise, you could hear it. Because of this atmosphere, tapings were thick with hostility at times that created a feeling of urgency. The fan response really did intensify matches the same as you might see a team getting "the home team advantage" in say basketball. This feeling of electricity from the audience helped the wrestlers work hard and also helped the angles play out.

House shows were, of course, an equally important part of the promotion during its time, as that is where a big part of the revenue was made. Florida cities such as Tampa, Orlando, St. Petersburg, Miami, Fort Lauderdale, West Palm

CHAPTER 3 – Training & Florida

Beach and Lakeland made up the loop that the promotion served for years. CWF did a great job selling out their venues using simple but effective storylines. They would build-up events and offer the possibility of title changes to bring in the fans.

To remind you, this certainly was a different era. At this age, we were still in the times of the "traveling world champion." The NWA would send its champion from time to time to unify everything under its banner. When they did, Florida was always a big challenge for whoever the titleholder of that moment was to get through. But in order to see the title change hands, the fans had to buy a ticket. By construct, the big title matches weren't happening on TV. Fans had to go out to the show and this is how they made money.

When the world champion wasn't defending on these shows, the Southern and Florida Heavyweight titles were big titles being defended. These too also changed hands during house shows for the most part. However, Florida was strong with continuity and didn't leave the fans out. To keep their followers in the know, their television program would usually air a highlight package of the major events at the big house shows, and show storyline stuff or title changes on the CWF television show to keep everyone in the loop. This was smart because it made people not want to miss a show.

By the time I got to Tampa, Joe's son Tully was already there and he was already wrestling full-time. I hung out with him some backstage for a few shows and picked up some more things I needed to know as a wrestler. It wasn't long before some more strings were pulled and I was about ready to walk the aisle on my own for my first match.

On February 23, 1977, I was off to a house show in Miami. That is when I put on my boots for the first time. The card read Crusher Verdu versus myself, wrestling under no gimmick name yet. In print, I was on the program listed solely as Merced Solis, just because of the lack of a better name.

Although some may not have heard his name before, Oscar "Crusher" Verdu was no lightweight, by any means.

Verdu was one of Captain Lou Albano's first high-profile partners. Albano always put over Verdu's very thick and stocky physique and insisted that the Crusher had never once been taken off his feet. With one look at him, you could see why. That big bastard looked impossible to move!

For those of you who don't know him, he had some press back in the day. In 1970, Crusher had a great little WWWF main event run against Bruno Sammartino. He even won his first Madison Square Garden match with Bruno, due to excessive bleeding by Bruno. One of their big matches the first ever wrestling sell-out at MSG in five years with a record gate for a wrestling event at that time, something like $85,000 in ticket sales.

Now, his match with me was not at all on the Bruno-level, but I was ready to give it my all.

I was being pitted against a 300 pound wrestler. I'll never forget the nervous tension beating me down before the match had even begun. I mean, I looked at him and figured I could outlast the overweight wrestler, cardio-wise. Also, letting an old school guy know that this was my first match was probably a big mistake.

Crusher had to protect the business, in case I wasn't long for the business. Therefore, he had to make me think a bigger portion of the work was real, just in case I was going to drop out.

The start of the match itself was nothing major. Wrestling in front of such a small crowd that night made it so there was very little pressure on me. However, a few more minutes into the match, Crusher started to lay into me, crashing his big forearm into my head. Immediately things turned around for the worse. He started putting the boots to my back while I was laying on the canvas. I knew he meant business; if he was holding back at all, he had me fooled.

He grabbed me by my hair to get me back on my feet, then slammed me to the canvas and came down on top of me. He was protecting the business, probably thinking that I hadn't been smartened up yet, because I didn't give him back a receipt.

I had practiced breaking a fall in my training, but I hadn't practiced it with a 300 pound man coming down on top of me at the same time! *Whaaappp!* When this happened, he knocked the wind right out of me!

All of a sudden, I heard the crowd getting into the match and rallying behind me for the first time in my career. Although I was exhausted, I stood up, ran to the ropes, and flew at him with a cross-body. He caught me in the air and gave me a back-breaker. At that point, I thought I was done. He dropped me and covered me for a pin. I raised my shoulder just in time to the roaring delight of the crowd. I was only moving on instinct by then.

Crusher quickly turned to the referee because he had thought he had beaten me. Then he focused on me again. As he went to body-slam me, I hooked his right leg and cradled him in a small package, pinning him to the canvas. As the referee went down to count his shoulders down, the bell rang.

Time had expired and the match had been ruled a draw.

I was disappointed but glad that the match had come to an end. I was dead tired and unsure if I could make it back to the dressing room on my own. The fans were still cheering me on, but I was too tired to show them any gratitude. I collapsed on the floor as I made it through the doors of the dressing room.

Once in the back, I was congratulated by the other wrestlers for my efforts, and the booker handed me my reward; a very generous $40.

Yes, forty bucks was a far cry from the $1,400 I was earning a week playing football in 1976. However, *I passed the test.*

Crusher eventually came over to my side of the dressing room, right as Eddie Graham was walking by.

"So, Oscar," Graham said to my opponent, clearly letting me hear their conversation. "What do you think of Blanchard's guy?"

"Not bad. Actually, the kid's good," Crusher said. "I think he will be alright."

And that was it… one for the record books.

After the show was done, I helped take down the ring despite the fact that I felt like a battered old man.

Eddie thanked me. "You in for next week?"

"Sure thing," I said.

I finally left the dressing room after all the matches were over and the ring was dismantled; a few fans were waiting for the wrestlers to show up in the parking lot that night and asked me for my autograph. That was the first time for me and what a good feeling it was to know that I had won at least a few fans' support.

After that, I headed back out to the road feeling proud that I finally had my first professional wrestling match under my belt. That night was a long one, and I was proud to have been so able to do whatever the business had thrown at me.

Although I was sore as hell, I resumed my training with Matsuda the very next day. I knew that I had a lot more to learn. My rise to stardom clearly wasn't happening overnight.

The next week came, and my next match was in West Palm Beach. I got there a few hours early, and I helped set up the ring. Then, I made my way to the back to look at the card that they taped up to the wall.

Battle Royal? No problem.

Even though I was green, I knew that my spot opening the show in a battle royal was essentially a night off. Basically, you got in the ring, threw some worked punches, and eventually jumped out with some help. The fans enjoyed the spectacle of all the boys in the ring. It didn't take much.

Curiously, I kept on looking down the card, however. After seeing my name with a bunch of the others, I looked at all the names and circles to try to figure out the psychology behind the rest of the booking, then something weird happened.

I saw my name again.

Yes, I was on the card twice! For my second appearance, my name was coincidentally written right next to one of the guys who helped train me, Bob Orton.

CHAPTER 3 – Training & Florida

Eddie walked by me as I was staring at the wall, just as my singles match started to register.

"That good?" he asked, referring to my match.

"Perfect," I lied.

My hands started to sweat.

Even more so than for my first match, I was nervous. My first match was against someone I didn't really know, and it was early on the card so nobody was really paying attention to it. I didn't get any sort of stage fright or anything. It never got to me. This time, however, I was facing one of the bigger names in wrestling at the time, it was later on the card, and I knew that people were going to take notice. This one was going to be tough. I was wrestling a bigger name in front of a much bigger audience.

Even more so, I knew that this was a test. It was just like school. I got a bunch of information from my teacher, and now I was going to have to show what I had learned.

As I made my way down the aisle, I felt uneasy. It almost was the same feeling I had back in my earlier days, waiting to see where the football coaches were going to place me.

The ring announcer called our names.

It was on.

Working a match against the guy who trained me and also the guy who would probably be giving me the nod or not for future matches was scary. I couldn't hide any mistakes. There would be no excuses.

Bob Orton came into the ring right at me. Just as we were about to lock up, I buckled up my fist and he ducked under the ropes.

Not knowing if he wanted me to follow him or not, I stood there stupid for a second, until I heard him.

"Don't hit me. Chase me," he said.

I ran around the ref in hot pursuit of my teacher just as he had instructed.

We got back into the ring and he did the same damn thing again. He waited for me to lock up, then bailed. As he hit the floor, he smiled a little, pointed at his head and said,

"Wait, then do it again!" So, I waited, then started running yet another circle outside the ring right after him.

Then, I got it. He was calling the match.

When he said something in the ring, it was not his character speaking. He wasn't taunting me. I had to follow his lead. That's just how it worked. Quite often, the heel would "call the match," meaning lay it out and direct everything.

So "chase" is just what I did.

The crowd loved it. I jumped outside of the ring and ran a few steps behind the coward, and the crowd was right behind me. That made the audience root for me, love me, and hate him all the more.

When I got back in the ring the third time around, Orton was waiting for me. He put the boots to me and the crowd started screaming. They hated this chicken shit move.

I put up a good fight but lost again. Just as he had instructed, I almost never even touched him.

When we got back to the dressing room, he thanked me for a good match. It was always customary to thank your opponent, especially in a case like this. Being a new guy, it was your job to go out there and make yourself look bad to make someone else look good. In some cases, you were actually giving up some of your value in the fan's eyes to help the other guy out.

Eddie Graham liked what he saw in me. He immediately booked me a few times a week and I started working matches with guys like Rock Hunter, Angelo Poffo, Paul Orndorff, Scott Irwin, Mike Hammer and Ivan Koloff. I started learning even more about calling matches in the ring and reading the crowd.

My matches with Paul Orndorff were brutal. "Brutal" is probably even too light a word.

One on March 24, 1977 was particularly stiff. We beat the living crap out of each other in a match that went to the time limit. That was probably the most painful 20 minutes of my life! Because he was green as well, it was pretty much the blind leading the blind out there. I know it must have looked good because 90 percent of it was real. We, of course, thought we did a great job. However, we were black and blue the next morning and knew that we had to lighten up if we were going to both continue on.

After a few months, I realized how lethal some of the guys in the business could be. Some of the guys I was working with were really tough. They could easily snap a guy in half. The fact that they didn't kill anyone in the ring proved they were pros.

What fans don't often hear about is what happens behind the scenes when the action from the ring spills over and the fight becomes real.

In some cases, fights will carry over from the ring to the dressing room, or hotel room, or to a bar later that night. Once you leave the ring, the rules change. There is no referee and no one to ring the bell.

ERNIE LADD

Around this time, Ernie Ladd was wrestling in Florida. Mike Graham featured him pretty well, but eventually, it came time came for him to drop the NWA Florida Championship title to Rocky Johnson. Back then, champions often had some kind of creative control clauses in their contracts so that things that promoters asked them to do could be more of a collaborative thing. If this wasn't the case, a promoter could do serious damage to someone's stock in certain regions. So Eddie talked with him, and Ernie agreed to do drop the title in Jacksonville as long as it wasn't televised. The only real concern Ernie Ladd had was footage of the title changing hands being used to make him look bad as he left the territory, and they agreed this would not be the case.

When the day finally came, Ernie Ladd came to the locker room like any other day. He played cards with some of the guys as a lot of them did to kill time before the show. He had every intention of doing what he had agreed to do. He looked at the paper on the wall, talked to Eddie, and received the finish in the dressing room. To the best of my knowledge, Ladd was fully intending to carry out everything according to the plan.

Ernie Ladd and Rocky Johnson (ABOVE) were wrestling in the ring fine until about 10 minutes into the match. All was well until Ernie happened to look up and see a camera pop up in the upper deck of the Jacksonville Coliseum. Apparently, the camera was not there when the match started but mysteriously somewhere in the middle of the bout in order to be on hand to catch the finish! The idea was, Eddie would use a clip of the ending to tell the story on television if necessary knowing that Ernie would be gone from the area by the time it aired and he would be none the wiser.

Because there was a change in what he had expected, Ernie decided that there would also be a change on his behalf from what he was expected to do. When Ernie Ladd saw that camera, he said something to Rocky like, "Nothing personal," then hopped over the ropes and left the ring. In the end, there was nothing the referee could do. He had to call the match a count-out and Ernie didn't drop the title that night. Before anyone in the back even knew what had happened, Ernie walked from the ring to his bag and straight to his car and back to his hotel.

CHAPTER 3 – Training & Florida

Back in the office, Eddie Graham eventually caught wind to what had happened and he was absolutely pissed! His right hand boys, the Briscoe Brothers, were also very upset by Ladd's actions and they were not having it.

That night, it is said that there were a number of late night phone calls followed between the Brisco Brothers and Eddie Graham on what to do about the situation. The NWA Florida champ was clearly going to leave the territory with the belt and this would leave things a bit of a mess on the storytelling side of things.

Now, I am not sure what really went down, but some say that promoter Eddie Graham decided to send the Brisco brothers out to rough up The Big Cat and teach him a lesson. Apparently, the plan was for the Briscos to double team Ladd and punish him. Whoever thought up the idea of punishing an almost 7 foot tall, 330 pound former football player was a good idea, however, probably wasn't thinking things through.

Around three in the morning, one of the Brisco brothers called Ernie's hotel room, and not for a late night cup of coffee.

"Ernie, we need you to meet us in the parking lot of the old Sportatorium in Tampa to discuss what happened tonight."

Ladd immediately noticed the words "in the parking lot." That was called "a red flag" in football. He figured that wanting to meet outside was a pretty strong indication of trouble. Ernie didn't hear the words "in the office," he heard them say "in the parking lot."

Ladd had been around the block and went on the defensive. He suspected something was up as would any able-minded individual, but he was no coward, either.

"I'll see you then," he said, trying to let them hear the smile on his face.

Ernie was confident and fearless. He agreed to meet both of the Brisco Brothers there, alone.

Ernie put down the phone. He acted calm, cool and collected. He fixed his hair a little in the mirror and went out to his car. He started up his trademark big Buick and put on the radio.

According to the story, a relaxing song like Al Green's "Let's Stay Together" came on. Ladd sang a long a little for a moment as he waited for his car to warm up, then got back out leaving the motor running. He walked around to the back and opened his trunk and pulled something out and gently placed it on his backseat.

Now, what happened in the parking lot is unclear, but a couple of things are known. There were two Briscos, but only one Ernie Ladd. Normally, this math wouldn't have looked good for the current NWA Florida champion, but not on this particular night. There was an equalizer.

When he finally pulled up to the famous Sportatorium, Ernie got out of the car, reached in and turned up the Motown playing on the radio. Then, he grabbed the tire iron out of the backseat. He walked right over to the Brisco brothers who were getting out of their car and without saying a word, he immediately knocked them out cold.

Ladd opened up his trunk again, but not to put away the jack. This time, it was to put the brothers away. He mashed their beaten bodies in the back and closed the hatch. Then, he drove them down the road and dumped them out on Graham's front lawn.

Before he left, he reached in his bag and added the championship title to the top of the garbage heap. As Ernie started his engine, he turned up the tunes again and honked his horn.

Eddie woke up and ran out to his yard in his underwear. He was just in time to see Ernie drive off. Eddie then started his car up not to chase the former champion, but rather to rush the injured brothers off to the local hospital for medical treatment. (One needed stitches in his head from a tire iron and the other needed treatment for a concussion.)

As for Ladd, he went back to the hotel room and went to bed.

After that, surprisingly both the Brisco Brothers and Ernie Ladd made amends like nothing major had really happened. Many crazy wrestling beefs end up this way.

According to Gerald Brisco today, it was just an incident that occurred and didn't have any lasting heat. That's just how the brotherhood of wrestling often works, I guess.

Incidentally, at some point after this, I remember Ernie grabbing me up and taking me out to a Cincinnati Reds game. He introduced me to Pete Rose and Johnny Bench. Despite the tire iron, he could really be a super nice guy!

MY FLORIDA LOOP

When I decided to become a wrestler, I had no idea what a wrestler's lifestyle was like. I figured that wrestling was like football and I would only have to wrestle in a match once a week. Little did I know that wrestlers making a living off of the business had to wrestle a match every single night of the week.

On the Florida circuit, a wrestler would have a match on Mondays in West Palm Beach and then on Tuesday night make an appearance in Tampa. On Wednesday, the wrestler did a morning TV taping in Tampa and then traveled for a match that night over to Miami. On Thursday, it was on to Orlando, and on Friday he'd be wrestling in Sarasota. Saturdays were usually spent wrestling in Savannah, and then on Sunday a show would certainly happen, but the show location usually varied.

In my short stay in Florida, I traveled mostly by car and there were usually four in a vehicle. I rode mainly with Angelo Poffo, a former wrestler who was also a promoter, in his nice Mercedes and paid him 30 cents per mile. Poffo, of course, is also the father of Randy Savage and Lanny Poffo.

A NEW OPPORTUNITY

The Imperial Bar was a happening place that was always packed with ladies and loud music. This is where all of the wrestlers went after their Tampa matches on Tuesday nights. As usual, there was a live band playing. (Incidentally, in the Brutus Beefcake book *Struttin' & Cuttin'*, Beefer talks about first seeing Terry Bollea's band, Ruckus, at the Imperial years before he was wrestling as Hulk Hogan.)

Even if wrestlers weren't on the Tampa card that night, if they were in the business and near the area, a lot of the boys would just show up to the Tuesday night Imperial scene.

I had just had my match with Ivan Koloff, so we made sure to sit on opposite sides of the room. Between us, however, I saw all kinds of wrestlers; Oliver Humperdink, Jos LeDuc, the Briscos, and even Dusty Rhodes.

As I was enjoying my drink and watching the band, Tom Renesto, a match-maker in Florida, came up to me and tapped me on the shoulder.

"Can I see you outside for a second?" he said, cupping my ear.

"Sure," I replied.

We excused ourselves and both walked outside and jumped in his car.

"So what's up, Tommy?"

"How'd you like to get the break of your life?" he asked.

"Well, I sure I would!" I replied, hoping for the best. I only had a handful of matches under my belt, so any sort of promotion of sorts was coming to me as a total surprise.

"Jim Barnett saw you on television," he continued.

"And?"

" ... and he absolutely loves you!"

I knew the name. All the boys did an impersonation of the Georgia-based promoter who sounded like Charles Nelson Reilly.

"So what did he say?"

"You'll be making $1,500 a week, and you can start on April first if that works."

I couldn't believe it. That was quite a jump in pay, and if there was ever a case of something sounding "too good to me true," it was right then. However, I decided that I had no other choice but to accept. Even if it were exaggerated, it had to be a step up.

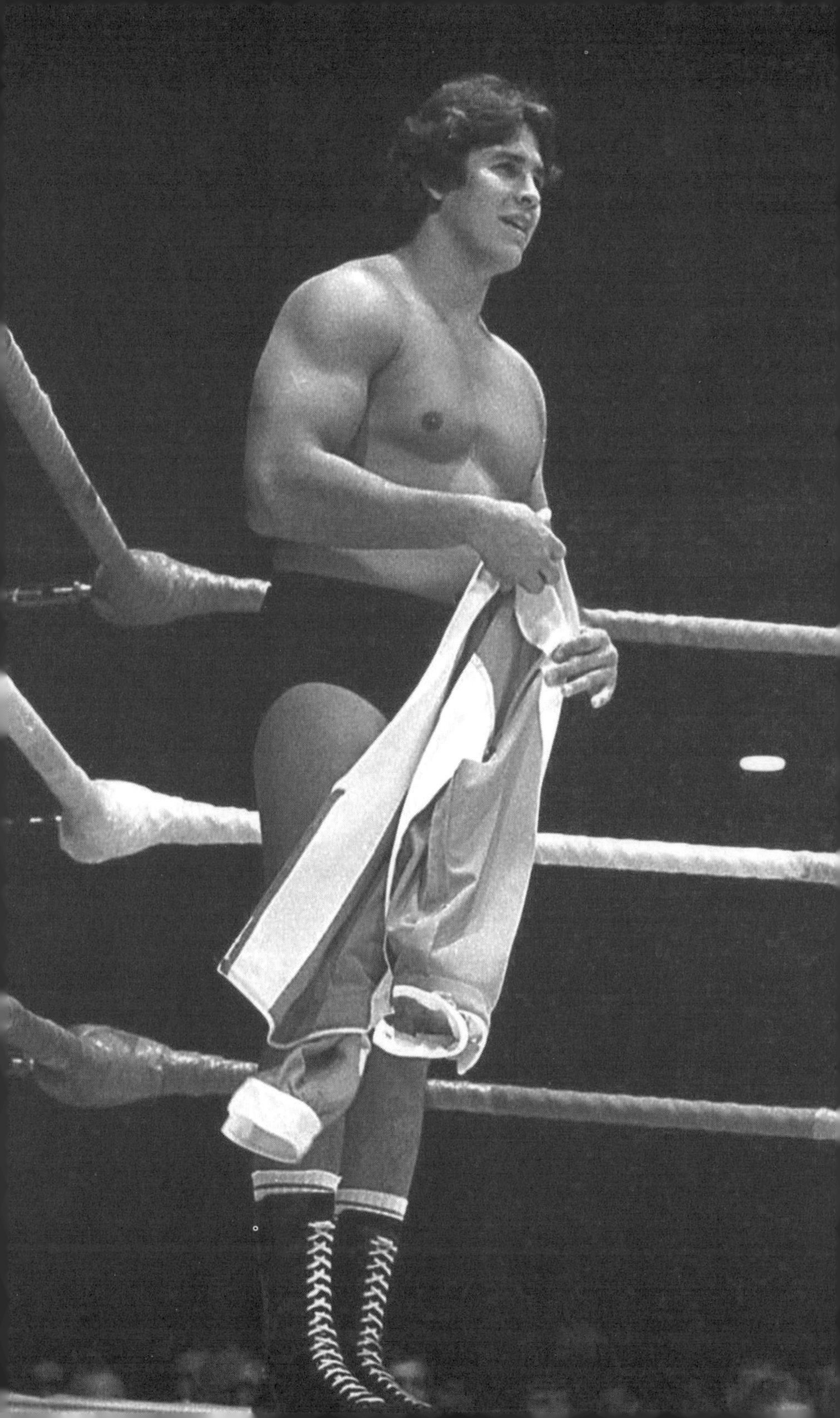

CHAPTER 4 - ATLANTA

I didn't think a phone call was best for negotiation. So, I arrived in Atlanta and spoke with Jim Barnett in person.

Jim seemed interested which further made me belive the money Renesto was suggesting. As our talk came to an end, Barnett offered me a guaranteed contract alright; a whopping $350 a week! Talk about, "too good to be true?" I was more than disappointed to say the least. It was so much less than what Renesto said. However, this was a life lesson that helped me prepare for others. Tons of future promoters would make empty promises that would never happen, and I would always first remember back to this moment. This is why I never got my hopes up for any of them.

Either way, I took the gig. To make thing work, I was able to split an apartment with a guy named "Wildfire" Tommy Rich to help save some money in expenses.

Despite the fact that the actual offer was way lower than had been discussed, I had to consider it. Georgia was starting to grow which at least meant more potential money.

GEORGIA CHAMPIONSHIP WRESTLING

Georgia Championship Wrestling was a promotion whose self-titled TV program started airing in the 1970s. Though based in Atlanta, the company also ran live wrestling shows throughout its outlined Georgia territory.

Before I got there, the promotion underwent some big changes. First, around 1972, the company started promoting matches at the then-brand-new Omni Coliseum. Next, their show switched from its regular channel, WQXI-TV, to a new UHF station owned by Ted Turner. The new WTBS showed a lot of promise.

That new television deal would the promoter Ray Gunkel's last decision. He died of a heart attack later that year after a match versus Ox Baker in Savannah, Georgia. This meant even more changes for the company. His death then set off internal issues. After two years power struggles within the promotion, a new face was called in to take over;

CHAPTER 4 – Atlanta   71

Jim Barnett, who had owned promotions in Indiana, Michigan, Ohio, Colorado and Australia.

So about a year before I got there, WTBS just started to air on satellite. The station started to pop up on cable systems all across the country and reached more households than anyone in the business thought was possible. This really started to change the game, and Georgia was the first promotion to really feel it.

Because of cable TV, Georgia's wrestling program really started to reach new heights. Therefore, Georgia Championship Wrestling became the first real NWA promotion to broadcast nationally.

Many of the NWA's regional promoters were unhappy that their stars were not being showcased, but Barnett argued that since he was only using his own Georgia-based wrestlers, that there was no harm done to the big picture.

Throughout the 1970s, Georgia Championship Wrestling was one of the main shows that really helped put TBS Superstation on the map. It was this show and the exposure it could provide me with that helped make my decision to take their offer.

FIRST BLOOD

This early in the game, I wasn't wrestling under my real name, Merced Solis, nor was I wrestling under the name Tito Santana, which wouldn't come along until my time in the WWF. My stage name in Atlanta (and later in Charlotte) was a name given to me by Jim Barnett. It was *Richard Blood*.

Oddly enough, the name "Richard Blood" wasn't a gimmick name at all, but it did have significance. This was Ricky Steamboat's actual birth name. I think maybe they wanted to call me Richard Steamboat but didn't want to straight up steal the gimmick directly, or just didn't have the balls.

You see, when I first got to Atlanta, Ricky Steamboat had just left to go to Charlotte. He had been a big name for them, so in a sense, they wanted a new Steamboat; a guy to fill his spot. After talking to me, Jim Barnett had a "great idea." He decided to make my Steamboat's replacement by connecting me to him somehow.

Now those are some big shoes to fill!

I wasn't too crazy about the idea of using this name because Steamboat was already big and established. I mean, sure, I liked the spot, but Ricky was over at the time and I didn't really compare. I guess Jim figured that we were about the same size and that I was young. Therefore, maybe I could just take over where Steamboat left off and nobody would really notice. I guess Barnett realized he could have had a real star in Atlanta had he known how to promote him correctly, but he had let him go. So in a roundabout way, I was his shot at a do-over.

Jim Barnett knew that he might work with Ricky Steamboat again, so he didn't want to piss him off. Therefore, he flew over to Charlotte himself to get permission for the use of a name that could somehow connect me to Steamboat. I'm not sure what Ricky thought of having another wrestler sort of riding his coattails in another territory, using his real name. Maybe he even told Jim "No" and didn't give him his blessing. I don't know. I guess the endgame plan for me was a rib to some degree because I didn't end up using the Steamboat name, but rather his actual surname.

Anyhow, once the name was set, they decided to throw me in a tag match to start. Wanting me to be this alive and energetic babyface, Barnette told me back stage to jump over the top rope when I got into the ring.

So on March 26, 1977, it was "First Blood" time for me in Savannah, Georgia. Scott Irwin and The Russian Stomper were set to take on Ted Oats and his new partner, me.

"And making his way to the ring, hailing from Mission, Texas, weighing in at 230 pounds, here is Richard Blood!"

All the boys were in the ring, and I came running down the aisle like a house of fire. I got up on the apron, waved to the fans. Then, I jumped up over the top rope, tripped, and fell flat on my face.

That totally threw off my game.

CHAPTER 4 – Atlanta

RICHARD BLOOD

Jay Youngblood, Paul Orndorff, and yours truly, Richard Blood

Ted Oates laughed and helped me up. "Are you okay?" he asked.

"Yes. Just call me gracious," I laughed.

That graceful start did mess me up for the rest of the match, though. I actually bumped a few times when I wasn't supposed to. The boys knew I was a little shook. You have to make mistakes in the ring before you learn, I guess.

My debut on TV as Richard Blood was on April 6, 1977, against a guy named Jack Evans. Fortunately, it went a little better than the first. People knew that Atlanta had just lost one of their top stars, Ricky Steamboat, and Barnett decided that I was the right new fresh face for the spot. He had the commentators even sell it by saying "Richard Blood has as many female fans as Ricky Steamboat did."

I was working a lot with guys like Jack Evans, Bill Howard, Randy Savage, Ken Dillinger, and Jerry Stubbs. I was still brand new. I was depended on picking up things about the business from the guys who had been it before me. One of them was Don Kernodle.

MY FRIEND DON

Being green, I quickly learned it was best to talk to all of the boys I could to learn as much humanly possible.

DON KERNODLE

CHAPTER 4 – Atlanta

Talking to Don Kernodle, I learned about the importance of respect. Respect was everything in the sport and respect could really open doors for you. From Don, I also learned that working really hard in the ring was one of the best ways to earn respect.

Don told me that he had an interesting start of his own on how he got into the business and it was all about respect.

As his story goes, Don wrestled four years in high school, and then four years in college. When he graduated from Elon College in 1973, he started thinking about professional wrestling. He started doing anything to get a name. He was power lifting and arm wrestling at the same time. In fact, he held the United States arm wrestling champion for two years.

Then, there was some kind of Judo try out at his local YMCA. He showed up and threw all the guys around and they let him right in, skipping all the formalities. He figured judo would help him break his falls, in the event he could catch a break in the wrestling business.

Anyway, he eventually entered the All-South judo tournament held in Burlington and won it by making a 460 pound guy tap out in about six seconds as a white belt, and he was just a beginner!

Soon after that, he figured he was ready. He went up and talked to the wrestling promoter for Jim Crockett Promotions in Charlotte, North Carolina, a man named Mr. John Ringley. He told him that he had wrestled heavyweight at Elon University, Elon College that he was interested in getting into the professional wrestling business.

Because they were doing something with Bob Roop on television, it was perfect timing. Ringley said, "Well, I'll put you on TV tomorrow night then in Raleigh. (Back then, they had matches in Raleigh on Tuesday night at Dorton Arena, and they had the TV show on Wednesday night.)

"Who will I be going against," Don asked.

"Bob Roop," Ringley responded.

Don couldn't believe it and probably looked a little scared.

"No, you don't want to be a wrestler," Ringley said.

"Yes, I do! I'll be there!" he said, knowing this was his only shot in.

Now, as they say, timing is everything. Right at this time, they were doing an angle with Roop where he was offering an open challenge on Mid-Atlantic TV. It was very old school. The way it worked was "if anybody could beat him in less than ten minutes, they would win $2,000."

He had beat everybody that the promotion could sacrifice he could with his "sugar hold" (which was basically a sleeper) in less than twenty seconds. Ringley needed to bring in some new faces so he didn't continue to bury the talent on his own card. He figured Roop was such a good shooter that Don wouldn't pose any real threat. Roop was a great amateur wrestler from Michigan. He was a bronze medalist in the 1968 Olympics, I think in Greco-Roman wrestling, so Ringley figured he was a sure win.

That Wednesday night, Don Kernodle was booked on the show airing on WRAL, as the latest in a string of competitors to Olympic medalist Bob Roop.

Don Kernodle had absolutely no idea that it was all a work, and in this rare particular case, it wasn't going to be. They brought him in the back. Just to mess with his head a little to further ensure that he would be not in the right mindset to win, they had him sign all these waivers saying that if he were to die in the ring, there was absolutely nothing he could do.

Next, they brought him to a totally empty dressing room where Roop was, alone, lacing up his boots. They were trying to intimidate him. Yeah, they were really trying to psyche him out, which they did!

Roop ignored him for a long time then finally looked up and said, "You must be the guy I'm fighting tonight."

"Yes sir, Mr. Roop, I am," he said, walking over and shaking his hand. "My name is Don Kernodle. This is nothing personal with you. It's just that this is the only chance I've got to get into professional wrestling, so I want to try it."

"Okay," he said, going back to work on his boot strings. "Good luck, kid."

CHAPTER 4 – Atlanta

Don was ushered out of the room. He wandered around the locker room nervously. Homer O'Dell was there. Jerry Brisco was there. Johnny Weaver was there. Rip Hawk and Swede Hanson were there, but nobody offered him any real encouragement. They all knew that he was a mark and just played it off like it was all real.

Just before he went through the doors and out to the ring, Homer stopped him. He was a big man. He was tall, and he was way over 300 pounds. He shook his head.

"Kid, there's gonna be a lot of people watching you tonight," patting him on the shoulder. "You just go out there and do the best that you can do. Okay?"

Don nodded. He walked down the aisle and got into the ring for the first time. The heat from the lights was tremendous in the old studio. He didn't know what to do, so he just did what he saw the other wrestlers do on TV when they came into the ring. He backed up into the corner and put his arms up on the top turnbuckle and waited.

The ring announcer went over the stipulations for the match. The deal was Don had to beat Bob Roop in ten minutes or less, in order to win $2,000. All he really had to do was wrestle defensively. He didn't have to beat Don; he just had to make sure he didn't get pinned. Roop certainly had a built-in advantage.

Don was scared. He didn't know if Bob Roop was planning on jumping on him to try to kill him. He figured that he signed all those papers, so anything was fair play. Angelo Martinelli was the referee. When the bell rang, it was on. Before Bob even knew what hit him, Don took him down! Now, that really got his attention, but immediately, Don thought, "Now, what the hell do I do with him now?!"

Roop then took over. Don tried his hardest to hang in there with Roop, which nobody expected he would ever do going in and actually did very well for himself. He wrestled very very well and took Roop to the limit.

It was a sold out show at the curtain backstage. All the boys were watching and thought there was an actual chance that some fan was going to possibly beat Roop. They even started to root for the underdog. They all laughed at the thought of Ringley making the mistake of booking someone who actually could beat his man, and also at the idea of him having to pay someone $2,000 after messing up their whole storyline.

All of the other challengers had pretty much been choked out in less than a minute, but Don just didn't let Roop get the sugar hold on him. The only thing Roop had going for him was experience and conditioning. As the match got to about the eight minute mark, the grueling heat in the studio started to get to Don and tire him out. He let his guard down for a second, and Roop put a front face lock on him. Don didn't even really know what a front face lock was! His forehead hit the mat, but he was still on his feet. He stood back up with him on three different occasions.

Roop weighed 285, and Don weighed like 220 pounds. He was bigger and a lot better wrestler eventually, he put some kind of hold on Don. Now, it wasn't the sugar hold, but Don had to give up because this lock felt like he was going to break his neck. Don held out as long as I could and almost took Roop to the ten minute mark before submitting. He was exhausted. The match was over.

As Don walked back through the curtain to the dressing room, the boys at the curtain quickly scattered. However, two onlookers remain; Ole and Gene Anderson. They knew Roop was supposed to be wrestling a mark that night, but they had no idea it would have turned out as it had. They realized this guy just wasn't your average mark.

"Man," Ole said. "You almost beat him... You almost beat him! Oh my god. That was great!"

Gene looked at Don then over at Ole and said, "I tell you what we are gonna do. I know you wanted to get in with us. Well, you got our attention. Kid, we are gonna help break you into the business."

He told Don to be at the YMCA in Charlotte at 9 a.m. on Monday. While Bob Roop defeated Don Kernodle by submission, Kernodle's skills impressed Ole Anderson and Gene Anderson who both offered to train him for free.

OLE THE ASSHOLE

When I went to work in Georgia, I had to deal with all new people. The wrestling matchmakers in Atlanta at this time were a pair of former wrestlers, Ole and Gene Anderson, the same guys who offered to train Don Kernodle for free. Incidentally, they were considered brothers in the wrestling world, but they were not really in real life.

Coming in as the new guy who Barnett wanted to use to pull in the Latino audience made sense on paper. However, it seemed like he didn't share this paper with the guys running his shows. Even if he did, I think the brothers had other ideas of what they wanted to do with me.

Now, before you go and think the Andersons were nurturing, all-around good guys for offering to help train Don for free, I want to tell you that they absolutely were not.

Ole Anderson, in particular, told others that he really didn't like me because of my inexperience. He didn't like using green guys because they were more work, and he didn't have the patience to work with them. However, I don't think being a rookie had anything to do with him being difficult. It turned out that Ole was just a self-centered, obnoxious individual whose power had gone to his head. That, and he also was an asshole.

Actually, both Ole and Gene had completely different personalities, but they did have one thing in common; they both liked playing stupid games by abusing their power and messing with wrestlers' lives and livelihoods.

It didn't take me long to realize there was more to the wrestling business than I had expected. I was learning though, and I was willing to do whatever it took to learn more. So, I put up with many Mexican jokes, and rude remarks from Ole because I had to. *Pick your battles.* He was always trying to bury someone and used any excuse he could. I remember him as being a really bitter person.

There is an Ole Anderson story out there that really shows how much of a jerk he could be, just for no reason.

I guess back when he was still wrestling, Ole was going to share a ride with some of the boys as we all do. So he got into a car to go to a show he was on along with a friend he usually travelled with. For this particular trip, there was also another guy in the car who was also hitching a ride to the arena. The other guy was Larry Simon.

During the ride, Larry was talking about some of the good wrestlers he had worked with over the years and eventually mentioned how good of a wrestler he thought Karl Gotch was.

"He really is one of the best," Larry said.

"One of the best?" Ole chimed in. "I heard Gotch is currently working for the sanitation department in Hawaii."

This was possibly true at the time. Gotch was a legitimate tough guy, but they say he was taking a little time off to recover from a wrestling injury.

"Ole," Larry said laughing a little. "Have you ever met Gotch?"

"No."

"Well, he really is that damn good," Larry said.

Not appreciating being preached at and not hearing any compliments about himself, I think Ole got rubbed the wrong way. He scratched his head. "You really think so? Well, how tough can Karl Gotch really be for Christ sake if he's in Hawaii off hauling garbage?!"

"So, you think you could beat Karl Gotch?"

"I don't know," Ole said. "But if he can't even get booked on shows and is picking up people's trash somewhere on an island, it's a possibility."

Fast forward a month later.

The same car pulled up to the lot after a show. Larry was driving and Ole's friend was already sitting on the passenger side.

"Hey man, get in," his friend said to Ole, after rolling down the window.

Ole threw his bag in the trunk, then opened the side door. He saw there was another guy back there along for the ride, so he walked around to the other side and sat next to him. Then they all drove off for the next show.

Eventually, Ole looked over at the guy by his side. He looked like he was carved out of stone.

Ole knew right away who it was.

CHAPTER 4 – Atlanta

"Hey, Ole," Larry said. "I'd like you to meet Karl Gotch."

Feeling set up, Ole didn't even try to save face. He turned to Gotch and said, "Okay, okay. If you want a piece of my ass, you getter bet in line and you better take a number."

Karl Gotch looking like a damn piece of steel didn't miss a beat. Instead of turning his head, he slowly turned his whole body until he was looking right at Ole.

"Is that so?" he asked. "Well, when I wrestle you tomorrow, you should pack a lunch. Because I am going to make good and sure that I take all fucking day."

Gotch stretched the hell out of Ole that night.

Ole was an asshole. He didn't think before he spoke. He insulting everyone he could, probably to make himself feel better. It didn't matter if he was wrestling or booking. He was always the same.

Ole was also a typical redneck. Working with him, he often insulted me, calling me every Mexican insult in the book. He didn't care who was in the room or not.

"Who is working with Jim tonight?" Gene would ask his Ole before a show.

"I put him with the beaner," he'd say referring to me.

Nice, right? He didn't even look before he spoke, because I was right in the doorway. *This was the norm.*

I was super appreciative of the opportunity Jim Barnett gave me in Georgia, but my problems with Ole Anderson just got worse and worse. That wasn't all, though. Then, if you paired up Ole with a guy like Dick Murdoch, who was also there at that time, and not giving receipts for all of the insults almost became impossible.

DICK MURDOCH

One example of Dick Murdoch taking his racist view of life a little too far happened to my good friend Tony Atlas.

Outside of wrestling, Tony was a bodybuilder who held many championships. One night after a wrestling show, however, Dick scribbled on a little piece of paper to give

Tony the address to a "meeting" that he told him would seriously help his weightlifting career.

You see, in order to go to regional competitions or national competitions, you had to first win a state title.

"These sponsors are looking for someone to push for the Mister Georgia competition," Dick Murdoch told him. "If you go, you will be the focus of the meeting, for sure."

"You think so?"

"I know so," he said.

Tony thanked Dick and then went to Tommy Rich. He asked Tommy to drive him to the meeting and he agreed.

Tommy followed the directions off the paper. They drove and drove and drove, until they were way out in the boonies. They eventually turned up a little dirt road.

"Get down, Tony!"

"Huh?" Tony said from the backseat where he was trying to take a catnap.

"GET DOWN!"

Tony dropped. He waited a moment, then snuck a look out the back window just in time to see a man in a pointed hood holding a shotgun.

"What the fuck?" Tony whispered.

Yes folks. It was some crazy backwoods KKK shit.

The next day at the next show, Tony confronted Dick about the tasteless prank that could have gone bad.

"Dickie, why would you do this to me?" he asked.

"I really didn't think you would go!" Dick Murdoch responded, laughing up a storm.

Good old Dickie never tried to hide it. He even claimed to be a card carrying member of the KKK himself.

"I should have known better," Tony said, walking away and shaking his head.

PLAYING THE GAME

Both Ole and Dick made it very clear that they didn't like blacks or Mexicans. What made it even worse was that Ole was in a position of power and still had absolutely no problem calling one of his employees a "wetback."

CHAPTER 4 – Atlanta

Can you imagine that happening today? I mean, you would likely be fired on the spot, right? But I guess these were just different times.

Ole was my boss, so I had to take all of his shit it if I wanted to get anywhere in the territory. Of course, being treated like a second-rate citizen hurt very much, but when you are trying to get somewhere, you have to play the game. I couldn't let a guy like that keep me from accomplishing my goals.

I believe you reap what you sow. They say Ole has had some bad luck with his health. Perhaps that is karma coming back to bite his bitter ass. I don't wish ill will on anyone, but he made it hard to ever be sympathetic for him.

STAN HANSEN

Aside from having some issues with Ole, the promotion had some really great names to work with. Some names that wrestling fans will immediately recognize include a very young Randy Savage, the oldest of the Von Erich brothers (David), and even a badass named Stan Hansen.

Stan played his gimmick well. He was perfect at being a loud, violent cowboy who wanted to fight everybody. This character was known for his great interviews. He was always seen in a cowboy hat and leather vest and came to the ring swinging a bull rope with a lip full of tobacco.

A year before I worked with him, Hansen debuted with Vince McMahon's World Wide Wrestling Federation - WWWF. Two months in, he was feuding with the WWF Heavyweight Champion, Bruno Sammartino. During one of their title matches, Hansen accidentally broke Sammartino's neck after a messy powerslam. To work Bruno's recovery time off TV into the storyline, both Hansen and WWWF announcers claimed that Sammartino's injury actually came from his vicious "lariat" clothesline.

Stan was known for his hard-hitting, stiff wrestling style, which he blamed on his poor eyesight. Some would say he hit someone as hard as he could, then apologize afterwards to them, saying his "depth of perception" was at fault for not being able to pull the punch correctly. Many people wonder if he was really that blind, or if he just used his thick glasses as an excuse to whoop ass and get over. After all, the harder you hit someone, the better you would look to the fans, then the more you are worth to promoters.

Stan was pretty stiff in the ring, and if he didn't like you, you were going to find out soon enough. Fortunately for me, I had an in with him. Hansen also played college football for the West Texas State Buffaloes.

In our match, however, he was just fine. I took what Stan had to give and made him look like a million bucks, so I earned his respect. In return, Stan started recommending me to promoters for lucrative Japanese tours!

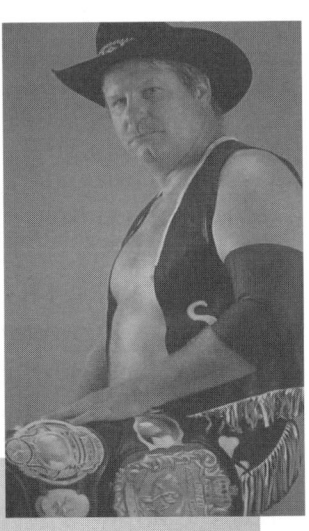

Stan Hansen

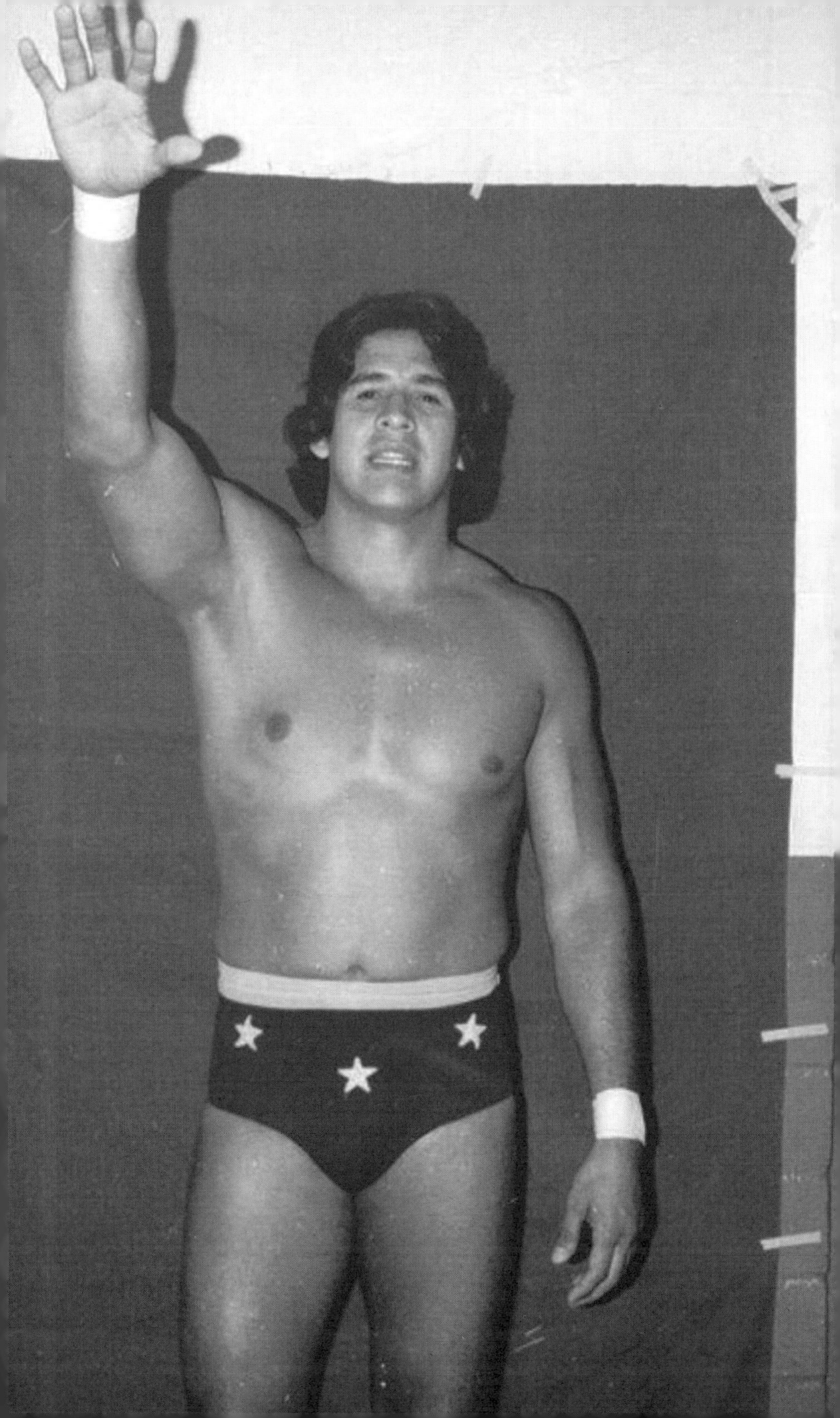

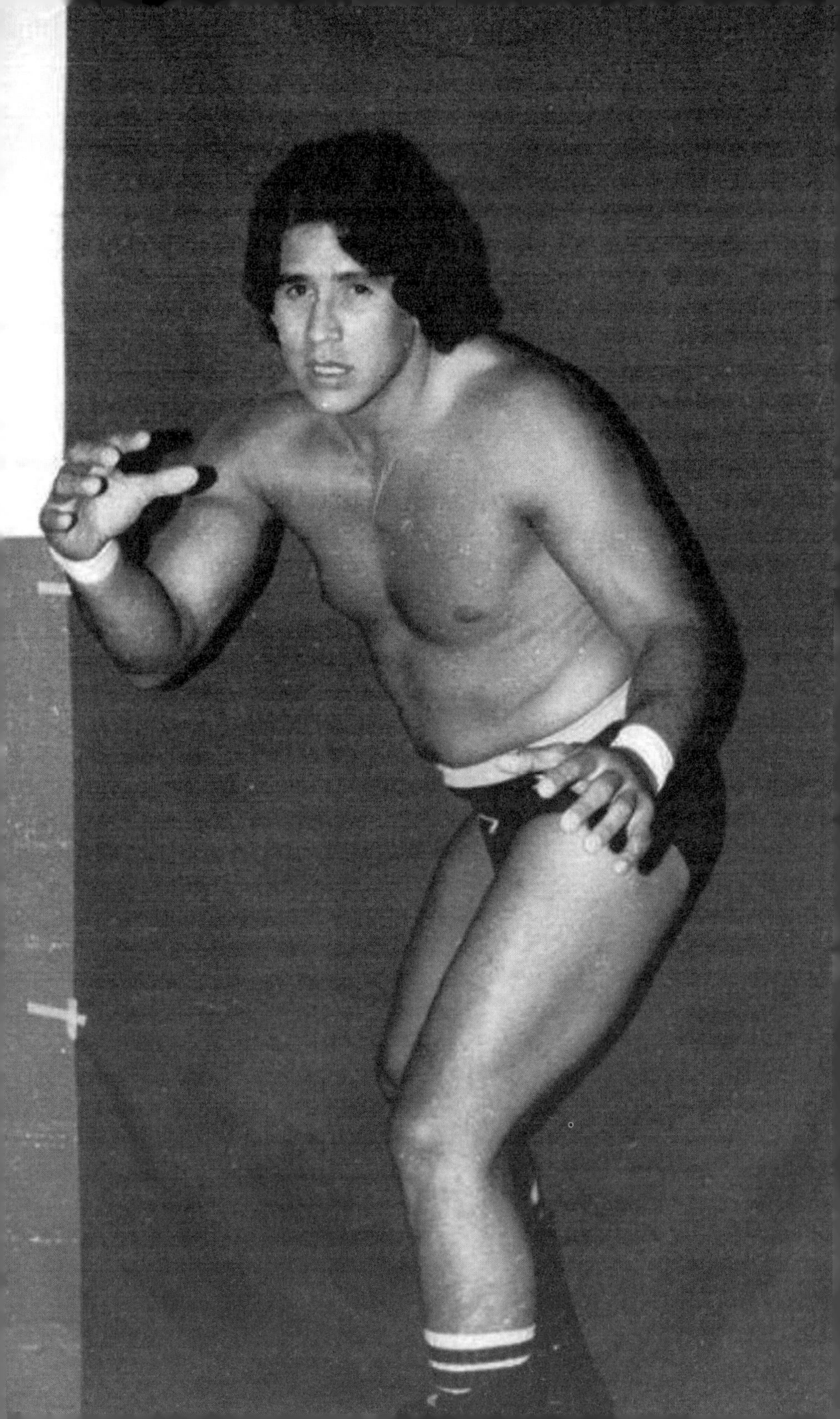

CHAPTER 5 - CHARLOTTE

After about ten months in Georgia, Ole booked me for some matches over in Charlotte, North Carolina, as a favor to the Crocketts. The Crocketts were also part of the NWA. They were down in talent and needed someone like me. Ole's move away was a blessing for me in disguise.

A guy by the name of George Scott was the head matchmaker there for the Crockett brothers, Jim, David, and Jackie. The Crocketts were the promoters who owned the Charlotte territory with the NWA, and George Scott ran a very tight ship for them. He was very organized.

One example of George Scott's organization was his rule that all of the wrestlers had to be at the building at least one hour before start time. While this may not sound like much of a rule, there were a number of guys all over the nation who had a habit of showing up very close to their own predicted bell time. This led to all kinds of problems, so Scott did away with it all by instituting this rule. (Soon after, other promotions started to copy it.) Another example was George made everyone dress nicely and in most cases behave like pros. He also made sure that the boys kept up with the stories that the promotion were trying to tell in that the "good guys" could not travel with the "bad guys."

During this time, I spent even more time on the road than I had before wrestling in cities like Raleigh, North Carolina; Richmond, Virginia and Columbia, South Carolina. In any given week, we typically drive between 2,000 and 3,500 miles. Middle card guys like me, Randy Savage, and Tiger Conway Jr. probably worked 330 days out of the year. The top guys didn't have it any easier. Ric Flair, Wahoo McDaniel, and Ricky Steamboat were all lucky to get more than a week off for the whole year.

While wrestling in Charlotte, I began to polish my skills in and out of the wrestling ring. Since doing interviews was very important to a wrestler's success, I practiced my interviews and speaking techniques in front of a mirror. I also used to practice with the boys during our long rides or downtime between shows.

I remember a number of times cutting promos on Don Kernodle, Tony Atlas, and Brian St James who were all sitting in the car as we drove from town to town. To really get it right, sometimes we would use a beer bottle as a pseudo microphone, and one of us would pretend to be the interviewer for the interviewee. I know this may sound crazy, but this mock-up approach really helped us all improve with our interviews. It was also funny and a way to come up with ideas of what to say, back in a time where there was no scripting or writers handing wrestlers what they had to say, like they do today.

During this point in my career, Paul Jones gave me sometime valuable. He taught me how to properly throw a real good pro wrestling punch. There is an art to throwing a believable punch, and like any art, it takes lots of practice.

What Paul did first looked almost as ridiculous as the beer bottle interviews did in the car. Just like the master in *Karate Kid* showing his student how to catch a fly with chopsticks, Paul had a weird way to do it.

One day, Paul came into the locker room with a brown paper bag.

"Hey, kid," he said to me. "I got you a present at the store. You are going to love it."

"Oh yeah?" I said, expecting to see some kind of delicious snack, or adult beverage.

"Here it is," he said, pouring the bag's contents onto one of the tables where the boys played cribbage.

I was surprised to not see anything edible. Sitting in front of me was a big ball of butcher's tie string and some thumb tacks.

"Thanks?" I said, not knowing exactly what I was supposed to do with the gift.

"Well, you threw a couple of potatoes last night," he said rubbing his chin for effect. "I think some of the boys would agree it would be a good idea to have you work on your punches."

"Sounds good to me," I laughed. "I'm game."

Paul had me tie a Styrofoam coffee cup to a string and attach the string to the ceiling with a thumbtack right in the corner of the dressing room.

"Now, I want you to shoot away at this thing until you just barely touch it without making it move at all."

That made sense.

When some of the boys came into shows with their bags, they would look over at me swinging away at this thing and kind of smile. Nobody really made fun of me though, because they knew my practice of precision meant that there was less of a chance that I was going to knock someone's block off with a potato in the face.

For weeks, I would head over to the show early with that rope and a cup. Then, I would practice throwing my "paper cup punch" trying to get as close to the cup as I could without making it move.

After a while, *I finally mastered it.*

Some wrestlers stiffen up when throwing their punch, and their punches don't come close to connecting, so they look unconvincing. On the other sides of things, sometimes they actually connect, and that shit hurts. My good stiff friend Greg Valentine is a candidate for the latter. He should have listened to Paul Jones and practiced right along with me on that Styrofoam cup, because, I'll tell you, he could have a pretty stiff punch at times. I guess that's why they call him "The Hammer."

THE CHARLOTTE LOCKER ROOM

Jerry Blackwell, for one, was just awesome for a guy built like he was. I don't even know where to begin. Nicknamed "The Mountain from Stone Mountain," Jerry Blackwell started his career in the 1970s and was the total package, a super heavyweight to boot. A crazy bumping machine who was versatile, great on the mic and had a vast amount of charisma. He might be the most overlooked guy in wrestling history. Despite being a super heavyweight at sometimes almost 500 pounds, Blackwell was a very nimble and gifted worker, able to throw a great standing dropkick! Putting him with me only made sense.

Jerry had seen it all. He had been there and done that and was the epitome of what you would consider a grizzled ring veteran. Blackwell was known for his ridiculous feats of strength. One of the most famous stunts that he sometimes performed during live interviews was driving nails into 2x4s using his head as a hammer.

We need more well-rounded round guys in wrestling like Jerry. I mean, 400 pound dudes who could go up for slams light as feather and also jump up and throw a dropkick right on your chin. It is a shame his body shape wouldn't get him through Vince's door today (figuratively and, quite possibly, literally.)

WRESTLING MONEY

My income went up with the move. I went from making $18,000 in 1977 to making $33,000 in 1978. That was a lot of money for a single guy who had few bills to pay. With the extra income, I was able to help my mom buy some land in Texas. The old-timers like Paul Jones and Johnny Weaver cautioned me to save my money, and I listened to them. I wasn't making the big bucks yet, but I was putting money away as much as I could and not wasting it on stupid crap like some of the boys used to do.

It was always sad, and a little scary to see some of the old-timers toward the end of their careers failing to make ends meet. The problem was, they had not properly planned along the way.

Early on, I listened closely to some of the horror stories of guys who were really making the big bucks in the wrestling business. Some of them earned over $100,000 a year, but at the end of the year, they had to borrow money just to pay their taxes. I didn't want to end up like them.

Wrestling contracts drawn up by promoters were, and still are, typically based on the idea that performers are "independent contractors." Back then (and even today) wrestling was not unionized so wrestlers were totally on their own. With no retirement plan and no health insurance, I was always taught that a wrestler has to be smart with their money. One way to do this was to eat out as little as possible. Eating at restaurants could really take a big slice out of your payoff. This is why guys like Nikolai Volkoff were known to carry a little hot plate around with him and just eat soup or canned food back in the hotel room after a show. They say that just before he passed away, he gave a ton of money to one of his best friends so that he could pay for college. That was what the saving allowed him to do.

However, some of the guys were quite the opposite of what you could call a "spendthrift." Making good money was actually a bad thing. Some guys would spend their money as fast as they could make it and quite often to their own demise.

Guys like "The Missing Link" Byron Robertson began his long wrestling career in the 1960s. He eventually showed up in the WWE in the 1980s, making more money than he had ever seen before. When he started headlining cards in New York, he didn't use the payoffs on his trademark green face paint or fancy hair products. The Link spent every last cent he made on drugs; everything from anabolic steroids to marijuana, cocaine and amphetamines. He was also an alcoholic, to boot. In the end, the business ate him up alive. His story included failed relationships, spans of real homelessness, depression and even suicide attempts. Link finally died in 2007 after a horrible battle with cancer without a dime to his name.

"Mister USA" Tony Atlas was another guy who had issues because of money. For one, he has been divorced four times. Think about it. If the first ex-wife takes half the first time, and the second ex-wife takes the other half the second time, by the third time around there is nothing left! Not planning all too well for himself, he also got into drugs and then the remainder of his money dried up. He tells horror stories now himself about once being homeless in Maine under freezing conditions, not brushing his teeth for about a year, and having to eat out of dumpsters.

So some guys on the card that I was working next to directly were excellent examples of what not to do. Guys like Wahoo McDaniel and Ric Flair would spend the money as soon as it came in. I mean don't get me wrong, it was nice for them to throw it around a little at a restaurant or a bar after a show, especially when they were getting paid way more than I was. However, I would do the math sometimes and know that what I was seeing couldn't be a good idea.

Ric Flair legitimately lived his gimmick. He was spending a huge portion of his pay on clothing, the best restaurants, and the fanciest hotels money could buy. Granted, this probably did enhance his stock in the game, but to what cost?

Coming from a poor background, I always look at the world through a fiscal "critical lens," right down to the detail of which sport had the cheapest uniforms in high school, right? It wasn't uncommon for me to say to myself, "Does this make sense money-wise?" Whatever it was, I often tried to figure out the money behind it, and I think because of this, I am still okay financially today. I would stress to the new wrestlers coming up to do exactly the same thing.

LEARNING FROM THREE

One of the best ways for me to learn was riding with the boys. I often had the opportunity to pick one of a few different cars to ride in with other guys who were heading out of town to the next show. Some of the car loads may have been more fun, but I often found that riding in the old veteran car was the one that would benefit me the most.

I spent about a full year in the Charlotte territory, driving around and learning a whole lot from guys like Paul Jones, Johnny Weaver and Abe Jacobs. For most of that year, when I wasn't in a car with one of them, I was following them around, constantly picking their brains. I was slowly learning all the tricks from these three guys.

Paul Jones was a big star from Charlotte and went to Atlanta. He was Mexican American, just like me. Because he had been around the block, he had learned how to use race to make money. One story about him that is funny came a little later than when we were working together.

A few years down the road when Paul was managing more, around 1982 or so, he was acting as the mouthpiece for guys like Manny Fernandez or Rick Rude in various

Paul Jones

Paul Jones' Mustache

Abe Jacobs

Johnny Weaver

different factions that he called the "Paul Jones Army." He wanted to have a dictator-like persona so that he could be even more hated, so he asked if he could do an Adolf Hitler type rip-off gimmick. The promoter he was working for at the time had Jewish relatives so he said, "no way." However, Paul thought it would be good so what he did was, every week before TV tapings, he would slightly shave off just a little bit off of his mustache on both sides, but a barely noticeable amount. Subsequently, his mustache got shorter and shorter. After a number of weeks of this, he was slowly starting to look more the way he wanted to. The promoter compared pictures, realized what he was doing, and told him to cut the shit. *That's classic Paul Jones right there.*

Now, Johnny Weaver was always chewing tobacco and watching car racing. I couldn't figure out why he was there. He was not muscular. He wasn't great in the ring. However, boy, did he give me advice on ring psychology.

Another guy I learned from here was Abe Jacobs. He was *country tough* and was the type who could tear you apart if he really wanted to. However, he probably was the guy who looked out for me the most where it mattered the most and really stressed that I should be careful with my money. I remember one day I was ordering something pretty expensive on a menu at some truck stop. I made a joke about just getting the money and paying it right out.

"It's not what you make," he said chuckling and shaking his head. "It's what you keep."

He's right.

A light bulb went off in my head. That was definitely a learning moment for me, though I can't explain why. I never forgot those words from Abe and almost made them my mantra. After that, I looked for ways to cut corners and I am one of the few who saved very well and still have my money to this very day.

On top of that good advice, Abe modeled how to roll with life on the road. Because he was all about the bottom line, he never messed around with drugs or even drank. Partying to him cost money, and put you at a risk to lose money. Living cheap was actually also living healthy, and that was a great side effect that helped you look dependable to promoters.

I quickly learned that the wrestling business was all about moving up that piece of paper that they taped up on the wall in the locker room. You wanted to be one of the wrestlers up on the top of "the card." The math was easy; the closer I got to the headlining match, the more money I would earn. Wrestlers would do whatever it took to climb the ladder or keep someone else from climbing it because it meant money for them. This is why I learned early on that there was plenty about back-stabbing going on in any promotion.

BACKSTAGE POLITICS

Charlotte is the territory where I really started to learn that there was more to wrestling than just what you could do in the ring. There was a lot of strategy outside of the ring that could really make or break a star that had absolutely nothing to do with wrestling.

It wasn't unusual for one wrestler who was already sitting at the top of the card to tell the promoter that he just wouldn't wrestle a certain individual. This would help protect his spot in headlining shows; a spot he would maybe share with a couple of other guys and that was it. The funny thing about it was, however, that back in the dressing room, this same wrestler always behaved like he was best friends with the very same guy that he was holding back. The promoter, of course, would listen to his star, and the poor guy who was being singled out would never get the opportunity to make a big payday.

In Charlotte, I became aware of cliques in wrestling, as well. I think that there were two or three very obvious cliques in the Charlotte territory while I was wrestling there. These groups were often based upon social/lifestyle choices; wrestlers who say drank or smoked marijuana and did other drugs usually stuck together. But top stars also formed cliques, because of financial concerns, so they could stay on top. The newcomers were often left to themselves, until they were able to mingle into one of the established cliques.

The last important element of wrestling that I became familiar with during this year was the "stooges," who were always around, ready to report anything they could to the promoters if it earned them a few points. Stooges were usually the referees, although once in a while a wrestler would break rank if he was told it was a matter of keeping his job. Promoters always wanted to keep tabs on what was going on after matches, what was being said and done away from the ring. Stooges kept the promoter in the loop.

GIRLS, GIRLS, GIRLS

The longer I stayed in the business, the more I grew to developing a passion for the profession. And I have to admit, part of that passion was fueled by all the partying I did. Although I was still socially shy around the boys because I was still really green, I no longer had to worry about not having a date when I wanted to head out for a night on the town. So many women flocked to the wrestlers in the Florida, Atlanta and Charlotte territories. It was unreal.

Promoters were very conscious of having a large number of women at the shows. Their thinking was simple; if one woman showed up and a wrestler flirted with her, pretty soon that one woman would return to a future show and bring her friends. It made good business sense because it put asses in seats. And the ladies came in droves.

The term for women who chased wrestlers was "ring rats." I saw lots of these attractive "rats," and at first, I just didn't get it. I quickly realized that it almost didn't matter to some of the girls just which wrestler some of them ended up with, just as long as they ended up with someone.

Many of the rats would even go after the filthiest and foulest wrestlers in the locker room, just because they were wrestlers! I remember some of them chasing after the bigger grosser guys like Ox Baker. Although Ox was really a great guy, he was also a hairy, unattractive bastard! As far as being shy, I lost that trait right away when I saw an attractive model-like blonde on Ox's arm at a bar after a show one night. I figured that if Ox could get a hot woman like that, then the world was going to be my oyster.

CHAPTER 5 – Charlotte

Once I started talking to a few of the rats, I couldn't believe just how many pretty girls would go after just about anyone who was on TV.

Now, this much is true. The lyrics to Bob Seger's "Turn the Page" told a real story about life on the road:

"On a long and lonesome highway, east of Omaha, you can listen to the engine moaning out its one note song. You can think about the woman or the girl you knew the night before, but your thoughts will soon be wandering the way they always do. When you're riding sixteen hours and there's nothin' left to do, and you don't feel much like riding, you just wish the trip was through… Here I am, on the road again…"

This was our lives. Words like these became very relatable to a number of the boys who were away from home 300 nights out of the year. Guys would get lonely on the road. Everyone handled it differently. Some would drink or party away their sorrow. Others would hook up with rats to forget about the road. Others even yet would sometimes take their check and pay women for sex.

The road really was a lonely place at times.

The term "ring rat" itself was not very nice. To me, it made it sound like that female fans who wanted to date one of the boys were all low class and nasty, which they really were not. Some of the female fans were actually very well-off, attractive, had a lot of money *and* even still had most of their own teeth. ¡Arriba!

It is true that some of the girls did live up to the stereotype, however. Especially down south, some of the "rats" did look like Dutch Mantell in drag. I, of course, would never hang out with any of the ones who had mustaches that long. For me, if I wanted to be with a woman, she had to less facial hair than I did.

Seriously though, when I dated a few girls, I was always smooth. I was super nice to women and never mistreated anyone. I treated the few girls I went with always with the utmost respect that I could.

There were rumors that some were even much smarter than resorting to the oldest occupation in the world.

Some say that the Junkyard Dog (a guy I would soon come to meet in Mid-South) decided that as a "great athlete and a word-renowned star," he shouldn't have to pay women for sex, the women should have to pay him.

The Dog wasn't called a "dog" for just nothing, you know. Take about opportunists? That's right, he would hook up with rats and often charge these women up to $100 a night with him.

The Dog was a really nice guy, however, I have to admit. He didn't discriminate based on social class. Rumor has it that if a woman didn't have enough money at the time that the proverbial doggy style was about to go down, then she would just have to find another way of paying him, like *layaway*. Sometimes this meant payment in alcohol or drugs. Whatever he was getting, I suppose this is definitely one way to make a little money on the side.

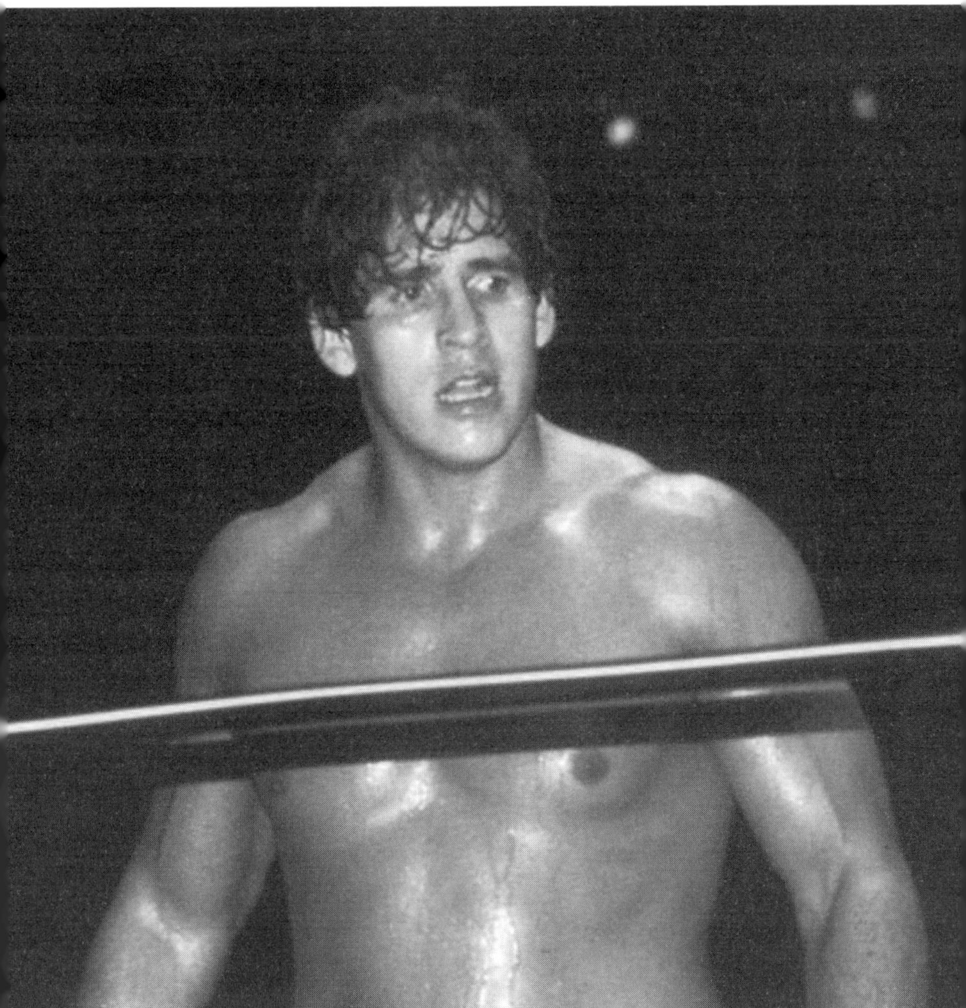

CHAPTER 6 - ALL JAPAN

After my Charlotte run started to wind down, I was already booked to go work for Blackjack Mulligan and Dick Murdoch who had just bought Amarillo from Funks. Being close to the border, they figured I would be perfect for the younger babyface, and figured I would be a big Mexican star. As great as that sounded, I also got another offer that I was going to squeeze in first, *a tour of Japan.*

Wrestling had always been big in Japan. American wrestlers who went overseas almost always made good money. This is why most wrestlers looked forward to being booked in Japan for a few weeks. I wanted to be one of these wrestlers. So, when the news came that Stan Hansen was going to put a good word in for me, I was excited.

And a good word for me he must have given, too! Soon after his promise, he said that Japan was thinking about bringing me in for some dates that fall. I didn't even have to think about it! If I got the green light, I knew where I was going!

When a guy was in between territorial moves, he could more easily get booked for a tour in Japan as he didn't need to take time off. Jim Barnette made a call for me and right after I was done in Charlotte, I was off to Giant Baba's promotion All-Japan.

The deal sounded great. Just before Christmas, I was ready for a five-week stay that would earn me $1,000 per week. That was more money than I had made in the business in all up to that point!

GIANT BABA

In October of 1978, I was brought into All-Japan Pro Wrestling to work a tour. This was a big deal for me because I had never been booked outside of the country like this for a major tour, especially in a land as foreign to me as Japan. I immediately realized how big wrestling was on a global level. Its shear size really opened my eyes.

CHAPTER 6 – All Japan

Speaking of big, in a land where most of its people stood around 5 feet tall, the man who booked me was quite the opposite. He was nothing short of enormous.

Shohei Baba was a giant pro wrestler, best known by his ring name Giant Baba. At 6 foot 10 inches and 300 pounds, Giant Baba was one of the most famous Japanese wrestlers of his era. His popularity in Japan riveled Hulk Hogan's huge run in America which would eventually come a few years later.

This three-time NWA World Heavyweight Champion, and he was also a co-founder of All-Japan Pro Wrestling. He won its championship back in 1973 and held it for 1,920 days only losing the title to Tor Kamata just before I got there. (He would then regain the title from Abdullah the Butcher sometime the next year in 1979, lose it to Harley Race in 1982, then win it again four times, holding it for 3,847 days which is something like ten years total!)

Baba's life outside the ring was always very protected from the rest of the world. He didn't socialize with other people in the business. He never went out drinking with any of the boys like the rest of the promoters did. Some think it is because he was rather shy when it came to socializing. However, this did not make him lose any credibility with anyone. Baba was highly regarded by anyone with whom he dealt.

When I first showed up to Japan, he came to my hotel as a sign of respect to welcome me, as he did most all of the foreign wrestlers that he had booked. He was all about hospitality in everything that he did. He always made sure all of the Americans that he booked flew first class, were put up in the very best hotels, and all accommodations were provided.

After we said our "hellos," I went down to the hotel's restaurant to grab something to eat. When I went to pay, the waiter shook his head. I thought there was a problem with credit, but that wasn't the case at all. I was then told that all the beer and food that I would want for the entire tour was already pre-paid by Baba.

I wanted to have the opportunity to grab a few drinks with Baba because I had already learned that getting booked on promotions wasn't solely on wrestling ability. A lot of times, getting work spawned from the social connections you made with the promoters, or boys in charge, more so than how good you were in the ring. So, I asked around to try to make it happen. I soon learned that having a social hour with Baba to try to connect with him just wasn't going to happen. He wasn't much of a drinker and just didn't consort with people in that way. I did hear that Baba had a ridiculous tolerance for alcohol, more than the common man. They say he could literally drink for hours and never get drunk. He also had a really bad smoking habit at one point in his career.

It is weird because being one of the biggest names ever in Japan, he wasn't really into working out or staying all that fit like one might think someone in his position would do. Just think about how menacing he would have looked if he had been in better shape. It just wasn't in the cards, however. They say Baba really hated weight training and that it led to bad things.

One of his later students, Kenta Kobashi, said that Baba told him to actually stop lifting weights at one point. Kobashi said that he and Baba were visiting America and Kobashi dragged his trainer along with him to a gym to kill time. It wasn't long before they saw two big muscle heads excuse themselves to go make out in the alley. After Baba saw that, he never went to a gym again, thinking maybe that what he saw was a result of working out and possibly catchy.

Could you imagine what Baba would have looked like if he worked out though? God rest his soul, but damn it if Giant Baba didn't look like a giant pop-tart with skinny arms and legs.

FIRST JAPANESE TOUR

Before I went over to Japan, I did my homework and I learned that the entire Japanese culture is also based on respect. I mean, very little Japanese citizens ever went to jail because it was a disgrace to their families to be there. Crime there was much lower than it was the States, so much so that people didn't even have locks on their doors throughout a large portion of the country. This lifestyle translated as such in their version of professional wrestling.

At some point, back in the States I was told that when you walk in as a new wrestler into a Japanese locker room, you really have to go out of your way to greet everyone, even people in the shadows. So that is just what I did. I respected my peers and the Japanese wrestlers returned the pleasantry. However, I wasn't told that if the Japanese wrestler about to meet me was green, they didn't just show respect in return, they practically treated you like royalty.

I never heard about the "being idolized" thing until I experienced it firsthand my first night there for the promotion.

When I first showed up for the tour, I already knew that the rookies in Japan are called, "young-boys." Being a new face from America, I was told young-boys would do anything to help you. I heard it was a tradition for them to even bow to veterans and thank them for just allowing their match to happen on the same card as they were on. This was the mindset young-boys lived by.

My very first day on the job in All-Japan, I saw this tradition, first hand. As I walked into the hall, the young-boys would actually rush ahead of me and push in front of me to open a door for me that I was practically just about to open for myself. They grabbed my bags out of my hands when I didn't really want them to just to carry them for me. They even rushed to bring me many presents of food and beverages, even after a just had a meal.

I felt like the Messiah.

They were so very nice, it was too nice. It really almost seemed ridiculous by our standards, like it was some kind of joke.

By the time I made it to the first All-Japan locker room, I sat down to get ready for my match. I opened my bag and started fishing through it to find my trunks. When I did, I stood up and unbuttoned my pants.

Immediately, a young-boy was all up my space, literally trying to help me take my pants off.

Boy was that a surprise!

"That is okay," I said in the nicest way possible. "Thank you so much, but I've got this under control."

Immediately after pushing a hand away, another hand was at my feet, untying and trying to remove my shoes!

It was then that I learned another old wrestling tradition in Japan. Young-boys always laced/unlaced the boots of the veterans. Later on in life, I would hear that this tradition mostly likely stemmed from an old Samurai practice of young Samurai soldiers having to dress the experienced Samurai Warriors for battle. I would also hear that this was like a superstitious rite of passage and that a young-boy would actually get some good luck/karma from doing this from helping the more experienced wrestler. It was almost like good fortune was contagious.

The locker room isn't the only place I found differences. Another thing that I noticed during an actual wrestling match that was culturally different was that the fans didn't boo, or scream or even cheer.

They marveled.

The most you would really hear from the audience is an occasional, "Oooooo," and maybe applause, but only polite clapping. Their applause was more like what you would see at an opera house, not a wrestling show.

My first few matches with All-Japan were fine. Baba booked me with some young-boys and established me. The people ate it right up.

The fans really found interested me, so much so that it was almost funny. After one of my first few matches, I went back to the locker room. Many of the young-boys bowed to me like I was a god. The match itself was really nothing special, but they put it over like it was the best thing ever.

I laughed and headed over to the showers. The showers, like everything else, were really low. The architects were designing for much smaller people. I had to actually duck to fit under the showerhead!

The funny thing is, I knew there was no way that Baba would have fit under the showers. I figured he probably would just wait to get back to the hotel to clean up, but I figured wrong.

CHAPTER 6 – All Japan

At the end of the first night, I was about ready to head out and there he was. Baba was in the corner shower of the locker room sitting on a folding chair absolutely naked.

It was time for his bath.

There was a large trough-like area there that I believe teams used to clean their cleats and/or equipment with a hose. In this instance, however, what Baba did was let the water build up on the floor by plugging the drain with some towels, and have the water rise up above his ankles. To my surprise, he was having the young boys give him a nice hose down and sponge bath after his match. His handlers were reaching down into the water and splashing him upwards, much like zookeepers would clean an elephant.

I thought this sight was just ridiculous, but it must have been common place to the other boys in the locker room, as they no sold the hell out of it.

"*Niiice*," I said, gesturing to the site of Baba's cleansing to Abdullah the Butcher.

Abby smiled. It was clear that he had seen it all before, but he put me over a little and nodded.

STAN HANSEN

Stan Hansen was not above getting a little help from the young boys, as well. They absolutely worshipped him. He was the corner stone of All-Japan for many years and over everywhere he went.

Kamala tells a funny story where the first time that he was booked in Japan, he felt like a monster. Everyone ran from him everywhere he went; everywhere, that is, except for the showers.

"What the?!" Kamala screamed as he felt a small hand start to soap up his back.

Just like they did with my clothing, it was a young-boy with a sponge trying to help Kamala get to those hard-to-reach-spots in the middle of the 6 foot 7 inch Ugandan Giant's back.

"No, no. I got it," he told him. "I'm all good."

The rookie bowed and headed out of the prison-style group shower Kamala was standing in. He looked over and learned that he wasn't the only one being offered a young-boy back scrub. Stan "The Man" Hansen, was in all his butt-naked glory, getting a shampoo and cream rinse.

I probably saw something like that too, but ran away before it was permanently engraved in my brain.

I don't think I mentioned it before, but I knew Stan Hansen from even further back than my wrestling days. Stan was my Texas State Freshman football coach! He was quite the character and I knew him well. Getting a little spa action was not the only thing that Stan did that was crazy.

I remember going in to one show and walking into the locker room.

"Damn it," I said half-laughing, covering my nose with the collar of my t-shirt.

"What's wrong?" one of the boys asked.

"What's wrong? That's the wrong question," I said. You really should be asking ...what died in here?"

The boys laughed, as one of them grabbed my luggage to help lead me to the dressing room.

"Seriously, it smells like hell."

They laughed again.

"Does not smell good? Good to us," one said smacking his lips.

I knew it wasn't a food odor I was smelling, either. That was just a lame attempt at a joke by one of the young boys.

Just as I ducked around the corner, a saw a line of toilets, and one of the booth doors opened. Stan walked out quickly to rush down the hall.

"Oh, hey Tito," he said, turning. "I'm in a hurry. I have an interview. Will catch up soon, okay?"

He rushed down the hallway and the young boys were holding their hands up over their faces. However, it was not to block out the foul fish-shit smell from a Texas redneck's asshole. It was because they were laughing.

"Look," one pointed, chuckling.

After closer inspection, Stan had a piece of toilet paper tucked into the back of his pants, strategically rigged up so that every step he took the roll would unravel and unravel more and more paper. We all looked down to see a TP trail chasing behind him down the hall.

"Mister Hansen!" they would say. Trying to slow him down only made him run even faster.

He knew. He kayfabed everyone who tried to stop him and break the growing chain of buttwipes. I knew this was actually an old Jackie Gleason bit they used in the movie *Smokey & the Bandit*. Stan didn't care.

Now, from what I understand, a lot of the Japanese venues didn't provide toilet paper rolls in their bathrooms like we do in the States. Many places were BYOT - *bring your own tissue*. But for us Americans, quite often, Baba would have rolls flown in just to make things feel more at home for the *Gaijin* talent.

That line of wasted perfectly good imported toilet paper made Stan's prank even worse!

JUMBO TSURUTA

That first night was taped at the City Gymnasium in Kurume, Fukuoka, on October 9th. My first match was a tag team bout: Me (as Dick Blood) with Big Red versus Giant Baba and his partner, Jumbo Tsuruta.

For those of you not familiar with him, Jumbo is probably one of the most famous wrestlers in the world that not many people in America know about.

At the age of 21, Jumbo competed in the 100 kg+ class at the 1972 Munich Olympics for Greco-Roman. The reason for this is that he desperately wanted to become a professional wrestler like his hero, Giant Baba.

After introducing himself to Baba who immediately took a liking to him, the generous owner of All-Japan did the opposite of what we often do here in America; he sent Jumbo to America to learn a different style. Because of this move, Jumbo and I both had a common thread; we both had ties to Texas.

In America, he was trained by the Funks in Amarillo, just a few years before I would go there for wrestling myself. The Funks would immediately see great potential in him.

The first time Dory met the new guy that Baba had discovered, he was walking into their camp in Amarillo to learn the finer points of professional wrestling.

"Mr. Funk?"

Dory turned and there he was. He was a tall, lanky, lean looking kid with his hair all buzzed.

"Yes?"

"Mr. Funk. My name is Tommy Tsuruta. I have never wrestled a professional match before in my life. This is my first time, so I hope you will please take care of me."

"A friend of Baba is a friend of mine," Dory said.

Dory says Jumbo went on to become the best student he ever had. "Tsuruta just learned so fast. It was unbelievable."

"The first time I met Tsuruta," Terry Funk recalls, "he was wearing a pair of size-14 sneakers, an old shirt and a pair of pants that had been worn way too much. It was the best stuff he had. He was just an overgrown kid. However, even though Tsuruta looked odd, he took to pro wrestling like a duck to water."

In less than two months after his debut in Texas, Jumbo was "on the top of the card" challenging Dory Funk Jr. for the NWA heavyweight title. His Texas tour put him on the map.

Upon returning to his home country of Japan, he immediately became one of the top names in All-Japan. Jumbo started teaming with Giant Baba. Within a year, he had gained another NWA World heavyweight title match, this time against Jack Brisco.

By 1976, Jumbo's career took off. He faced Baba for the first time, and other huge names like Billy Robinson, Abdullah the Butcher and Harley Race. By Baba booking Jumbo with these experienced veterans, he created a star.

Two years after his start, he was off to Amarillo, just before going back to Japan where he would ultimately work with me. It was always a small world in wrestling!

DICK BEYER

I only worked for All-Japan for a little over a month, maybe six weeks total. Besides wrestling with Jumbo, I also had matches against Great Kojika (who started the Big Japan wrestling promotion,) Masao Ito, Kim Duk (aka Tiger Chung Lee,) Rocky Hata, and Munenori Higo. I also worked with a guy in a mask known as "The Destroyer."

Now, being a Latino wrestler, you would maybe think that I would have a lot of experience working under a mask as the Luchadores did, but I really didn't. However, when I was over in Japan, I worked with a guy who had a whole lot of experience under a hood.

Being in Japan with not a whole lot of English speakers to talk to, you would get to learn a lot about the few people there with you. It wasn't long before I learned that The Destroyer a.k.a. Dick Beyer was a huge name in All-Japan and he was someone I worked with him many times while I was over there.

Dick was trained by Ray Stevens and Dick Hutton and learned some really great technical skills. He debuted back in 1954 and was chosen in 1955 as "Rookie of the Year" by *Wrestling Life* magazine. At this time, he worked the first seven years of his wrestling career close to his home in Upstate, New York, home, due to his football coaching job and his work with the Army Reserve.

On tour in Hawaii, Freddie Blassie was first impressed with what he saw from Dick Beyer. By Dickie's second Hawaiian tour, he was trying things out as a heel, working as "The Intelligent Sensational" Dick Beyer. This made him look even more valuable. Blassie saw this and became even more impressed. That is when he decided to pull some strings for Dick by recommending him to a big California promoter, Jules Strongbow.

Before Strongbow booked him, Beyer was mostly focusing on being a scientific-style fan favorite. However, Strongbow liked the idea of his heel work and asked Beyer to wear a mask and call himself "The Destroyer." Beyer reluctantly agreed, but immediately found that the traditional wrestling hood was super uncomfortable for him. It turns out that the first mask that was given to him was from a guy named Vic Christy, a huge practical joker. It was made out of wool with small eyeholes and you could barely breathe through it.

After his first masked match for Strongbow, Beyer returned to the dressing room pissed.

"Tell that Strongbow that he's seen the first and last of 'The Destroyer'!" he said, pulling off the mask, not realizing that he had just been ribbed. "I don't see how people wear this shit!"

However, the next day, he went shopping at a local Woolworth's and something strapping caught his eye.

Right there in the women's underwear section, in the middle of the aisle, Dick Beyer was trying on women's girdles on, but on his head!

He told me he went to work on that thing like Betsy Ross. After he made the purchase along with some thread and a needle, he was cutting and sowing in the passenger seat on the way to his next show. That's right, he started crafting his own mask out of a woman's girdle that would allow him to breathe during a match and not itch to holy hell.

After stitching the top closed, he admired his handiwork. The mask had wide holes for his eyes, nose, and mouth. When he was done, he pulled it over his face for the first time. He looked like a pantyhose-bank robber. The distortion of his features made him look even more like a monster.

"It's perfect."

The creation was life-changing. The look inspired a new character out of him, and the gimmick took off. Putting his own spin on that promoter's idea character and really owning it won him many wrestling magazine covers during the 1960s. The exposure was priceless.

It was learning stories like this that really helped me understand what I had to do even more so to become successful. I learned that it was a good idea to take the ball that the promoter hands you, but not half-ass. *Take the ball and then really run with it.*

I decided to apply this idea to myself. I had heard more than once that I was someone promoters thought could quite possibly be a clean-cut babyface that Latino fans could look up to. However, I never really embrassed the idea. I then started thinking that maybe I needed to listen to what the promoters wanted, then really learn how to give it to them the best that I could.

ALL-JAPAN OVERALL

Working for Baba was educational. I learned a lot and experienced many eye-opening experiences.

On the last bus ride to the last stop of the tour, Baba had the driver pull over the bus. We were in the middle of nowhere, so I thought he was going to just give like a motivational speech or something while he still had everyone's attention. That is not what happened, however.

Giant Baba went up to the front, nodded to us all, then went down the stairs out to the road. Then, he angled his body facing oncoming traffic, pulled out "Tiny Baba," and proceeded to urinate in the road.

A few of the young-boys looked over at me to see my reaction. In turn, I nodded slowly while smiling hard like I loved it.

"*Niiice*," I said to the young-boys sitting next to me.

I learned in All-Japan that, much like Baba's penis, everything was pretty much harsh and right in your face. The Japanese style of wrestling was almost a shoot. You really had to work your ass off in the ring. I was lucky I was in good shape because if I wasn't, I was going to be in for a really rough tour. Man those guys worked solid. You really had to earn your money.

I will say this; the money was good... *very good!* However, I just wasn't really a big fan of Japan other than what it did for my wallet. Some of that first tour left a bad taste in my mouth.

For one, the food was crazy. I remember going to the Tskujiki Fish Market one morning on a sight-seeing kind of trip and seeing the biggest sushi fish I had ever seen along with other sea creatures that the Japanese people I guess ate. Some of that stuff didn't even look like it was from the planet Earth. "I'll never eat that," I remember saying, pointing at some big pink squid-looking thing laying in ice.

Before I learned about yakitori houses on a later tour, I didn't have a whole lot of meat in my diet in Japan. Being a Latino, I was used to eating all kinds of protein with my vegetables, but not really a whole lot of fish. Not being a big fish eater, it was a real treat when I could get a hold of a good piece of steak.

One night, I had a Yakuza sponsor at the Ribera Steakhouse in Tokyo. The Yakuza were a group of what some like to call the Japanese mafia. They were big fighting-sports fans and often had some good money to blow. A couple of guys asked if they could take me out to a meat house, and I couldn't accept the offer any faster.

"Meat? Show me the way!"

It was actually nice to have the Yakuza around to pick up a tab for the boys, from time to time. Letting a sponsor take you out was a regular practice in Japan, and later on down the road, some of my best meals ever came out of these get-togethers. See, what would happen is, these guys who had a little "hard earned money" would take the wrestlers out to both be seen with them and hear their stories. It was usually a win-win situation.

After the invite without any hesitation, I was immediately ready for my first sponsor, and I was ready for meat.

When we entered the restaurant, I was in heaven. I could smell steak cooking and my stomach started to pop like it was the main event.

They walked us back to a discrete little area in the back of the establishment and there were all kinds of the wrestlers' pictures on the wall.

Now, before this, I hadn't eaten very much more than a couple of crumbles of meat on some cheap dish I was living off of called "Spaghetti Napolitan" ever since I got there. I was happy to have those guys treat me, mafia-connections or not.

CHAPTER 6 – All Japan

Japan is a very fish-centric country. Cattle in Japan was harder to come by than in the States by far, and because of its scarcity, a Kobe beef steak would cost up to almost $300 in small towns, and I just wasn't making that much to warrant spending that much on one meal. A $300 steak twice a week, and I wouldn't have anything left for beer, right?

I didn't have a whole lot of money at this time, and this was the first real tour where I was making something that I was actually going to be able to save. However, most of the money was coming at the end, and I was really looking forward to this big feast that they had raved about.

It was a nice gesture. We sat down at the nicely made table, and the sponsors ordered for us in Japanese.

We drank some tea and some saké. We had these little bowls of salad with some kind of ginger dressing. While we were waiting for the main course, my sponsors laughed as I told some stories about wrestling with Terry Funk.

Finally, they brought out plates.

"Here it comes!" I said rubbing my hands together.

Then, before my hungry eyes, I saw these little slices of raw fish. Saddened that it wasn't the Kobe I had been anticipating, I was famished so I dug in.

I put a giant bite in my mouth and... *it tasted horrible!*

"You like?" one asked.

I nodded.

"Have more!" they said.

Trying to be polite, I ate more and pretended I liked it to keep my hosts happy. It smelled like sour milk and had the worst fishy taste I ever tasted.

"More?"

"Nooo," I said, pantomiming a full stomach. "Thank you. I'm full."

I sat back in my chair, and my stomach started churning but a BAD churning, not because I was still hungry.

I excused myself, ran out to an alley and puked.

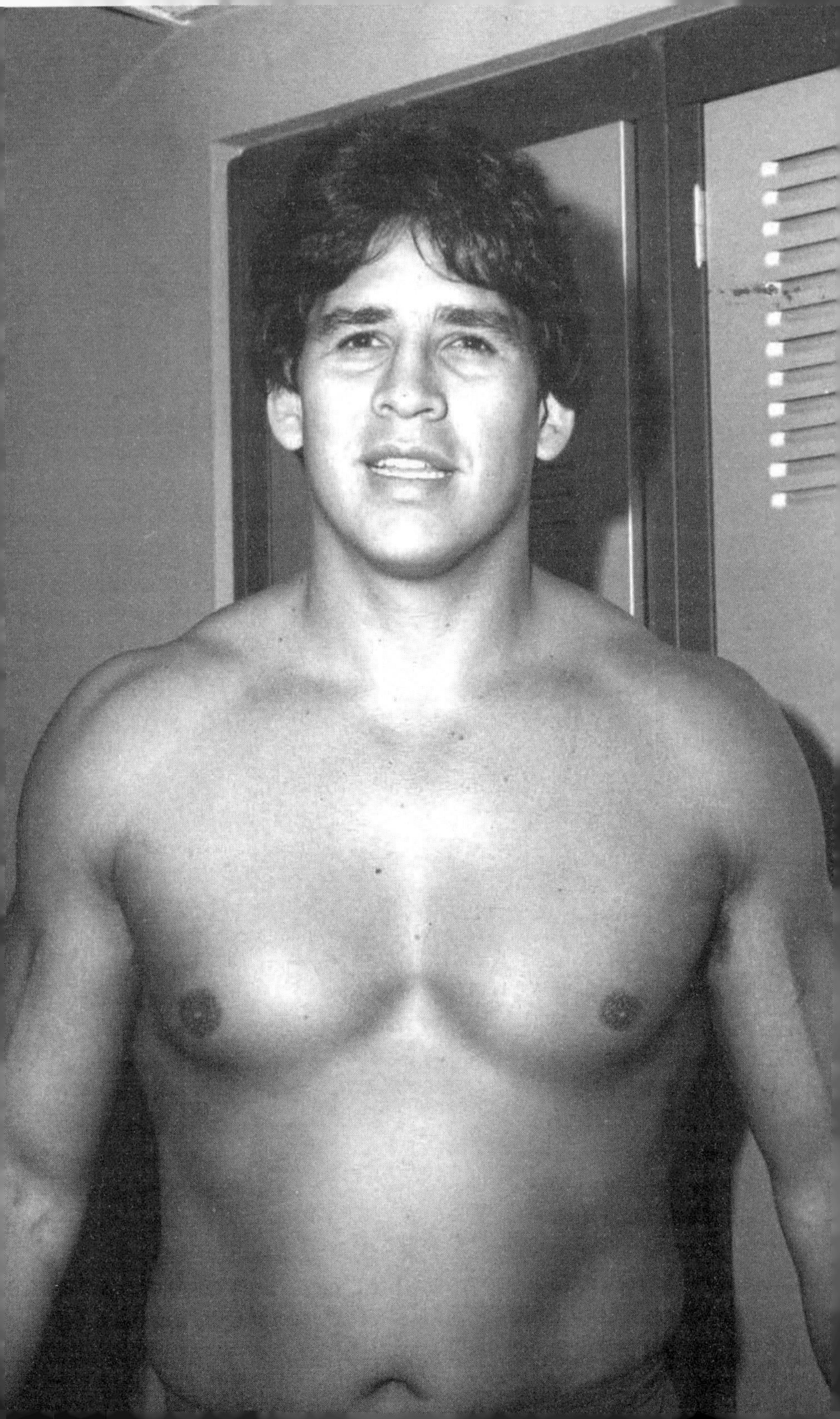

CHAPTER 7 - TEXAS

As planned, I finished up my final dates in Charlotte in the second week in January of 1979 after my tour of Japan. Then, I started up work in the newly owned Amarillo territory of Texas, right in my home state. For the first time in my career, a promotion was finally willing to take a shot at using me as a main eventer. That is right, I was making it to the top of the card and doing so in Texas.

As a kid, any wrestling I would have been exposed to would have been something taped in San Antonio, Texas. I was vaguely aware that a wrestling program was televised on Saturday afternoons. These shows were, of course, promoted by Joe Blanchard who promoted in the mid-to-late 60s for San Antonio/El Paso. (He would later break off of the Dallas booking offices with Fritz and call his promotion Southwest Championship Wrestling, it just wasn't called this when I was growing up.)

I wasn't a huge wrestling fan, for one, because I was out playing sports when it was on, but remember also seeing Amarillo wrestling at least a few times when I was at away games with my sports. When that show was on, I think it had guys like Johnny Valentine, Wahoo McDaniel and Fritz Von Erich, as well as the Funks. My memories are a little fuzzy, but I seem to remember something about Karl Von Steiger hitting Ricky Romero and Lord Alfred Hayes with a devastating Heart Punch.

Getting booked in Texas was somewhat nostalgic for me, in that I would soon be wrestling for a promotion just north of my neck of the woods. It felt like a homecoming to some degree.

For those of you history buffs, Amarillo ran wrestling shows in several cities in the Southwest, including Amarillo, Lubbock, El Paso, Odessa, Abilene, Albuquerque and also in Colorado Springs. They also had occasional spot shows in smaller backwoods towns like Lamesa, Hereford, and over in Hobbs, New Mexico.

Amarillo's one-hour television show aired weekly. It was filmed in a studio in Amarillo and broadcast throughout west Texas, New Mexico, and southern Colorado. Like Florida, the Texas show was mostly comprised of studio matches with little highlight clips from big house show matches. They also featured occasional clips from a significant match from another region.

The territorial promotion was very typical for its time. However, one aspect of Amarillo set it apart from the rest, and that was they had The Funks.

THE FUNKS & AMARILLO

In the late 40s, Dory Funk Sr. and his wife Betty traveled throughout the country with their sons Dory and Terry in tow wherever their father had a wrestling booking. "Tow" is the operative word here in that the Funks actually lived out of a trailer mobile home that was being pulled behind an Oldsmobile.

In 1949, the Funks moved to the Amarillo area permanently and pretty much took it over. Wrestling did very well in Amarillo and the West Texas Region, partly because of Dory's contributions. He was a big rugged Texan that the fans could relate to. In the ring, he epitomized the phrase he used in his promos when he said that he was, "meaner than a rattlesnake and tougher than shoe leather."

Dory held the North American Title on seven different occasions in the 1950s. In the 1960s, Dory won the North American Title on ten more occasions, defeating guys like Danny McShane, Fritz Von Erich, Clubfoot Inferno and Buddy Colt.

The 1960s also brought the debuts of Dory Funk, Jr. and his brother Terry. As the 1970s approached, Dory, Jr. captured the NWA World Title which he held for over four years, defending it frequently in the region. As the 1970s continued, Amarillo got huge! Dory Senior, Junior, and Terry became top draws on every card. (This is when Dory, Sr. made and an agreement with Baba for talent exchanging between Japan and the U.S, that not only helped the

Amarillo product, but also helped to turn the Funks into names overseas.)

On June 3, 1973, Dory Funk Sr. sadly passed away at 54. Even after his passing, the territory remained hot. Terry won the NWA title in December of 1975. Dory, Jr., and Dick Murdoch were the top faces at this time going against guys like the Brisco brothers and Harley Race. However, by the time 70s were coming to an end, so was Amarillo.

The Funks just became too big to stay in one place. They became international stars and were wrestling all over the world. Dory, Jr. took a job with Eddie Graham in Florida. Terry was all over the place, and the promotion was eventually sold to be repackaged by Bob Windham (a.k.a. Blackjack Mulligan) and Dick Murdoch who continued to run it until roughly 1980. After that time, Fritz Von Erich would take over to promote World Class Championship Wrestling.

Now, to back it up a little, I was set to step into Amarillo right after the Funks were stepping out. My spot there came as a favor to Terry Funk who took a liking to me to and was plugging me to one of the new Amarillo territory bookers, Black Jack Mulligan. Now, on top of Terry's recommendation, I had also befriended Blackjack back in Charlotte. Because of this, he decided to take a shot with me. The idea, once again, was to try to use me to my fullest potential to better connect to Texas' big Latino audience.

Blackjack was a big man, 6-foot 6-inch and around 300 pounds. He had long dark hair and a thick mustache and was rugged looking, like a cowboy. His partner, Dick Murdoch, was also a cowboy-type but a little more unrefined. He was that big rough and tough cowboy-type with a big belly and a few missing teeth. Both of these wresters had been main event wrestlers themselves, and I knew they would be great resources to learn from. They both had a lot of experience working heel for a big part of their lives but had also both turned babyface at this point, later on in their careers.

See, having made good money as wrestlers in the Charlotte territory, the two cowboys decided to invest and cut out the middleman so to speak. Blackjack teamed up with Dick Murdoch and they planned to pool their money with aspirations of becoming wrestling promoters. Finally, when a territory become available, they jumped at the opportunity. They purchased the northwest Texas promotion from The Funks so they could both wrestle and promote cards themselves, subsequently cutting out middle-man promoters.

Blackjack Mulligan sincerely wanted to give me my first really big break. The promotion's headquarters in Amarillo was just 17 miles from Canyon, where I had played football in college. Since my real name carried with it some celebrity in that particular area, he asked me to go back to using my real name, Merced Solis, which I did. Blackjack was banking on my name to help put fans in seats.

MY NEW LOOK
For my new Texas run, I wanted to reinvent myself, so to speak, so that I would really stand out. I decided that I would look like a traditional Mexican. For my new gimmick, I got a big sombrero and wore a matching serape, which is a brightly colored wool shawl that wraps around the shoulders.

I tested out my new look for a number of weeks and it really was getting over. The gamble worked out well for both Blackjack and me. The fans loved it, and more than ever before, they wanted my autograph. I was getting hit up at gas stations, in restaurants before shows, and even in the bathrooms by the urinal. My autograph was finally in high demand and I knew this meant good things for my future.

Blackjack continued to push me as much as he could. Unlike Blackjack, however, his partner Dick Murdoch still never had a positive thing to say to me, no matter how well I was doing for their company. His remarks to me were often rude, if not borderline racist. Some of it was probably also steaming from a fear of losing his headliner spot and fame.

My first Amarillo TV appearance in the new sombrero gimmick was on February 24, 1979, in Muleshoe, Texas. I was super excited about this finally happening for me as I knew positive television exposure could really be just what I needed. However, despite having the support of Blackjack, I didn't predict the professional jealously factor that would be coming from the other side of management.

Dick Murdoch was wrestling on this same card that night and didn't want me to "steal his spotlight." Therefore, when it came time to book the show, as the promoter, he pulled me aside and made it good and clear that I was not to outshine him. He booked me against Stan Lane and made sure that our match was uneventful and ended in a draw.

I was very upset. Being awarded a draw on my first TV match with the new gimmick wasn't going to help me get the big push I wanted. A TV debut can make or break you.

A couple of days later, I walked into the dressing room feeling dejected. Right off the bat, Blackjack read my body language, knew something was up, and pulled me aside to talk about my frustrations. I remember walking down a creaky hardwood-floored hallway off to a dark side of the venue in Lubbock. I was nervous because I was about to "stooge" on one of my bosses to his own partner.

I told him what the finish was, and he shook his head.

"I'm sorry I wasn't there, man," he said. "Honest. That wasn't how it was supposed to go." The fact that he wasn't there at the taping did hurt me. It gave Murdoch the opportunity to change things up, but he was sincere. I truly didn't think that Blackjack was playing good cop/bad cop with me. He seemed legitimately sympathetic.

After I finished complaining, I could see his face turn from sorrow to anger. He was clearly mad.

"You were supposed to get that big win on TV so you could get your push," Blackjack told me. "Look, I am a man of my word, and I will fix this."

We shook hands, and he walked off.

Dick Murdoch was the exact type of person I spoke of a few chapters back; the kind who would smile to your face but would stab you in the back the next instance. He was also too ignorant to see I would be helping his new promotion by drawing Mexican-American fans and more young kids to the matches. I had two years of wrestling behind me and had been wrestling a minimum of 25 matches per month against some pretty good competition.

I decided right then that I was not going to let Murdoch get the best of me, and I was not going to let him hurt my career. I started working harder.

Blackjack knew his partner had a rep. In fact, I wasn't the first non-caucasian person to say I wasn't treated the best by the man who called himself "Captain Redneck." Thankfully, Blackjack went out of his way to get me over.

ROCKY VS MURDOCH

Rocky Johnson, father of Dwayne "The Rock" Johnson, made similar accusations against Murdoch. According to Rocky, Murdoch sometimes didn't pull back at all on his kicks and punches in matches against him.

One night, it was Rocky versus Dick Murdoch again. After a number of stiff shots, Rocky had had enough. He told Murdoch to start "taking it easy" or else he would have to retaliate. Murdoch didn't seem to care and continued to kick him really hard in the ribs. After continuing to take the assault, Rocky locked up with Dick and said, "Listen, if you keep hitting me like this, I am going to hit back."

Dick hit him again…

Then Dick hit the mat… *¡Arriba!*

Rocky Johnson, you see, was a former boxer who sparred with the likes of George Foreman and Muhammad Ali. One punch knocked Murdoch out cold!

Rocky covered him for the win, then left him sprawled out in the ring and headed back to the locker room.

TAG TEAM CHAMPIONS

At this point, the New York territory really started to take off. All of the guys started looking to go in that direction. However, way before Ted DiBiase would change his look and take on the "Million Dollar Man" gimmick that earned him his fame with the WWF, he was hanging with me in Texas.

Believe it or not, Teddy was yet another teammate from West Texas State I ran into during my stay in Amarillo.

I don't know what it was about that school. Maybe it was something in the water, but that school's football team cranked out some of the biggest legends in wrestling ever.

CHAPTER 7 – Texas

Beside Tully Blanchard, Terry & Dory Funk, Stan Hansen, Blackjack Mulligan, and Ted DiBiase, there was Kelly Kiniski, Manny Fernandez, Bruiser Brody, Bobby Duncum, and even Dusty Rhodes. That is eight WWE Hall of Famers right there who played football at West Texas State!

Out of them all, DiBiase and I hit it off the most. We were already friendly during our time together on the field, but we became even better friends in ring and on the road. He was the more experienced wrestler by this time, but not at all selfish. Ted had probably been wrestling about two years longer than I had, but made it a point to bring me up to his level. He spent a lot of extra time with me. He didn't have to, but he really helped me improve my skills in Texas.

Everyday before a show, we would try to get to the event before anyone else did so we could get in the ring and practice. I remember many times arriving to a show so early that we would actually help set up the ring, just so we could use it. Then, once nobody was around, we would wrestle a match in front of an audience of nobody.

Teddy was impressed by our chemistry. We were both quick and fearless and just worked really well together. Seeing value in us possibly working together, Ted wisely suggested to Blackjack that we should be booked as a tag team, and then go after the Texas Tag Team Titles.

I felt honored that Teddy wanted to make that pitch to the powers that be. It didn't matter that I was going to be taken out of the singles category to make that happen. I knew that working side-by-side with Ted DiBiase would only continue my success in the long run.

The promoters agreed to the pairing. Our energy was just what the promotion needed. The fans ate it up, so we started winning matches, working our way up the ladder to become the number one contenders to the tag team champions.

In early 1979, the crowds were really responding to us, so we finally got our shot and became Texas Tag Team Champions. I had used all that I had learned up until that point and become much better at playing off the crowd, bringing the fans' emotions right in the ring with me. I gave

them 100-percent effort each match, knowing that they would be there for me.
I started getting really good at being a babyface.
Our time as champions was brief, however. Since Teddy and I were moving up the ladder and drawing a large fan base, I think Murdoch felt threatened again and decided to cut us off and intentionally squash our rapid success. One week after winning those tag team belts, DiBiase and I were told we had to drop the titles!

Ted didn't take the news well at all. After doing the favors, he immediately put in his notice. He left Texas for New York and signed right up with the World Wrestling Federation.

As for me, the same option in New York wasn't quite there yet, so I had to stay in Texas a bit longer. I wanted to leave just like Teddy, but at that time, I honestly had nowhere else I could go.

HOPE

Just by chance, my friend André the Giant was just passing through the territory. He was booked to wrestle for only one week in Amarillo. During this time, I drove him around from show to show for his handful of appearences.

André knew that I was miserable in the Texas territory and understood that Dick Murdoch was sabotaging my career to keep the spotlight on himself, and quite possibly to spite me for stooging him out to Blackjack.

With great empathy for my situation, André decided to have a meeting with Mario Savoldi, a well-respected referee in Amarillo, about me.

CHAPTER 7 – Texas

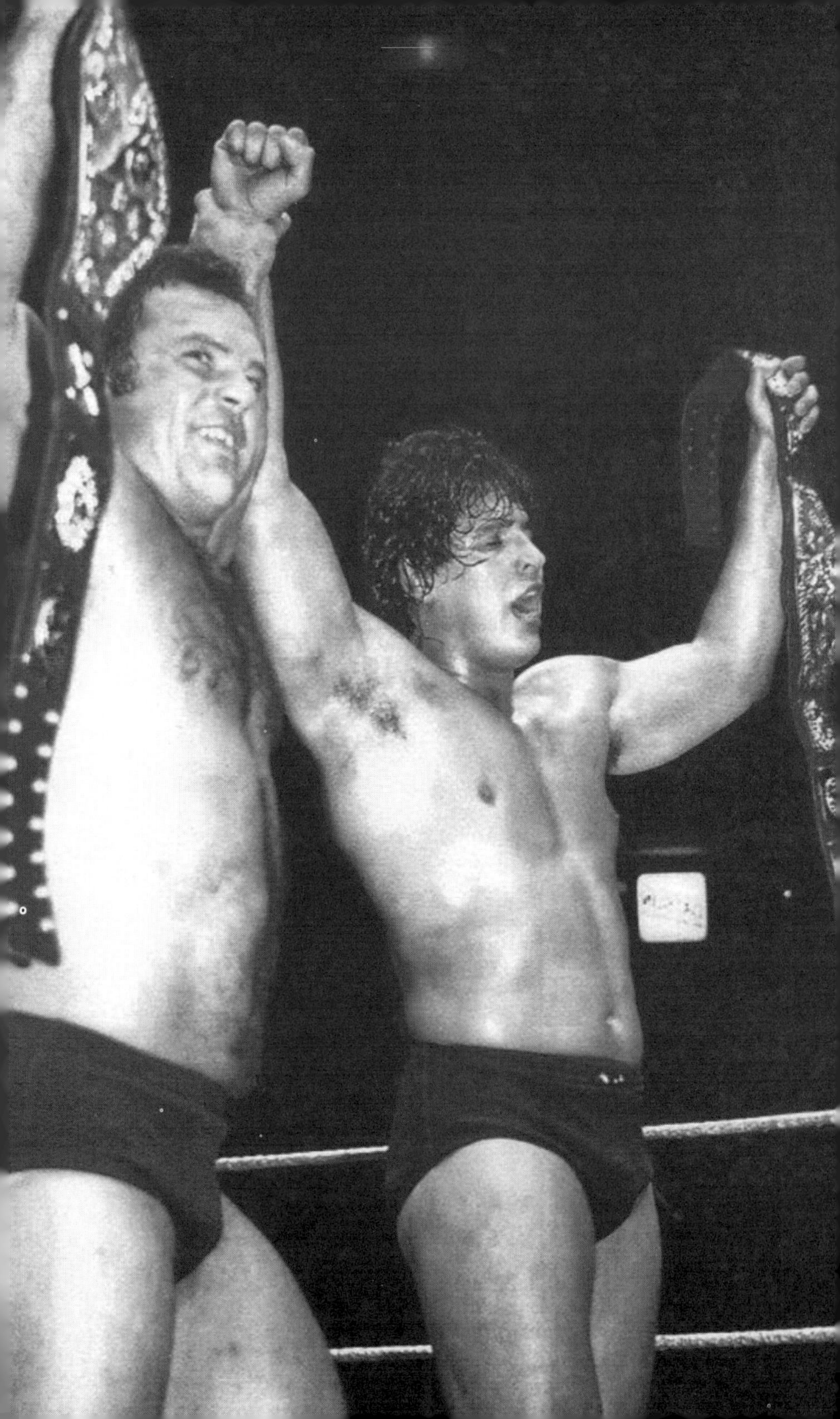

CHAPTER 8 - WWWF

André the Giant talked to referee Mario Savoldi and, in the end, convinced him to help. They both decided to put in a good word for me to try to land me a spot in New York. André borrowed some tapes from Blackjack, and Mario did the same. They both mailed them out, and they both made some calls. Then, one day, Mario called me.

"Now, Merced," Mario said, "Vince McMahon Sr. is probably one of the most respectable promoters in the business."

"Oh, I know," I replied. "You don't have to tell me."

"Well, we called my father, Angelo, and I think we have finally have him interested in you," he said. "Don't let me down."

"Are you serious? Oh my God, thank you so much, brother!" I said, promising him that I would not let him down.

I had never dreamed of getting to New York so soon.

The good thing about the timing of it all was that Vince wanted me to come to New York right after Ted DiBiase had debuted. This was great news because, again, Ted would be there for me. I wouldn't ne swimming into unknown shark-infested waters by myself. I had someone there who could watch my back while I watched his.

WWWF

Today's measuring stick of pro wrestling, WWE, has an interesting background. The promotion's roots go way back to 1915 to a guy named Roderick "Jess" McMahon, a sports promoter who dabbled in basketball and boxing, and one who also booked wrestling matches in Madison Square Garden for over 20 years.

In November 1954, Roderick McMahon died from a brain hemorrhage. Then his partner, Toots Mondt, teamed up with Jess' son Vincent to help run some shows. The younger McMahon with Mondt clicked. They were very successful and soon controlled roughly two thirds of NWA's booking, mostly because of the location of their heavily populated New York territory. They made a lot of money.

However, there was trouble in paradise. In 1963, McMahon and Mondt caught heat with the NWA offices for booking "Nature Boy" Buddy Rogers as the NWA World Heavyweight Championship. After this, Capitol Wrestling left the NWA banner out of protest for some time.

Eventually, Mondt left Capitol in the late 1960s. Vince McMahon quietly rejoined the NWA in 1971 and eventually renamed it the "World Wide Wrestling Federation" in 1979, just a little before I debuted with them.

My first impression of Vince McMahon Sr. was he was a very classy, smart and intelligent man. He was in his early sixties when I first met him. He was tall, fit and always looked good. He was also a good speaker with great ideas.

McMahon was a very sharp dresser with a large wardrobe of stylish suits. He had two homes; he lived in Cape Cod throughout the year, but spent the winters in Florida. While he wasn't at every show, he had several road agents who reported ticket sales to him every night, and others who also filled him in on how the shows had gone.

SAY MY NAME

When I first came into the WWWF, I had a meeting with Vince. Just like Joe Blanchard had suggested, Vince also saw money in me as being someone Latino fans could grab onto and relate to.

Believe it or not, I was the one who picked my new wrestling name; at least the last name. Before my first match with the company, Vince asked me to come up with a catchy name. A couple of days later, at a TV taping, I mentioned to Vince that I liked the name "Santana." He wanted to know if it was a common name. I gave him a little history about the name, telling him there was a Spaniard named Santa Anna who had switched sides and fought bravely for Mexico's independence from Spain in the early nineteenth century. Santa Anna also later led Mexican troops at the Battle of the Alamo and the Battle of San Jacinto.

"Hmm," Vince said. "Let me think about that one."

CHAPTER 8 – WWWF

About a week later at another TV taping, Vince came up to me and said that my wrestling name would be *Tino Santana*. I enthusiastically accepted.

For my first televised match for the WWF, I was set to wrestle as "Tino" Santana. When I got to the show, some fans were waiting outside in the back parking lot hoping to see the wrestlers come in. I went over to a few and signed some autographs as "Tino," then headed in for the event.

After my match, Vince was waiting for me in the dressing room. I was worried at first he didn't like my match.

"From now on, I think we want you to wrestle as 'Tito' not 'Tino' Santana," he said. "Is that okay with you?"

"I Like it," I replied, happy my match was fine. "If it is good enough for you, then it is good enough for me!"

That very night, on the same show, I found myself signing my autograph for the same group of people with a different spelling.

I can only imagine what they thought if they compared the signatures.

He must really be from Mexico. Look! He misspelled his own name!

MY HOMETOWN

When I started wrestling as Tito Santana, the ring announcer Howard Finkel kept announcing to the fans that I was from "Tocula" Mexico.

Try to find that shit on a map somewhere and good luck! There is no such town by that name in Mexico.

The reason for the fictional town name wasn't to hide something or anything. It was just that the Fink was supposed to say "Toluca" but for some reason, Howard just couldn't pronounce it properly.

Backstage, I remember trying to correct him and to have him repeat after me.

"It's Toluca," I would say. "Now try it. *To-lu-ca.*"

"*To-Cula*," he would repeat, incorrectly.

"No no…**To-luca**."

"*Col-tuca*," he would say.

What in the hell?

After several attempts to correct him, I finally gave up. (He did, however, say "Tijuana" correctly when we would switch things up with the El Matador gimmick.)

BUSY SCHEDULES

WWF wrestlers were always on the run. In addition to all of the house shows we did for live audiences, we also had to film for TV every three weeks. And let me tell you, those tapings were not easy, either. The way the TV tapings worked was, we would arrive at the venue usually around 2 p.m. and we wouldn't finish up until usually after midnight!

Now Vince himself didn't make it to a lot of the shows, but he did not have a closed door policy. When Vince McMahon wasn't being tied up on the business side of things, he always made himself available to the wrestlers. Of course, the more important the wrestler was, the more time Vince would allow to talk with him. But either way, these meetings gave us an opportunity to air any complaints in private. McMahon had a way of making the wrestlers feel good about themselves and he was smart to do this.

These meetings were important because the wrestling business was confusing. We had no set pay scale, no union to protect us, and no benefits whatsoever. We were paid weekly, but we could draw (borrow) $100-$200 each night whenever we wrestled. The problem was, we had no way to predict what our pay would be, because our checks changed from one week to the next. There was never any real stability. We were considered self-employed, yet we could only wrestle for the one company that we were bound to. That prevented us from wrestling in multiple territories at once, and to a degree, also limited our exposure. This was the nature of wrestling everywhere, and because of this, it was good to be able to talk to the boss himself.

In a few cases, I had to really fight for my money. I didn't have an agent, so I had to handle everything myself. One time, I remember wrestling in Philadelphia against The Iron Sheik somewhere in the middle of the card. I was paid $1,200 for the match. The very next month, I went back to Philadelphia and again wrestled the Iron Sheik, but this time it actually was the main event. I was higher up on the card, and the attendance increased, but my pay actually went down to $750.

This makes no sense at all!

Rather than to go in like a house of fire, I very politely brought it to their attention, and they immediately agreed. Because of my gracious attitude, they gave me another $750. Now, if I had acted all crazy, they may have given me a few extra dollars, then stopped using me altogether.

I didn't come into the WWF with any promises, but I didn't need any. I just focused on working hard and being dependable. I'll never forget the first time I wrestled at Madison Square Garden. The attendance that night was 22,000, and I wrestled against Johnny Rodz. It was easily the biggest night of my young career, and I made the most of it. Vince gave me a chance, and I didn't let him down. I was as nervous as could be, but I managed to get by without messing up the match.

In 1979, I decided to introduce a different type of wrestling to the company; taking things to the air. At this time, everyone in New York were giant monsters who mostly brawled. My roots in the Southern territories provided me with exceptional training and plenty of experience wrestling against some of the best in the business. I also learned to use skill, finesse and creativity to my advantage.

The WWF was very different from the South. The WWF has big, powerful guys. The fans were used to these hulking wrestlers, not wrestlers who preferred flying maneuvers to brute force. This really made me stick out.

When I started, I threw drop kicks, did flying head scissors, and arm drags, and a few other aerial moves. I had a lot of energy, and my repertoire of moves was quite different from the style of the big guys I was wrestling against. My different style helped me catch the fan's interest. Almost immediately, I had a supportive fan base.

After I started to catch on, I developed a fan in the locker room. Mister Fuji of all people liked what he saw and decided to help me out. He actually requested to work some matches with me so he could help me with timing and how to call spots better in the ring. This "polishing" helped me tremendously and bought me even more TV time.

MISTER FUJI

Ninty-five percent of the wrestling business was traveling. Because of this, guys had to find stuff to kill time. Constantly traveling is one of the worst things about being a professional wrestler. When you don't see a wrestler in the ring, he is either probably driving, making hotel reservations, or setting up flights. As if figuring out your travel is not already bad enough, factoring in ribs on the road was brutal.

Now, Mister Fuji helped me out quite a bit. He liked me so I was relatively safe. But if you got on his bad side, you were a goner. Most of the guys loved Mister Fuji and even affectionately called him Uncle Harry. While he was beloved, he was the king of pranks. His jokes were both legendary and borderline evil. He would pull them in the locker room, in hotels, in airports, in restaurants... nobody was safe anywhere.

Fortunately, I never fell victim to any of his antics. However, he really was an instigator and an innovator when it came to practical jokes and pranks.

He was actually usually considerate to me. We roomed together some to save money. I remember the first night Mister Fuji said, "Tito, you go to sleep first. I snore."

So I did. A few hours later, I woke up and it sounded like the apocalypse. He was snoring so loud, he was waking the dead. Somehow, however, he woke up and knew I was miserable. So he took off and feel asleep in the lobby, or something. He wasn't so thoughtful to everyone, however.

I remember one night after a show, we were taking the redeye out somewhere and there was a guy on the plane who recognized that we were wrestlers started "talking shit." Yes, he was saying how the business was fake and making a point to say it loudly enough so that we could hear it. Fuji, being the master ribber that he is, waited for this guy to fall asleep and then went in to the bathroom. Once he came out, he started back to his seat, but then turned around for a second trip to the bathroom before finally returning to his seat and sitting back down next me.

"Uncle Harry," I said. "You had to go twice?"

"No," he said. "I needed to wash hands."

We flew for a few minutes, then the whole plane smelled like feces.

What Mister Fuji did was wash his hands after he took a shit and placed juicy turd on the shoulder of the sleeping passenger. (Yes, you read that right.)

When the passenger awoke, he took one sniff and found that someone had left a present on his jacket.

"I'm going to kill me a wrestler!" he screamed.

The shit literally hit the fan. ¡Arriba!

Another time, I was actually rooming with Mister Fuji. One night, I saw Fuji down at the hotel bar drinking. There was nobody around, so I went over and sat next to him.

"Looks like you had a few to drink already," I said.

"A few?" he confided. "Maybe six or seven."

We talked for some time, and he drank another six or seven on top of whatever he had had before I got there.

"I'll be right back," I said, excusing myself to the rest room. "I'm surprised you haven't gotten up to take a piss yet, yourself, with all you have been putting down."

Fuji laughed.

"How do you do it?"

The devious one pointed down under the bar. I looked down and realized that drinks weren't the only thing going down.

At some point, he had pulled little Fuji out of his pants and it was just dangling there. When I realized what I was looking at, he unloaded, streaming yellow down on the floor.

I got up and ran in horror. Fuji laughed.

That wasn't the first time. Fuji had a history of pissing in public. Whenever he could get a reaction, he would pee and no-sell it all together. That was his joke. He had no qualms taking out his junk and leaking where ever he damn well pleased. Another time, Fuji was talking to the manager at some hotel in their bar. I go over to Fuji, and he whips it out and just starts pissing away in a potted plant… while he was still talking to the manager the whole time. The manager was so shocked that he didn't know what to say!

Seriously, nothing was off limits to Mister Fuji.

In my first run with the WWF, there were very few people in the locker room who were more respected than Hulk's heel manager, "Classy" Freddie Blassie. Even though Blassie was the man, that didn't mean that he was off limits for a Fuji prank.

If you remember ever seeing Freddie Blassie, he was always known for his fancy outfits and his flashy wardrobe. He spent some serious money on his costumes. One of Fuji's favorite ways to mess with a guy was to go after their weak spots. This way, he would get the biggest reaction. In this case, that meant Fuji had to do something to Blassie's clothes.

One time in the dressing room, Fuji saw that Blassie had a whole suitcase of costumes with him. He probably brought his whole bag so he could do some costume changes between appearances. (We were at a television taping and he always liked to change things up to look fresh for TV.)

When Blassie went out to manage a guy during one of his matches, Fuji rubbed his hands together and got ready to strike. Then, piece by piece, he stapled and superglued all of Blassie's clothing to the ceiling.

Another famous prank of Mister Fuji was the time that he put laxatives in Haystacks Calhoun's coffee at the airport. What happened was, Haystacks got up to go to the rest room just before their flight off to Tokyo because he knew that he couldn't fit in the little tiny lavatories in the air plane. This was a great plan because it was a long flight. However, his one mistake was leaving his coffee, unguarded.

After Haystacks returned, he finished his brew and the two of them boarded the plane. Not even a half hour after takeoff, his stomach started brewing on its own.

Calhoun was dying. He started sweating first. Then, his stomach was making all kinds of noises. He was squirting out farts. He was getting the cramps. He was just dying.

    Calhoun got up. He ran to the bathroom and saw what he already knew; there was no way he was going to fit in there. He couldn't even get one leg in there, let alone his whole body. So went to the back of the plane behind a curtain where two poor tiny Japanese guys were. They held a big trash bag up to his ass. The boys could hear him moaning and squirting shit into the bag.

    Everybody was laughing their asses off.

ANDRÉ IN WWF

    I remember driving André around some in the WWWF. After all, he was instrumental in getting me there, so it was the least I could do. The thing about it was, he broke about three of my car seats until I got wise and reinforced the springs underneath them with bricks. After that, everything was just great.

    He stayed in my apartment a few days here and there. It was always quite a sight to see. I would let him have the bed when he did because my couch was kind of on the small end. When he went in the bedroom, his legs still went off the side of the mattress, so we would rig up some chairs with pillows on them to sit at the foot of the bed for his feet.

    I remember one night, Terry Funk had just divorced his wife. We all went out to the hotel bar after a show, and he was really sad and spilling his heart to us. We were essentially his shoulders to cry on.

    In the wrestling business, you see, some of the boys more than you see your actually family sometimes, so he was like a brother to us. We tried to console him the best we could. We were out drinking after a show in a public place and not really paying attention to our surroundings being engrossed in conversation. When we had let our guard down, that is when some drunk asshole came over to where we were sitting.

    "I couldn't help but hear you guys," he said. "But I wanted you to know that I am the guy dating Terry's wife."

Now, fans could often be stupid when they were around wrestlers. Sometimes they would try to show they were just as "tough" as we were. Other times, they would try to impress us in the most stupid ways you could think of. Now, I don't know if this guy was telling the truth or just full of it, but that was the wrong thing to say at that moment.

Terry looked like he had just been shot in the stomach. André patted him on the shoulder.

"I got this, boss," he said.

The fan laughed a little at Terry's response, but when André stood up, he stopped laughing.

"Tito," he said. "Let's go outside with this guy and have a little talk."

"Okay," I said. (Who is going to tell a giant, no?)

André called for another drink from the bartender and put his arm around the guy harassing us. I followed suit. We both walked out of the bar with the guy and moved around the corner to the alley.

André grabbed him by the shoulders and slammed him against the wall. I figured we were going to have to beat the shit out of this guy, so I got ready. Then, before it got worse, André looked down at me. "Thanks, Tito," he said. "I'll take care of this from here."

I nodded and left. He knew I didn't get myself into trouble much and decided he would be the one to "take out the trash."

As I walked around the corner, I heard some screaming. I don't know if he checked his oil or what, but that guy didn't come back.

When André returned, he ordered another round of tasty drinks for everyone around us.

"What happened out there," Terry asked.

"A little misunderstanding," André said.

"Misunderstanding?" I asked, chuckling.

"Wrong guy," he said.

Now, I don't know if he meant that fellow had mistaken Terry for a different person, or he was just messing with "the wrong guy." It didn't matter though. André took care of it.

Anyone who messed with any of the boys, André was always there to defend them.

ANOTHER NEW GUY

Speaking of "hulking" wrestlers, around this same time a newer wrestler like myself was getting his bags together and taking a flight to New York.

Vince McMahon himself was a proud Irish man and wanted a hero for the Irish population. On top of bringing me in to really reach the Latino population, Vince also wanted to bring in an Irish wrestler to attract more of that ethnic fan base that lived in the Northeast. That is why he suggested that Terry "The Hulk" Boulder take on the Irish surname, Hogan.

Terry wrestled as Terry Boulder at this time on some shows I was on, but the idea was, he was soon going to get that new gimmick and a new name that would end up changing the business.

At the time, Vince McMahon told Terry that he wanted him to dye his hair red, and Terry said he would. However, Terry told most of the boys in the locker room that he never really had any intentions of ever doing so. I remember to make the boys laugh, Terry took the hair dye that Pat Patterson, waited for him to walk out of the room, then flushed it right down the toilet.

"My hair is already starting to fall out," he said. "That dye would probably just melt the rest away."

Soon after that, Terry was wrestling his first match under the name Hulk Hogan, but starting out as a villain. The fans ate it up. During that initial run as a heel, Hogan was paired with "Classy" Freddie Blassie, a wrestler-turned-manager who could really guide Hogan and show him the ropes.

After that, Hulk made his Madison Square Garden debut, defeating my ex-partner, Ted DiBiase. McMahon next put Hogan with Bob Backlund and then started his first big run with the legendary André the Giant.

Terry and I would shadow each other a lot, ending up in the same territories and on the same cards as I would because of timing. I didn't know it at the time, but our intertwining bookings and his success would later be very impactful on the success of my own career.

Around this time, however, Terry hadn't made it quite yet. Like the other promoters, I thought he was just another big dude in the locker room. I did, however, think he could eventually make an impact in the future.

BRUNO SAMMARTINO

Before Hulk Hogan would turn into the fan favorite he would become, the most popular wrestler at this time on the top of the cards was Bruno Sammartino. He was the WWWF World Champion and the main draw for Vince Senior.

With his name on the top of any card, shows would sell out. It didn't matter where he was booked, his name would fill the biggest of all arenas.

Bruno wrestled for over 20 years and held the title of World Champion for something like 13 years. He was never a superstar national or international like Hulk Hogan because he only wrestled in the eastern part of the country. But still, Bruno was the best wrestler of his era.

Bruno was less of a showman than Hulk Hogan. He was a big and tough, rugged, powerful wrestler that everyone respected.

Toward the end of his career, I had the opportunity to work with him and enjoyed it very much. We got to tag team together and we had really good chemistry in the ring. He was very proud of himself and the business, and he was a great role model for younger wrestlers like me.

GAINING VINCE'S RESPECT

It seemed like by the time most wrestlers got the call to go to New York, they were already veteran, polished wrestlers. I had only been in the business for about two and a half years, so I had some work to do before I could be considered for main-event material. I was just glad to be in New York and part of the best wrestling territory in the world.

While Bruno Sammartino didn't really teach me, I learned a lot from watching him in the ring. In fact, I learned mostly all of my moves by watching other wrestlers like him. If I liked a move that I saw on a particular show, I would sometimes try it out for myself the very same night I noticed someone do it. I modeled my matches after a lot of different wrestlers, but no one in particular. I incorporated what I had learned into my own distinct style while providing a fresh younger face for the WWWF.

I had seen the other Latino guys out there like myself. There were Lucha guys out there, and, yes, they were flashy, but they didn't wrestle in the fast aerial style back then that they do today. I saw guys like Chavo Guerrero and thought to myself, "Yes he is decent, but I think I can offer something much different than he does."

Whatever I did, I guess it started to work. Vince McMahon started to notice. He liked my aerial moves and the style I was developing in the ring. He took an interest in me and often took me aside to offer little pointers.

He had been around far longer than me, so I listened. That was probably the best thing I could do for my career.

Fine-tuning my craft, I began to move up the ranks from the earliest matches on the WWWF card as a "curtain jerker" to wrestling higher up on the middle of the card. This told me that Vince was making plans for me.

After only a few months in New York, Vince McMahon told me he wanted me out for an interview on TV. Then, he presented me with a huge trophy and named me "Rookie of the Year."

The trophy presentation was filmed and shown to the entire WWWF viewing audience, which at that time included all of New York, New Jersey, Connecticut, Rhode Island, Massachusetts and Pennsylvania. The WWWF had a potential viewing audience of 80 to 100 million people at this time, and this even more so increased my stock.

Soon after the award ceremony, my stock went up. People really started recognizing me wherever I went.

I remember among one of the first times I was really being recognized by a fan, I was at a urinal at a rest stop. Someone was rushing in to use the facilities after a wrestling show, and I was just rushing out to beat the traffic.

"Tito Santana?" he asked.

"Yes, that's me," I replied.

"Oh my God," he said kind of squirming around. "I am your biggest fan.

"Oh, thank you," I said.

"Please," he asked, "Will you sign my program?"

"It would be my pleasure," I said.

The fan ran back to his car, but stopped for a second, because I think he was turtle-heading; holding back a crap.

He ran back to me with the program and a pen trying his hardest not to pinch a loaf off in his pants.

"I really have to get in there, man, because I ate a lot of hot dogs and drank a lot of beer tonight at the show watching you," he said, "but I just don't want to miss this opportunity."

"No problem," I said, kind of flattered. I mean, after all, this fan really, really had to go, but he actually risked shitting himself to get my autograph! I felt a little bad for him so I agreed to wait for him to get the wrestling program out of his car. However, since it took him longer than I had hoped, I decided to have a little fun and make him wait for me to sign his paper.

As he waited, he was clearly doing the pee-pee dance. As a rib, I took an even longer extra-long time removing the pen cap to sign his program.

"So, how would you like this made out? I asked. "Sign it, or to your name?"

"Yes," he said crossing his legs. "Just your name if fine."

"Are you sure?" I asked, trying not to laugh. "I mean, it's really no problem."

When I finally finished up, he thanked me and ran into the bathroom faster than a cheetah in heat.

He probably almost crapped himself over my signature, both literally and figuratively.

GETTING COLOR

From what I had learned, getting color was a great way to make money when used correctly. Now, I rarely did it much, and that really was the way it should have been. If you did it all the time, you would end up with a forehead that looked like an air vent. Look at Abdullah the Butcher and you will know what I mean.

Blood was usually really reserved as a means to get over a feud between two guys and typically for a return match, a money match. Not everyone followed this rule, however.

Enter Captain Lou Albano.

Captain Lou who was one of the greatest managers and one of the greatest talkers in the business ever. But boy could Lou drink! You would always see him with a big pastic thermos, walking around, sipping on that thing and you just knew that the clear liquid in the jug was not water.

One time before a show, I saw the Captain drinking like a camel and said, "What do you got there, Lou?"

"You know, your body is like 90 percent fluid. I have to replenish my fluids," he said.

The thing about it was, your body is supposed to me like 90% water, not 90% vodka!

Later that night, I was working with Lou. Not even a minute or so in, I whipped him to the ropes and he fell out on the apron. Despite the fact we were only one minute in, Loue was already cutting his head. I think he thought that he didn't get enough color so he went back to the well. I looked again and saw him cutting his shoulder and cutting his neck! Red fluid was flying everywhere.

I laughed. He had to have been messing with me.

Ridiculous!

IVAN PUTSKI

Vince Senior was smart. He really knew exactly how to bring a wrestler along and turn him into a star. His sense of timing and pace was exceptional and I can't say enough good things about him.

Four months into my WWF career, he decided to give me a title push, teaming me with "Polish Power" Ivan Putski.

Our pairing was a good one. Ivan was bigger. People couldn't sympathize with him if he was getting beat up in the ring, because he looked like he should be able to take a lot of pain with all that muscle. So what we would do is I'd take the heat and get the audience behind me, and Ivan would come in for the save. We just blended well.

As a team, we were great. I'd do fast stuff, and Ivan would do power moves. We were very well-rounded.

Professionally speaking, it was also great for me because working with Ivan really helped get me polished. He helped me even more understand the importance of positioning in the ring. Also, with the age difference, he taught me about life-lesson stuff that I needed to know so that the business didn't eat me up. He helped sharpen me to life on the road and what I needed to do to survive.

At the time, the Valiant Brothers (Jerry & Johnny) were the champions. Vince had us beat a number of contender tag teams first to give us some credibility, before our big title match on March 6, 1979, in Allentown, Pennsylvania. That is when we won the WWWF Tag Team Championship belts. Thanks to that push, I began making more money than I had ever made in my life.

I was getting tons of TV and magazine exposure with my tag team title run. It was insane. There I was, only three years in the business, and already a tag-team champion in the number-one wrestling league in the world. Every match I was getting booked in, I was competing against the promotion's very top stars, and I was also doing weekly interviews to put over our team.

A lot of the boys were happy for me, but maybe not so much for Ivan. Some of them were pretty jealous of him at the time. He had a pretty sweet deal. All of his boys were playing football at the time, and he had it in his contract that he could go and watch them play on weekends when the rest of his peers were usually working for Vince. Quite often, Vince would actually fly him to go see his sons play. The boys hated it, but you can't really blame him. He was a big name and could command perks because of it.

Ivan and I held the titles for close to six months before we lost them to The Wild Samoans in April 1980.

VINNIE

During this time, I got to know Vince McMahon's son, who we all called "Vinne." I didn't know it at the time, but by befriending him, I was able to lay the groundwork needed to eventually step my game up even more in the future.

In 1980, and at this point in his career, Vince's son was just a commentator. He was about 35 years old in 1980 when I met him, and the locker room treated him like just one of the boys. He was athletic and liked to work out, so the wrestlers naturally took to him. He was well put together and became a weightlifter.

During our interview sessions, I first noticed that Vinnie had a work ethic like you could not believe. He could work, work, work, like nobody else and barely needed any sleep. I remember watching him interview wrestlers for seven or eight hours at a time, non-stop, and he never complained. They say he is still like this today, and even considers "sleep" to be his number one enemy.

Vinne in 1980 was very much like his dad. He was a super nice guy, down-to-earth and treated everyone with a certain amount of respect. He had a way of making you feel important and his charisma helped him get done what he wanted to get done.

Now, the father was never much around at shows. He was more of a businessman who was at the office more, taking care of business. What a lot of people don't know is he had partners at this time. He was still the real "owner" owning about 51 percent of the pie, but the partners mostly ran the show. The partners, I believe, included Gorilla Monsoon, Arnold Skaaland, and Phil Zacko, who was also small part-owner. Angelo Savoldi was an agent, and he too helped run the shows.

Now, for all I know, maybe one or two of them could have been ripping Vince off because the father was never around to really see the money. People may have been skimming off the top. I remember at one point, I was making only about $75 a match before I won the tag titles, but a few of the boys think I was being reported as making higher than that to Vince because of conversations they had had. None of that would matter though, as it was all about to change.

LEAVING WWWF

Of course, I didn't really go, but back then everything was mostly done in cycles, even the talent exposure. Most of the guys found success in touring with one promotion and moving to another one when they got stale. Fans then really liked fresh, new talent that they hadn't seen before, and the territorial system provided a great way for you to bring your show on the road when one area's fans had had enough of you. Then, one you had done a number of other promotions, you could return fresh with new material and ideas, plus the fans will have missed you because absence makes the heart grow fonder.

So when I lost the tag championship, Vince came to me and kind of gave the hint as to what should happen next, after explaining this.

"Well, what is it you think I should do, Vince?"

"I think you should go out, get some more experience, and then come back."

So that is just what I did.

I really liked Vince's honesty with me. In fact, he became a bit of a mentor for me when I really needed it back then. Whenever I would contemplate moving to a new territory or sometimes a change with how I was doing business, I would call Vince for advice.

Vince didn't leave me high and dry though, either. If you were in good with the bookers, back then they would often call another territory and find you a gig on your way out, sometimes facilitating a trade for their own promotion. In this case, however, Vince found me another tour in Japan.

Bad News Brown, Tito Santana, Osamu Kido, and Dusty Rhodes - 1980 NJPW

CHAPTER 9 - NEW JAPAN

My second trip to Japan was a better experience than my first one. This one was from May 1, 1980 to June 11, 1980 and it was for New Japan Pro Wresting, run by Antonio Inoki, the rival promotion to Giant Baba's All-Japan.

A QUICK JAPANESE WRESTLING LESSON

Before All-Japan & New Japan existed, the biggest promotion in Japan was JWA: The Japanese Wrestling Alliance. This promotion was founded by Rikidōzan, a man who is credited with bringing pro wrestling in Japan to the mainstream.

In 1963, their leader Rikidōzan was killed by a member of the Yakuza. With Rikidōzan gone, JWA had to then rely on two of their younger stars to fill the seats; Antonio Inoki and Giant Baba. Baba and Inoki were top stars in the promotion for years, both as singles wrestlers and as a tag team. The JWA remained successful until they began to lose fans to a new rival promotion called IWE.

By 1972, Inoki and Baba were both unhappy with the direction that the JWA was going. They were eventually both fired for trying to change things behind the scenes. As a result, both wrestlers decided to start their own promotions. Baba founded All-Japan Pro Wrestling, and Inoki started New Japan Pro Wrestling. Immediately after that, the JWA went out of business.

Antonio Inoki appointment himself as the president and the top star of NJPW from day one. Within the first year, NJPW had a TV show and the NJPW Dojo was also established as a training system for many of the company's top stars and is still crafting many young talents to this day.

Initially, NJPW did not bring in wrestlers from out of the country. The only exceptions to this were Karl Gotch (Inoki's trainer,) Lou Thesz, Billy Robinson and André the Giant. NJPW was a "purist promotion" promoting technical wrestling ability over theatrics and characters.

In 1974, NJPW started a yearly tradition of having a tournament between the company's best heavyweights every summer which would become called the G1 Climax, and soon became a part of the National Wrestling Alliance.

In 1976, arguably Inoki's most famous match took place when he had a special attraction bout with Muhammad Ali. During this time, New Japan was second to All-Japan in terms of popularity. Despite the poor quality of the bout, Inoki's popularity in Japan grew. In 1978, New Japan then formed a working relationship with the WWWF when Inoki went to America and was awarded by Vince McMahon with the WWWF World Martial Arts Heavyweight Championship, a title that would be defended solely in NJPW despite being branded as a WWWF title.

After that, Inoki started to play catch up with what Giant Baba was doing over in All-Japan. Baba's formula of booking foreign talents to headline events had been working very well and had placed All-Japan above New Japan for many years. However, at the tail end of the 70s. Inoki began bringing in a lot more foreign talents, many of whom would go on to become huge names in the WWWF.

Growing competition between NJPW and All-Japan led to increased ruthlessness and higher paychecks in order to compete for the best talents which directly leads us to a tour that I was booked on.

OUR 1980 TOUR

Hulk Hogan was booked to go over to NJPW in 1980, through a bit of a talent exchange with Vince McMahon. I was booked on that same Hulkster tour along with André the Giant, Dusty Rhodes, Chavo Guerrero, Bad News Allen, Bob Backlund and a few others.

On this tour, Hulk Hogan instantly become a big star. In order to fit in in New Japan's world, Hulk actually used a more technical style than we are all used to seeing from him. NJPW fans nicknamed him "Ichiban" (number one) as a result.

This time around, I would not lose any weight. André the Giant was also still a big star at the time in Japan, so sponsors would take him out every night and wine and dine him. As part of the deal, however, he would always bring me along for the ride. Therefore, I ate like a king.

The sponsors had no problem paying for my dinner. It was a small price to pay in order to hang with André the Giant. Every night I was eating Kobe beef, and the finest foods they had to offer. It really was great.

One night, however, we had a night off from the shows. There were no sponsors. Just me and André.

"Let's go on a date," the big man said.

"A date, huh?"

André laughed. "Yes, boss. You and me."

"You and me?"

"I'll buy."

He was too big to say no to, so I went on the date.

We went out to see a movie first and fortunately for me, he was a perfect gentleman.

I kind of got the gist of the film, even though it was all in Japanese. Watching, you could get an idea of what was going on, so it wasn't all that bad. The characters, however, were drinking wine throughout the whole movie.

After it was over, André and I went to a restaurant for dinner. There were no sponsors to foot the bill, but sure enough, he ordered an expensive bottle of wine. I mean, the moment the waitress came to the table, "wine" was the very first thing he said, even before she handed us the menus.

"So, why are you ordering wine?" I asked the giant sitting before me.

"That movie made me thirsty," he winked.

As I looked over the menu, I struggled trying to understand the language. It looked like something from another world. But as for the prices, I understood numbers all too well. I had to.

When the waitress returned, the first bottle was gone. André immediately ordered another. I looked in the menu and quickly identified what we were about to drink, and figured out what we were going to have to pay.

I couldn't believe it.

"André!" I said. "This bottle cost $200.

André just laughed and said, "Drink, Boss!"

So drink I did, and I drank a lot. (I'm glad André didn't try to take advantage of me that night!)

André always treated me like a younger brother. He was so good to me, and he made my time overseas so enjoyable. I will say this though. I didn't much like going to Japan because you were just so far away from home. During my period over though, my sister lost a baby. I could only call once a week to offer condolences. It was like $80 for three minutes. It just costed too much to call as much as I wanted to.

By the time I had returned to the states, she had already buried the baby. Trips to Japan were just so far away that if an emergency were to happen, it was almost impossible to get back early, souring me on future ones.

ANTONIO INOKI

A word about Antonio Inoki... Despite the fact that Japan was looking to not really be my cup of tea, Inoki was just as generous to me as Giant Baba was.

However while Inoki was generous, he was very against losing in his own matches. He'd invested in himself for his own promotion, and was almost never on the losing end of the stick, especially in his earlier days. Because of this, a win against Inoki would be a huge feather in anybody's cap because they were so far and few between.

A few years after this tour, I was invited once again to join the Hulkster on an NJPW tour but politely declined. On that tour in 1983, Inoki was taken out on a stretcher during a match with Hogan legit, and was hospitalized!

See, Hulk's Japanese wrestling style was far more technical than the kick, punch, leg drop stuff that led to Hulkamania was running wild in the WWF. Over there in the "Land of The Raising Sun," Hulk was using a different finisher; a running forearm called the "Axe Bomber."

Apparently, Hogan nailed Inoki with it and something was wrong with their timing. As a result of this miscue, Hulk accidentally knocked Inoki out for real! Because Inoki never lost a match, this accident instantly made Hogan an even bigger internatiaonal name!

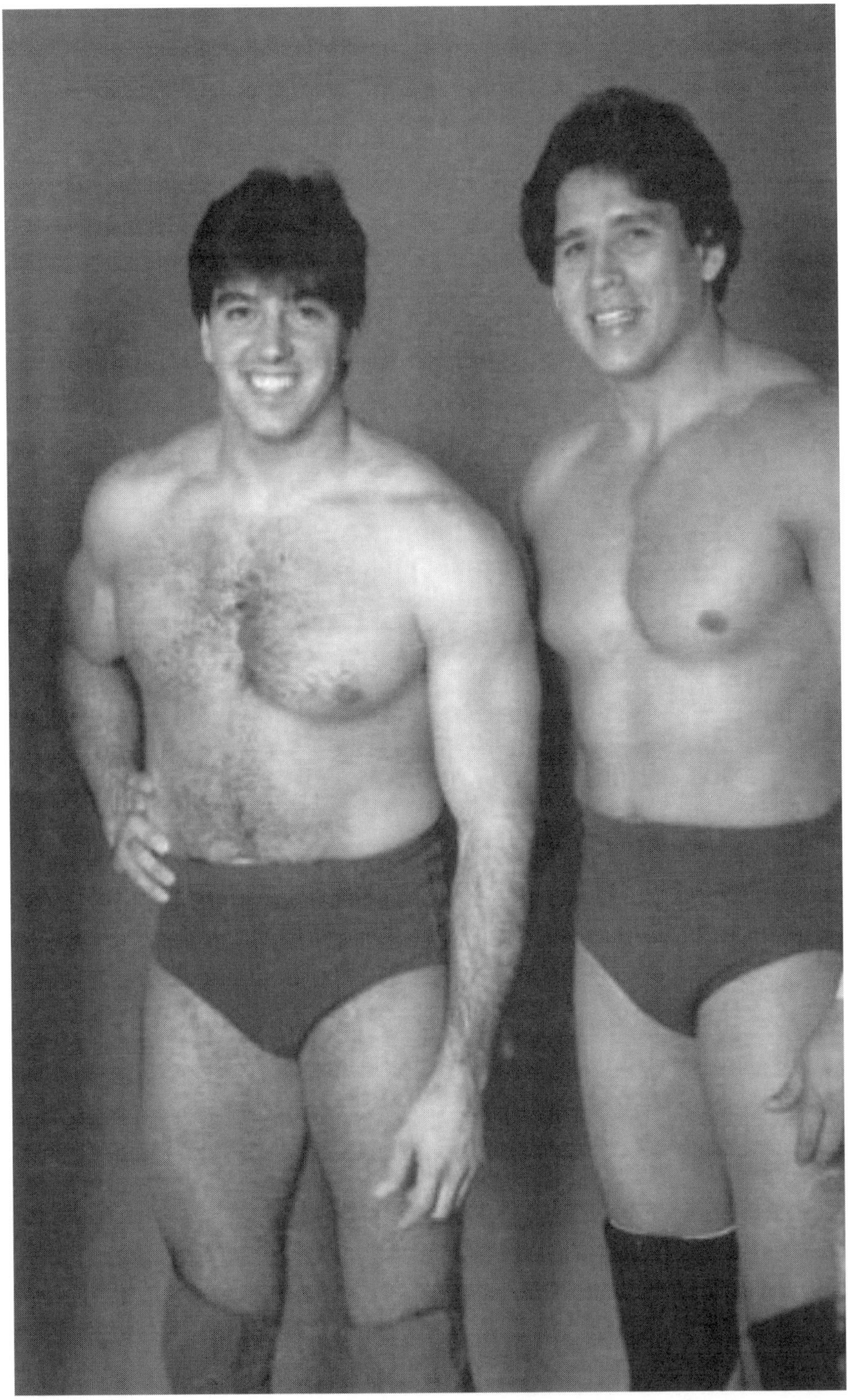

CHAPTER 10 - AWA

Continuing to gain the experience that Vince McMahon Sr. (my mentor) told me to get, I was all set to wrestle in the American Wrestling Association in what would be a decent run from 1980 to 1982.

When I first stepped foot into the promotion, I walked into the locker room and saw a familiar face. I was reunited with a good friend of mine from my Atlanta tour and an incredibly strong Italian guy who had received his biggest push from the Montreal territory; *Dino Bravo.*

Dino was awesome and a classy guy. He immediately took me under his wing, gave me some pointers, and trained with me at the gym. We were inseparable, and he made my transition to the AWA a simple one.

I actually roomed up with him and he was the one who suggested I use *"¡Arriba!"* at the end of my promos to add excitement and a finish to them. He was right, and that catch phrase would follow me for the rest of my career.

AWA HISTORY

The AWA was technically the Minnesota territory. It had a rich history in its 30 years of business and was known and loved around the world by its fans.

The AWA started after a dispute over who the NWA World champion was. See, back in July 1957, Eduardo Carpentier defeated Lou Thesz for the NWA championship in a two-out-of-three falls match. However, since one of the falls was a disqualification, promoters who wanted to continue to call Thesz the NWA champion started to question whether or not Carpentier should rightly be recognized as the champion. Ultimately, the NWA's official decision was to return the title to Thesz. However, several promoters continued to recognize Carpentier as the NWA World champion so that their cards too would draw better and make money. Eventually, one of them (Wally Karbo) booked an NWA title match in August of 1958 and had Carpentier lose to Verne Gagne.

With some promoters recognizing Gagne as NWA champion and others recognizing Thesz, some kind of unification match was really needed, but everyone was stubborn and it never happened.

By 1960, promoter Wally Karbo lobbied for his man (Gagne) to be recognized as the champion, but the NWA stood their ground. Subsequently, Karbo split off from the NWA and formed the American Wrestling Association.

As a peace offering, the newly formed AWA recognized the sanctioned NWA World champion Pat O' Connor as their first champion, and gave him 90 days to defend his title against Verne Gagne "or be stripped of it." The NWA ignored this challenge, and Verne Gagne was awarded the AWA World title in August of 1960.

The AWA continued to grow nationally. Operating mostly in the mid-west and Winnipeg, Gagne defended his title in NWA mainstay cities against former NWA champions. And for the better part of those 10 years, not much else happened of note in the AWA. From the late 60s until 1980, the AWA only had two people wearing the AWA title, and they were Verne Gagne and Nick Bockwinkel, whose victory over Verne Gagne in 1975 was the first one in seven years, and he would hold the belt until 1980.

By 1980, however, wrestling was changing. Promoters stopped working together and became even more greedy. There were less cross-promotional cards with different guys working together. The more competitive nature of the business just got worse and worse because of egos. This change came about from promoters stepping on each other's toes because of the expanding reach of television. (And it goes without saying that Vince Jr. was a big proponent of this.)

AWA VS WWF

The AWA was not at all like WWF. The AWA had a reputation among the boys as being an easier place to work than some of its competitor promotions. While they didn't always pay as well as other territories, their schedule was so much lighter that they made it worth it.

Generally speaking, there was probably somewhere in the area of over a hundred dates less than what other promotions were running a year. Wrestlers worked only 200 to 220 days a year, leaving plenty of days off. In the WWF, I was lucky if I had two days off a month. The AWA only had about 16 regular wrestlers and only one event per night. The WWF, by comparison, had 40 regular guys and ran in two different towns per night.

Verne Gagne ran things in an entirely different way than Vince McMahon did. The two were actually complete opposites; Vince was a tall, well-dressed man, but Verne was short and bald. Vince never wrestled, but Verne was in his late fifties and still the AWA World Heavyweight Champion. (He held the title well into his sixties.)

The two companies had completely different attitudes about the business. Vince's focus was on moving the company into the entertainment category, but the AWA was more old school and interested in just selling out arenas.

Verne wanted everyone to think the business was on the up and up. He did not want the good guys hanging around with the bad guys; he expected believability. However, I don't know why he thought that people would believe that a 60-year-old man could beat Hulk Hogan.

BIRTH OF HULKAMANIA

In 1979, "Sterling Golden" debuted in Memphis. While he didn't impress many with his actual wrestling skills, his look and his personality set him aside from the rest.

In 1981, Vince McMahon scooped him up as a heel under the name Terry Boulder, then later Hulk Hogan as a heel against André the Giant. Eventually, Hogan left to tour of Japan. The ball started rolling. Late in 1982, he returned to America.

Hollywood casted him as Thunderlips in *Rocky III*. Hulk's major role in this third Rocky movie with Sylvester Stallone, gave Hogan immediate mainstream attention. Vince Senior didn't want Hulk to star in the movie because it would have taken him away from wrestling and he would have also lost control. So Hulk didn't go back to the WWF, he went to the AWA.

Verne, on the other hand, decided to take full advantage of the situation and mainstream attention Hulk was getting. The AWA actually played scenes of the movie on their wrestling program to help promote Hogan, which it did.

When Hulk finally came to the AWA to work for Verne Gagne, he was actually a heel, like he was in the Rocky movie. He brought in Johnny Valiant to manage him. Vern told me that he originally was supposed to be a villain in the AWA, but the fans just were not going to let that happen. He looked so out there that the fans were cheering and eating it up. So Vern quickly turned him face and fired Johnny Valiant.

From that point on, Hulk was as a newly turned babyface. Hulkamania was on fire and he was the biggest attraction in wrestling. Both starring in the Rocky movie and also being impressive in the ring had a lot to do with the new-found success that AWA was seeing. They started selling out everywhere.

I saw the fans around him. People couldn't believe their eyes. He was solidly built and stood 6-foot-7. For his size, he was very quick. His physical attributes were only part of the reason he became beloved. More importantly, he was exceptionally charismatic. Fans loved everything about him. So did many of his fellow wrestlers. Money fell off him.

When the arenas were full with Hulk on the card, we all made money. And the good thing about it was, the arenas were always full! I consider myself lucky to have been with Hulk for most of my career. He made my career a success.

Throughout the years, I have heard and read others who would knock Hulk's success. But I honestly think it all has to do with jealousy. The wrestling business is about who can get people to buy tickets or tune in on TV. Without reservations, I can say no one did it better than the Hulk.

So there in the AWA, they were selling tickets like never before. There was a buzz around one Supercard show

CHAPTER 10 – AWA

where it was said that Hulk Hogan might have been set to beat Nick Bockwinkel for the AWA title. This was the perfect opportunity to finally change the title and usher in new young talent that AWA desperately needed. But that's not what they did. They left the belt on Nick.

The AWA didn't take the risk and, in the end, they missed the boat on Hulkamania and the money around it.

BIRTH OF THE BURRITO

Before my time in Minnesota, my finisher was a flying cross body. I would hit the ropes, jump in the air, and turn to land on my opponent flat in a pinning combination.

Somewhere along the way in the AWA, I made a mistake. As a high spot, I randomly went for a flying cross body but quickly realized that was the finish for the match, so I added a flying elbow to it, at the very last second.

Whoa! That got a big pop.

Immediately after that, I changed my finish to that.

It wouldn't be until the next promotion that I worked for (in my return to the WWF) that Bobby Heenan would end up naming it in commentary, calling it "The Flying Burrito."

UP IN THE SKY

Up until this point in my career, like any wrestler, I always had to drive to all the different cities. This was the norm in most territories. That was pretty much the nature of the business when the cities were within driving distance. However, in the AWA there was another option that we took advantage of from time to time… *the AWA airplane!*

In the AWA, some of the wrestlers actually flew from show to show in Verne Gagne's small Cessna plane. Infact, some of them actually took advantage of the plane most of the time, meaning they used it even more than driving.

The way that it worked was we would leave our house at five o'clock in the evening and could actually be home most of the time by midnight. That meant no need for hotels!

There was one problem though about flying. You try squeezing a bunch of rough pro wrestlers into a small plane and see what happens. I have to admit, we had more than a few close calls on that plane!

One time, I was just minding my own business in the plane, when all of a sudden, a loud blast came from behind me. My hair flew backwards and the pressure changed. We turned around to see that one of the wrestlers, who was drunk, opened the rear door in flight! He had dropped his pants and was actually trying to urinate out the back hatch. I couldn't believe it. Imagine being below on the ground, maybe walking to church or something and then feeling some drops on your forehead and realizing you were getting pissed on. Talk about golden showers! ¡Arriba!

I mean, I never pissed out the back, but there was more than one occasion on that plane where I pretty much shit my pants. Another time, the pilot forgot to switch gas tanks and we barely had enough fuel to land. Another time, we had an emergency landing at an air force base due to fog because our lights were faulty. Whoever said you are safer in the air, never rode the AWA airplane.

MEAN GENE OKERLUND

I believe that the two years I spent in the AWA were the most valuable to my career. The only way to get to the top is to compete against the best, and I did just that for those two years in Minnesota. However, the other part of wrestling is what happens behind the microphone. The AWA vastly improved my interviews.

Practice makes perfect. I gained so much good experience by both practicing and learning from the other AWA guys who were already great on the stick. I remember talking for hours to guys like the Crusher, Baron Von Rashke, and Mad Dog Vachon about how I improve my promos. They taught me that it wasn't really just about trash talking, but rather how to progress the story as a whole.

Eventually, I came up with a promo-cutting formula; giving the history or setting the stage, putting the opponent's ability over, and explaining how I would do everything I could to overcome the odds and beat them. This formula worked and helped get me over even more.

The AWA television commentator at the time was Gene Okerlund. He handled all the interviews. He was absolutely excellent at doing his job. Having him there to lead me while I was really getting the hang of it even further helped me sharpen my skills and make me even better.

Gene could lead you along, and if you messed up, he was right there to get out of a mess. Gene knew I was young and inexperienced when it came to TV interviews, so he was always there with the right questions to move me in the right direction. His questions helped me along that formula above that I tried to outline for you here. He always made sure to get the very best out of me, and his questions did just that.

He would later becoming almost a house hold name with his "Mean Gene" gimmick in the WWF. However, he was hardly mean spirited in real life. He was simply the best. I would argue to say that Mean Gene was to wrestling in his heyday what John Madden was to the NFL.

SGT. SLAUGHTER

A guy named Robert Remus (better known to fans as Sgt. Slaughter) is still one of my best friends to this day.

In 1977, I first met Sarge working in Atlanta. When I entered that territory, Sarge was already getting a big push, but he still took the time to be nice to me backstage while I was still learning. In return, I put him over (in a handicapped match with Don Kernodle), and I did everything I could to make him look good. I took crazy bumps, I sold my ass off for him, and I made him look like a monster.

Sarge today says that match totally raised his stock in the eyes of the fans. He says that match was a turning point in his career and that it actually helped put him in line to make thousands and thousands of dollars.

As a result, Sarge became a loyal friend of mine and wanted to return the favor. In fact, as he was on his way out of the AWA when I showed up to Minnesota, so he personally asked Verne to book us together in matches in which he lost just to help put me over and help me shine.

By the time I made my way to Minnesota, I was past just trying to figure out the fundamentals and that made things easier as far as being able to socialize with another wrestler outside of topics related to the business. Our time together in the AWA is when Sarge and I really were really able to get to know each other and would lead to an even better friendship in the future.

JERRY BLACKWELL

I worked with a number of AWA big men, but one who really stood out was Crusher Blackwell. Known as "The Mountain from Stone Mountain," Jerry Blackwell started his career in the 1970s. Despite being a super heavyweight at sometimes almost 500 pounds, Blackwell was one of the most agile big men I had ever worked with and a truly a gifted worker. He was able to throw a great standing dropkick! Putting him with me only made sense.

Our different styles made for some great matches. Like Bruiser Brody, he was the kind of guy who if he gave it to you, you had to give it back. If you didn't, he would just kill you in the ring.

Blackwell was known for his ridiculous feats of strength. One of the most famous stunts that he often performed during live interviews was driving nails into 2x4s using nothing but his head. During some of our matches, I became a softer target than for Blackwell's hammering head than a board with a nail in it.

BIG AWA MATCHES

The biggest matches I had in the AWA included ones against Nick Bockwinkel. The first real big one was in Saint Paul, Minnesota, on March 1, 1981, and the second was in Winnipeg, Manitoba, on May 13, 1982. Bockwinkel, of course, won both of these matches by cheating, the bastard!

When Verne came to me and told me he wanted me to work some matches against the AWA Champion, I was ecstatic. I knew Nick Bockwinkel was a shooter and a hooker. His dad was Lou Thesz's best friend, so if his son was anything like that crowd, I was going to really have to bring my A-game.

When doing my homework on our upcoming matches, I was told that when working with Nick, I had to watch out for "his weight." What he would do in various "rest holds" to keep you on your game was put all of his weight on you. If he had you in say a headlock down on the mat, he would put his weight on it and smoosh the jelly out of your skull. "Now, don't do the same to him," they would say. "You will only make him angry."

I first time around when I wrestled Nick Bockwinkel was the end of 1980 into the start of 1981. Our matches turned out to be just great. We actually had some one hour Broadway matches, which were a first for me, where I really learned how to read the crowd. Working with him really upped my game.

We got a pretty good rivalry going by the time Nick started his second reign as AWA champion. Our AWA title matches made it to nearly every stop on the AWA circuit. While I never beat Nick for the AWA title, this run established me as a national main event singles star probably for the first time in my career.

One time, I was wrestling AWA Champion Nick Bockwinkel. My 300-pound brother was in the audience watching the show, and he was never smartened up on how things worked and thought it was all real.

FAMILY AFFAIRS

Wrestling "secrets" were usually shared on a need-to-know-basis. There were a lot of guys like myself who never really told even their family how things worked.

At the end of the match, we had wrestled to a 60-minute draw. The referee raised my hand, as a show of respect. My brother mistakenly thought I had won the belt and become the new AWA Champ and bum rushed the ring. He grabbed me. he picked me up and started hugging and squeezing me. Now, I had just wrestled nonstop for 60 minutes and was completely exhausted. I had to scream at him to put me down and let me go because I could barely breathe.

At that moment, security came into the ring to drag him away. Things got rowdy, and there was pushing and shoving.

"No. It's okay," I told security. "He is my brother!"

When the ring announcer finally told the crowd that a title doesn't change on a draw and that Nick Bockwinkel was still the champion, my brother calmed down.

He was heartbroken and in tears!

"Don't worry, I'll get him next time."

On July 4, 1982 in San Antonio, Texas, there was yet another "family affair."

I teamed with Terry Funk to battle Gino Hernandez and Tully Blanchard in a match for the AWA. During the course of the match, I was thrown over the ropes and fell down hard on the concrete floor. Gino climbed out of the ring and started putting the boots to me.

As I sold his kicks for the audience, I noticed that a lady was hitting Gino, and I started laughing. Because I was still selling the kicks, I couldn't really see her face, and I didn't think anything of it at the time other than him getting bitch-slapped by a fan was pretty funny.

Shortly thereafter, the match ended in a disqualification for Gino and Tully, the heel team.

When I got back to the dressing room, Gino said to Tully, "I can't believe it! As I was putting the boots to Tito, this fat Mexican girl came over and was slapping me on the back."

He was livid.

"Tito," he said. "Would you look at this shit?" As he turned, he pulled up his t-shirt and showed us the marks on his back.

I laughed, thinking it was another rowdy fan, over excited by the realistic picture that we were painting.

After I cleaned up, I met my family at a local restaurant for dinner. My mom, brother, sister, aunt, and her family had all drove up that evening to watch me wrestle. As we were eating, my brother told me that my sister had hit Gino during my match.

CHAPTER 10 – AWA

All of a sudden I put two and two together. The big Mexican girl that Gino was talking about was my sister. I told my family how Gino was complaining about such a girl in the locker room. My sister said, "Yes, it was me. I was mad at him for kicking you." We all had a good laugh, but I continued to protect the business.

HIGH FLYERS

Another set of great matches I had in AWA were actually in their tag team division in a series of babyface versus babyface bouts. For this program, I was teamed up with Rick Martel against the High Flyers, Greg Gagne and Jim Brunzell.

One thing about Greg, he wasn't very big, but he had psychology. He really could work like his father. He often got a bum rap trying to live up to his father's name, which he could never really do, but he really was a good performer.

On August 29, 1982, in Saint Paul, Minnesota, we lost probably the highest profile match in our series. Why? Well, because one of The High Flyers was the promoter's kid, so what can you do? ¡Arriba!

But the most important point worth mentioning here is that I was teaming for the first time with a future tag team partner who would eventually hold the WWF Tag Team Championship with me. (More on this later.)

JIM BRUNZEL

Speaking of The High Flyers, Jim Brunzell would later follow me to the WWF and become one of The Killer Bees (the one that the Iron Sheik didn't want to make humble.) I have a funny Brunzell story, so I thought I would tell it here.

One time a bunch of us were at a bar. Jim Brunzell and I were drinking a cold beer after a match which really was a great thing to do to unwind. We were pretty much minding our own business when Ric Flair comes over to our table.

Now, as I mentioned before, some guys don't spend their money very wisely. Flair was on a mad tear that night and was buying rounds of beer for the whole place. He had done it so much that they forced him to pay his tab, and wisely because he had spent his whole night's earnings.

"Hey, Jimmy," he said, leaning on the bar already three sheets to the wind. "Can I borrow $20?"

"Sure, Naitch," Brunzell replied.

Flair ordered a drink.

"That will be $4," the girl said.

Flair gave the $20 bill to the waitress, smiled his sexiest smile and said, "Keep the change."

"Ric! But that was my $20!" said Brunzell.

"I'll pay you back."

I saw Brunzell recently at a comic book convention and asked him if he remembered that night.

"Sure do. He still owes me $20."

HULKSTER LEAVING THE AWA

The problem was that Verne Gagne didn't want to change the AWA's old school style. He didn't like the idea of rock-n-wrestling.

Also, Verne didn't want to share merchandising with Hogan, who was hot off his Rocky appearance. Hulk wanted to sell t-shirts and really push the gimmick, but he wanted a piece of the pie that Verne did not want to agree to. Verne said no to the idea of splitting merchandise profits, so Hulk eventually decided he had had enough, and made a phone call to someone who was willing to pay a little more.

Hulk went back to Vince.

Letting the Hulkster go was perhaps the worst business decision by Verne Gagne that he could make. Any money they lost in the merchandise would have easily been made up by additional revenues from house shows or the additional merchandise they would sell overall because of Hogan.

The bad business decision by the AWA turned out good for Hogan, and also good for me, as we would follow each other once again over to WWF.

Hulk Hogan, after basically being told that the AWA World title was not coming his way, left for the WWF by the fall of 1983, and never looked back.

CHAPTER 10 – AWA

As you all know, Vince would put his World title on Hogan almost immediately after Hogan's entrance back to the company.

The war between the "Big Three" (which at the time were WWF, NWA and AWA) suddenly looked very different. This move with Hulk Hogan put WWF on top of the world, it put Jim Crockett struggling to find direction for the NWA, and Verne Gagne watched his fan base shrink.

The essential problem was that Verne Gagne was old school. He believed that wrestling should be depicted as a sport and not as "sports entertainment." If you go back and look at some of his matches in the 70s, you can see Verne locking in wrestling holds that could go on for ten minutes at a time. I think this mentality is possibly what hurt his promotion.

Verne didn't really go for gimmicks. He didn't like the cartoony, circus-like feel that the WWF was going for. He continued to push the stars of the olden days like The Crusher, Mad Dog Vachon, Baron Von Rashke and Nick Bockwinkel, but he didn't make way for new talent.

Verne had guys could continue to be used effectively in the upper card, while the new breed of power wrestlers such as Ken Patera, Scott Hall, and even top draw Hulk Hogan, were more of a side attraction to be used to build to the older Bockwinkel's title defenses.

There was one guy who was willing to take Hogan on.

BOUNCING OUT

In the end, they had me finish that program with Rick Martel because we were starting to get over and couldn't surpass The High Flyers. The High Flyers had the top babyface tag team spot. There wasn't really room for another.

So they ended pulled us apart without really any direction, and they also didn't have anything for us really as singles. I wasn't getting beat, but I also wasn't getting pushed on TV, nor even mentioned much as all. It was like I wasn't even there.

Eventually, that was it.

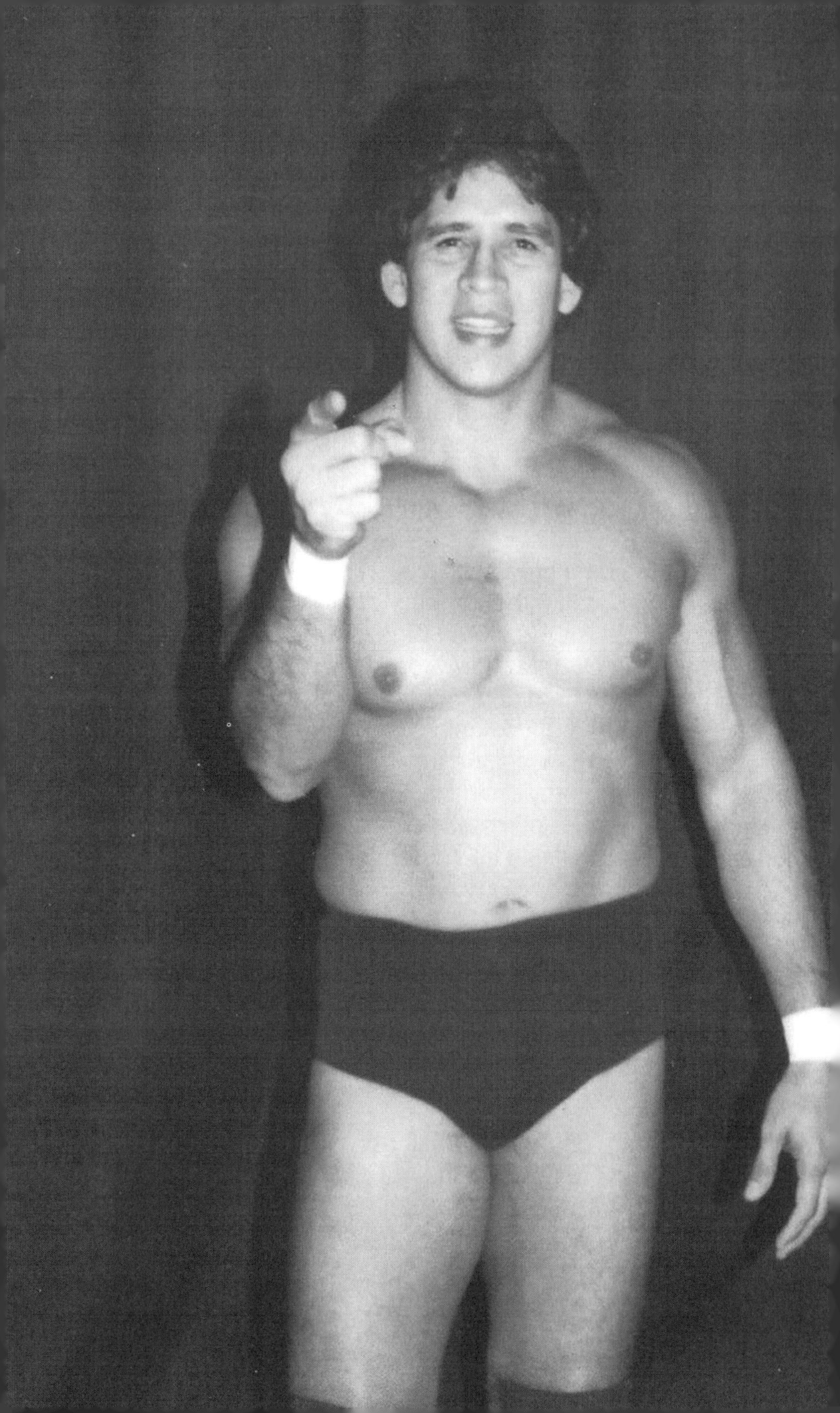

CHAPTER 11 - MAKING CONNECTIONS

As much as some may think, I didn't date much at all early in my career. Sure, I had met lots of girls who were wrestling fans, but I never remained anywhere long enough to where I really could develop a serious relationship. I had always wanted to meet someone who knew nothing about the wrestling business, and one who could appreciate me for who I am. One day, my prayer was answered.

THE QUARRY

I was living in New Jersey when I headed over to a bar in Lake Hiawatha called "The Quarry" with buddy of mine. Steve Travis (RIGHT) was staying at my apartment for the night, and, after a WWF show he was booked on, he wanted to go out and get a beer. I didn't really feel like it, but he said he was buying. I've never been much into bars, but I've also never been one to pass up a beer, so I headed out with him. It was the first time I had been there in probably a year.

We walked in. It was a nice little dive. We had just settled in at our table when all of a sudden a beautiful woman opened the door. She was wearing a long, blue dress and had big beautiful green eyes.. Her light brown hair was flowing. My eyes popped out of my head when she walked passed our table. I continued to stare at her and Steve could tell I smitten. "You like that?" he asked.

I turned to him and said softly, "I think I'm in love."

The woman and her friend sat across the dance floor from us. She didn't even acknowledge me.

"See those two girls?" I said. "I'll buy you another beer if you go over and talk to them."

"Sounds like a deal!"

Before he could act, I added a special stipulation to the offer... "But the one with the long hair is mine."

"For a beer, I'll do it," he laughed

Steve wet his fingers. He straightened his hair nicely and smoothly went up to where they were sitting. I'm glad Steve was there because I was too shy to go up and talk to a woman out of the blue. Steve on the other hand, was bold as hell.

"My friend and I are lonely," and said pointing at me. "Do you mind if we join you?"

The girl in the blue dress nodded. I guess she liked Steve's line, so she said yes. I was waved over by Steve and then I introduced myself to both girls, but I was only interested in the woman with the stunning green eyes.

Leah was very soft spoken. She hypnotized me with her lovely smile. Our conversation flowed with ease. She was a very good-looking girl, but I could tell she was not hung up on herself. It was also wintertime, so I was intrigued as to why she has such a gorgeous tan. After we chatted, I found out that she was living in Hawaii and was in town visiting her parents who lived nearby.

The rest of the night just flew by.

Twenty years later, I still can't believe I'm married to such a beautiful and compassionate woman! Through both the good and bad times, she has always been by my side.

To this day, despite the fact that I'm a cheapskate, I wish I could buy Steve another beer. We lost him a few years ago, but I am eternally grateful to him breaking the ice that night. Here's to you my friend!

ON THE MOVE

During the end of my time with the AWA, I found out that my new wife, Leah, was six months pregnant! ¡Arriba!

CHAPTER 11 – Making Connections

Verne Gange came to me right after I had heard the news. He had news for me of his own. He admitted that I had been overexposed. He said that the AWA also had a number of new babyfaces coming in and that I was about to get lost in the shuffle. That is when he served me my notice telling me it was time to move on to another territory. The move couldn't have come at a worse time for me personally.

Verne recommended me a few places and left the decision up to me. The promotions he recommended were Joe Blanchard's in the South Texas territory, and Jim Barnett's Atlanta territory. I, of course, knew them both.

Since Joe gave me my introduction to the business, I called Tully, his son, first. He told me that they could guarantee me a spot, but could not offer any guaranteed money. Now, Jim had given me my first steady job in the business. When I spoke to him, he promised me both a decent spot and guaranteed I would make $1,000 a week.

I was leaning toward going to Atlanta, but I called my mentor, Vince McMahon Sr., first for some advice. Although Vince left the decision entirely up to me, he too recommended Atlanta over Texas. He said going to Atlanta would get me a considerable amount of TV coverage, as the territory's matches were often televised by Ted Turner's *TBS Network*. He said that Atlanta was now the "bigtime" because TBS was broadcasting nationwide. It was a no brainer. I listened to Vince and decided to go to Atlanta.

I called Jim Barnett and accepted. Once again, Jim treated me with a huge amount of respect. In addition to the pay, Jim gave me an additional day off every other week.

With the good also came the bad. Ole Anderson was still the matchmaker in that territory. It was known that I wasn't crazy about him, and I know he wasn't crazy about me. But I was positive and thought that maybe we could work through our differences and work together this time.

Ole said they planned on making me a big star because of their nationwide TBS TV coverage. Although I was skeptical, I also wanted to believe him.

FROM GOOD TO BAD

It only took three months in Atlanta for me to realize that Ole had no intention of living up to his word. At that time, Ole was making his move behind the scenes, trying to take over the Atlanta territory from Jim. Eventually, it worked.

Somehow Ole double-crossed Jim and took control of the company. When I agreed to go to Atlanta, Ole was only the matchmaker. If I had known that donkey's asshole was going to take complete control, I would never have gone.

Before that, I had a verbal agreement with Jim that my weekly pay would be no less than $1,000. The deal included an arrangement for me to travel to Ohio every nine weeks or so. For this extra effort, Jim promised me anywhere between $1,400 and $1,800 per week. the key word in all of that unfortunately was "verbal" agreement.

Once Ole took over, he made it pretty clear he wanted me out. He never had any plans for me to get a push, and if that wasn't clear enough he cut my pay to $850 per week when I was traveling to Ohio, and to a measly $350 per week while in Atlanta.

Ole, you are a cheap, cheap bastard.

One day, Ole came up to me to let me know he was in charge. He arrogantly came right out and said it.

"You know, Tito," he said. "It was Jim all along who wanted you here, not me. Since I'm taking over, I don't really have the same spot for you he did, but will honor Jim's agreement. You can keep working for me if you really want."

I knew he was lying and didn't want me there because, in the same breath, Ole asked me if I was interested in going to work for Bill Watts in Louisiana.

Leah was very pregnant (*¡Arriba!*) and due soon. I had no plans on moving and told Ole just that.

"Fine," Ole said, "but there are no guarantees."

Now, I knew that Bill Watts was very interested in me wrestling for him. However, he and Ole were good friends, and my gut told me they had a game plan to get me to Louisiana. It almost worked. Bill and his matchmaker, Ernie Ladd, had traded phone calls with me to convince me to join them in the Bayou. But they balked at my asking price of $2,000 per week guarantee.

The main reason I didn't want to go to Louisiana was Paul Orndorff smartened me up on the deal. He had already told me all I needed to know about the Louisiana territory. Paul wrestled for Bill in Louisiana and told me just how long the trips were and how the money you got was not what you really deserved. Watts' monsterous territory stretched from Houston, Texas, through all of Oklahoma down through Louisiana. It was not unusual to travel 400 miles each way by car just to do a single match. The wrestlers were also expected to work seven days a week for peanuts.

As a new wrestler, I was used to some of these conditions in moderation. However, Paul told me the deciding factor. Bill Watts was in the business of taking advantage of young wrestlers and actually made a profit off of their ignorance.

In the end, I didn't want to go somewhere where I'd be gone from my family most of the time and not compensated for it. So I politely declined to sign on with Bill.

BELATED CHRISTMAS PRESENT

Soon after the first discussions with Bill Watts, my wife went into labor on Christmas Eve! This led to me cancelling my tour in Ohio that week to be sure I was there for the birth. Ole, that miserable prick, was not at all happy that I stayed behind. He wanted complete control of my life, but he was not getting it.

"My family comes first," I said.

We spent that Christmas Eve at the hospital, but it was a false alarm. But then, our son, Matthew Ryan, was born two days later on December 27, 1982!

He was healthy and so was my wife. That was the only thing that mattered at the time. That was the best Christmas present ever.

I was the happiest man in the world.

I had both a beautiful wife and a healthy son.

CHAPTER 12 - SCREWED BY OLE AGAIN

I remember scraping up some meals and literally eating tuna out of the can. I was in Atlanta for a short time but wasn't seeing eye-to-eye with Ole again, because he really was a miserable old bastard. He took away my guarantee, and I was back to making peanuts. Any money he handed me was getting eaten up by my expenses.

Just as the money dried up, Bill Watts over in the Mid-South territory coincidentally expressed interest in me again. Nothing had changed. His promotion was also all over the place and required all kinds of driving that would really take me away from home so I decided against it, again. But it did seem odd that right when my guarantee went away, another option magically appeared.

When I turned Bill down, I figured that was the end of it. Sadly it wasn't. I was about to get an education on how bookers and promoters like to mess with wrestlers' lives.

Even though I told Ole that I wasn't going to Louisiana, he went ahead and booked me in matches out there the first week of February 1983. You see, both of them had already made the decision for me, *I just didn't know it.*

"You are only going to be out there for eight days, and that Bill has agreed to pay you $2,500 for that tour," Ole said. So I was off to some matches in New Orleans.

I really didn't have a choice in the matter if I wanted a paycheck that week. Little did I know, I wasn't the only one; they were playing the same game with Butch Reed.

So along with Butch Reed, I headed to Louisiana for the eight-day stint. Neither one of us had any idea what to expect. The only thing we knew is that Ole was ready to get rid of both of us, and we both needed the money.

MID-SOUTH PITSTOP

The Junkyard Dog was the big name out there at the time. He was super over, almost like their Hulk Hogan. JYD always drove the best cars and threw his money around like it was water. He was very generous, which I appreciated. He always picked up the tab and even paid for our hotel rooms

CHAPTER 12 – Screwed By Ole Again

and stuff. See, the Dog knew our situation and decided to take care of both Butch and me.

His generosity was great because our payoffs were just like everyone else's payoffs at Mid-South at the time. *They were the drizzling shits.* That cash itself would have been good, but Mid-South was famous for long drives between shows and we saw them first hand. We wrestled eight nights straight all right, and they were eight days of hell on the road. We started in Shreveport, before traveling to Tulsa, and then to Oklahoma City, then to Baton Rouge, Little Rock, Houston, and a few other cities.

I knew that the initial payoffs wouldn't last. The only reason they were paying me well at the start was because Ole wanted me to go work for Bill and it was a game of bait and switch. It wasn't likely that my pay would remain that high because Bill had already told me what he wanted to pay me when I declined his initial offer. So I took what they offered knowing that eventually the well would run dry.

After that eight-day tour ended, it was back to Georgia. When I returned to Atlanta, Ole kept me around a few more weeks, but cut my pay more and more.

In March, I returned to Louisiana for a five-day tour. Bill paid me more money than I was making on similar trips from Georgia to Ohio. The message from the two promoters was clear; move to Louisiana or else. Ole had cut my pay by such a staggering amount, I could no longer afford to live in Atlanta. I then had no choice but to sign with Bill.

After all the misery that Ole put me through, I finally was ready to move on. I was sure from speaking with Paul Orndorff (a Mid-South territory survivor) that I wasn't going to like working there, however. But at that point, I decided to take the pain I didn't know over the pain that I did know.

I discussed the move with Leah, and she agreed that if Bill were to make me a decent offer, I should go ahead and sign on with him. The next day, I figured that Bill would be happy to hear I was ready to negotiate. But his response lacked any kind of emotion.

"Okay, Tito," he said. "I will talk to you in a few days."

It was all a game. They had run me down so much that it was easy to see that I had lost any and all negotiating power with Bill.

As they said on *Seinfeld*, "He had hand."

When I realized what their gameplan was, the wheels in my head started turning. I had to act quick, or else be destined to work for peanuts again and blow it all on gas.

LAST STITCH EFFORT

That Wednesday morning, I got up early and called Vince McMahon Sr. in New York. I told him how Ole had been treating me so poorly and that I couldn't take it any longer. I explained how Bill had showed an interest in me, and that I would be talking to him Friday about making a permanent move to Louisiana.

"Well, Bill is a good man to work for," he said. "It sounds like that could be a good move for you."

Oh shit. That wasn't the response I wanted to hear.

I had hoped that Vince would tell me that I had suffered enough, that it was time to pack my bags for New York to return to the fold. Didn't happen.

The next day, Bill Watts had a car waiting for me. When I got in, I found that I was riding with the Junkyard Dog from Tulsa to Houston. The idea was I would work a spot for him, and talk business after the show. It was there that we would meet, under his terms. This was probably so he could have some kind of home court advantage.

I entered the dressing room and the boys were all there. After saying my hellos, I sat down and started to lace up my boots when I saw Ernie Ladd. He looked around and pulled me off to a corner where nobody else could hear us.

"Tito," he said, "Tonight you'll have to make the biggest decision of your life."

"What are you talking about? My talk with Bill?"

"Well, not just that. I was just talking to Vince and he mentioned you," he said.

"Is that right?" I asked. "I really like him."

"Well, I think he likes you too. And I'm pretty sure that he has something for you," he said.

CHAPTER 12 – Screwed By Ole Again

I just looked at him, dumbfounded. I had no idea what he was talking about.

"You think?"

"Oh yes," Ernie continued, "He didn't only talk to me about it, though. Vince also called Bill and told him that he wants you back in the WWF. He wants you to call him Saturday morning."

I was the happiest man in the world.

If the decision was between Bill Watts and Vince McMahon, the decision was not going to be a difficult one. The decision was obvious. It was almost like a waitress coming up to you and asking, "Would you like a peanut butter and jelly sandwich, or the prime rib?"

My wife just had a baby. Less miles. More money. More exposure.

I was off to New York!

About a half hour after talking to Ernie, sure enough, Bill walked into the dressing room with his game face on.

"Tito," he said, motioning to follow him. "We need to talk." I followed him off to an abandoned room in the venue. It didn't take him long to let me know I had two options. I acted surprised when he told me about Vince's call, but he knew that is where I wanted to go.

"Listen, I also think you are a great talent which is why I have been pulling to get you out here."

"I really appreciate that, Bill," I said.

"And that's why I want you to know that I really want you to stay out here working for me."

I thought that this was actually a great place to be in. Back in my football days, when two different teams wanted you, there was a bidding war. The one that wanted you the most was going to have to pay for it.

"Look, Tito," Bill continued. I can help you with little areas that maybe you are still lacking in on the business end of things, like how you are with your interviews. We can work on it, and I think you will become an even bigger star for it!"

I believed Bill was genuine. I really think he felt he could help me out, but I didn't want to hang around to find out. Why prepare me for New York, when they were already calling?

"Just do me a favor," he said. "Take some time before making a decision and really think it through. And whatever you decide, you will remain in good standing with me."

"Thank you, Bill," I said.

To be fair, I gave it the proper time. Immediately the next morning, I called Vince.

When he answered, I identified myself.

"Hello, Vince," I said. "This is Tito."

"..."

There was only silence on his end. The silence lasted about 30 seconds, but it seemed like an eternity.

I started to think that maybe Vince was in on this whole thing with Ole and Bill. I had anticipated a warm response from Vince, and for him to launch into the terms of his offer; but I was greeted by silence.

What the hell?

I couldn't take it any longer, so I spoke first and made sure to put on my best tone of a disappointment.

"The reason I called is because I was told to do so."

At that moment, he finally responded.

"Yes, Tito. It's time for you to come home."

He could probably hear me smile through the phone.

"Your start date will be May the tenth (1983.)"

I was absolutely ecstatic! I'll never forget that day either because it was also my birthday. What a present?!

"Vince, that's all I needed to hear," I replied. "Thank you!" I couldn't wait to hang up and give my wife the good news.

FAREWELL

When I got back to Atlanta, I didn't think twice. I immediately gave Ole my notice.

He tried to talk me into staying. I couldn't believe he had the nerve. For what? To torture me? What a scumbag!

He revealed his plans to take wrestling down to South America and told me that he wanted to make me one of his top guys. I had never heard any of that before and doubt it was real. It all sounded like a load of crap. I thought, *"Ole, have you no sense of decency?"*

Rather than to cut a promo on him and tell him what a piece of shit I thought he was, I babyfaced the hell out of him. I didn't want to give him the satisfaction of letting him know he got to me. So instead, I decided to kill him with kindness.

"That sounds great, Ole," I lied. "Thank you so much, but I already promised Vince, brother."

I respectfully gave him my three-week notice.

When I finally got home, Leah and I had a small celebration and began counting the days until our move back to New York City.

ito Santana is like a cue ball. The more you strike him, the more English you get out of him.

–Bobby Heenan

TITO SANTANA

TITO SANTANA

TITO SANTANA

TITO SANTANA

I first met Tito when we worked together for Eddie Graham in the Florida territory, where he had started a few months before me. However, I got to really know Tito later on when we were both part of the Georgia territory. Because we were both former college and professional football players, we bonded immediately. He had a passion for competition and a spirit that was unmatched. Unlike others, Tito was honest and straightforward. He would tell you exactly what he was willing to do and what he wasn't. As time went on we became very close friends and could always count on each other.

After leaving Georgia, Tito and I both went to work for Vince McMahon and the WWF. Although other guys initially were getting the push, neither Tito nor I were going to be denied. He was very talented; he wasn't going to be held back. He was a very unselfish person in the ring and had tremendous psychology. Some of the best wrestling matches I ever had- and I mean matches that went thirty to sixty minutes long-were with Tito Santana. We had a passion for the business and worked our butts off in the ring. We could always steal the show. We knew how to work, how to control the crowd, and how to get the people right where we wanted them.

In fact, when Tito and I first started with the WWF, we wrestled for thirty minutes in Kansas City. Vince McMahon Jr. was at ringside and after the match he came into the locker room and said, "That was the best wrestling match I ever saw!" I can say without reservation that Tito was one of the best workers in the business. Tito was and is a great person outside the ring. He never stabbed anyone in the back and everybody liked Tito. If you ever needed anything he would be the first to help you out.

- **Paul Orndorff**

CHAPTER 13 - BACK IN THE WWF

In wrestling, they always say to the new guys coming up, "Make sure you bring your gear. You never show up to a show without your gimmick." This means never to just go to a show to network because you never know if they will need an extra body which could be your foot in the door. This advice is very true.

Some of the biggest breaks for athletes come from being in the right place at the right time. Fortunately for me, the right time to return to the WWF was May 10, 1983.

At the time, Jimmy "Superfly" Snuka was one of the biggest stars in the WWF. He was selling out arenas everywhere and was the hottest name around. However, there was an accident and he found himself in a world of trouble that continued to haunt him for the rest of his life; *Jimmy's girlfriend died from a fractured skull.*

There were rumors back in the day that Snuka was truly a wild-man, just as his gimmick depicted. One talked about him bringing girls back to the hotel with him after shows to party with. One girl talked about him actually slamming her on the bed, then climbing up on top of the hutch and "superfly-splashing" her completely naked on the hotel bed.

CRACKKK!
After the bed collapsed, she ran out of the room naked. As the story goes, Jimmy chased her out of the hotel room and through the lot, letting his coconuts dangle freely in the wind. Some say this was a normal night.

One night, however, a woman ended up dead. The way Jimmy explained it was that the girl fell while they were fixing a flat tire on a car rental and hit her head just right and she was gone. I wasn't there, but Jimmy was a rough and tough wrestler and worried at how things may have looked. Before he called the police, they say he called Vince who was a better talker than he was. Vince spoke to the police for him.

During what became an ongoing investigation by authorities, Snuka took some time off and missed a bunch of bookings. I was both the lucky and unlucky one to take his place. The reason I say "unlucky one" is because when fans pay to see someone that's who they want to see. When I got bumped into Snuka's spot, thousands of fans didn't hesitate to let me know they were not pleased to see me instead of him.

So for my big return to the WWF, I was getting booed out of the building every single night. However, Vince knew that they were making the best of an awkward situation and that I was showing up to work as a fill-in. I did my best to ease the transition for the WWF, and Vince appreciated it.

"Thank you so much, Tito," he said, shaking my hand. "Anyone else and it would have really been a nightmare out there. I'm glad to see you back here and know we made the right decision."

As for my first WWF TV tapings upon my return where I was not being a replacement on the card, those turned out very successful.

Vince McMahon Sr. continued to reinforce the fact that I had made the correct move. I had become more polished and made a return with more value to the company.

Vince Senior was a great guy and a great coach. He had a gift for making me feel great about myself. I believe that gift played a large role in why I have never heard anyone say a bad thing about the man. And it's very rare to be able to say that about any promoter, as most of them often get a bad rep with the boys due to business decisions.

ANOTHER GIANT

A few words about a fellow named, Big John Studd. When he first started getting the big push in New York, he started stepping over the top rope. André was the only one who used to do that, and I think when the "Eighth Wonder of the World" saw John Studd do it, he felt like John was engaging in "gimmick infringement."

To make matters worse, John was having the ring announcer announce him as "The Giant Studd."

I remember, eventually, the bookers finally started booking them against each other. I remember watching those matches and André just destroying him! If Studd tried to leave the ring, André would chase him back to the locker room, and if he got ahead of him, he would drag him back to the aisle and lay in on poor John. He really let him have it!

You did not want to get on his bad side. André would stomp on your foot in the corner so you couldn't move, then grab you by the hair. If you tried to take off, he didn't care, he'd rip big clumps of it right out of your head.

Studd angered André by doing things that André believed only he should do. It is like Studd had to actually be able to read his mind to really know what the problem was. Other than something obvious like stepping over the top rope, Studd may have just sold something like a "big man" and that would could piss André off. Studd could not even have known it was an offense to the French Giant.

One time, Studd came running back to the locker room after a tense match with André. He had the fear of god in his eyes! He was quickly putting on his shirt, grabbing his stuff, and getting ready to get the hell out of dodge. When we asked him where he was going, Studd sad, "I have to get out of here, right now. He's going to kill me!"

FIGHTING OUTSIDE THE RING

Whoever Paul Orndorff was riding with one day didn't want to give him a ride back from Columbus back to Dayton, because he was in a foul mood. So Tony Atlas, Brian Blair, and Tommy Rich let him jump in with them. It wasn't long before they second-guessed their generosity.

They drove a few minutes, and Paul wrinkled up his nose. *Mister Wonderful smelled something not-so-wonderful.*

"What the fuck is that smell?" he asked, referring to something coming from the back.

"Those are my barbecue ribs," Tony said from behind the front on the passenger side of the rental car.

"Well, throw them out! Those son of a bitches smell bad," he said. "I'm going to throw them out."

"If you throw them out," Tony replied not wanting to lose his lunch, "I am going to throw you out with them."

CHAPTER 13 – Back In The WWF

Tony was just joking, but Paul didn't take it as a joke. He starting hitting the back of Tommy Rich's seat saying, "Pull the fuck over! Pull the fuck over!"

Tommy looked over at Tony in the passenger side seat and said, "I better pull over before we crash."

So Tommy pulled over. Paul jumped out of the car and headed over to the passenger side where Tony was seated. Tony looked over at Tommy and said, "Does he really want to fight over this?"

Tony opened up the door, just as Paul was about to punch him.

Tony was a collegate wrestler, not a football player like Paul, so he immediately went into grappling. He side stepped the punch, hooked his arm and cradled him, down to the ground.

Tony would not break the hold. He pulled Paul's knees up to his face and held him there to try to make him calm down. Brian Blair and Tommy Rich eventually broke it up and everybody got back in the car.

"I'm sorry," Paul said. "I don't know what came over me."

Tony knew that the road made guys crazy and readily accepted his apology. They drove down a little way and Brian realized that Tony's ear was bleeding. Upon closer inspection, they realized that he had bit his earlobe and it was dangling off the side of his face.

"We better bring you to a hospital," Blair said. "You don't want to leave that alone or it will look a mess for the rest of your life."

They went and got it stitched up and Paul felt terrible. The two of them made up and it was over.

These days, Paul Orndorff said he whooped Tony's ass, but Tony said the only thing he could do is bite, "he could never whoop me in a hundred years."

THE NEW BOSS IN TOWN

I had only been in the WWF a few short months when a large meeting was called to inform us about a "change in leadership."

Vince Senior got in front of the locker room with some tears in his eyes. "I would like to announce that my son, Vinnie, will soon be taking over," he said, choking back a sob. "I have been training him for some time and I think that he will do a great job. As much as I would like to stay, I physically can't continue at this time."

We knew this was coming so this was no surprise. Declining health had everything to do with the father handing over his portion of the business over to his son. He became ill with prostate cancer shortly after the meeting. He was not able to continue running the company. It was a done deal. He had sold his shares to his son. Vinnie had bought out the remaining shares and would soon be taking over.

As I recall, he promised Gorilla Monsoon a job for life as part of the buyout, a promise which Vinnie would keep. The other shares were purchased for around $100,000 a piece, which is pennies compared to the billion dollar company it would eventually become!

Vinnie started out like his dad, but as the WWF grew, his personality changed. When Vinnie took over for his father, he was no longer our friend, Vinnie, and that name would die He became the boss, and we called him "Vince."

Upon taking over the reins Vince went from being a friend to being my boss. Vince let us know that there were many changes ahead; he had big plans and predicted a major growth period for the WWF. Vince was a workaholic and had a tremendous amount of energy and enthusiasm. It anyone would be able to initiate such a growth, it would be the new Vince.

The new "Vince" became far more ruthless than his father ever was. I don't know if it was because he wanted to impress his father, who wasn't around much in his life growing up, or what reason, but he started to break traditions in the business as a whole to achieve even more success.

Back then, territories weren't crossed. If you ran shows, you ran them in your area. Once in a while, an "outlaw" show would happen, meaning a promoter would run in a clearly defined territory, but if he did, he was often shunned. With the advent of cable television, however, Vince decided anywhere they had TVs, it was his product he wanted people to see. Subsequently, he wanted to go national and be the biggest "outlaw" of all time.

His strategy was to air his show in markets all across the country and swipe up a few of the wrestlers who were big in those regions to air on his shows. By doing this, when people turned on their televisions and saw a wrestler they were familiar with on WWF programming, they would continue to watch.

KNOCKING ON TED TURNER'S DOOR

Ted Turner had owned the television airing rights of Georgia Championship Wrestling since 1972, and he was very proud of the success of this show. The two-hour long program aired every Saturday night from 6-8 p.m., or later from 6:05 to 8:05. Because of its growing fan base, it had become the main NWA, and also the first NWA territory to be carried by many cable and satellite providers across the country.

In 1982, Georgia Championship Wrestling changed its name to WCW, World Championship Wrestling. At this time, the promotion itself was being operated by Jack Brisco and Gerald Brisco, Jim Barnett, and Ole Anderson who was the head booker. WCW was a great alternative wrestling program for traditionalists who didn't like what Vince McMahon was trying to usher in. Many hardcore wrestling fans believed that McMahon's attempt to mainstream wrestling as a form of entertainment instead of a sport was horrible, because of an emphasis on cartoon-like gimmicks. WCW, in turn, emphasized a more athletic sports-based product. If you have ever heard Gordon Solie commentate, you will know what I mean. He was an NWA announcer who I knew from his days with Championship Wrestling from Florida. He also hosted programs for various other NWA affiliated promotions at the time and brought a sense of realism to WCW that was unparalleled.

In 1983, Vince McMahon began his master plan to expand the WWF to a nationwide audience by use of cable television. Many felt he was throwing away the gentlemen's agreement seemingly all wrestling promoters had by doing this. As I said previously, before this time, there were very well-defined borders of where promoters could run their matches. They would never cross the borders with their product. Everyone respected this tradition and worked together, subsequently. "You stay on your side of the fence, and I'll stay on mine, then everyone will be happy." However, Vince's first step was to ignore the old way of doing things. He wanted to get a national timeslot on cable television with the intent to do it as a commercial for his product, then ultimately compete in every market.

Vince's first real victory was purchasing Southwest Championship Wrestling's Sunday morning timeslot contract on the USA Network. He replaced that programming with his own show, *WWF's All American Wrestling*. In addition to that, he created two more shows for syndication to reach other areas called, WWF Championship Wrestling and *WWF All-Star Wrestling*. Then he made a wrestling talk show called *Tuesday Night Titans* to also air on USA.

I am sure that Ted Turner saw what McMahon was doing. Rather than to secure his own new timeslots to feature his product, Turner felt he was buying out his competitor's to take their place and defeat competition at the same time. Eventually, McMahon decided that he wanted to control all nationally-televised professional wrestling in the United States by taking over WCW. However, when he made Turner an offer to buy the historic GCW/WCW time slot on Saturday night, Turner scoffed at the thought.

McMahon was a workaholic, however. I remember talking with him into the wee hours of the night with Hulk and him saying "sleep is your enemy." It is this "never say never" attitude that made Vince McMahon into the success that he is today. I don't think Ted Turner at the time knew that McMahon was going to do whatever he could to find a way to securing the last remaining national cable slot for the WWF.

The WWF with this plan was set to indeed grow, but Vince's father would never get to see it. Shortly after the

CHAPTER 13 – Back In The WWF

syndication plans began, Vince Senior passed away from cancer in May 1984. Sadly, none of the wrestlers were able to go to his funeral. We were all too busy wrestling in a business that never stopped. I will say this, however, when Vince Senior passed, I shed a tear at the news. He was my mentor. We had lost a great man and a true credit to the wrestling profession.

Vince's son would continue on and so would WWF.

While WCW had a loyal fan base and was very popular, Vince learned that things were not as great behind the scenes. Putting some feelers out there, Vince learned that Ole Anderson was locking horns with his fellow owners by the way he was operating the promotion. McMahon identified the weakness and decided to strike.

Knowing he couldn't buy the timeslot from Turner, Vince set up a secret meeting with the Brisco brothers and Jim Barnett. McMahon offered them roles in the WWF, as well as some good money and all three men agreed to sell their stock. This gave the WWF the controlling stake in WCW. Ultimately, by hook or crook, McMahon took over the Saturday night timeslot.

July 7, 1984 was the end of an era for a group of fans. That was when the last *World Championship Wrestling* episode aired. Many of them a week after that referred to July 14, 1984, as being "Black Saturday," the first week of WWF programming on TBS. First off, that initial WWF episode had no Gordon Solie. He had either resigned, or was terminated, but the staple voice of the program that everyone knew from that timeslot was gone. Then, the former show's co-host, Freddie Miller, introduced Vince McMahon who many felt stood for what was the direct opposite what the fan base wanted. McMahon promised the fans that they would love the new show even more. The WWF's TBS show, however, was not live wrestling matches shot from the TBS studio. It was mostly a highlight show derived from using clips of their other programs, and some occasional house show footage.

Ted Turner was beyond pissed when he saw the new WWF product. On top of that, hate mail was flooding his office from angry WCW fans, often accusing him of being a sell-out and accusing him of being the catalyst of change in the programming.

Soon after that, Vince's plan became evident. *WWF Georgia Championship Wrestling* on TBS quickly became an infomercial-like platform to promote the first *WrestleMania*. The purchase of GCW was all part of his big gamble; he needed it for more exposure. On March 2, 1985, the WWF began airing in-studio squash matches commentated by Freddie Miller and new play-by-play commentator Gorilla Monsoon. These programs ran until March 30, 1985, the day before a massive event that Vince McMahon was betting all his chips on …

WrestleMania!

Tito Santana battling "The Duke Of Dorchester" Pete Doherty

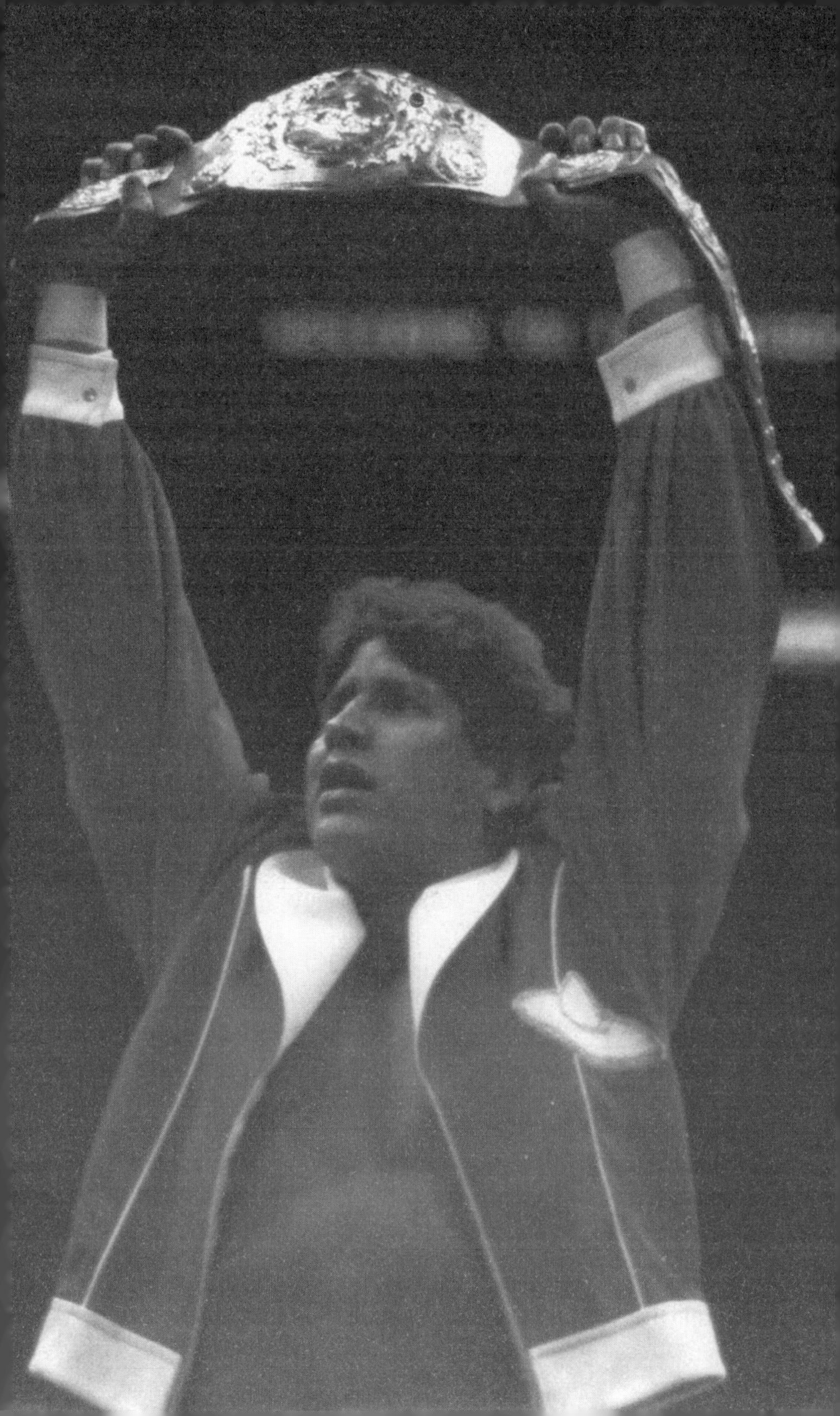

CHAPTER 14 - INTERCONTINENTAL CHAMPION

After some hard work, I won the Intercontinental belt for the first time on February 11, 1984, by defeating Magnificent Muraco at the Boston Garden. We had a great match as Muraco was always great to work with, but there was just one little problem; too bad they never got the whole match on film so people could actually see it. It was actually pretty good.

That night, Hulk Hogan and I wrestled in an earlier match, and then Don and I went on last. I was already ticked off because Vince and all the WWF big shots left the arena before my match was over so they could beat the crowd traffic out of the area. In the process, they took some of the gear with them and they actually took the truck that had the most of the camera supplies in it. Yep, you guessed it. By the end of the night, they ran out of film.

Ran out of film?! They would have never treated the Hulkster with the same cheap, low-rent, shoe string lack of respect. ¡Arriba!

After the match, I found out that the filming crew just happened to "run out of film," so the finish that I used to beat Muraco that night was never seen by anyone other than the fans in live attendance.

My hurt feelings were patched up just a little bit when I found out just how much money I was going to be making that year.

Before winning the IC title, I had been making about $60,000 a year during my first couple of years in the federation. I was still saving up to purchase my first house in Flanders, New Jersey, for in the area of $119,000. I thought I was going to have had a hard time scrounging up the money to afford the home, but when I called the WWF office and asked if they could help me out a little, they told me that my projected income for 1984 would be $176,000!

You can imagine the look of shock on my face when I heard that. Needless to say, we bought the house. I stopped caring that they didn't tape the whole match that helped me make the money to do so.

TITO BEATS MURACO - Boston, MA - Boston Garden - February 11, 1984

A TYPICAL DAY AS IC CHAMP

To the victors go the spoils. Even though I am both charming and shockingly handsome, my wrestling schedule didn't leave much time for beauty sleep.

I think I averaged about maybe three days off every 90 days of work, and that was being generous.

As the intercontinental champion, my regular routine became very robotic, to say the least. I was part of the machine.

Mostly every day, I typically got up at 5:30 a.m., showered, and headed to the airport to catch the first flight out to whatever city I was booked in for that day. I was always worried about being late for an event, so I made good and certain to be at the airport early to catch the first plane. (In my twelve years of working with the WWF, I only missed two flights, and in both cases, it was due to a wake-up call that somebody else had forgotten to make.)

After checking in at the airport, I would eat breakfast. As I waited at the gate, I would call Leah from a pay phone. (Do you remember those things? It's too bad cell phones weren't around back then. I would have been living on them!)

Next, I would board the plane. I would try my hardest to get good and comfy, with one of those pillow gimmicks behind my head. The flight itself always gave me a chance to make up on some lost hours of sleep. It gave me a chance for a nap and I almost always took advantage of the opportunity. (I know that some people have a hard time sleeping on a plane, but I was not one of them. I got good at it. The sky was my favorite place to catch up on some quality sleep.)

Upon landing, I would immediately head to the rental car desk. There, I had to make all my own car and hotel reservations, as well as pay for everything upfront. Whenever I could, I tried to go for larger vehicles like Lincoln Continentals, because I knew I wasn't going to be the only one in it. Nine times out of ten, I was sharing the car with other wrestlers which only made good sense. We would split the costs and share driving duties, and it just made the time pass that much quicker.

CHAPTER 14 – Intercontinental Champion

A word on who I rode with back then ... the idea was that faces should ride with faces, and heels should ride with heels, but that didn't always happen. Because of the competitive nature of the business, heels didn't get close with other heels, and the same with the babyfaces. Both teams generally were always at least a little bit nervous that their counterpart may be interested in taking each other's spots. This is why whenever I grabbed a rental car, I was probably sharing with some heels if I could because I got along better with the heels.

From the airport, we would head straight to the hotel and check in. Then, I would eat a pretty big lunch. Food on the road for most of the boys was usually a lot of pasta and grilled chicken. We didn't really know it at the time, but our bodies would process the carbs in the pasta and would turn them into sugar, but we were always working out in gyms so we could work a lot of that off. For me, I love burgers and fries. I wasn't nearly as strict as "Mister Wonderful" was with his diet!

After lunch, I would go straight to the local gym for usually an hour-and-a-half-long workout and burn off those lunch calories. (Gold's Gym was my preference, but any gym close to the hotel would work.) Lifting weights and staying in shape was very important to me, so I worked out four to five times a week regardless of my travel schedule.

I learned how to put together an efficient travel workout plan from advice that I got from Tony Atlas and Paul Orndorff. I mean look at them! You know they must have been doing something right.

I usually did 20 minutes of cardio, then I would switch to weights. One day I would work on my chest, triceps and shoulder. The next day, I would focus on my back and biceps. On the third day, I would work on my legs. If I had some extra time, I would always try to do some additional cardio exercise, because it was key to my endurance in the ring.

After my workout, I would head back to the hotel, clean up, and then head out with the boys for a light snack and to chew the fat. Afterwards, I would take a break, usually between an hour or two. During that time, I would watch TV or take a nap, and be sure to call Leah back again.

Then, it was off to the arena.

At the venue I would first check in with the road agents; guys like Chief Jay Strongbow, Rene Goulet, and Pat Patterson. They were the ones who would post the card and help wrestlers with any concerns they may have. Then it was off to the locker room to "hurry up and wait."

While I waited for the night's events to get underway, I would start a big game of cribbage with André. After that, I would stretch and get dressed for my match.

Wrestle. (Yes this would happen, but that was the easy part. The wrestling itself was usually 15 minutes or less of the entire day. The rest is what we really got paid for. We got paid for everything else in between.)

After my turn in the ring, I would shower and maybe wait for the other wrestlers I traveled with to finish up. Then we would jump in the Lincoln, leave the venue together, and head back to the hotel often around 11:30 p.m.

Back in my room, I'd check in with my wife for the third time, then head to the hotel lounge or restaurant for a late dinner and drinks with the boys.

I usually ended up back in my room by 1 a.m. to catch a few hours of sleep before my 5:30 wake up call.

After that, the whole thing would happen all over again.

Rinse and repeat.

DON'T CALL ME CHICO

During one of our daily grind loops, I think I was traveling from Los Angeles to San Diego. By this point, fans were eating the WWF up more than ever before. As I arrived to San Diego and grabbed my bag, there were a number of fans there. They had done their homework and predicted they would see some of us because of the flight schedule, and where we were the night before.

CHAPTER 14 – Intercontinental Champion

"Hey look," one of them shouted, as I was waiting for my luggage to come out from the conveyer belt dock. "It's Chico!"

"Chico!" a kid repeated as a handful of fans came running my way.

Chico? What the hell is that?!

I signed their magazines and rushed off.

I didn't say anything to them, but boy did that piss me off! I figured they just had a racist grandfather or something who watched wrestling with them and they just didn't know what they were repeating.

I hurried off to the next show shaking my head. I didn't think much of it. Some of the black heel wrestlers got spit on and were called a hell of a lot worse than that, so I shrugged it off.

I wrestled on the event, headed off the hotel, and left the next morning for another show. When I got to the back of the next arena, there were a bunch of fans waiting to see the wrestlers go into the building. One of them pointed at me.

"Chico!"

Chico again?! Wait. What the hell is going on here?

"Um, hello kids," I said signing a few autographs and trying to be polite. "It's Tito, right? Okay?"

"Yes, Tito! Thank you!" they said.

"Chico means like a little boy," I said trying to correct them the best that I could. "And I'm much bigger than you are. Right?" I laughed it off, and the kids laughed with me.

This happened a few more times until I about lost it. I remember pulling up to an arena, and I actually saw a sign that said "CHICO" on it in capital letters. I walked over to the fan knowing that I was a babyface, trying to figure out how to best handle the situation.

Now this is a time in wrestling where it was not cool to really openly route for the bad guy, and it was not cool to go against the good guy, so the whole thing was really dumbfounding me. It made no sense.

As I approached the fan with the sign thinking of what to say, he pushed it in my face and wanted me to sign it! It was clear that he was a fan and really liked me, so I signed his poster, "Tito Santana."

"Now, let me ask you something," I said as I was handing him back the poster. "Why is it that you have Chico on your sign? You know my name is 'Tito' right?"

The fan shrugged. It was apparent that he was not going to say anything because he actually didn't want to upset me.

"Do you not like me?" I asked.

The fan shook his head. "No! Of course we like you!"

"Well, then maybe don't call me Chico?"

I didn't fucking get it. I shook my head puzzled. The fan was not going to tell me where he had heard it because he didn't want to offend me, so I went off into the arena.

You see, it took me a while to figure out why some fans were calling me "Chico" because I never had an opportunity to watch any of the WWF programing. Every time one of the shows would air, I was either traveling or we were actually in the ring wrestling.

Eventually, however, a fan smartened me up.

"Jesse The Body Ventura!"

I should have known.

When I finally learned the source, I hunted him down and we had a good laugh.

Jesse was so over as a heel, by him calling me "Chico" I would actually get over more because people hated him and would stick up for me. Once I knew what was going on, I actually wanted him to bury me more to get the sympathy vote from the fans ... And bury me more he did.

Jesse was the master of trash talking, and actually a good friend of mine. I first met Jesse "The Body" Ventura in the AWA. We enjoyed many great matches with each other. He was a master in getting the most from the crowd with the least amount of work. He was a true credit to the business.

After his career ended due to injury, Jesse became a commentator for the WWF. On several occasions, he referred to me as "Chico" or a "taco vendor." It's easy for me to understand why such comments are viewed as discriminatory, but let me be **very** clear in saying that Jesse

CHAPTER 14 – Intercontinental Champion

is not a racist person at all. He never said those things maliciously toward me. He was simply playing a role in time where race was more acceptable in comedy than it is today, acting in a way that would help me to get over with the fans.

Jesse made me money, and did a great job at it, too.

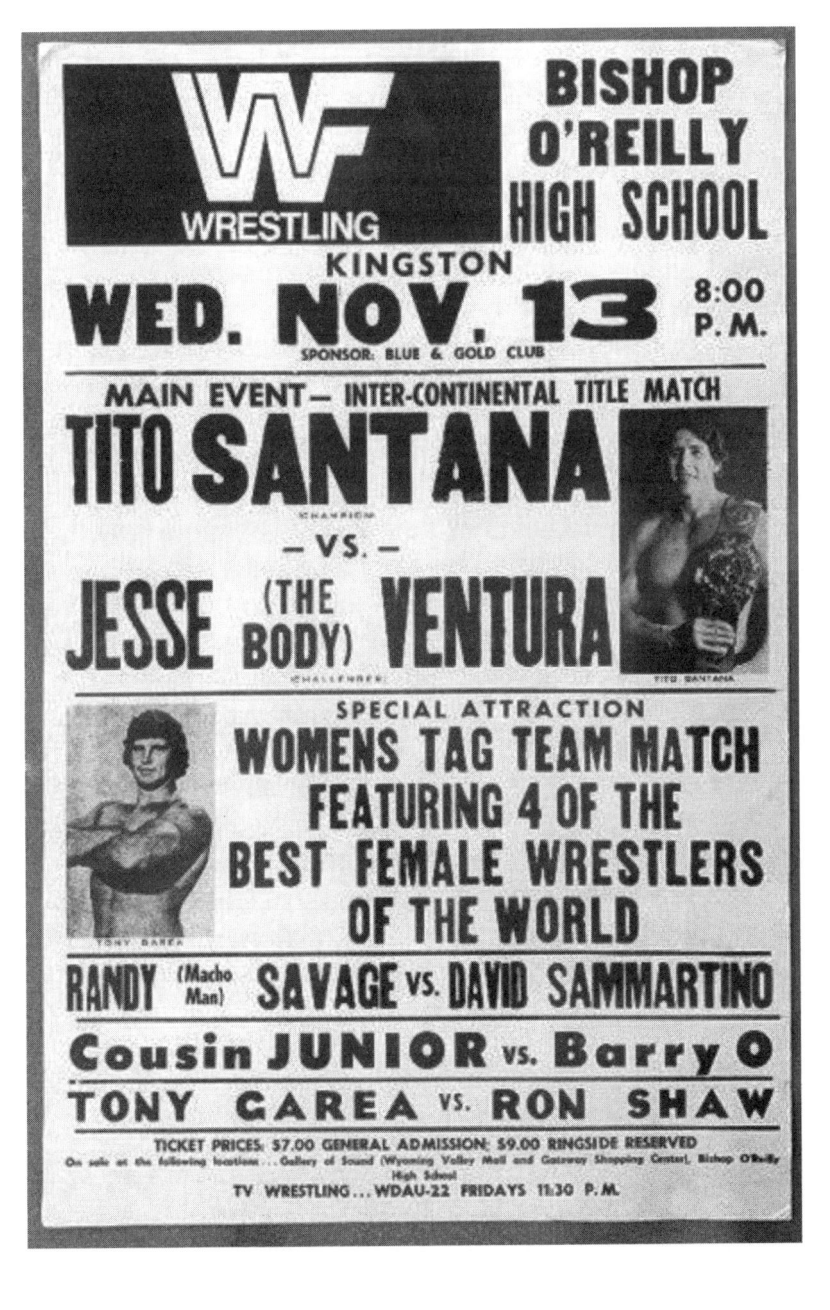

SPEAKING OF BOBBY ...

Bobby Heenan had been part of the wrestling industry for some four decades. He had done it all, from wrestling, to managing, to TV commentator. When Jesse left to film *Predator*, Bobby was tapped to be his replacement. Before he started, however, I actually asked him to hit me with the same kind of Mexican jokes that Jesse had.

When Bobby started up doing color commentary for the WWF television shows, he picked up right where he left off. He regularly insulted me and spoke poorly of me, which is a good thing for me because he was a heel. This continued the empathy from the fans.

He did everything possible to help me get over, and he did a great job at it. When he commentated, he said crazy things like referring to me as "Chico," telling people that "my family lived in a 1957 Chevy," and insinuating fans could always find me "at a taco stand in Mexico."

One of the biggest things he did for my career was name my flying forearm "The Flying Burrito." This name stuck so much so, that it is what the move became called backstage. I even called it that when I called matches.

Bobby's insults were aimed at helping me to get over as a babyface, and they unquestionably did just that! They didn't call him the "Brain" for nothing.

I did feel that there were more real examples of prejudice and racism back then in wrestling, but never from the kind of stuff that guys like Jesse or Bobby were saying. They did for comedic effect to be part of the show. The stuff I mean as being "real examples" was behind the scenes.

The real racist crap came from guys like Ole Anderson and Dick Murdoch, as I stated before. Stuff that would actually hurt your bottom line and make you bring home less money to your family.

If you really want to call someone racist, Dick Murdoch legit showed me his KKK membership card once. Now, that is about as bad as it gets.

Dick and Ole's blatant actions and words towards me (and others) were very insensitive and hurtful.

CHAPTER 14 – Intercontinental Champion

DEFENDING CHAMPION

After getting the title, I remained at my peak for a good couple of years. I had finally been established as a top wrestler and received world recognition as well as respect from many of my fellow wrestlers.

I defended that Intercontinental title against anybody and everybody, taking my lumps in the process.

One night at Madison Square Garden in a match against Paul Orndorff, I took my first really nasty spill. As I ran toward him to try to land a flying forearm, he ducked at the last second. He dropped down and grabbed onto the top rope, so I had nothing to grab onto as I went flying.

I literally took to the air.

I flew over the top rope and out of the ring to the floor. I was able to turn in the air and land on the concrete floor on my back. My sweaty back caused me to slide into a crash landing and probably kept me from a real serious injury.

Everyone watching thought I had just killed myself, but I was relatively okay. After a few days, and lucky that I hadn't suffered a serious injury. However, my knee felt a little off. This was the start of knee problems.

By October of 1984, I had been champion for eight months. I was gaining momentum, holding my own in all my title defenses, and building a really solid fan base. I didn't know it at the time, but the end of my run was near. The company was planning on having Paul eventually beat me for the championship. Then, something happened that would kind of mess up their plans.

Now, if Paul Orndorff actually was the next in line to win the title, I would have had no problem with it. He was one of my close friends in the business. Because we were so close, he ribbed me often, busting my chops because I always flossed my teeth in the locker room, or playing tricks on me by putting tabasco sauce or salt in my coffee.

Paul had a great look and was one of the best heels ever. The way he could work the crowd was unequaled by his peers. But, he had a temper that worked against him. He was sometimes an atom bomb just waiting to explode.

If Paul wasn't happy with one of his payoffs, he would just lose it and walk. He was capable of just quitting on the spot. He really didn't give a shit. He didn't take crap from anyone. I think his lack of politics hurt him in his quest of becoming the WWF World Heavyweight champion which is why that never happened.

DRIVING ON A BAD WHEEL

One night in a match with Paul in Los Angeles, the arena was packed with mostly Hispanic fans. After he gave me a piledriver, the Hispanic fans started throwing things in the ring. Paul was being pelted by batteries, oranges, cans, bottles, half-eaten hotdogs, you name it. At first, he just egged them on, but then he realized that things were truly bordering on pandemonium.

By the time a fan hopped in the ring and jumped on Paul's back, he had had enough. Paul flung him off and went running because there was almost a full-fledged riot.

It felt good to be loved. ¡Arriba!

On my way out of there, however, I somehow had twisted my knee. It started to swell up right away. It hurt like hell and then just got worse and worse.

A few days later during a match in Erie, Pennsylvania, Paul locked me in a move that popped the cartilage in my already bad knee. It was very painful and I couldn't walk or put pressure on it. Somehow, I made it through the match, but to this day, I don't know how.

André the Giant had to help me back to my hotel room that night and up a flight of stairs. The following day I hobbled to the airport to catch a flight to the next town.

We were working a crazy schedule and I was taking on all comers. As the Intercontinental champion, that was pretty much the gimmick; you were the one people saw wrestle, and wrestle well. The whole point to the title was you were the "workers' champion."

Limping my way from town to town, I remember ending up in Rochester, New York on August 21, 1984. I was in the main event against Roddy Piper for the IC strap, in front of a packed crowd.

CHAPTER 14 – Intercontinental Champion

During our match, all was going fine until Piper went for his "Three Stooge Eye Poke" that he did all the time. However, the timing was off and accidently stuck his finger way into my eye - hard. He had probably done it a million times before, and dozens of times with me, but this one just got messed up and it was an accident.

Holy shit! I can't see!

Piper felt really bad, so bad, he didn't want to continue and went to the opposite corner. When I told the ref I couldn't see, the referee relayed the message and Piper got worried.

Things must have looked odd to the fans out there who could see well what was going on during that time. Roddy just left me alone in the corner of the ring to hopefully recuperate. He kept apologizing from across the ring and didn't touch me.

What he did to kill time was actually kind of funny in hindsight. He literally pulled the referee over to the other side of the ring and started pointing at different fans' t-shirts in the audience and having a discussion with the official about what he saw them wearing. He buried a few people calling them white trash. It was hysterical.

Here I was in a lot of pain, but laughing at the same time at the shit Piper was saying. This went on and on until I regained my sight, about three minutes later.

After the match finally ended, I went back to the locker room. I was beat up. My eye was sore, and my knee was getting worse.

"Brother," he said. "I'm so sorry about the eye, man."

"Oh, I think it will be just fine," I said, shaking his hand. "It's my knee I'm more worried about. I think it's about had it."

On the flight later on that night, Piper came by again to apologize about the eye spot. Whoever I was sitting with, traded seats with him and we had a long discussion.

It was actually very good for me in a number of ways. Roddy Piper was one of the most intelligent guys in the business. He gave me some great advice and, in the end, he suggested I take the time off for the knee operation, but have Vince parlay the injury into an angle on TV.

"That is perfect," I said. "You are absolutely right."

The next day when I saw Vince, he was shocked to see me on crutches. "I'll be okay for a bit," I said, "but we do need to talk."

Vince immediately took me into the makeshift office at the venue.

I asked him about doing an angle with Paul where he would injure my knee and take the title from me. We would make it a very vicious attack that would put me up on the shelf for a month or so, which would allow me to have surgery and rehab my knee. "Then, I when I return, I could go back against Paul, and win my title back in a grudge match."

"I love it," he said.

Vince appreciated that I was a trooper. I was working on a bad wheel and I know he liked the fact I was so loyal that I was working on an injury for the good of the company. He also liked the idea that Piper and I came up with so much that he practically gave it the greenlight on the spot.

We were finally all set to run with it on TV when we learned that there would be one minor change in details. The whole thing wasn't going to be with Paul, it was going to be with someone else.

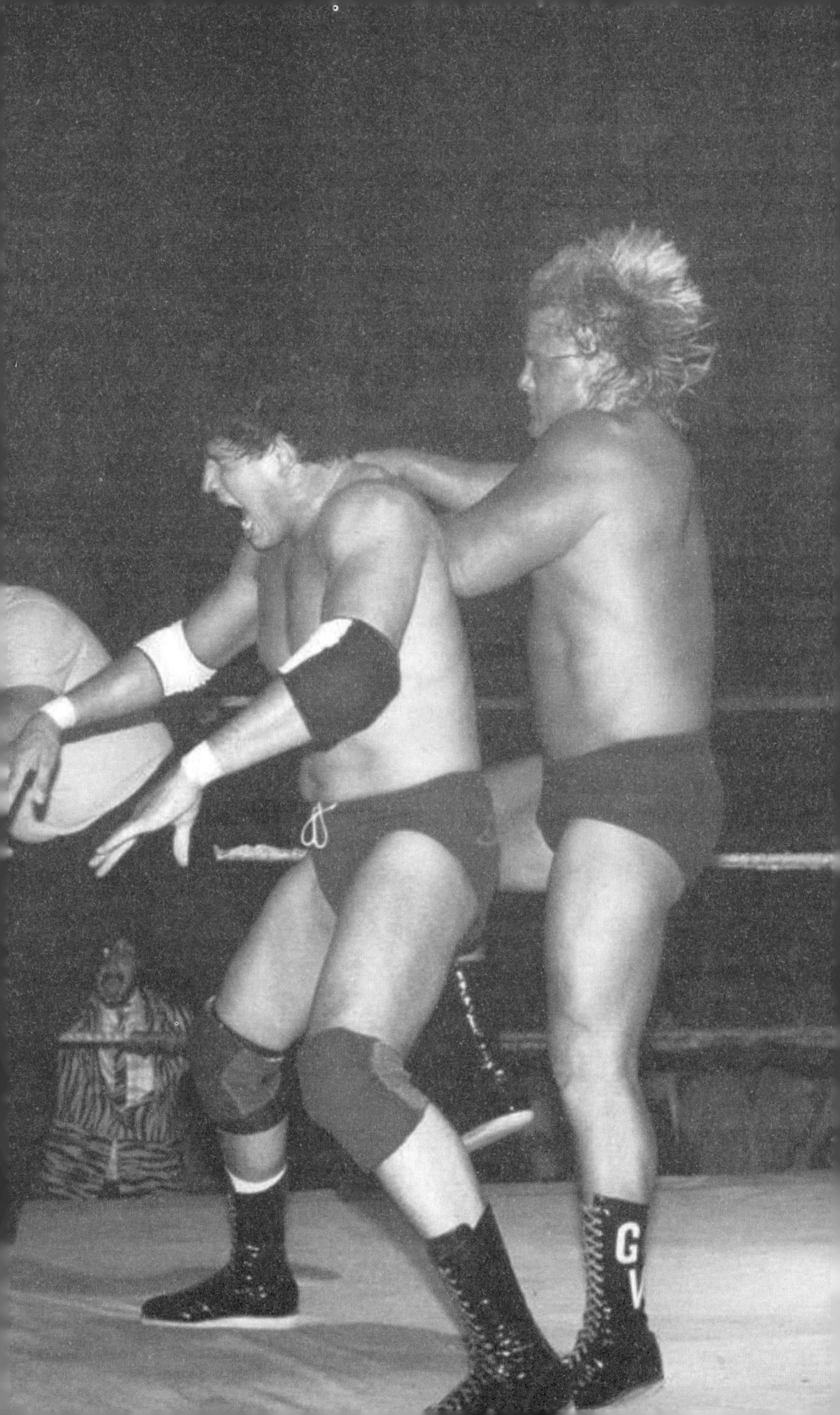

CHAPTER 15 - GREG VALENTINE

One of the biggest feuds of my career, bar none, was with Greg "The Hammer" Valentine. It was the classic brawler versus the scientific babyface and the fans loved it. We were opposites and that is what made us complement each other so much in the ring. Before I get into detail about the proverbial "yin to my yang," I think it is first probably best to hear a little bit about his father.

JOHNNY VALENTINE

For those of you who don't know a whole lot about Greg, he was the son of the legendary and very creative, Johnny Valentine.

While in the Mid-Atlantic Championship Wrestling, Johnny Valentine came up with a gimmick match that would entertain fans for years to come. In 1974, Johnny Valentine was the Mid-Atlantic Heavyweight Champion and wanted to do something different to draw money. That is when he came up with the first ever, Johnny Valentine 1000 silver dollar challenge!

What Greg's father did was, he began bringing a large fishbowl full of silver dollars to the ring and promised to give it to any wrestler that could pin him or make him submit in 10 minutes or less. During the early months of these 1,000 silver dollar challenges, Valentine defended his money against a number of different opponents a number of times each month.

Being the heel that he was, Johnny always said he would take on "all comers," but he generally defended the $1,000 only against lower and mid-card wrestlers that fans felt he could beat. He made it fun though for the fans, even when he was pitted against lesser name opponents. He always had them just about win, before pulling out some crazy surprise to make the timer pass the 10-minute mark and infuriate the fans. He was great at timing it just right.

Valentine continued to go undefeated in his 1,000 silver dollar challenge matches. After beating challenger Bob

CHAPTER 15 – Greg Valentine 201

Bruggers on the Mid-Atlantic Championship Wrestling TV show that aired in many area markets on Saturday, July 20, 1974, Johnny was confronted by none other than my mentor, who was going by the name "Mr. Number One" at this time, Paul Jones!

Paul challenged Johnny, and Valentine blew him off saying, "Get in line, boy! You're not good enough to wrestle me!"

"I'll give you some incentive!" Jones replied. "I will match your 1,000 silver dollars, and bring the money next week, making it a 2,000 silver dollar match to the winner."

So at WRAL TV Studios, on July 27, 1974, the match was on. As promised, Paul Jones brought his 1,000 silver dollars poured them into Johnny's fish bowl that already held 1,000 silver dollars. There were so many silver dollars that many were falling out of the bowl and onto the floor!

"Ladies and gentlemen we have a very, very special event tonight," the ring announcer Joe Murnick said, before explaining the 10-minute stipulation rule to the match. Chief Wahoo McDaniel (a future rival of Greg's) joined Bob Caudle at ringside for commentary and the bout started.

"You can tell how much Johnny loves money. Just look at him! Look at the expression on his face!" Bob Caudle said as Valentine stared off at the fish bowl overflowing with silver.

Wahoo laughingly replied, "That man, he doesn't trust anybody."

Johnny took his own sweet time taking off his ring robe. The psychology was Johnny had to be beaten to get his money, but he didn't have to beat Paul in 10 minutes to win his. Therefore, precious seconds ticked away for Jones, and it was all about stalling.

During the match, whenever the opportunity would present itself, Valentine would waste more time and get heat from the fans. He would jump out of the ring. He would duck under the ropes to break interaction away from Paul, anything to allowing those vital seconds to tick off the clock. The commentators told the story, and even Wahoo admitted the Valentine was smart by his approach of killing time.

In the match's final minutes, Jones pulled out all the stops. He got Valentine in his famous airplane spin, to no avail. He also frantically put Johnny into the Indian Death Lock hold, also to no avail. As the final countdown approached, Paul locked in the abdominal stretch, but Valentine held on until the time limit. The bell rang.

A flat-out in the ring Valentine had once again defied fate and held on to his 1,000 silver dollars. But this time, the "Champ's" 1,000 silver dollars had doubled and had become 2,000 silver dollars!

Johnny Valentine continued with his silver dollar matches for another year or so, but because of Paul Jones failed attempt, the ante had been increased and it became the 2,000 silver dollar challenge.

Now, the reason I brought up this match is important. When Johnny's son (initially referred to as his "brother") Greg Valentine revived the silver dollar challenge in 1976 when he entered the Mid-Atlantic area, it went back again to being a 1,000 silver dollar challenge.

During this run, my first match with Greg Valentine was, in fact, for 1,000 silver dollars.

I guess I couldn't have made much of an impact, at the time, however. If you ask Greg about this today, he doesn't even remember that our match even happened!

JOHNNY'S RIBS

Johnny on the road a long time and comfortable with "entertaining himself" to make the time pass and was known for his pranks.

Johnny, for one, was the master of shitty hotel room pranks, literally. For instance, one thing he would do was get access to a fellow wrestler's room who was not around. Then, he would turn the heat up in there, full blast, even (especially) in the dead of summer. He would then shut all the windows and take a nasty steaming dump in the middle of the bed and wipe his ass with the sheets. For the finishing touch to his masterpiece, he would make the bed up again perfectly, so that you couldn't tell where the smell was

CHAPTER 15 – Greg Valentine

coming from until it was just too late. Imagine sliding into that bed after a hard match at the end of the night!

Another one of his famous pranks was the time that he took Jay York's asthma inhaler and filled it with lighter fluid. (Don't try this at home kids!) After a match, Jay came back to the dressing room and used his inhaler. He got immediately light headed and passed out. (Some say he could have even died!) Now, for whatever reason, Jay thought that Buddy Rogers had spiked his inhaler, so when he came to, he immediately went out to his car and got a shotgun. He waited in the lot, and when Buddy left the arena that night, he fired right at him, blowing a briefcase right out of his hands. Nobody to this day knows if that was the plan, or if the plan was to actually shoot Buddy. The funniest part about this story is, the very next week, Johnny had come clean about the rib, then Jay and Johnny ribbed the whole locker room. They staged an altercation in which Jay pulled out a gun and shot Johnny (with blanks) and Johnny used ketchup packs to make the whole place think he really got shot.

Johnny also liked to get the new guys, breaking greenhorns in the hard way. Greg tells a story about one particular annoying rookie who was "up Johnny's ass" trying to get his attention like a puppy does its master. He desperately was trying to get over with him to the point of annoyance. He would follow him around, open doors, and carry bags and little things, worse than any Japan young boy. Then, he would constantly sit down to shoot the shit with Johnny at the worst possible times and bum his chew off him to try and look cool. It was obvious to everyone that this kid didn't like chewing tobacco. Not really knowing who Johnny was, he had no idea how literally "shooting the shit" was soon going to be.

Johnny had enough. He was tired of sharing his chew with someone who didn't even appreciate it, so he devised a plan. He went out into a cow pasture and collected up some nice choice mounds in a shopping bag. Then he pounded those turds out and spread them in the sun to dry on some stones. The next day, he cut the dung up the best he could and put the shredded goodness into some of his old chewing tobacco bags that he saved just for the occasion. For the finishing touch, he sacrificed a small bit of real chew to mix it into the mash to make it look legit.

While they were on tour, the greenhorn came by and watched Johnny chewing his tobacco.

"You want some?" he asked. The kid nodded. He reached into his suitcase, grabbed the little bag, and handed it to the rookie. He watched with great delight as the newbie began to chew and suck on the poop-juice. "Pretty good, aye?" Johnny asked, spitting his tobacco spit into a cup.

His eyes watered up like he just ate the world's hottest pepper or something. Then, his face shriveled. "Yeah. Mmm. Good," he said, trying to kayfabe the horrible taste in his mouth and look cool.

"You can keep that bag. I got more."

It was the gift that kept on giving. For the rest of that week, whenever the new kid saw Johnny around, he would take out his pouch and pack a huge dip in his lip of "dip-shit." He would just sit there and rough through it, chewing on that bag of cow poo and smile, still trying to get over good with Johnny.

I guess you could say that was a crappy thing to do.

Speaking of shitty pranks, he would play pranks on his own son, Greg, that were just ridiculous. One thing I remember he would do is call Greg like something terrible had happened, "Hey kid, you gotta get over here!" He would describe all the symptoms of a heart attack without actually saying the words.

Greg would then hop in the car, fearing the worst not knowing exactly what was wrong. He would jump out of the car and rush right to the front door. He had no idea that there was a large glob of shit smeared under the doorknob, just waiting for him to put his hand in it.

On October 4, 1975, maybe five years into his son's budding career, Johnny Valentine was in a private airplane, a twin-engine Cessna 310 and off to a show. He was with Ric Flair, David Crockett, Bob Bruggers and Tim Woods. While the recommended occupancy was technically correct for the small plane, the maximum weight limit was greatly exceeded because wrestlers are typically heavier than your average person. Because of the weight of the wrestling passengers, the pilot Michael Farkus knew before takeoff that he was going to have to reduce the amount of fuel that the plane was carrying in its tank.

Everything was fine, until halfway through the flight, the pilot realized they were flying on fumes. Subsequently, the worst happened and the aircraft ran out of fuel.

It crashed near Wilmington, North Carolina. The impact was life-altering. The impact broke the backs of Bob Bruggers, Ric Flair and Johnny. Greg's father had a bone fragment lodged in his spinal column that paralyzed him for life. It was so bad that he also had to have a clamp implanted in his back to hold the bones in together.

GREG TRAINING

One might think that this would have immediately thrusted him into wherever he wanted to go at the time, due to his father's popularity with promoters, but his father didn't want that. He wanted him to come up on his own so he could be his own person. A young Greg Valentine didn't immediately capitalize on his father's fame. Instead, Greg got his start training in Stu Hart's dungeon, in addition to timely advice from his father.

Back in 1948, Stu bought the Canadian territory from a guy named Larry Tillman. He had the rights to promote wrestling shows in Calgary, Edmonton, Winnipeg, Seattle, Vancouver, Salt Lake City and lots of other Northwest states that nobody else was running, or even really wanted to run in. Stu was actually commuting to all of these places out of Great Falls, Montana, where he lived. When he first started promoting, he would drive up to Calgary or Edmonton and it was a bit of a hike every time he had to do it. On one of his trips in 1951, he finally saw a house in Calgary for a decent price and bought it. Then, he relocated his family to Canada.

Stu started training students to wrestle soon after buying the house for a few reasons; one was to offset the cost of the home, and the other was that he was running out of fresh talent and needed to create new talent to fill out his Stampede Wrestling shows.

One of the very first guys he taught was Nikolai Volkoff. He wasn't even 20 years old yet when he started training in the basement of that house that soon took on the name "Stu Hart's Dungeon." Soon after him, former AWA World Heavyweight Champion Gene Kiniski was next. A number of guys went through there and Stu Hart stretched every one of them; the Iron Sheik, "Superstar" Billy Graham, and even Ole Anderson. Gorilla Monsoon trained with Stu who broke his nose on the first day of lessons. Mad Dog Vachon, Fritz Von Erich, Paul, and Jos LeDuc, Archie "The Stomper" Gouldie, and even Greg "The Hammer" Valentine.

Greg tells a funny story today how Stu would be on the phone setting up deals. He said the house was filled with cats and that one particular one became accustomed to hanging out with Stu while he was on the phone. In fact, it became conditioned to do so, almost like Pavlov's dog.

"Stu didn't realize it, but whenever he got on the phone, the same cat would jump up on the counter and turn his back to the famous wrestler. Then, he would take a pencil and play with the cat's asshole, just circle it and all. Then he would move down to the balls. The cat seemed to enjoy it, and this became a regular thing, so much so, that when the phone would ring, the cat would get into position!"

Valentine had already learned a lot from his father before he officially started training. The Dungeon was different, though. There would be no exceptions or going light on Greg because he was a family member, as it might have been if he had trained with his father. The dungeon was as close to hell as physically possible, being in the dark basement of Stu Hart's house. They trained hard on some old nasty wrestling mats on the floor, and if Stu got ahold of you, he'd try to make you scream!

Greg said the training was hell. They had 13 kids, and probably 25 cats. He didn't have any boots yet at the time, so he first started his training barefoot. However, because the mats probably hadn't been cleaned in 15 years, he caught some kind of filth on his feet from them called

CHAPTER 15 – Greg Valentine

Impetigo. Impetigo often appears as red sores on the face, especially around a child's nose and mouth, and on hands and feet. The sores burst and develop honey-colored crusts.

After the infection, Stu was trying to stretch Valentine and saw his ugly foot condition.

"Geesh, you can't wrestle in here with your feet like that. You will get it on my mats," Stu said.

"But I caught it from your mats!" he replied.

Valentine eventually finished and was ready to go. Stu had him go and referee to learn that side of the business first, the same as I did. Greg officiated for the original Sheik out of Detroit some, until he was ready for his own matches.

Eventually, he was given the name "Babyface Nelson." Soon after that, another promoter changed his ring name to "Johnny Fargo" to work as one of the Fabulous Fargo brothers, teaming with Don Fargo from 1971-74.

Eventually, Valentine went to Florida and changed his ring name to "Johnny Valentine, Jr." but that didn't last either. You see, this name was before the plane crash. His father was still wrestling and afraid that the name would imply the elder Valentine was too old to be in the ring. That is when he took on the name, Greg Valentine.

His snug style had earned him respect from the locker room. He had picked up the name "the Hammer" for how hard he seemed to be hitting people in the ring.

"People believed what I was doing," Valentine says when asking him about his name. "I never wanted anybody to be able to see through any of my stuff, so when I threw it, I threw it hard."

Long before pairing up with me, Greg went to North Carolina for Jim Crockett and teamed up with Ric Flair. They won the NWA Mid-Atlantic and the NWA World Tag Team Championship Titles. They worked a program with Ole and Gene Anderson, trading the world tag titles back and forth until Valentine was ready for his first headline singles feud with Wahoo McDaniel.

Now, this is important, because this is where some of my eventual feud would get its "legs" from, no pun intended.

In a nasty feud with Wahoo, Greg "broke" his leg.

Valentine who was using the figure-four leg lock as a finisher said that Wahoo's legs were so thick that he couldn't really get the traditional figure-four on him, so he mostly just "scissored his leg and fell backward."

To get heat, for weeks after the leg-breaking angle, Valentine wore a T-shirt everywhere he went that said, I BROKE WAHOO'S LEG" on the front and "NO MORE WAHOO" on the back.

This taunting drew money and fans came from everywhere in hopes to see Wahoo exact his revenge.

After this, Valentine made his way to New York for Vince Senior in the WWWFs success with Wahoo in the NWA and make him a wrestler who would attempt to break the leg of every opponent he stepped into the ring with.

Back then, you had a lot of creative license as a wrestler. It is not like today in the WWE where everything is written out for you and you are essentially a body going through their motions off a script. Back then, you could take a feud or storyline that worked very well for you in one place and then recreate it into other territories without having to be afraid of getting sued. You owned your own creativity. So, just like Greg did with Wahoo, a Native-American Indian, he did practically the same thing with, Chief Jay Strongbow, also breaking his leg in the ring.

Before recreating the angle with me, Greg took a tour in the Mid-Atlantic territory. There, he elevated his name even more working a brutal feud with "Rowdy" Roddy Piper. I remember seeing various wrestling magazines at the time with the two of them fighting for the territory's top title, the United States championship. The pictures were jarring. At Starrcade 1983, Valentine and Piper had a dog collar match with each man chained to the other by the neck and totally covered in blood.

After these pictures scarred fans' brains everywhere, Vince McMahon smelled money. Expanding his father's old territory, Junior decided to offer Valentine a deal to return back the WWF. Valentine agreed. He dropped the U.S. title immediately to Dick Slater and packed his bags for New York.

I'm glad he did.

GREG VS. TITO

Now, I had just started to take off. Vince had me beat Don Muraco at Boston Gardens, and gave me my first singles run as Intercontinental Champion. This was a huge leap of faith for him to do for me, and I was very grateful. However, I was wrestling on a bad wheel and didn't want to tell him. I was afraid that if I took time off to let my leg heal, someone else would come along and take my spot.

I also knew that my next opponent, Greg Valentine, was a star and perhaps going to mean even more for my career than I had so far. Now, Valentine had heard I was a good guy. Because we were on opposite sides of the heel/face dynamic, they weren't able to "hang out," really, but he too felt we could really do some good business.

"I was really impressed on how quickly Tito moved up the cards," he said in an interview for this book. "It had taken me many years to become a headliner and Tito got there much faster, so I knew that he was something special."

Eventually, word got out to the office that I was hurt. It was pretty hard to hide seven-foot giant André carrying me up a staircase to my hotel room after a card here and there when there were no elevators.

In fact, the first idea was using Paul Orndorff to become the new IC champ so I could time off for knee surgery. He would injure me somehow, then I would return eventually to regain the belt. However, Orndorff had some kind of heat with George Scott, the WWF booker at that time, so Valentine was next in line.

In hindsight, that change actually turned out to be gold, for me that is.

I took a few days off before I agreed to drop the title. I needed to nurse my knee to a point where I could wrestle in an action-packed match before getting "injured." I needed to be in good enough shape to really put him over before going under the knife.

Come September 24, 1984, in Ontario, I was ready. This angle was set up to be very similar to ones Valentine did with both Wahoo and Strongbow only a few years before. Little did we know, this time it would be even more impactful.

Coincidentally, Strongbow was actually the agent for our match. He helped us with our finish so that we would be building to an eventual rematch that could mean more money for us down the road. Strongbow was the perfect guy to help put it together. Afterall, he knew Greg's strengths in the ring, first hand.

Before our match, my knee felt great. Because it was pretty tender, I had it all taped up like crazy for extra support and it seemed like it was working. When I stepped up the ring stairs, I was conscious of each step, but it didn't realy hurt. I did know, however, that I was literally walking on my last leg so I was playing it extra careful.

For the story, Greg was an excellent wrestler and experienced pro. So the moment the bell rang, he immediately got on me and went right to work on my knee. We were actually playing up the injury which was real. During the match, I worked the best I could and was able to hit him with a good flying forearm early on. We did a good job making it look like I should have been able to pin Valentine, too, until his manager, Captain Lou Albano, interfered. After that, Greg got the upper hand and illegally pinned me using the ropes. The story was great.

Outside of the story, my knee was not so great. In real life, I was in massive pain after the finish, and my whole leg was throbbing. I had been "robbed of my title," but at that point, I sold it like wanted to get out of the arena and find a doctor, quick, *because I really did.*

As I was exiting the ring, Greg put the icing on the cake. He blindsided me, dragged me back onto the mat, and put the dreaded figure-four leg lock on me. Captain Lou kept the referee occupied, and Greg used the top rope to pull himself up and apply extra pressure.

The crowd couldn't believe it. They were pissed!

CHAPTER 15 – Greg Valentine

I had to be carried out on a stretcher, and all of a sudden, my Intercontinental title was the last of the fans' worries because my future was in doubt. The fans gasped. They were shocked and in total silence. We had them eating out of the palm of our hands.

Three days later, I finally had surgery. Luckily, in surgery, they found no significant ligament damage and were able to put me back together easier than they had hoped for. I was elated to find out that my operation was only going to keep me out of action for a couple of weeks!

I still had to go through some very rigorous rehabilitation on my tendon, but as an athlete my entire life, I managed the pain and did additional rehab at my home gym, so things were looking good. Things looked so good that I came back only ten days off after going under the knife.

"Ten days? Why?" you might ask. Well, to be honest, I didn't want to miss an MSG payday. I just taped the hell out of that knee again and prayed to God that it would hold together. I was looking at such a good payday in New York that I figured if my knee were to fall off and roll out of the ring - that would be just fine! I would just pick it up, put it in a paper bag. With the amount of money they were talking, I could just pay for a second operation and still have a boatload of money left over!

Roddy Piper came up to me the day I returned. He was the one who came up with the injury angle idea and was super impressed that I was back already to see it through. He just couldn't believe I was back as soon as I was and pulled me off to the side.

"You know kid, if that knee just happens to fail out there tonight, you probably could make Vince pay for your medical bills and you could probably get some kind of temporary severance pay to help you out as he recovering from surgery. Do you hear what I'm saying?"

I laughed. "Yes, Roddy."

However, Piper was planning on quitting that same day, so I wasn't sure this was the best advice.

Some good advice did come from Jack Brisco, however. Jack was the one who suggested that I learn

Greg's finisher and use it against him upon my return "to get the best of him." In the storyline, I also think it was Jack who taught me "how to master the figure-four" as part of the TV angle. After this, I started using that submission hold as part of the storyline, and also for the rest of my entire career.

Fortunately, the tape on my knee held up and, even though I had rushed back to the ring before the doctors said I should have, all turned out just fine.

I didn't win the title back on my return. That would have been way too soon. We had a number of matches set and ready to milk everything we could out of our feud.

I didn't work a bump-heavy style in my first few matches back. I focused more on brawling to avoid my knee getting reinjured. The fans knew me as a scientific wrestler, but they didn't seem to notice the change in style because my character was angry at Greg Valentine for trying to "end my career." It only made sense that I was going into the ring to fight. So fighting we did, and the chase began.

One of the best ways to get the fans behind you is to not give them what they want right away. In this case, having me chase Greg for the belt but always come up short was a perfect way to build to something even bigger.

Our rivalry was pretty intense. Looking back at it, I think it was a very believable feud for fans to buy into basically because I was a good seller, and Greg was so stiff!

Business for us boomed as our feud really gained heat. "Detroit, in particular," Valentine recalls, "Detroit probably grew four or five times over in crowd size for the WWF as our feud developed!" See, Vince started taking the show on the road, using WWF programming as a commercial for shows outside his territory. The WWF "invaded" the Omni in late 1984. Now, much like me, Valentine didn't get along with Ole Anderson who was booker for GCW in that territory, so we were taking the feud to areas where we were unfamiliar and still doing very well with it.

One thing that really helped our program is the Hammer REALLY laid in on the shots, so snug that it wasn't hard to sell. I wasn't used to taking hits that snug, but I knew the fans were eating it up so I tried to give it right back the best I could. Then when he would least expect it, I would retaliate with some stiff potatoes of my own and laugh watching Greg block mine the best he could.

No matter how hard I hit him, his chops were always a hundred times worse. I absolutely hated taking those chops. They really were bullshit! I thought they were lousy for ring psychology and also caused legit pain.

In return for taking those chops, however, Greg would sometimes get color for me and really make me look good. Generally speaking, Greg bled a hell of a lot more than I ever did, so it didn't bother him. Plus, he had the hair for it. Gigging just wasn't my thing. In the past, would do shitty blade jobs so the promoters would stop asking him to bleed.

One night, I remember hitting Greg with a chair shot, and blood was everywhere, instantly.

Wow. That was some good color work!

Then the ref checked on Greg and came back over to me. He actually got color the hard way. I guess there was a seam on the chair that caught him just right and split his head open. It looked like roadkill on his head.

When he got back to the dressing room, I met up with him to check on him and apologize.

"Where is Greg?" I asked one of the agents.

"Back there yelling about getting stitches."

Worried he was upset with me, I remember walking down the hall thinking of the best way I could to apologize. But when I got back there, Hammer jumped up, hugged me, and thanked me for the match.

I soon found out that the chairshot was the furthest thing from his mind. He actually encouraged working snug with me, because he knew we were making money and the fans were buying it. Come to find out about the "yelling," he was actually arguing with the doctors over having to get his head shaved for the stitches.

His hair, after all, was his money.

We started to sell out arenas on shows through the end of 1984 and well into 1985. This was impressive because in areas that were not getting the A-card with Hulk Hogan who was the major WWF draw, we were the only attraction that could do the same for the company. Both of us waged war across the country. We competed in some very classic bouts, and also in gimmick matches.

At some point, there was talk about Don Muraco coming back into the picture. Before all this, he no-showed an event somewhere which led to him having to drop the Intercontinental title to me in the first place. However, over time, he got back into good graces again, and Vince decided he wanted Greg to drop the belt to me, so we could shift back to what they had originally planned for Muraco. Fortunately, Valentine refused to do the job, arguing on the basis of the booming houses. He won.

One of the agents came to his defense and broke the news to us all. He said that our feud was actually outselling Hulk Hogan matches in some areas! This both humbled me and empowered me to do an even better job in the ring.

Finally, WrestleMania was about to happen, and I then learned... *Tito vs. Greg was not on the card?!*

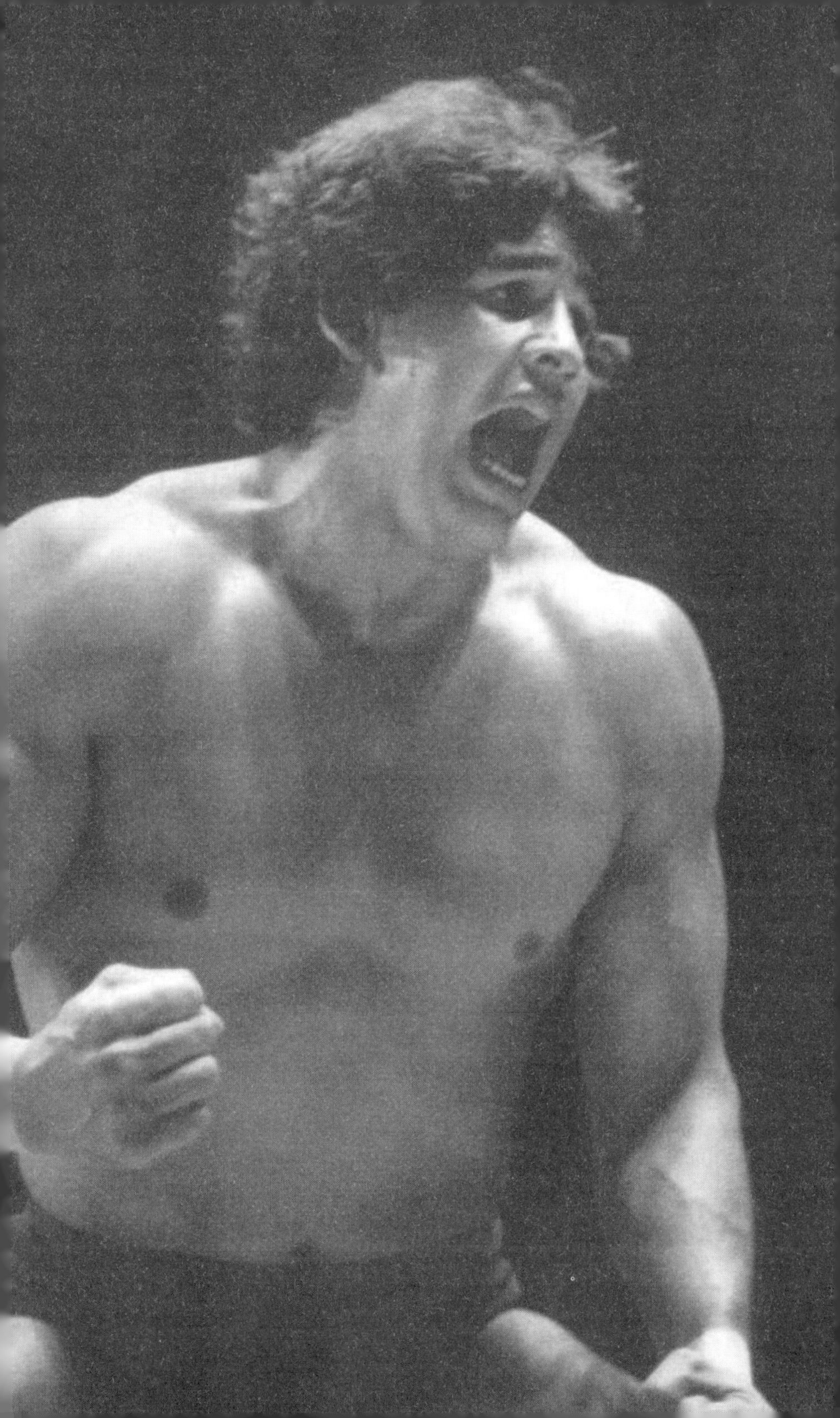

CHAPTER 16 - WrestleMania I & II

When Hulkamania hit, it hit hard.

Hulk and I started almost at the very same time in 1977. He was right behind me there in Florida and, at the beginning, he was a really humble guy for sure. Maybe that fed into his success? I think that I was really blessed because everywhere that Hogan went, that territory just seemed to be on fire, and I wasn't booked far behind. I was quite often in the same locker rooms that I was in.

We were together in New York in 1979, then both of us went to Japan, and then both of us went to the AWA, and then WWF. When Hulk did that Rocky movie, it was a real game changer for him. When he came back to AWA wrestling, Verne Gagne missed the boat on him over financial differences, but Vince scooped him up. He got mainstream exposure and had the best body in professional wrestling. He hit it at the right time, and he got over.

Because Hulk drew money, we all made money. I made a lot of money throughout my entire career just because I was lucky enough to be in the same building as Hulk Hogan. Because we got paid a percentage of the tickets, we learned quickly that being on the same card as Hulk meant that you were going to make a whole lot more money. Therefore, everyone wanted to be on his shows.

Vince knew that Hulk Hogan could be his connection to the national mainstream connection he wanted, so he did what Verne didn't do. Vince pushed him to the moon and did whatever he had to in order to find success.

When Vince McMahon announced his idea for the first *WrestleMania*, other wrestling promoters around the country thought he was crazy. They figured he had signed his own bankruptcy papers and that they could also finally lure their own talent back that Vince had pulled from them. They just weren't thinking "big picture" like Vince was.

None of the other territories believed that Junior would be able to take over the business. New York had a historic reputation for not looking real, not bringing in the toughest wrestlers. Nobody thought he had a chance. He

CHAPTER 16 – WrestleMania I & II

was mostly disliked by his competition. His rival promoters were actually pulling for *WrestleMania* to fail and were hoping for the ultimate demise of WWF, although that wasn't in the cards. They felt he was robbing from their talent pool, and the syndication of his television program was infringing on their territories. Nobody outside of the promotion wished him well.

"WrestleMania was the ultimate in calculated risks," Vince has often said. "If Mania had failed, the future of the WWF would have been bleak."

WrestleMania was officially the first real professional wrestling pay-per-view event ever. It took place on March 31, 1985, at Madison Square Garden in New York City. While the setup wasn't much different than any other house show at MSG, Vince's gamble had paid off. Vince McMahon's main competition in the wrestling industry at this time was with Jim Crockett Promotions' NWA. Vince wanted to offer a mega-card, and he decided to piggyback off of the success of Jim Crockett's annual big show Starrcade (which began airing in 1983) by also making his show available in multiple locations on closed-circuit TV.

While the numbers weren't really record breaking, the attendance for the event was, in fact, a hot crowd of 19,121 fans. You really could feel the "excitement in the air," as they say. When I pulled up to the garage that day, I knew the hype had paid off. The hall right below MSG held another 10,000 people who were there because there were not going to be any seats left in the arena. All of those people were fully willing to watch it live on a closed-circuit TV in the hall.

The venue's seating limitation wasn't a concern. Again, Vince was thinking "big picture," not tickets sold. The almost 20,000 people in attendance were just a scratch on the surface. The event was also seen by another million viewers through closed-circuit television in many big halls across the country, making it the largest showing of any event on closed-circuit television in America at the time.

It was outside-the-box thinking. This had never been done before. Vince had all kinds of media reaching different people than your traditional redneck "wrasslin'" fan.

The boys in the locker room all really stepped up in loyalty. Nobody was holding Vince up for more money, or anything. We knew the risk he was taking on us. We knew we needed to be there for each other; promoter and talent. He was betting on a lot of really good wrestlers, and nobody wanted to disappoint.

The turnout that day was spectacular. It didn't happen by mistake. Vince planned this and bet everything he had on this one single event. The strategic placement on the calendar of WrestleMania's date in itself was very important. Vince couched it on the Sunday between NCAA men's basketball Final Four on Saturday and the championship game on Monday. There was virtually no competition. There was no football, no baseball, no Olympics, and no college basketball. The date selection was perfect.

Everybody was psyched. There was a different feeling there. The audience really was a smattering of all walks of life. I saw rich people. I saw poor people. I saw attractive women. I saw ugly men. I saw people of all ages all gathered in the name of professional wrestling, like never before. So how did this happen?

ROCK 'N WRESTLING

The WWF decided to cross-promote the WWF with pop culture, to bring in this new mainstream audience and create a "Rock-n-Wrestling Connection." His hopes were that if he used celebrities from pop culture, he could pull in a whole new diverse demographic to his show. He wanted the first *WrestleMania* to have a larger than life feel to it, with a combination of special guests from both the entertainment world, as well as sports. Vince McMahon had signed a deal with MTV and aired two wrestling specials to drum up interest for *WrestleMania* to help make this happen. The first MTV wrestling special was the one where Hillbilly hurt his leg.

So on July 23, 1984, *The Brawl to End It All* aired live from Madison Square Garden. There, Wendi Richter beat The Fabulous Moolah to win the WWF Women's title, with Cyndi Lauper in her corner. Six months later on February 18,

CHAPTER 16 – WrestleMania I & II

1985, *The War to Settle the Score* had Leilani Kai, beat Richter to avenge Moolah and capture the title, with Cyndi Lauper again at ringside. Cyndi Lauper, a pop star, brought WWF into the popular eye. (Many people argue inversely that Cyndi Lauper's singing career was pushed into the mainstream because of *WrestleMania*, and all the media she received for the participation in it. Who knows? Either way, it was a win-win situation for sure.)

Promoting *WrestleMania* for almost a year before the payoff, interest had time to marinate. Other celebrities were booked for the buildup for Mania including Muhammad Ali, Liberace, Andy Warhol, The Rockettes and Major League Baseball's Billy Martin. But the cream of the crop was a celebrity that was actually going to wrestle and further legitimize the sport; Mr. T agreeing to team up with Hulk Hogan for the main event!

The celebrity names helped *WrestleMania* receive crazy amounts of publicity all over the place which pro wrestling would never have accomplished on its own before this. The awareness helped not only sell out MSG, but also secure multiple closed-circuit viewing locations around the country in the days before pay-per-view was available to all on cable TV. (*WrestleMania* was, in fact, the first to tap the few stations experimenting with PPV.)

MY MANIA MATCH

It was March 1985 at the Madison Square Garden. I was in the big city and ready to walk out in front of 20,000 plus people, to open up for the first WrestleMania ever.

Before the show, I walked around some backstage. I met a bunch of people that night that seemed outside my regular circle. One was the iconic artist Andy Warhol. It turned out that Warhol wasn't just a professional wrestling fan, but also a fan of mine! Andy actually made his way to the locker room in hopes of meeting me. We chatted for a while, and I was impressed with his personality and character. I gave him my autograph and we had some pictures taken with each other.

Tito Santana, Cyndi Lauper and Brian Blair

CHAPTER 16 – WrestleMania I & II

I also met up with Liberace that night who was with The Rockettes. I watched as he put on a great performance right in the middle of the wrestling ring. Later on, I would get a chance to meet him. He was very polite and quite a small person.

"I really respect what the wrestlers are doing and how hard you work," he said to me. That was a compliment from a world-wide entertainer that really meant a lot to me.

In hindsight looking back at this momentous event, you would think that I should have looked at being included as being a real honor at the time. However, I did not at first.

I was very upset at my spot on *WrestleMania*. Traditionally, the first match was not looked at as being all that special, because in many cases, fans were just settling into their seats. Quite often, the wrestlers in this spot were looked at as so far down on the ladder that fans barely cared about this match and often some didn't really watch it at all.

At the time of *WrestleMania*, Greg Valentine and I were in the middle of that huge program and drawing very well! Aside from Hulk Hogan, if our match was on the top of a card as the main event, we were selling out arenas. Because of this, I couldn't understand why Greg and I couldn't have a semi-main event match at what was being promoted as one of the biggest wrestling cards ever.

To make it feel even worse, George Scott, one of WWF's bookers at the time, booked me against a no-name masked wrestler name The Executioner. The Executioner wasn't even a part of WWF's regular roster. The gimmick was just like a jobber attraction. Now, the person playing the role of The Executioner was actually a well-known name from AWA, Buddy Rose. I figured if he wrestled without the mask, that would have at least drawn some eyes to our match. However, George didn't want to waste a loss on Buddy in such a big platform, in case they were going to use him for something bigger down the line.

I found out later that I was not being punished, and I was not an oversight. Vince came to me and told me that that the reason I was on first is that he knew I would deliver and he really wanted something good to open the show, not just another throw away match. He wanted to set a tone.

Before I went out to the ring for my match, Vince pulled me aside. "Tito, I have everything riding on this pay-per-view. If it doesn't work, we are going down. If it is successful, we are off and running and nothing can stop us."

"I understand," I said.

"I also understand you didn't really like your spot," he said. "But I want you to know that I put you in the first match because I want to get people off their butts right off the bat, and I think you are the only one who can really do it."

The genuine pep talk made me feel real good.

"Well, I will admit. I didn't look at it that way," I said. "Thank you very much."

I believed him. I knew that he appreciated my work ethic. If making me first for this reason really was the case and not just lip service, it made sense. I always tried to make it hard to follow any of my matches. Some of the boys didn't like to have to work after one of my matches because they knew they would have to really up their game or have their match seem lame in comparison. Because of this, Vince was in a weird way complimenting me by putting me on first. Looking back, it is kind of neat to say that I was the first person to ever wrestle at a *WrestleMania* by wrestling in the very first match.

Later on, George Scott would also tell me that another reason why Greg Valentine and I didn't wrestle a main event match at 'Mania was that our matches were so good that they didn't want to give it away. The program wasn't finished yet. We really were selling out arenas still with it and the WWF wanted to continue to use us in every individual city we toured in. By not exposing it at a pay-per-view event and bring some finality to our feud, we could continue to make money with our match around the country.

Finally, my match came. It felt like any really big show to most of us in the locker room, but that was because we had no idea it was the start of something as massive as what it would become.

CHAPTER 16 – WrestleMania I & II

After about five minutes, The Executioner submitted to a figure-four leg lock, giving me the win. The crowd was going crazy. As the hype man, I was happy I had accomplished Vince's goal of hyping the audience.

The early match also worked out well in helping me continue to promote my program with Greg "The Hammer" Valentine. During a match later on in the evening, Greg pinned JYD in their match by rolling him up and holding the ropes for leverage. I did a run-in and told the referee about Valentine's cheating. In turn, the ref reversed the decision and restarted the match. Valentine refused to continue and walked out of the ring. The referee disqualified him and JYD was declared the winner. Valentine was pissed off and of course, blamed me for the loss. This action added fuel to the fire for our rivalry and gave ample opportunity to the commentators to explain why this happened, which they did. That spot then became a national commercial, in a sense, for people around the country to come to see us fight when we were in town.

My good friend André the Giant was also on the card in a $15,000 bodyslam gimmick match against Big John Studd. After the match, André took the prize money and threw real money into the crowd! And I would be remised if I didn't mention the big main event; Hulk Hogan and Mr. T versus Roddy Piper and Mr. Wonderful.

At the end of the show, Vince was happy. Getting the fans up and on their feet was just what we did, and it really did set the bar for the rest of the show.

"I was glad he had me, and I had him," Buddy said in an interview. "Tito was great and was always a night off. He would sometimes fill in for other wrestlers, but everything he did was always gold. He always worked his ass off. He never hurt you, even with his flying jalapeño."

"Looking back on that match at *WrestleMania* though, I remember we were told we could only go five to six minutes," Buddy Rose also said regarding our match. "And for me, that was when wrestling became commercialized. It was around then that it stopped being where you could just have a match that you and your (opponent set up,) and it became something where you had to make it short and fit within an exact time so they could get the next match on."

After the show, "Playboy" Buddy Rose was celebrating in the locker room. He wasn't used much by WWF at this point, but he was known by all the boys. They were all pretty cool to congratulate him for a great appearance with the company. The boys weren't the only ones to compliment Buddy, however.

Once he had unmasked backstage, I remember Cyndi Lauper coming up to him and being all funny. She grabbed him by the arm and kept pulling him around to anyone who would listen.

"I love this guy," Cyndi Lauper would say.

Rose laughed, blushing as she pulled him from person to person.

"His name is 'Playboy'. I love it, I love this guy! He's mine now!" she said.

Now, if you have ever seen Buddy Rose, especially in the later days of his career, the funniest part about this adoration from "the girl who just wants to have fun" was that Buddy looked the furthest thing away from being a "Playboy" pretty much most of his life. That just goes to show how deep Cyndi was to not judge a book by its cover.

While *WrestleMania* was the first time Buddy Rose and I ever worked together, we would wrestle again together around the world for years to come.

MANIA AFTERMATH

That first WrestleMania was an unprecedented first for pro wrestling in different ways. It brought professional wrestling to a national audience and successfully made the WWF mainstream. Before Vince's brainchild, wrestling was a regional sport that only really catered to a rough crowd. However, after the first WrestleMania, everything changed.

Vince made sure that *WrestleMania* would be a yearly event to see and be coupled with famous Hollywood actors and celebrity personalities. The mainstream appeal opened up an audience of all ages.

CHAPTER 16 – WrestleMania I & II

GREG VALENTINE FEUD CONTINUES ...

In hindsight, I now realize that *WrestleMania* had enough drawing power already. Adding another major grudge match (mine) would have maybe been burning out too many angles at once, and could have possibly slowed down the momentum. It's sort of like the argument people had with the Batman movies; having more than one major villain in one storyline was just too much.

Greg and I continued to work hard in front of sellout crowds on the top of cards everywhere. Usually, they were basic one-on-one singles matches with a classic "good versus evil" theme. Eventually, as time went on, we started to introduce gimmick matches to keep things fresh. One night, Greg Valentine and I battled in a lumberjack match. The next night, it was a strap match. The next night, it was a best two out of three falls, or a death match. However, we never had it out in a cage, because "Hammer" thought we should build up to that, and make it the final crescendo of our story.

Finally, Vince came to us before a show and said, "It is time." He went on to warn us that a change was coming in about a month. It was finally set to have me exact my revenge and defeat my archenemy for the Intercontinental Championship.

We were on the final stretch, building up to what would end in a big 15-foot high steel-cage match. We both knew that final match would ultimately end our war. We also both knew that final match had to be our greatest bout of all.

By this point, Valentine had held the title for nearly an entire year. His title reign established him as one of the most hated villains in the WWF and arguably the entire industry at that time. This was to say a lot because Vince was collecting a roster full of super outstanding wrestlers that he was stealing from promotions all over the country.

Baltimore was chosen for the city that would host the title match, but this was no accident. In fact, it was strategy booking at its best. The change of the Intercontinental title was slated for this city because it was the home of Jim

Crockett Promotions. The hope was this big match would help to further take from their fan base.

I remember the big night very well. Howard Finkel came up to us before the match early in the day. "In case you didn't know, you two now have the longest running feud in WWF history."

In looking back, we had wrestled each other seven times in MSG alone between 1984 and 1985.

Gorilla Monsoon was the one who came up with the finish for our cage match. It was perfect with Valentine having the cage door kicked in his face as I was climbing over the top.

MY TITLE BREAK

When we finally met on July 16, 1985, in that steel cage in Baltimore, Maryland, it was a perfect opportunity for The WWF to introduce a new, sexier, updated belt. The championship itself had undergone a makeover from the days of Pedro Morales and Don Muraco, and with the national expansion going on, Vince wanted an even sharper image for the working man's championship. So the plan was for Greg to destroy the old belt after I won it back.

I had chased Greg for over a year, trying to regain my belt. The fans loved watching us go at each other every night everywhere. We gave our fans a great show every time, beating each other black and blue. During that time, we wrestled in all kinds of matches; lumberjack matches, taped-fist matches, hour-draw matches, no-time-limit matches, no disqualification matches, you name it, but we saved the cage for last. The company finally pitted Greg Valentine and me in a "one and done." It was an anything-goes steel-cage match in Baltimore.

The wrestling that took place in the cage that night was typical of our battles. We beat on each other for 15 or 20 minutes and laid in the punches snug. He ran my head into the steel cage and my forehead started bleeding. Before it was all over, though, he was bleeding worse than I was. His old scars caused him to bleed more, and again, it was easier to see the blood on him because of his blonde hair.

I didn't have many scars, so I didn't open up easily. That was just fine with me. I didn't want any scars on my head. I was a pretty babyface, after all. ¡Arriba!

To make sure I avoided any unnecessary cuts that would lead to a forehead that looked like hamburger meat, when the bookers asked me to blade, I always did a very poor job at it. Eventually, they quit asking me to do it. If you look at my head today, there is only one scar. And that scar didn't come from a blade. In a match against Brutus "The Barber" Beefcake slammed my head into the side of the ring apron at the Omni in Atlanta. The stiff blow busted me wide open, which resulted in 14 stitches.

Thanks, Beefer!

I finally beat Greg in that steel-cage match to regain the Intercontinental title. When I went back into the ring to accept the belt, Greg had already taken it away from the referee and smashed the belt against the cage. He took that old championship and beat the dogshit out of it repeatedly against the cage, tearing the gold away from the leather.

In the end, I was awarded the busted-up belt while on my knees, and I still lifted it up over my head in victory. The fans were cheering me on. It was both a great feeling and a great way to end that chapter in our careers.

When I got back to the locker room, Vince was right there to congratulate me. He pointed at the beat up belt and laughed. "Wait until you see the new one, pal. It's absolutely beautiful."

I was excited knowing the new sexy belt was on the way. When I got home, I showed my wife the old belt. It was dented and marred and totally falling apart. I figured that I would never wear it again so I just had my wife toss the old IC title belt in the trash, and we forgot about it.

Boy, do I wish I didn't do that, today.

"I had to give the belt back to Tito at the end of that match," Valentine said recently, regarding the end of the feud. "I had no idea that he was just going to throw it out!"

He's right. What was I thinking?!

When I saw The Hammer a few years ago at a comic book convention, he thought about asking to borrow the old IC belt for a photo opportunity.

"Whatever became of that old belt?" he asked, thinking I just kept it after that angle.

"I know you are not going to like the answer," I said. "But my wife knew I was getting another one, and she threw it out."

"She what?!" Greg said, almost laughing and crying at the same time. "Do you know how much money I could have made with that belt now?" Valentine works a lot of autograph and convention shows these days.

"I know, I know," I replied. "But who would have known though back then that any of our stuff would be worth any money?"

"Don't you think people would have paid for a picture with that belt?" he laughed, but it was easy to see he was only half-kidding.

If you ask him today, Greg will tell you that he thinks our feud still had more juice in it and ended prematurely. "Maybe we could have broken Tito's other leg to build for another round of matches!"

"Hammer" loves me though and admits that our feud was the best money feud in his entire career.

At this time in the WWF, Greg Valentine will tell you that he rose to the greatest point in in his career. During our program, Valentine became the #2 heel in the company, just as he had been in the NWA with Crockett. The difference here is, the WWF had become a much bigger company. Holding the IC title at that time meant that Valentine was perceived by a large portion of the US audience as being the second-best wrestler in the world.

Shortly thereafter, the WWF received the new belt, the iconic Intercontinental design still in use by the WWE today. To award it to me, Mean Gene simply jumped in the ring before a random six-man tag match and told the audience that the new belt had arrived, and handed it to me.

I wrestled Greg a few more times, but the feud was officially over. If you ask Greg today about the 1980s WWF

CHAPTER 16 – WrestleMania I & II

wrestling scene, he will tell you that life on the road was difficult, but the money he made really made up for it. There were weeks when Valentine was bringing home $20,000 a week!

That wasn't just $20,000 either. It was $20,000 in cash!

"When I started out with Vince, they always paid us in cash," he said. "It was amazing how much you would get paid, and then, you always had all of this cash on you when you were out on the road." He was exactly right. I remember having these big blocks off money on us and trying to think of where I could hide it in hotels, or even in rental cars. I often felt like I was money laundering.

After the blow-off to our feud, Valentine wasn't forgotten for all his hard work for the company. They teamed him with Brutus "the Barber" Beefcake and made them the top heel team in the company. Then, come August of 1985, "The Dream Team" went on to defeat the U.S. Express (Barry Windham and Mike Rotundo) for the WWF World Tag Team Titles. They held those belts until losing them April of 1986 to The British Bulldogs at *WrestleMania II*.

Greg told me that working with the Bulldogs was tough because they were very "new school" and wanted to plan out spots out in advance. Valentine had an old school work ethic. He just wanted to go out there, feel the crowd, and "call it in the ring."

Greg told me he refused to go over spots with the Bulldogs out of principle.

"I thought Brutus was very good. He was actually a lot better than he gets credit for being. But when the Bulldogs wanted to work spots, I told them they would have to get with Brutus to do that because I just wasn't going to," Greg said. "I'm the heel, and I'm the veteran. I'm going to lead the match, and I just don't work that way."

Valentine was very old school and just wanted to wrestle. He didn't really like the cartoony-like comedy that WWF was attempting to push with their product. In fact, he once almost resigned because they wanted him to and Dino Bravo to "kidnap" the Bulldogs' mascot, Matilda.

THE CARTOON

Speaking of cartoons, building on the success of the first WrestleMania, Vince produced a Saturday morning cartoon series featuring most of the big-time WWF wrestlers, including me!

The show was titled *Hulk Hogan's Rock 'N Wrestling*. It also featured "Rowdy" Roddy Piper, Superfly Snuka, the Iron Sheik, Nikolai Volkoff, The Fabulous Moolah, Junkyard Dog, André the Giant, Big John Studd, Wendi Richter, Captain Lou Albano, and Mr. Fuji.

The thing was ridiculous, but pretty cool at the same time. I mean, diehard wrestling fans already said the WWF wrestlers were like cartoons. And then, there we were, actual cartoons!

I made some okay royalties off of the airing of the cartoon, which ran for nearly two years beginning in September 1985. However, it wasn't crazy money. I think the reason for that was that I didn't do the voiceover for my character.

From what I understand, Vince didn't want any of the wrestlers to use their real voices for the cartoon, so he hired actors to do our voices. But on occasion, they would fly me out to Los Angeles to tape some promotional commercials for the cartoon. The commercials were live action. I actually received more money for those than the actual cartoon, because it was actually me.

Either way, the money didn't matter. My kids got to see me as a cartoon character. That happiness was something that money couldn't buy! I professionally taped all the episodes and still have them in storage for future grandchildren to enjoy! Now, if only they have VCR players in the future, we will be back in business!

MY FIRST ACTION FIGURE

On top of all the merchandising that *WrestleMania* spawned, action figures started to be released by a company called LJN. They didn't really move like the ones they make today do. They were more like hard rubber statues that bent some when stressed, but would bounce back into shape.

I was not one of the very first guys to get an action figure made of me. I think I was in the third or fourth line, and mine came out in 1986. The first guys to see their likeness pressed into a toy received something like $100,000 in royalties! This is because when our contracts were initially written up, nobody figured in a million years that merchandising like this was going to happen, so the clause was overly generous. After the first few lines of figures came out and the office saw what they were paying out in royalties, they made a special addendum to our contracts to cover all the new pieces of merchandise that were being produced.

By the time my first royalty check came after the action figure had finally been released, they had already figured it out. I had heard there was going to be a cut back, but I had no idea just how much.

"Hey, Tito," Arnold Skaalund said. "Your check is $18,000."

"What?!" I said, expecting to make maybe $80,000 - which would have still been less than what the guys got for the first run of action figures.

I pinched my nose at Arnold Skaaland, who was cutting the check. I made a big fart sound with my mouth to let him know I thought that the payoff absolutely stunk. I did not pass go, I did not collect $200, and I did not say *Arriba*.

He went on to give me the new breakdown that differed from what I was expecting. He explained that the decision to specify merchandise payouts is what did it, and that is why it seemed like a big cut back on our share of the profits.

The rumor turned out to be true. I guess the last thing the WWF wanted was for its wrestlers to become too wealthy and grow independent. Then, they wouldn't be able to control us, right? Sadly, the day of giant pay-offs was gone, but it was still more than I had ever made for a royalty anywhere else in wrestling, so it wasn't all bad.

ANOTHER SINGING SANTANA

After *WrestleMania* and the success of the *Rock 'n' Wrestling Connection*, Vince wanted to keep the ball rolling with even more merchandising. Vince's ultimate goal was to push his product under the spotlight of pop culture. He wanted to continue to grab the attention of the MTV audience, but this time in the medium that their network was familiar with, a hit music video. A music video?!

Why not make Tito Santana sing? Just because my last name was Santana didn't mean I had any musical talent!

Dammit, I knew I was a horrible singer. A toilet flushing was more melodic. All I can remember when I first heard about the idea of a wrestling album was thinking, "Where does all this crossover stuff end?"

To continue to associate the WWF Superstars to the celebrity world, Vince asked Cyndi Lauper to help him first produce a record album. Suspecting it may be a little campy, Lauper agreed to help, but only under a disguise and credited with the fake name "Mona Flambé." (After hearing the splendid finished product, I still wonder why she felt she needed to do go anonymous to this very day!)

Vince also secured David Wolff, Cyndi's boyfriend and manager, as the executive producer of this auditorial gem. David was also incidentally a huge wrestling fan and the real reason why Cyndi agreed to promote *WrestleMania* in the first place.

CHAPTER 16 – WrestleMania I & II

As a record producer, David Wolff had all the contacts he needed. David contacted his friend, rockstar legend Rick Derringer, to be the producer. He had been doing some cool multi-platform stuff with Weird Al Yankovic that he thought would make for a good match.

Vince also tapped "The Mouth of the South" Jimmy Hart to be heavily involved in the music-making process. What many people don't know is that before Jimmy stepped foot into a wrestling ring in Memphis, he was part of a successful band called The Gentrys that had pop chart hits.

David decided that using the wrestlers as talent would further push the idea that Vince was looking for. David, Rick and Jimmy had to then figure out where the real "Rock and Wrestling" connections were, as far as wrestlers having musical talent was concerned. It turned out that some of the wrestlers on the roster really were actually good singers. David, Rick and Jimmy had to then figure out where their strengths and weaknesses lied. Of course, the main idea was to use some of the songs on the album as wrestler entrance theme music. What better way to make this happen than to have a wrestler participate in his own theme?

Before this, The Fabulous Freebirds from Texas were considered the first wrestlers to play rock music for their entrances. When they saw the pop that their entrance music helped to create, Michael Hayes eventually cut his own track, "Badstreet USA," to personalize it even more. After that, other wrestlers followed suit.

For *The WWF: Wrestling Album*, even more attention was being placed on what a wrestler's theme song would sound like, and how it reflected who they were as a personality. In short, the music had to match the character. This project really changed the way that the business looked at ring entrances at the time and how they would forever thereafter.

The funniest thing for me was, they booked the album much like a major event, or how they still book pay-per-views today. For the individuals who didn't have their own specialized track on the album, they needed to figure out a way to squeeze everyone together and get them all into one song. That is when they decided to make a battle royal-like track featuring everyone without their own single.

The big cluster fuck single was a remake of Wilson Pickett's "Land of a Thousand Dances," famously known for the "Na, Na Na Na Na" hook.

Jimmy Hart took the creative license to change the lyrics, here and there, so that individual wrestlers could sing personalized solo lines in the song and put over their characters in a wrestling twist. For instance, Freddie Blassie said, "I'll rap you with my cane, you pencil neck geek." Brutus Beefcake sang, "I'm gonna do the strut, up and down your spine!" You know, stuff like that so that the listener could picture which wrestler was singing just from listening to the song itself off the record.

However, for the rest of us that had absolutely no singing ability whatsoever, we would just be part of the chorus and sing the "na-na-na" part.

I, of course, was selected to be in the chorus, due to my soothing crooning abilities and fine golden throat.

When the day came for us to shoot the music video for "Land of a Thousand Dances," we all showed up to the studio in full gimmick. It really was a "who's who" of the 1985 WWE locker room, all getting together to belt out the tune and rumble on a recording studio soundstage.

The whole experience was one of the oddest things I had ever seen in wrestling. Here we were, faces with heels, all hanging out together wearing our full ring gear, singing in unison and dancing. You heard me right. Yes we were choreographed to dance along from side to side to the beat!

That little few seconds you saw of all of us on screen took nearly all day long to shoot. It was all laid out to look really chaotic, but in reality, it took a lot of work to get that look of insanity. Then, later that night, we were all rushing off to wrestle on a show.

Rick Derringer was also there on stage with Cyndi Lauper. Cyndi Lauper was in her disguise, probably because she didn't want to be associated with such a group of bad singers!

CHAPTER 16 – WrestleMania I & II

For my spot in the video, they had me standing on the babyface side of two different rows of bleachers. I was next to the Fink, and Windham and Rotundo were one level down in the row in front of me. We were doing our best to sing, but it, of course, sounded like shit. It's a good thing that we were only pretending to sing and our voices weren't on the track.

Looking down on the front of the stage, I could someone else pretending. Meatloaf was there! He was sitting at a drum set with dry ice smoke drifting up all around him. It was epic and it was crazy. He was there posing like he was laying a track, but he was not really playing the drums at all. He was just there to look the part.

We had a long day on that stage, over and over and over, non-singing that horrible song.

The whole thing was ridiculous. Our entire group was singing, "Na, na-na-na-na, na-na-na-na, na-na-na, na-na-na..." I was lipping the words but laughing over and over again under my breath and shaking my head.

"Why are you laughing, Tito?" Brutus Beefcake asked me, between takes.

"They definitely booked the wrong person," I said. "I think I probably have the absolute worst voice that anyone could put on an album," I said laughing.

Every wrestler had to film their individual parts separately, and then we had to film the group parts, as well. Then, get this, in the evening at the show, we had to perform the bit for the live crowd for even more footage.

For the next two weeks, all I had in my head was that stupid riff. "Na, na-na-na-na," Those bastards must have played that song a hundred times that day.

The music video played everywhere, though, despite my poor singing. It was on MTV, NBC's *Friday Night Videos*, *Saturday Night's Main Event*, and all the WWF programming. The video's reach was surprising and pretty amazing.

In the end, a lot of the songs came out to be very catchy. Being produced by Rick Derringer, they had a rock and pop appeal and turned out okay, for a bunch of wrestlers. To really add to the whole wrestling feel, David had all of the album's tracks interlaced with commentary from the WWF's announce team; Vince McMahon, "Mean Gene" Okerlund and Jesse "The Body" Ventura.

In October 1985, *The Wrestling Album* was finally released with ten awesome tracks worth of WWE wrestlers trying our best to sing.

The fold-out cover of the record was pretty cool. It featured McMahon, Okerlund and Ventura in the front, with all the wrestlers going crazy behind them on the performing stage in the recording studio.

None of the singles received any real heavy radio airplay, but *The Wrestling Album* as a whole reached #84 on the album sales charts! Kids everywhere owned it.

As far as the featured singles were concerned, Junkyard Dog, Mean Gene, Nikolai Volkoff, Hillbilly Jim, Jimmy Hart, Captain Lou and even Roddy Piper all got to sing their own tunes.

Junkyard Dog sang "Grab Them Cakes," which would replace Queen's "Another One Bites the Dust" to become his new ring entrance theme song. This was not an original song, however. It was a cover that was first recorded by a little-known hip hop star at the time named Captain Chameleon. They liked it so much that another Captain Chameleon cover tune (of his song *Jive Ol' Foe*) would be produced for Slick come the second Wrestling album with some minor changes, renamed *Jive Soul Bro*.

Piper's song, "For Everybody" is also a cover tune of "Fuck Everybody," by Mike Angelo & The Idols. The Piper version includes Rick Derringer on guitar, Cyndi Lauper on backing vocals, and the Tower of Power horn selection. However, the WWF could not allow any profanity on a product targeting children, in part, which called for the chorus change and the words "kiss my ass," being changed to "kiss my trash."

Hulk Hogan had an anthem that sounded like the Rocky theme recorded for his ring entrance, however, the use of this song was only short-lived. They ended up using this track for maybe a few months, and then it became the

CHAPTER 16 – WrestleMania I & II

exclusive theme for his cartoon, *Hulk Hogan's Rock 'N Wrestling*.

The real winner of the album was "Real American," a song made famous after Hulk Hogan decided to adopt it as his entrance theme. It wasn't really made for him though, however.

Before any of the songs for the album had been recorded, Rick Derringer had already recorded a rough demo of the tune. Written by Derringer and a guy named Bernard Kenny, they set out to just create a great, patriotic song that Vince would maybe like. When the WWF first started working on the project, they were all trying to figure out what songs would be on it, and if they would all be original tunes, or not. When Derringer played the track for Vince McMahon, he fell in love with it right away.

"Oh, wow," McMahon said. "We can really use this!"

Vince originally decided to assign "Real American" to The US Express, so that Barry Windham and Mike Rotundo would have a good theme song. If you listen to the commentary between the songs on the album, Vince McMahon actually says the song is, "dedicated to Windham and Rotundo." However, shortly after the album's release, Windham left to go to the National Wrestling Alliance.

Rather than to let the great track go to waste, Hulk Hogan decided to abandon the use of his Rocky-sounding, piano-heavy "Hulk Theme" for his ring entrances.

"Even though it's never been a single," Derringer says, "it turned into maybe my most successful song, ever." Hulk Hogan walking out to "Real American" for so many years has kept the song recognizable, but Derringer's guitar work is great, and the message continues to resonate with people beyond the wrestling. You hear it randomly played at sports events, political gatherings and just about anywhere.

The Wrestling Album marked the first big initiative by the WWF to create their own original entrance themes for their wrestlers. Years later, WWE's original entrance themes have often become cult classics, and they have since released dozens of sequels.

RANDY SAVAGE

I won back the Intercontinental title in Baltimore and was set to lose it again in Boston eight months later to WWF newcomer Randy "Macho Man" Savage.

When Randy Savage first came into New York, he got a big TV push because of some connections. He came in without what would be his trademark eye-candy manager, Elizabeth. They did a whole "battle of managers" thing for his "free-agent" contract, and eventually, Elizabeth beat out the other managers for Randy's "contract." To start, she was not around much and was really only booked for TV tapings.

On Aug 23, 1985, Savage started a new feud with me for the Intercontinental heavyweight championship.

When we first met up, I told him that I was going to let him call the match because he was the heel and that was the way I operated. Usually, it was the heel that called the match unless you were the vet or the champion. I had worked him some before in Atlanta, but we were both really green at the time and I figured all would be just fine.

When we went out there, it seemed like to me that Savage was doing stuff just for the sake of doing stuff. With all of his high-spot wrestling style and reliance in aerial moves, the crowds were not getting into our matches. It was just too much. Even though he had worked in other places like Georgia and Kentucky before coming to the WWF, he was still kind of working like a rookie. In fact, there were many old timers in the company who saw his matches and immediately considered Randy to be nothing more than a curtain jerker. They felt he was nothing more than an opening act, and they were reconsidering plans for his spot.

The problem was Randy wasn't used to wrestling with top workers and wasn't accustomed to the WWF's style. His timing was off and he did high-spots just for the sake of doing them, meaning he did them because he could do them. It was like he wanted to show what he could do, but didn't know where to put things in a match, or at what amounts. He was squeezing in way too much to show off.

CHAPTER 16 — WrestleMania I & II

He actually had a list of things he wanted to do, a physical list of things he had written down. A number of us agreed, Randy had to get out of the habit of writing down in advance all the moves he wanted to use in the course of the match. Wrestling at this time was about impromptu action and reaction. It was an art, and the goal was for us to paint a picture and tell a story. I know things are a little different today, but back then, the only thing that any wrestler needed to know before the match was the outcome.

I was a good sport. I rolled with his calling matches like that a few times, and we didn't get any kind of good response from the audience because we were really having some jabroni matches. Eventually, I knew that something had to change. I had to figure out how to explain to him what fans in New York liked, while not coming off too preachy.

Despite his shortcomings, I could see that Randy had awesome talent and a great work ethic. He respected the business. He wanted to get better in the big league. So finally, one night after a pretty bad match, I pulled Randy to the side trying my best not to insult him, as he had technically been wrestling for a number of years before this.

"Randy, the fans in this territory like a lot more power moves and mat wrestling. We are giving them too much too fast and they are missing it. They aren't responding."

Randy nodded. He was cool and listening.

"New York wants a little bit of wrestling and some ass-kicking, I explained. "They don't want to just see bump after bump after bump. You called more dropkicks in one match than I had done in the last two years combined."

I watched for his reaction. He was being receptive to the constructive criticism so I continued.

"You also have to realize that if you work like this every night with the schedule you have now, you will burn out in a few months, or just get hurt. Then, it will be all over."

To his credit, he listened and learned. As Randy worked with me and some of the other top guys in the company, we taught him how to work and showed him how to tell a story in the ring. We taught him where to put the high-spots so that they really meant something. He picked up the style he needed to pretty quickly, figuring out what the New York people liked.

He learned that as a heel, he shouldn't be out-wrestling the babyface. He needed to be breaking the rules more to make himself a hated heel, and to make the fans pull for the babyface. Eventually, he got it.

As far as our run, he also improved in interviews with just a little tweaking. For instance, when I was the IC champion and Randy and I were in a program, Randy was supposed to be chasing after me, right? However, in his interview, he talked about how he was the best in the world and would also soon become the World heavyweight champion ... *not the Intercontinental champion.* Putting his focus on another title, even if only for a moment, not only depreciated the Intercontinental title but me, as well.

"Randy you can't talk about getting a shot at the world title when you're supposed to be chasing me," I told him. "Forget about the world belt. Your focus and attention should be on both our match and the intercontinental title. That is what you want to win here."

He understood. With patience and practice, Randy improved to eventually become a master at the microphone. "*Oooooh Yeah!!!*"

When I first got to New York, I was in the same boat as Randy. Guys like Don Muraco and Greg Valentine took me under their wing and helped me adjust and become a smarter wrestler and better worker. I didn't help Randy out of preferential treatment, but because it was the right thing to do. Because we were a family and fraternity, and each wrestler was supposed to look out for each other.

Randy chased me for the IC belt for about six months. On the November 2, 1985, episode of *Saturday Night's Main Event*, Savage won the match by count out, but not the title. In our rematch on February 24, 1986, he finally beat me for the title at the Boston Garden by using a foreign object stashed in his tights.

Man, did he finally "get it." What a change that was from our first match together back in August!

A capacity crowd at the old Boston Garden screamed like mad throughout the entire 20-minute match, which left both of us drenched in sweat. Miss Elizabeth, Randy's manager, was ringside for the match. She was a very beautiful woman who was adored by the fans. Randy was really mistreating her, and the fans hated Randy for it.

Toward the end of our match, Miss Elizabeth gave Randy a small piece of iron that resembled a dumbbell and fit perfectly over his fist. He hid it from both referee "Dangerous" Danny Davis and me. As I was lifting him back into the ring, he punched me in the forehead. It was lights out for me.

The match was over, and I lost the title.

Randy took criticism well. He finally found all of the pieces of the puzzle and took off. The rest is history.

With the title, he clearly got more comfortable. That confidence made him even better in the ring.

One time, I was chasing Randy Savage trying to regain my belt. I did a move on him called a sunset flip. As I bounced back off the ropes, he was bent over facing me, in an effort to flip me into the air. But I jumped over him and grabbed his waist with my hands, taking him down into a pinning combination.

1, 2, kick out!

I didn't pin him.

Later in the match, he figured that "turn-about was fair play" and got back at me using the same move. This time, however, as he flipped over me for the pinning combination, he grabbed my trunks. He pulled them down so hard that my whole rear end came out. I just stood there. I had my pants down and everything. Shocked because that spot wasn't at all planned, I didn't go down with the move.

I just stood there, flapping in the wind.

Now, this ass-spot is an old school thing that babyfaces sometimes did to the heels, but I was always babyface so I never took it before. I didn't know how to sell it, or even if you could sell it as a fan favorite.

To say the very least, I was really embarrassed, but since Tito was known for his burrito anyhow, I just shrugged it off, pulled up my pants, and punched him in the face. ¡Arriba!

WRESTLEMANIA II

WrestleMania II took place on April 7, 1986, at three separate locations; New York, Chicago, and Los Angeles.

It was an organizational nightmare because of the unprecedented three-venue pay-per-view. Each venue had to have its own agents, its own crew, and its own announcing team.

Our venue was Los Angeles in front of 15,000 people. For my match, I was tagging with the Junkyard Dog against the Funk Brothers, Terry and Hoss (a.k.a. Dory Jr.).

Our announcing team was a little odd, to say the least. It was Lord Alfred Hayes calling the event, Jesse Ventura on color commentary, and Elvira (yes, *that* Elvira ... the "Mistress of Darkness") offering her own very special "analysis."

Keep in mind, part of the allure for WrestleMania again was that we had celebrities on hand, helping to blend us into the mainstream to give us celeb street cred.

While I didn't like them taking up spots, I will admit, I did enjoy meeting he celebrities. I talked to many celebrities including Elvira, badeball manager Tommy Lasorda, Robert Conrad, and even Ricky Schroder. The funny thing to me was when the celebrities came up to us and were actually asking for autographs!

I'll be honest in saying that I didn't really like them on the actual show as a paid means to draw. Like a number of the boys, I was also turned off by paid celebrities at 'Mania. You see, outsiders took big bucks to produce. In my opinion, I just didn't feel like they drew that money back in return. While Mr. T may have drawn a little bit, the only real draw, perhaps, was a guy like Mike Tyson who was an actual fighter, on fire, and booked at a time where he could still make a difference in ticket sales. Most everyone else, however, seemed somewhat second-rate to me, and just leaching off of the money that the actual wrestlers were drawing for the event and could in return be paid for.

Case in point: Burger King's Herb.

Do you even know what I am talking about? "Where's Herb?" was an advertising campaign for Burger King from 1985 to 1986. The TV commercials featured a fictional character named "Herb," who had never eaten at Burger King before. If a customer spotted this *Herb* at their Burger King, he/she would win $5,000, and then everyone in the place would be entered into their one million dollar drawing.

Do you really think Herb was a draw? Well, Herb was a guest ring announcer at *WrestleMania II*!

Besides the oversaturation of low-rent celebrities, our match turned out okay.

It was always cool to work with the Funks.

Terry pinned the Dog after clocking him over the head with his manager Jimmy Hart's megaphone. After this, Terry was off to Hollywood I think to do some movies.

Although the Dog and I lost the match, I always enjoyed working with the Funks and JYD. Both the Funks (especially Terry) and The Junkyard Dog played a role in the development of my career, so this night was something pretty special for me, despite the fact that I was splitting the gate with Herb, and the "Where's the Beef" Lady from Wendy's.

THE ANIMAL

George "The Animal" Steele was a very knowledgeable guy of all parts of the business, having served as both a wrestling promoter and talent. For those of you who have seen the wild-man character that he portrayed in the ring, some are often surprised to learn that he held multiple college degrees and also was a college professor.

Although George never captured any major titles while in the WWF, he was an admirable heel and later got over with the crowd as a babyface. His longtime feud with Randy Savage where which he fell in love with Miss Elizabeth is still talked about today.

For all his hard work, he was inducted into the WWE Hall of Fame in 1995, but before that, he was also made into a ring agent.

As a practical joker, you never knew what to expect from George. Like all of the wrestlers from that era, George protected the business, never letting on to fans that anything was scripted or fake. He had a very unconventional character, and part of The Animal's gimmick was that he couldn't speak coherently. He would just mumble and make unintelligible sounds, saying very little of any real words. But George made up for his silence with some witty humor both inside and outside the wrestling ring backstage.

I actually have two funny stories I would like to share with you here about The Animal.

For a time, George was a road agent with the company. Part of an agent's responsibility is to critique a wrestler's match. Although we were professional about it, most of the boys would laugh at George's critiques because he wasn't really well known for having the scientific wrestling skills that would have allowed him to really critique anyone. We all know he meant well, and I personally understood where he was coming from. However, as more of a brawler his whole career, he just didn't have the wrestling know-how to tell anyone how to wrestle scientifically-speaking.

After one of my matches, George saw that Vince was around and knew that he had to "do his job." In an act of job-justification, he made sure to call me over while to put me in ears-length of the boss. Then, he went into full detail on how I had not done a move correctly.

During that match that he was compelled to critique, I did a leap-frog over my opponent, which basically is where you just jump over a standing person.

"Tito," he said, "you had a great match out there. The only thing is that I would suggest that you don't do leap-frogs anymore," he said.

"Why is that?"

"Well, the leap-frog is a spectacular move that takes precise timing and communication with your opponent," he said, as Vince took notice, then walked away. He continued. "When you went up in the air, you were at a slight angle. You weren't balanced and I noticed you leaned toward one side. This positioning could surely end up in injury."

I had to do my best not to laugh out loud. The boys and I later had a good laugh at The Animal's expense. We knew exactly what he was doing in that façade.

As far as his advice went, I kept on doing leap frogs.

Another time, on the flight back from a show, George "The Animal" Steele decided to perform one of his notorious magic tricks on a beautiful flight attendant.

"Place your hand out, sweetie," he said.

She placed her open palm out, as directed and George put a foam ball in her hand.

He motioned for her to close it, which she did. He then tapped her hand, and she opened it to find two foam balls in her hand.

The flight attendant was amazed.

George again motioned for her to close her hand, and she once again did as she was told,

Then, George tapped her hand a second time.

When the airline attendant opened her hand, she blushed with embarrassment.

In her hand were not only two balls, but also a matching foam penis!

THE IRON SHEIK

The Iron Sheik was a good man, and we all loved to be around him, but man did he have a serious drug problem.

One time on a flight, I remember the Iron Sheik was worried that he was going to be caught with a stash that he somehow ended up bringing on to the plane unnoticed. So what he did was, he waited for one of the boys to go into the bathroom, then slipped it into the wrestler's carry-on bag

The other wrestler looked clean, so the Sheik honestly figured that the other wrestler would never be searched.

Now, by this time, the Sheik himself already had a criminal record, having been busted for cocaine only months before this. He had also just failed a couple of the WWF's drug tests, been suspended, and also put into rehab.

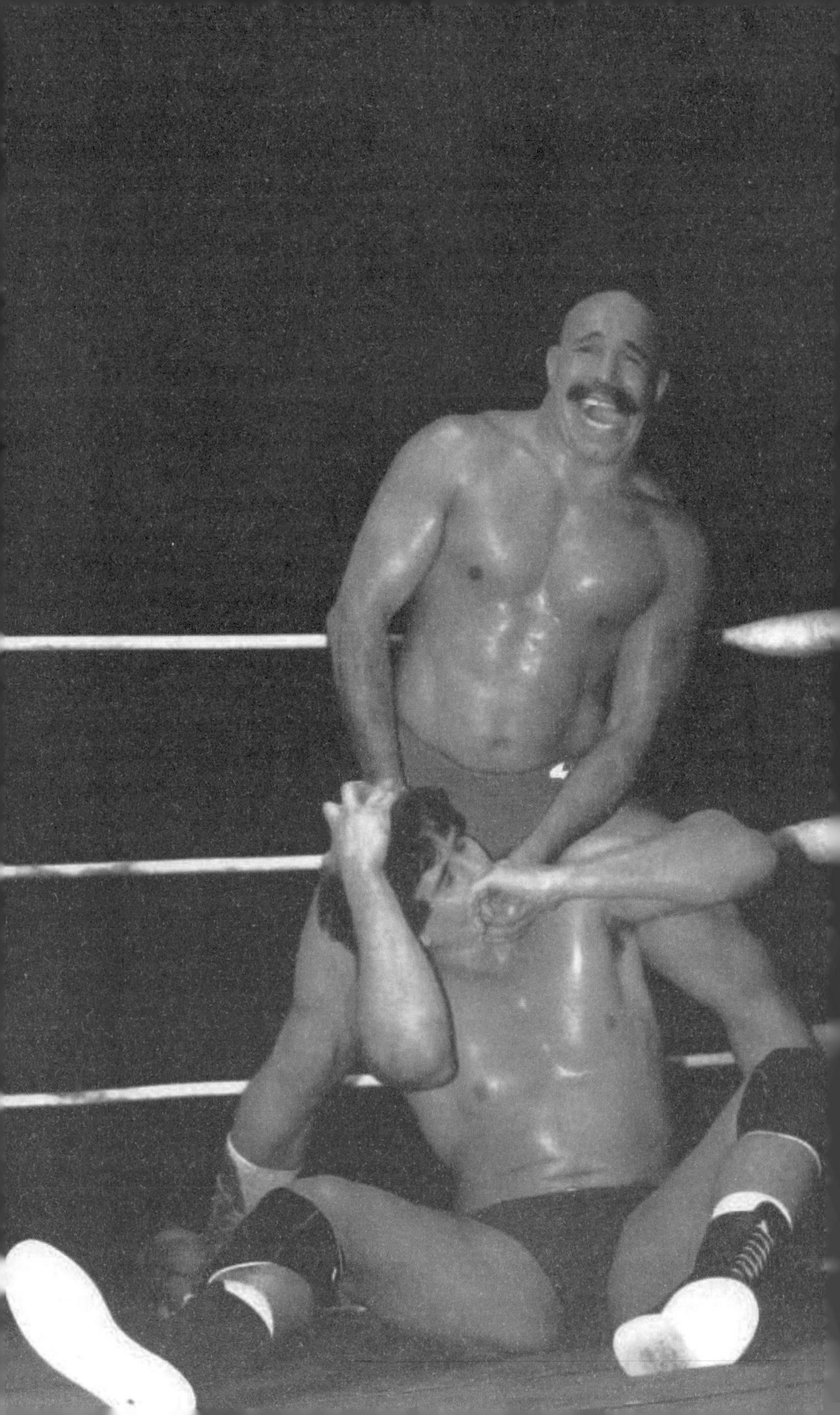

The other wrestler got off the plane ahead of the Sheik and made his way through the airport. Sheik had to chase him down through the terminal to catch up with him.

"Hey, Bubba!" he yelled. "Bubba! Wait!"

The other wrestler finally slowed down. "What do you want, Sheiky?"

"You have some of my medicine?"

"What?"

The Sheik then zipped open the other wrestler's carry-on and pulled out a little bag in broad daylight.

"What the fuck, Sheiky?!"

The Sheik patted him on the shoulder and put the stash into his jacket pocket for safe keeping.

Luckily for both the Sheik and the other wrestler, no one got busted with the goods.

Many of Sheik's less than proud moments have also included some kind of illicit substances. Most of the Iron Sheik's most outlandish stories also include moments where lines are blurred between his wrestling character and the real man behind it.

According to Marty Jannetty, one story he tells famously pitted him and The Sheik at a hotel bar in Iowa with a number of female fans. As the night unfolded, appearently Marty was going to take one of the girls back to his room but had to figure out something for her friend.

Marty looked around for any of the boys, and ended up going over to the Sheik as a last resort. "Hey Sheiky," he said. "I have this one girl coming over to my room and was hoping that you could keep her friend company for me."

"For you, Marty," he said, "I will do the favor." The Sheik agreed and took a look at the girl in the hallway and nodded.

Now, Marty said that things were going really well for him and the other girl. Everything was great and he had pretty much forgotten that the Sheik had taken her friend off his hands to babysit her.

Sheik brought the woman into his own room for a drink. Then, soon after that, the drink at her request was chased down by cocaine and some pain killers.

As time went on, the unlikely couple didn't really hit it off like Marty and her friend were in a room down the hall. She drank a bunch of his booze, and took a lot of his drugs, but that was about it.

Then, she just kept talking about Marty over and over again. Figuring the Sheik was investing too much energy into an avenue that was not going to put out for him, he eventually threw her out of the room on her ass.

When the police arrived, they knocked on Marty's room. Marty played dumb and said he had no idea which room the Sheik was in. When the police finally left, he ran out of his room and down the hall to see what all the commotion was. He knocked on Sheik's door. When he did, he looked out the window to the lot below and saw the woman being put into an ambulance on a gurney!

"Sheiky!" Jannetty asked. "What the hell happened?"

"Come in and sit down," Sheik said. "Now, I give her the beer, and I give her the coke, but all she wanted was you."

"So?"

"So then I give her a short clothesline."

"A SHORT CLOTHESLINE?!"

"Yes, Marty. But it's not my fault," he said. "She didn't know how to work!" suggesting that he hadn't really meant to hurt the woman, but it was her fault because she took the bump wrong.

HILLBILLY JIM

Speaking of almost going to jail, one time, I almost ended up in jail because of Hillbilly Jim!

One night, Leapin' Lanny Poffo and I were riding with Hillbilly to an event in Canada when he got pulled over for speeding. Now, Hillbilly Jim didn't give a shit. Back then, if you got pulled over and had been trying to avoid speed traps, you always pulled down the radar detector in the event that you did get pulled over. If you didn't, the police officer would see it, and then try to make things even worse for you for "trying to cheat the law."

So when Hillbilly Jim got pulled over, he didn't hide the fact that he had a radar detector, and that only made things worse.

The cop confiscated the illegal detector.

Now, Hillbilly didn't like that at all. He didn't want to part with his precious "Fuzz Buster," so he told the officer a piece of his mind.

"You don't have a warrant and have no right to take my property," he said. "So I would rather go down to the station with you and have you learn from your own sergeant the hard way that what you are doing is against the law!"

Lanny and I could not believe what we were hearing. We just sat there in total amazement.

We listened to Hillbilly curse the police officer in the most filthy and vile ways possible. The thing that really got our goat was the arresting officer just happened to be a woman. Here he was saying stuff that we just couldn't believe, stuff that was so bad that we actually started laughing because it was so uncomfortable.

Despite the insults and profanity, the officer refused to take us to jail. Lanny and I breathed a sigh of relief as the cop issued us a ticket, and more importantly held onto the radar detector.

The ticket cost us $60 each in the end, but at least I didn't have to spend a night in the slammer with a hillbilly.

DAN SPIVEY VS. ADRIAN ADONIS

Locker room fights almost never happened in the WWF. They happened in places like Mid-South where they were actually encouraged, but in the WWF while I was there, the wrestlers were like your family. We all rode together, we ate together, and we spent more time together than we did with our actual own families.

There was one pretty good tussle in the WWF that I saw, and it was probably the bloodiest one I ever saw, too.

We were all at a TV taping in Toronto on May 4, 1986, for *Primetime Wrestling*. After the first *WrestleMania*, Barry Windham had left and was eventually being replaced by another tall blonde guy by the name of Danny Spivey.

Spivey hadn't started tag teaming up yet with Mike Rotundo, and he was still wrestling in singles matches starting out. He was told he had to wrestle with Adrian Adonis that night and wanted no part of it.

Spivey had worked two matches with Adrian back in January of 1986 in Waterloo, Iowa, and Denver, Colorado and apparently Adrian stiffed him pretty hard in the match, but Spivey never said anything because he was still relatively new in the federation.

I have to say, that Adrian Adonis was a pretty tough customer. In Amarillo, he legitimately offered any of the wrestlers on the roster $1,000 if they could last five minutes with him shooting in the ring. Nobody could do it. He also was a little bit of a bully, at times, and beat up some of the guys on the undercard who wouldn't say anything about it.

Adrian was being groomed to work as the foil for Hulk Hogan soon, so he could do whatever he wanted in the ring with jobbers to look strong. They were booking him in a lot of job/enhancement matches at this time where he beat the crap out of all of his opponents.

Spivey worked his match that night in Toronto with Adrian, and just as he thought, he got potatoed. Adrian kicked him hard, hit him hard, and knocked the wind right out of him for real.

After the match, Spivey was waiting for Adrian behind the curtain in the locker room. I went over to calm him down.

"What's wrong, man?" I asked.

"Wrong is what that guy did to me in the ring," Spivey said. "But don't you worry about that. I'm going to right the wrong. I'm going to fucking kill him, that's what I'm going to do."

I wasn't the only one who could see that he was pissed. Scotty McGee, another one of Adrian's victims recognized the fact but knew that Spivey needed to calm down.

CHAPTER 16 – WrestleMania I & II

Along with The Dynamite Kid, they grabbed up Spivey and rushed him out of the arena.

The crazy thing is, the next night, Spivey was booked on another card that had Adrian Adonis on it at The Civic Center in Brantford, Ontario, Canada.

When Dan Spivey showed up that night he went right to Adrian's locker room. "You are lucky the boys pulled me out of there last night," he said to Adrian.

Adrian didn't skip a beat. He was applying makeup in a mirror and ignoring Spivey. That even made him madder.

"I'm warning you. If you ever pull anything like that with me again, I am going to let you have it."

Adrian continued to kayfabe him. He didn't say anything back. He just kept on with the makeup and ignored the threat.

After Spivey saw that he was getting nowhere, he left. Adrian had a few choice words for the wrestlers that had gathered around to see the backstage show. "The next time I get the pleasure of working with Mister Spivey," he said, rolling on some lipstick, "I am going to teach him a lesson."

The very next night in Flint, Michigan, Adrian Adonis was going to get that chance.

Like they say, telegram or tell-a-wrestler. Everyone already knew what was said and what had happened the night before between the two.

The way it worked was when you showed up to a venue, we would first go and look for the list of matches taped up to the wall by the booker. The wrestlers would look it over and that was about it. When everyone showed up to this show, however, everyone gasped at what they saw.

Pat Patterson decided to book Dan Spivey against Adrian Adonis once again!

Apparently, as the story goes, George "The Animal" Steele called in sick with what they said was "a bad case of the shits."

Talk about stirring the pot!

Therefore, Spivey was George's replacement.

Dan Spivey saw that atrocity and immediately went to Pat. He told Pat he refused to work with Adrian, not because he wasn't a team player, but "for fear of what he might do to him."

"Okay, okay," he said. "I'll see if there is anything we can do." Pat left to see if anything could be switched around. When Pat returned again, he shook his head. "Vince said we are stuck with this match tonight, and that you have to work with him tonight. But he did say it would be the last time you have to work with him."

I am not sure that Pat really called Vince. He had the power to do whatever he wanted with the matches. Maybe he was feeling like Bill Watts that night and wanted to see them fight himself.

When the match finally came, Jim Brunzell and I gathered by the curtain to watch. Spivey went to his corner. Then, Adrian went to the ring with his manager, Jimmy Hart.

The bell rang.

Just before lock up, Adrian shot a snot-rocket all over his arm. It was dripping gooey white and green slime.

"You are fucking disgusting," Spivey said.

Adrian immediately grabbed Spivey. He was talking trash and trying to rub his juicy, throat-load snot all over him. Then, he was punching Spivey stiff, and he was kicking him stiff, too.

"Spivey has got to be pissed!" Brunzell said to me, looking around the curtain kind of laughing at the train wreck we were watching before us in the ring.

He was pissed. Even more pissed than the night before.

Finally, Spivey reached his boiling point.

Adrian went to put the sleeper on, but Spivey put his hand up and blocked Adrian's arm from going under his chin.

Spivey broke the hold, broke kayfabe, and got ready to break his face.

Spivey shoved Adrian into the corner, and unloaded on him with right hands, just as stiff than what he had taken the whole match, or worse. Before Adrian could get his guard up to block more from the right, Spivey nailed him with a left uppercut. Adrian staggered then fell.

"I think he knocked him out!" I said.

CHAPTER 16 – WrestleMania I & II

Adrian Adonis dropped. His face was a busted open.

"Ref, that's not right!" Jimmy Hart shouted into his megaphone, maybe laughing a little, knowing the situation.

Spivey covered Adrian.

The ref refused to count, but he didn't really know what to do. All he knew was that was not the finish. He argued with Spivey a second, but that didn't matter.

Spivey covered Adrian's dead body again. The referee tapped Spivey again and continued to argue.

Spivey stood back up.

"Okay, then," he said. "I think I made my point. Count me out then."

Spivey turned around to leave, but before he did, he kicked the bully as hard as he could in the face.

There was already blood, but after that field goal, there was even more. Red freckles splattered the mat.

Spivey walked back to the locker room. He made eye contact with me behind the curtain and knew he had an audience. I'm not sure he knew it was me, or who it was, but he smirked and pretended to dust the dirt off his shoulder.

The ref counted him out and called for the bell.

Nobody expected that. Backstage, the boys all knew Adrian Adonis was a tough guy, but nobody really knew anything about Dan Spivey. We all thought he was just some naive twenty-something kid that Dusty Rhodes booked for a quick stint in WCW. Nobody knew he had lied about his age and was really in his 30s. We also had no idea that he was a bouncer and an ex-bookie hitman that collected money for the mob. Nobody knew he had served time in jail for assault. Nobody knew he was a legitimate tough guy himself.

The audience backstage went wild as Spivey went to find his locker.

Most of us knew it wasn't over.

If a real fight happened between the boys, it was always something fast. There is an unwritten rule regarding these types of fights; when they happen you break it up right away, *but only after someone wins.* The reason for this is, if there is no closure, it always meant another fight was just going to happen anyway.

I looked over at the Junkyard Dog who also had seen the whole thing. He nodded. He didn't have to say a word. We both knew there would be a round two when Adrian came back. So we did the only responsible thing we could do. JYD and I started moving the furniture out of the way.

"What are you doing?" Brunzell asked.

"Making room," I laughed.

"Hell yeah!" Jimmy Brunzell then ran off to the bowels of the locker room running around yelling, "Danny buried Adrian! There's going to be a fight!"

Everyone came circling in like high school.

Finally, Adrian drug himself up from the dead and made it back to the locker room. He was a bloody mess.

"Where in the fuck is Spivey?!" he shouted, coming in past the curtain looking like a zombie from Walking Dead.

He came in hot looking for Spivey, and all the boys gathered around.

"Right here asshole."

Adrian rushed to where Spivey was. Spivey got up. Trying to take him down, Adrian lunged at him, looking for a leg dive. Spivey stepped out of the way. Adrian went to tackle him again, and Spivey calculated it, then drilled him with another left uppercut!

Holy shit! That shot busted him open even more!

Thinking it was finally done, Junkyard Dog grabbed Spivey so he didn't kill him.

Adrian got up. He was dazed like he didn't know where he even was. His face looked like a ghost. As far as the blood, it was all over him. You could actually see the whiteness of his cheekbone poking through the wound.

Then, Adrian got some kind of energy surge.

"Shit! Danny, here he comes, again!" the Dog said. He let Spivey loose, as to not hold him and allow Adrian a free shot. Danny sized him up. Right as Adrian reached him, JYD nudged Spivey out of his grasp. Spivey buckled a fist.

POWWW!!!

Another textbook, perfect left uppercut!

CHAPTER 16 – WrestleMania I & II

That was it. After that, Spivey jumped on top of Adrian, pounding down into his face. He was dropping bombs. Dan Spivey was the clear winner.

Closure.

Everyone jumped in and separated them.

Adrian was covered in is own blood. He was so bloody, even his blood was bleeding.

Randy Savage dragged Spivey away down the hall to end it for good.

"Alright, brother. It's over. You got him," Randy said, taking Spivey off to see the medic.

"Where are we going?"

"Take you to the doctor."

"Why?"

"To get some ice for your hands," he said, trying to distract Spivey and get him laughing a little.

It's true. Spivey had been punching on Adrian's head so hard that he had to ice his fingers!

A little ice for Adrian, on the other hand, just wasn't going to cut it. He ended up with something like 200 stitches in his face. His run with Hogan definitely was going to have to be delayed until he was healed.

After that Spivey became a legend in the locker room. Chief Jay Strongbow started calling him, "Dangerous Dan, The Left Hand Man."

The next show that Spivey and Adrian were booked on together, Adrian Adonis walked by Dan Spivey, and that was it. They never had a match together, again, and the whole thing was squashed.

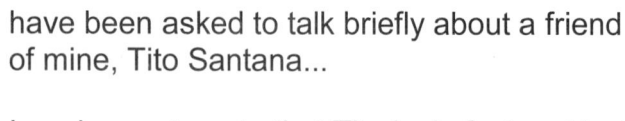

I have been asked to talk briefly about a friend of mine, Tito Santana...

I am happy to note that Tito is, in fact, not just a friend, he is a great friend. He is also an excellent professional wrestler, a great family man, and a caring father to his sons. And to top all this off, Tito is, and has always been, a classy superstar who respects the fans as he does all the other wrestlers.

Tito loved riding with the heels, probably because we were the exact opposite of who he was. He was always a babyface. Many times, we would want him to jump in with us (Demolition) to go along for the ride to shows - and we would always make room when we could. It was sometimes a tight fit to try to make room for him when it was me, Barry, and Fuji with all our luggage and Demolition gear in the car, but somehow we would manage. Sometimes We'd pick him up down the street so nobody would see the good guy getting into the bad guy's car. Once Crush got into the mix, it was a little more difficult, but we would still find time to meet up with Tito at the gym, or maybe go out and get something to eat together so we could hang out. He was just so easy going, and he was exactly the kind of person you wanted to have around on the road.

–Ax, Demolition

CHAPTER 17 - FAME

As the company expanded, the WWF became more and more "famous" in the public eye.

I think I first realized this when I was getting recognized almost everywhere I went. I was signing autographs more on the road at random places, more so than just in front of the wrestling venues that I was pulling up onto in the rental car.

When I would go into a gym for a workout, quite often we would hear "your money is no good here." I would work out for free. Then, they would be showering me with their merchandise as I was leaving the place.

The same thing seemed to happen in restaurants and bars too. If the place was not refusing my money to pay for a meal, then a fan at the other table would be picking up the tab. The amount of free meals I got was crazy!

The same thing happened with the salaries of some of its wrestlers. Along with that salary increase for a number of the boys, came a lot more prominence. Guys like Jake Roberts and Roddy Piper were making more money than ever before, but admittedly, some of them couldn't handle their newfound stardom.

A bunch of the boys made a ton of money in cash and blew it all partying. The difference between them and me was I was always smart and saved everything I could.

I also think that many of my fellow wrestlers at this time didn't really understand who was giving them their fame. Quite often, they would believe the work.

Even today, some boys don't get that Vince was the one who made them stars. Yes, they may have been good workers, but Vince made them superstars because of his investment in them and the way he promoted them on his television programming. I realized this, even more, when I got into the production side of the business. Vince had his hand in everything, and it was he and he alone who decided who was going to be a star. He could pick the worst wrestler in the world to put over, and that guy would fly to the top.

ENHANCEMENT TALENT

Not everyone on a WWF card made the big bucks, however. There were a number of guys who didn't make a lot, and didn't find fame but helped make us look like a million bucks in the ring.

"Jobbers" were often booked as one-off kind of guys. They were regional and only used when WWF was in town. Unlike them, there were other guys who were also paid to lose for the most part, but they were actually on the WWF payroll and looked at as talent to get over the names. This talent was called "enhancement talent." Some of these guys included Lanny Poffo, SD Jones, and Jose Luiz Rivera.

For the enhancement talent, I liked to throw them a bone whenever I could. If this meant giving them some good spots during one of my matches, I was all about that. If this meant picking up the tab at a restaurant, I did that too for them. Investing in them was almost an investment in yourself, because it seemed they would try to make you shine even more as a show of thanks.

Just to name drop a little bit, I used to drive around a lot with Demotion. I used to room with Steve Keirn (a.k.a. Skinner,) Paul Orndorff, and also Rick Martel. However, sometimes I would room with one of the enhancement guys. You see, if one of the boys was not doing as well at the pay-window, I would room with them then pay for most of the cost to help.

Back in the day, I had a 1978 Oldsmobile. I was riding to a show from home when all of a sudden, smoke started coming out of the hood. I was rushing off to the airport and didn't have time to deal with it, so I called my man, Jose Luis Rivera, who knew a little bit about cars.

"Hey Jose," I said. "My car just broke down."

"Oh, man, I'm sorry to hear."

"Well listen, man. Can do me a favor?" I asked.

"Sure, Tito. Anything for you."

"I don't have time to deal with it right now. Can you go get it? To repay you, you can keep the car."

"Keep it?" he asked.

CHAPTER 17 – Fame

"Yes," I said. "It's like 6 or 7 years old, but it's in great shape. I'm sure you can fix it up."

"No problem," he said. "Thank you, my friend!"

And he did just that. He fixed it up and gave to hissister. He told me recently that she had that car for another ten years.

I really liked Jose. I couldn't understand why they didn't use him for anything bigger than they ever did. It was probably the English thing. He spoke mostly Spanish and had a hard time with promos.

Another time, I knew Jose had been hit with some unexpected hardships so I took up a collection for him in the locker room. The boys were very generous when they heard the cause because they all liked Jose.

"Jose," I said, handing him an early Christmas card. "This is for you and your family from me and the boys. We want your kids to have the best Christmas they ever had."

He opened it up. In the end, I was able to give him $1,000 from the boys to help out for Christmas. His eyes teared up. This was something he never forgot.

One of the most famous enhancement talent wresters was "Iron" Mike Sharpe. A funny story about him was that he had a terrible germ phobia and had to clean himself from head to toe after every match to remove any possible germ from his body that he may have picked up in the ring. This, of course, was a sanitation process that could really take some time.

One night after a show in Boston Gardens, Mike was taking so long that he was still showering when the place actually closed. Nobody suspected he was tthere and he got locked in!

On a sad note, he eventually married a gold-digger girl who really took him for a ride.

From what I understand, she really "cleaned out his account." ¡Arriba! (That was a bad one, I know.)

FAMOUSLY CHEAP BASTARDS

My friend Nikolai was a funny guy. He wouldn't go up to a couple and introduce himself. Then, he would say, "Are you happy or are you married?"

Nikolai Volkoff was a famous wrestler with a Russian gimmick that everyone remembers. He was famous for singing the Russian National Anthem before every match. Despite his success, he was so cheap that he almost never went out anywhere with the boys for a bite to eat or a drink. He was always packing a bag lunch.

What he often did was carry a crock pot and a hot plate around with him for every tour. Then, what he would do is find a grocery store before every show and get something cooking before he left for his match. That way after the show, he could just go back to the hotel room and eat the nice $5 pot roast that was waiting for him.

Another famously cheap story comes from the Steiner Brothers. I remember Rick Steiner laughing about how cheap his brother Scott actually was.

"Scotty was so cheap," he once told me, "that I actually had to watch him whenever we would go out to eat somewhere."

It wasn't because he stole the ketchup packets or something. What Scott would is, if his brother wasn't looking when they were leaving, he would quickly turn around and pick up the tip.

ARRIBA ALOHA

I was beat. I had just worked for over 30 days straight in a row without seeing my family. I finally had two days off and was also closing on my new home. When I was able to take a few days off, I was beyond ready.

As I was getting the paperwork together for the real estate agent on my first day home, the phone rang.

Time froze.

I looked over at the phone and knew that I shouldn't answer it but, like an idiot, I did anyhow. And, of course, who do you think it was?

CHAPTER 17 – Fame

"Hey, pal," Vince said. "Guess what?"

"*Um*, what?"

"You just won a trip to Hawaii!"

My heart sank.

Vince wanted me to cover a match in Hawaii for the Junkyard Dog who called in sick for an event. I told Vince I couldn't go because was literally just about to close on our first house.

"Well, that's too bad. Ok, though, I understand," the man who never sleeps said. "No Problem."

After my two short days off, I was back to work bright and early. My batteries were recharged and I was ready to go. I called to get my bookings for the following week, and lo and behold, my schedule was the drizzling shits.

It looked like I had been demoted!

I looked at it again, shook my head and had to laugh. It was a quiet laugh, more like a chuckle. (What do you call a short quiet laugh in Hawaii? *A-low-ha*.)

Vince had pushed me down from the "A" team to the "C" team, probably cutting my pay in half for those matches. Although I didn't do anything wrong, he was punishing me for the Junkyard Dog's unreliability!

That was bullshit for even him!

RUDE AWAKENING

Late in 1986, during a TV taping in Nashville, I had a match against "Ravishing" Rick Rude that ended up almost as embarrassing as my sunset flip contest against Savage.

Rick Rude was all about sex appeal. After winning a match with his signature maneuver, a neck-breaker he called "The Rude Awakening," he would give some lucky lady a "Rude Awakening" of her own.

What Rick would do is have his manager invite women who were "sitting at ringside" into the ring, and Rick would plant a big kiss on them. The big joke behind the scenes was that usually these girls were friends of the wrestlers, rats or whomever they could scrape up last minute. Rick never really knew what he was going to get.

After a match with Rick in Nashville which he won, he was getting ready to do his "Rude Awakening" on a beautiful female fan and ham up his shtick as usual.

I had already left the ring. I was heading for the dressing room when the festivities were beginning in the ring. Bobby Heenan helped a young lady in between the ropes. Then, unplanned, I turned and ran back into the ring.

Not knowing what to do, Heenan bailed. Then, I knocked Rick out of the ring and took the girl into my arms. I leaned her back as far as I could, I held her for the camera, and we kissed just like Rick would do.

The joke was supposed to be on Rick, but then something else unplanned happened. I was going for a slight bend, but I got carried away and leaned too far forward.

As I kissed her, we just kept going down like Rick always did, all the way to the mat, but I ended up losing my balance. I slipped and fell.

I ended up on top of her, which was embarrassing, because I'd screwed up Rick's move, but it was still pretty sexy if you ask me.

It turned out okay and the fans loved it.

(I think that it probably happened due to a lack of blood flowing up to my brain. ¡Arriba!)

WRESTLEMANIA III

The WWF went from being just an east coast promotion to a national sensation and even became an international company.

In a short period of time, the company left behind its hotel room office in Manhattan and moved into a huge office building in Stamford, Connecticut. We went from traveling a little to traveling a lot and the wrestlers' pay also went up significantly; mine quadrupled! ¡Arriba!

Vince's dream had unfolded into an even bigger one than he had expected. *WrestleMania* started in Madison Square Garden with a capacity of 20,000 people. However, *WrestleMania III* was held at Detroit's Pontiac Silver Dome and featured over 93,000 fans. I don't think anyone envisioned that kind of growth! That's right, *WrestleMania III*

CHAPTER 17 – Fame

took place in March 1987 in front of a record-breaking attendance. It was an event loaded with great wrestling talent and plenty of celebrities, including rock star Alice Cooper, comedian Bob Uecker and movie star Mary Hart.

This was a great wrestling event to be a part of, even though I didn't have a real big role this time around. I ended up being part of a six-man tag-team match, teaming with The British Bulldogs against The Hart Foundation and Danny Davis.

Danny Davis was initially just a very good referee with the company. Then, Vince created an angle for Danny to become a controversial referee, which I thought was a genius move. I never expected the fans to buy into the character, but Danny did such an outstanding job that he went from being a referee, to an occasional wrestler, to the big time in a semi-main event!

Now, Danny had worked double duty for many years on shows as a referee, and a masked wrestler named "Mr. X" who was a jobber. What he would do is maybe ref a few matches, quick get changed, and then come out and wrestle under a hood. Nobody knew the difference and he helped to fill out cards that may have been short in talent. He too was a loyal company man to Vince and was finally getting his time to shine because of it.

So what they did on TV was to have him be the first "bad guy referee" who would essentially befriend the heels and help them win matches. That spearheaded his move from a referee everyone knew to a wrestler.

The Bulldogs and I lost our nine-minute match after the Harts' manager, Jimmy Hart, hit Davey Boy on the head with his megaphone.

Later in the show, I attacked Butch Reed's manager, Slick, and soon thereafter ripped his clothes off. This set up a short program between Butch and myself.

Since Ricky Steamboat was the Intercontinental champion at this time, Vince put Butch and me together to determine if one of us should work our way back up into contention for the belt. (Butch and I had some very good matches over a two-month period. But our program was simply mid-card matches that didn't amount to too much for either of us.)

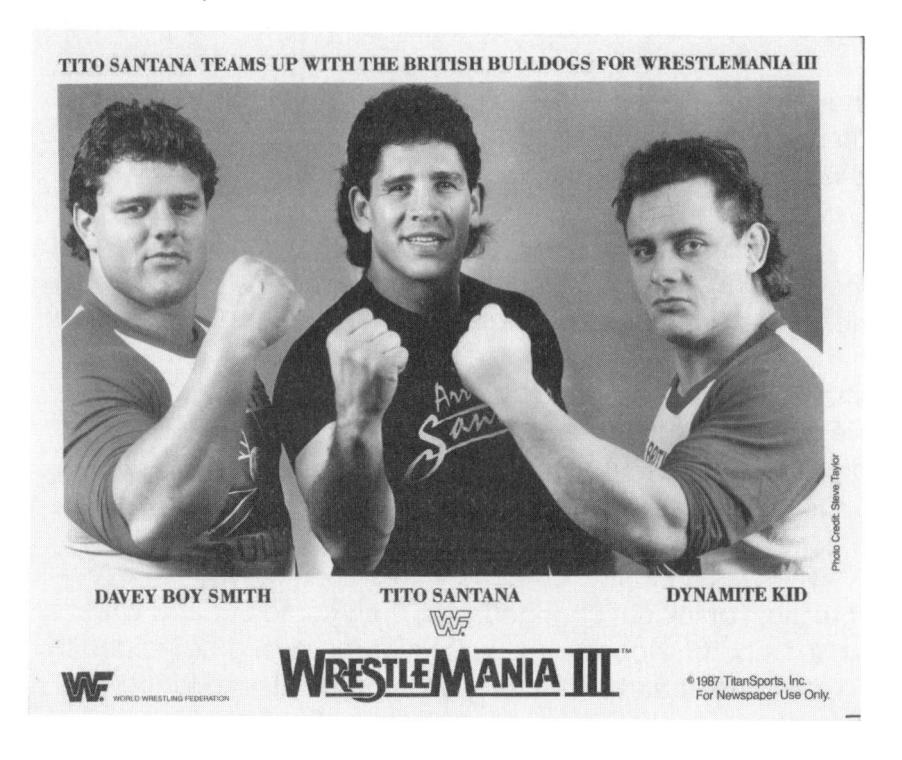

TITO SANTANA TEAMS UP WITH THE BRITISH BULLDOGS FOR WRESTLEMANIA III

DAVEY BOY SMITH — TITO SANTANA — DYNAMITE KID

WrestleMania III

© 1987 TitanSports, Inc. For Newspaper Use Only.

HULK VS ANDRÉ

The match that everyone really came to see at *WrestleMania III* was the epic battle between champion Hulk Hogan, and challenger André the Giant. Although Hulk beat André, neither my fellow wrestlers nor I had any advance knowledge of the outcome of the match. Like the fans, we were all in the dark and excited to watch the match backstage.

Now, as you may or may not recall seeing, the locker room for *WrestleMania III* was a hike. They had special "ring entrance carts" built just to transport the wrestlers to and from the ring. They were built to look like mini-rings with ropes and turnbuckles, and they seemed to add an extra degree of specialness to the event, but they served two purposes. One was to keep the wrestlers' entrance time

CHAPTER 17 – Fame

down because it really was a long trip from the locker room to the actual ring. And the other reason was so that André the Giant didn't have to endure an extremely long walk to and from the ring, due to his health. He was pretty worn down at this time in his life. Walking was even a chore for André at this point in his career.

There seemed to be some jealousy and static between Hulk and André, which led to my belief that Hulk and André would never agree to put on such a stellar match. The friction existed because André had been the man for years, and a lot of the boys didn't think that André would accommodate Hulk and officially pass him the torch on national television.

Although André and I were good friends, he never told me anything about what was planned for the match that night, and I had enough respect for him to not pry. Despite the build-up for the biggest match in the history of the company, both wrestlers protected the match and kept their mouths shut. So I just pulled up a chair to the backstage TV monitors to watch the show.

It was a sellout "at the curtain" as well with the boys. I remember a whole host of guys sitting with me there, waiting to see what was going to happen. Brutus Beefcake, Jimmy Hart, Randy Savage, Ricky Steamboat, Bobby Heenan, myself and others were all glued to the TV monitor ready to catch the action beside me.

I personally didn't think André would sell a lot for Hulk, but boy was I totally wrong. He worked his tail off in that match. André really gave it his all.

When the finish came, we couldn't believe our eyes. When Hulk body slammed the 500-pound André, there wasn't a single person in the locker room who trusted what they were seeing. Everybody jumped out of their seats and started cheering.

In the first place, André had a lot of physical problems; his ability to position himself in a manner to allow Hulk to lift him up is a true testament to André's drive and ability. Nobody was going to do anything to André unless he wanted it done. Equally amazing is the fact that Hulk was physically able to body slam André. All of us watching let out a collective, "Wow!" It was a good slam, and I think Hulk hurt his back in the process.

When the match was over, all the boys congratulated both wrestlers on a job well done. Hulk hugged and thanked André for passing the torch. Their match went far beyond anybody's expectations and set a new standard for the league. The immense effort netted both men something like a whopping million dollars each! Most importantly for the business, André helped get over Hulk Hogan. And with Hulk at the helm, he took professional wrestling to another level.

THE BRITISH BULLDOGS

As stated earlier, I teamed with The British Bulldogs for a six-man tag match at *WrestleMania III*. I was especially glad to have The British Bulldogs on my side. Although we lost, I have nothing but good things to say about Davey Boy Smith and The Dynamite Kid.

It is widely-known that the Bulldogs pulled many mean ribs on the boys. I do want to go on the record and say that they never pulled any of their shit on me, even though they had many opportunities to do so.

One time, a gopher was sent to the convenience store to buy the Bulldogs some coffee. When the lackey returned, the Bulldogs took the coffee but pretended they already paid him, which they absolutely didn't do.

The guy was upset and rightfully so. For some reason, he came up to me for some advice. He was a good kid and made far less than any of us. Because of this, I understood his concern.

"Look," I said. "I'll go and say something to the Bulldogs for you."

After promising him I would try to have his back the best I could, I went off to find Davey Boy and Dynamite.

"Hey, Tito," they said as I walked into their dressing room. "What's up?"

"Come on guys," I said to them.

"What?"

CHAPTER 17 – Fame

"The kid with the coffee. After all, this guy has done for you two, why not just give him his money and not put him through the ringer?" I asked. "With all the money you are making, you can't even spare a couple of bucks?"

They agreed and gave him the money for the coffee as well as some extra for a top.

After that, however, I kept looking over my shoulder to see if they were going to pull a rib on me because of the exchange we had had. For a few months straight, I remember that whenever we were on the same card together, I would rush back from the ring, and immediately look in my luggage. I had expected to see cut up tights, or some dogshit, or whatever, but it just never happened.

To their credit, I guess they had enough respect for me to not hook me up with any kind of revenge. In looking at some of the antics they did engage in, for this, I am very thankful!

Shortly after that, I am sure many of you have heard the story about The Dynamite Kid and Jacques Rougeau. For those of you who have not, Dynamite was laying in on the ribs pretty hard on the Canadian brothers, and eventually, this led to Jacques taking some time off from the company. He did not take time off to go vacation, however. Jacques decided he needed to learn how to box.

Jacques then went to the only person who he truly trusted to lead his training, his own brother Raymond, who was a very good boxer in his own right. In the process of training, Raymond taught Jacques how to throw some really good right hands, and not the kind I was throwing at Styrofoam cups hanging from the ceiling on strings.

After a few good weeks off, the Rougeaus returned. One night, the wrestlers were all eating lunch together before a TV taping, and Jacques went to get his food. The Dynamite Kid was already in the buffet line and a few words were exchanged. Jacques had had enough and went back to his dressing room.

A moment later, I watched as Dynamite left the catering room and heard a loud commotion in the hallway. *POWWW!!!*

All of the boys went running to see what was the matter. It was then that we learned that Jacques punched Dynamite right in the mouth with a thunderous punch, knocking out a bunch of Dynamite's teeth!

Jacques cashed in on his receipt and a stunned Dynamite did nothing to further the event. Regardless, Vince found out about the incident and eventually sent both guys home. He warned Dynamite that it was over and that he better not try to get revenge.

Unfortunately, after that, The Dynamite Kid was never the same.

THE GREATEST IC CHAMPION?!

I'm sure if you are reading this book, you also know who the Honky Tonk Man was. He famously called himself "The Greatest Intercontinental Champion of All Time," but he got that wrong. We all know who that was … ¡Arriba!

Wayne Farris began his career right around when I did, in 1977, but in a different neck of the woods. He got his start in Missouri and wrestled alongside his training partner Koko B. Ware for a promoter named Henry Rogers.

As "Dynamite" Wayne Farris, he moved to Memphis Wrestling in 1978, and also wrestled in Birmingham, Dothan, Mobile, and Pensacola. He later climbed the card when he started teaming with Larry Latham (the future Moondog Spot) finding success as The Blond Bombers in Florida Championship Wrestling in a team created by Gerry Brisco. When they took the show on the road to Memphis, the team jumped into a heated feud against Jerry Lawler (Wayne's cousin) and Bill Dundee that culminated in a "Tupelo Concession Stand Brawl."

The reason some people still talk about this match some forty years later because it was the first time anything like that had ever been done in wrestling anywhere. It was a hardcore match before hardcore existed.

Memphis wrestling historians will tell you the concession stand brawl was created out of desperation. Memphis promoter Jerry Jarrett had lost a lot of talent and

CHAPTER 17 – Fame

ticket sales were hurting. So Jarret created this stunt to get people talking again about his struggling promotion.

So back in 1979, on a hot June night in Tupelo, four wrestlers engaged in a brawl that became the stuff of legends. Bill Dundee and Jerry Lawler took their match with Larry Latham and Wayne Farris outside of the squared circle and up into a concession stand at the old Tupelo Sports Arena. Some say this was the start of hardcore extreme wrestling. Incidentally, the second one of those "Concession Stand" matches they did, they had Onita in it who took the idea back to Japan and created FMW.

Once Jerry threw the jar of pickles, it was on. Anything not bolted down was fair game.

"I'll never forget, Herman Sheffield, the promoter, was running up and down screaming!" said Lawler. "He didn't care about the mustard. He didn't care about the candy bars. He didn't care about the popcorn. He just said, 'please don't break my popcorn machine,' because that was his moneymaker there at the venue as the promoter!"

After that, Wayne had stints in the American Wrestling Association, Jim Crockett Promotions and another of other places that were my stomping grounds at one point.

Eventually, Hulk Hogan helped The Honky Tonk Man get his break in the WWF. The two had become friends in the Portland territory, where Honky had become overexposed and needed an exit strategy. Like any good friend, Hulk helped him land an opportunity in New York.

Once under contract, Vince gave Honky his gimmick, as an Elvis impersonator, and had him work as a face. Vince pushed him hard so his character would gain traction with the fans, but his character just wasn't catching on. Nothing was working, so Vince changed strategy and decided to make Honky a heel and give him a manager, "The Mouth of the South" Jimmy Hart. The change worked and the gimmick gained support from fans. As a matter of fact, the Honky Tonk Man got red hot with his audience.

On the June 13, 1987, episode of *WWF Superstars*, Honky defeated Ricky "The Dragon" Steamboat for the WWF

Intercontinental heavyweight championship. He was a one-time champion but held the belt for fourteen months!

In every interview that he could, he would tell the fans that he was, "the best ever Intercontinental champion," which is bullshit, we all know. However, he does still hold the record for longest reigning champ (which also is bullshit.)

It actually is impressive that he still holds this accolade today. Chris Jericho holds the record for the most reigns with the IC strap at nine times. But the Honky Tonk Man still holds the longest reign at 454 days.

I honestly never had a problem with Honky. I thought he was a good guy and thought well of his character. I will say this, however. The first time I had to put him over, I felt really weird, because I just didn't think this guy could even break an egg! ¡Arriba!

MEETING MIL

When I was first getting into the business, people were telling me that I had something that maybe other Latino wrestlers did not. I had the potential to reach and connect to the Latino American mainstream. Maybe they were right, but there was one name out there that had already reached levels for Spanish-speaking wrestlers. He was one I had respect for, and his name was Mil Máscaras, "The Man of a Thousand Masks."

For those of you who do not know, Mil was like the Hulk Hogan of Mexico.

Máscaras is one of the original "Big Three" of the Lucha libre wrestlers in Mexico; the other two being El Santo and Blue Demon. Mil is considered one of the most influential wrestlers of all time in his country, responsible for popularizing the high-flying Lucha Libre style in Mexico, and now around the world. Mil was years ahead of his time and helped revolutionize the sport. He inspired a countless number of future stars ranging from Jimmy Snuka to Rey Mysterio. If it weren't for him, there would be no Jushin Liger, no Ultimo Dragon, or no Great Sasuke of more recent times.

Mil was known as "The Man of a Thousand Masks" because he always wore a mask in the ring. He was one of

CHAPTER 17 – Fame

the first Mexican wrestlers to make it big outside of his home country, and he was also one of the original high flyers. Not only was he a big name in the wrestling ring, but his fame actually led him to become the star of twenty films! He has even appeared on three his country's postage stamps!

I first met Mil Mascaras when he was working for Paul Boesch, the promoter of the Houston territory. I was acting as a referee for Boesch during that time.

As a new guy behind-the-scenes who was just wetting my feet in the ring, I remember that for one particular show Paul asked me if I minded driving Mascaras from venue to venue.

"Are you kidding me?" I said to the promoter. "It would be my pleasure."

I idolized Mil, so it really was an honor for me to chauffer him around. I was like a kid in a candy store.

The masked Lucha Libre wrestlers have been a national phenomenon since the 1930s.

Early on in Mexico, El Santo, Blue Demon and Mil were the ones to really popularize wearing wrestling masks. Because of their contributions to the sport, now everyone has masks. Mil explained to me during one of our rides together that in Mexico the mask has become a mystical symbol and a projection of the wrestler's soul.

The early masks that were made when Mil was first starting out were very simple, basically colors to distinguish the wrestlers from each other. Today, Lucha Libre masks are now an identity. They are colorfully designed with symbolic images of animals, gods and ancient heroes the luchador takes on during a performance.

I learned from Mil that virtually all wrestlers in Mexico start their careers wearing masks, but over the span of their careers, a large number of them will be unmasked as part of their journey. Sometimes, a wrestler slated for retirement will be unmasked in his final bout or at the beginning of a final tour, signifying a loss of identity as that character. Sometimes, losing the mask signifies the end of a gimmick with the wrestler moving on to a new gimmick and mask.

The mask is now considered sacred, so much so that fully removing an opponent's mask during a match is grounds for disqualification and the most horrific thing a wrestler could do to another luchadore.

During the time that we shared together, Mil had never worked without his mask and had no plans to take it off. Yes, he had worked many gimmick matches over the years where his mask was in jeopardy, like Lucha classic hair vs. mask match ups, but in the end, it was always him taking his opponent's scalp in the end.

Back then, the mask was so much of the luchador's identity that they never took it off in public. When they were away from home touring, they would check into hotels and even shower in locker rooms with the mask on, not wanting even wrestlers from other promotions to see their faces.

One night after a show, I was driving Mil to the next town. He had just wrestled a pretty hard match and asked if I could stop at a local convenience store to grab him a six pack of beer.

"Sure," I said.

Mil handed me some cash. I hopped out, made the purchase and got back on the road to drive out of town.

As I was driving, I looked over and there Mil was, drinking away.

He took off his mask.

I had never seen his face and was totally shocked. He never took off his mask in the ring or in the locker room. In fact, he sometimes would even wear two masks, one over the other as a backup plan, in case some wrestler were to go rogue and into business for themselves and try to pull it off.

It was not like a fat homely guy getting into radio because he wasn't photogenic enough for television. To his credit, Mil actually was a good-looking man. His good looks surprised me because American wrestlers who wore masks were usually ugly as hell! ¡Arriba!

I wondered why he covered his face, but I never asked him. At the time, I didn't see myself as worthy enough to ask such a personal question of a superstar.

Over a decade later in 1987, I would meet up with Mil once again. Paul Boesch sold what was left of his promotion to Vince and had a contract with Mil to work some in the States. This allowed Mil to come to the WWF and Vince thought it would be neat if we were to team up together.

So on August 28, 1987, we were able to team up in a great match with two other guys who wore masks to the ring as part of their entrance, Demolition.

We won the match, and it was truly an honor to be in the same ring with the wrestling legend, one who took a liking to me so much so early on that he felt comfortable enough to let me see his face.

RAT TRAPS

Because of the success of the WWF, the rat thing got even crazier. It became a world-wide infestation.

Now at this point, I was happily married and did not partake in such carnal temptations. But there were many of the boys who did! (Shame shame!)

There were two kinds of rats at this point; one was the random no-name rat hook-up, and the second was the regular rat who was connected and looked after the boys.

Most of the guys liked to go out after the shows. The random no-name rats knew this so they would herd up. Then, the rats would predict which local bars, nightclubs or restaurant the wrestlers would go to. Droves of them would infest an establishment, hoping to bag a boy and then bang a boy. Believe it or not, these more desperate rats didn't care where this happened, just as long as it happened. There are stories of these no-name rats who were willing to service a guy in the most unromantic places you can think of, like junkyards, gas station restrooms, or behind a Chinese restaurant dumpster. (Now, that is hot!)

Oddly enough, there were also ring rats who were the go-to regulars for the boys. I did not partake in this world either, but some of the guys had a regular girl in practically every territory.

The professional rats had their own territories and treated the boys like it was their job to services the boys in those areas. There were a few regulars in different areas that you knew if you looked for them, you would see them every time wrestling came to that town.

I mean, when we would literally get off an airplane and come down the escalator, we would see three or four of these familiar faces waiting to service us.

These girls would drive 150 miles, pick the wrestler up, bring them to their shows, bring them out to eat after the show, and then bring them to their hotel after their show and "tuck them in" ¡Arriba! Then, they would pay for the hotel room as they left the building!

CHAPTER 17 – Fame

It was almost like some of the boys had their own female sugar-daddies that would pay for every little expense. Some of them, sadly, were probably being played. These regulars would give the boys expensive gifts like a boyfriend would do to a girlfriend. Watching from afar, it was almost like they were in competition to be the best rat of all. They would buy the boys expensive gifts like thousand dollar gold chains, or fancy rings, or even Rolex watches.

Some of the wrestlers took advantage of the rats for sure. It was pretty bad, almost like they were ribbing them. I think a few of the guys actually believed that you had to somewhat mistreat a ring rat so they would "know their role," and not risk affecting a guy's personal life beyond wrestling and start to think they were something else. These guys said they had to be mean as to keep the idea out of their heads that whatever they had could blossom into anything else. This is because, sadly, a lot of them had families at home waiting for them.

Jake "The Snake" Roberts and The Rockers were great examples of rat traps. These guys were famous for running the rats hard and also playing nasty pranks on them that they would fall for every time. Whenever the rats were around they would fall into the same trap again and again and again. They would take the bait and end up leaving witha sore tail in the end. If guys today did stuff like some of the boys did back then, they likely wouldn't be in wrestling. They likely would be in jail!

THE ROCKERS DEBUT

Now, I wrestled with injuries, illnesses and personal problems for the majority of my career, but I've always given my 110 percent as they say in the world of sports. In my whole time in the WWF, I only missed two major appearances in eleven years. The first was to bring my wife home from the hospital after giving birth to our second son in 1984, and the second happened a few months later when I was stranded in an airport due to a blizzard.

A lot of the boys I worked with had a very excellent work ethic as well. However, I did have some peers in the

WWF who were not always so diligent about showing up to work as we were.

From time to time, the company suffered a rash of no-shows. Some wrestlers simply weren't dependable. A good example of showing some early red flags right off the bat came from Shawn Michaels and his tag-team partner, Marty Jannetty.

Marty and Shawn were making waves in wrestling as "The Midnight Rockers" and really had a great future ahead of them. Unfortunately, they were also young and wild. While they were very talented as wrestlers, they also partied hard on many occasions and would miss their show the following day or night as a result.

CHAPTER 17 – Fame

They debuted with the WWF in 1987 as the tag-team, The Rockers. They were a very energetic and enthusiastic team, and they had great chemistry together in the ring after working out the kinks in places like the AWA. Things were looking great for them in New York at first, but they just were not getting the push they felt they really deserved.

On a plane ride home from a European tour, Marty came over to me one night and asked me for some advice.

"So, Tito, Why do you think The Rockers aren't getting a shot at the belts?" he asked, being the most level-headed of the pair.

"Look, Marty," I said. "My only advice to you and Shawn is to sit low and do whatever the company asks of you. Both of you are very talented. When the time is right, and Vince figures out what he wants to do with your tag team, you will get your break. If you try to rush him, he will go the other way and not do it at all."

"So what do I do? Wait forever?"

"No. In the meantime, you give your best in the ring, and watch your Ps and Qs outside the ring," I said, in my most politically correct way. "Hang in there, your time will soon come."

At this time, rumor had it that while the office loved what they were doing in the ring, they really did not appreciate their nightlife antics after the shows.

That really was my best way to kill two birds with one stone. They really needed to not rush Vince, and also behave more like champions before he would consider putting the belts on them. The stuff they were doing outside the ring with rats was just ridiculous.

When The Rockers showed up to an event, they would go right to the front door to see what was "on the menu." They would walk up and down the ticket line to see what little dish they wanted. During the show, they would "order their take-out." Sometimes, they would bump near a girl during a match and tell them to meet them after the show in the parking lot. Other times if they were really hungry, they would have a ring crew guy or security bring a girl back to the locker room and have them "make a special delivery" in a back alley.

I heard a story once where Marty had to start a match without Shawn because he was in the parking lot with a girl. Shawn finally joined his partner five minutes after the match had already started. I guess he made it there just in time for the hot tag, ironically after he just tagged some hot girl!

Every night after a show, The Rockers always had an after-party. They would always find the prettiest girls you could imagine and invite them back to their rooms as party guests. I don't know what they were partying with, but those girls weren't drinking Shirley Temples. The guests would often say it was always the same scene; the girls would party hard, probably have some crazy naked wrestling match and then eventually pass out. Then, the pranks would begin.

Anyhow, a few weeks after Marty and I spoke, Vince figured out exactly what to do with them *when he fired them.*

Almost a year later, The Rockers were granted a second chance and brought back into the company, which wasn't surprising. If you had talent, then Vince was a big believer in second chances.

KEN PATERA

Sometimes fame can go to a guy's head, especially a wrestler, and make them think they are above the law.

Now, late in 1984, a legit record-breaking Olympic powerlifter by the name of Ken Patera was brought back to the WWF, but he was awaiting trial for something he had just done before he was hired back.

The famous "McDonalds Boulder Legend" happened on April 5, 1984, when an all-star wrestling card was brought to the Watertown High School gym for a fundraiser for their Athletic Booster Club. Besides Ken Patera, the show had some pretty big wrestling names from that time including The Fabulous Ones, Buck Zumhofe, The Crusher and even Jessie "The Body" Ventura.

After the fans left the high school gym that night and headed for home, Masa Saito and Ken Patera hung out a bit to avoid any stragglers. The plan was to head over to their

CHAPTER 17 – Fame

motel in Waukesha where they were to spend the night before flying from Waukesha to Stevens Point for yet another wrestling show.

"I'm kind of hungry," Patera told Saito. "Mind if we stop first to get something to eat?"

Tom "Rocky" Stone, overhearing the conversation, walked over to where Patera and Saito were getting dressed.

"Hey, brother. There's not much open late in this area. If you hurry though, you may be able to catch something at

McDonalds down the way on Moorland Boulevard. I'm heading there now if you want to follow me."

"I know where it is," Patera said. "We will just see you over there. Thanks."

"Okay," he said. "You probably should hurry though. They close at midnight."

A half an hour or so later, Patera and Saito slowly pulled into the McDonalds parking lot. It was about 10 or 15 minutes before closing and Rocky's car was already there. The two former Olympians stepped out of the car ready to grub out hard.

Before becoming professional wrestlers, Patera was a highly-decorated Olympic weightlifter, and Saito was a freestyle wrestler for Japan at the 1964 games. Both with their eating games on at full force, they approached the entrance anticipating piles of tasty McGoodness. However, just before entry, a scrawny pimple-faced McEmployee rushed to the front door and turned the lock.

Saito checked his watch in disbelief. "Wait. It's not midnight yet!"

Patera's stomach growled. Everything went dark. One of the employees shut off the dining room lights. "No way," Patera pulled on the door just in case. Much to his chagrin, he went through the motions only to find it was, in fact, truly locked. The darkness in the lobby that Patera saw turned red. "What in the world? That little bastard saw us coming in. That's bullshit!"

Patera ran around to the other side to find another door and looked for signs of life. Saito followed his partner's lead and went to the side window to peer in. The two big, hungry wrestlers stood in the darkness of the night with their hands cupped up to the glass like two little kids looking in a candy store.

"Look!" Saito said.
There in all his glory was Rocky Stone, with his tray of food. He was enjoying a delicious Big Mac, some crispy fries and a scrumptious frothy shake.

Rocky saw them looking in from the outside and made eye contact. "I told you!" Rocky said. He pushed as many fries into his mouth as he could at once to mock the wrestlers out in the cold. Then, he pointed at his watch and shrugged. "Maybe next time," he laughed.

"We'll see about that," Patera said elbowing Saito lightly on the arm. Patera rushed around to the door again and started pounding on it with the side of his fist. "Open up, guys. It isn't twelve yet!" Patera yelled, pounding harder on the door.

No answer.

Looking in again, Saito could see that the employees were ignoring them and had already begun their closing cleanup rituals. Saito shook his head and ran over to Patera. He joined in on the pounding until the one skinny employee couldn't continue to ignore the sound anymore. The employee set his mop against the counter and came to the door. Thinking they had won, the wrestlers were surprised when the employee did not open the door but had only stopped his duties momentarily to point to the hours of operation sign on the window next to Patera.

"What's it say?" Saito asked.

Patera read the sign. "Looks like the restaurant closed at like 11:45, but drive-thru is still open. I'll handle this." At that, Patera walked directly up to the drive-thru window, ready to make his order and pounded on the glass.

At around five minutes of, the skinny teenager not wanting to cook on the now-clean grill fearfully opened the window. "I'm sorry but we can't take your order unless you are in your car."

"What's the difference?!" Patera asked.

"Company rules."

"Company rules?" Patera scoffed. Patera walked around the side and found Saito who was looking in at Rocky. Rocky was still laughing and pointing and Saito pointed back with his middle finger. "Get in the car. We have to DRIVE up to the drive-thru."

Saito got behind the wheel and just as the car pulled up to the drive-thru speaker menu, the employee hit the lights. The menu went black. Saito looked down at his watch. It was midnight. A voice came over the speaker.

"I'm sorry guys but you are too late. We are not open now. Please come back tomorrow."

Their jaws dropped. Saito shook his head in disgust and started to drive away. Just before leaving the parking lot, Patera grabbed his arm.

"Stop the car, Masa," Patera said. "We may not get any food, but I'm not going to let this 110 pound little asshole get the best of us."

The enraged "Olympic Strongman" Ken Patera got out of the car and looked back in the front window. Then, he curiously started digging around in the bushes right under Rocky Stone's window.

Rocky was about on the floor with laughter at about this time, knowing that the kid's running the joint had pulled one over on them to get out of doing more work.

A minute or so later, Ken Patera, a world-class shot-putter, stood up with his newly-found prize; a fifty-pound rock. "This will have to do."

Rocky shook his head. "No, you wouldn't," he said, knowing damn well that Patera was actually the kind of guy who would. Rocky grabbed his tray and rushed to the back of the building. Patera took a few steps back and launched the stone. The glass came crashing down like an avalanche.

About $500 in damages later, Patera walked slowly back to the car.

"Looks like they are closed," he said to Saito, making sure to be loud enough for the employees inside McDonald's to hear. "Let's just get something from the vending machine at the hotel!"

They drove off and checked into their rooms.

An hour or so later and maybe a 12-pack or so later, two police officers came pounding on Masa Saito's door looking for Patera. As they story goes, Saito denied Patera was in his room, when all of a sudden, a drunken Patera came flying in from an adjoining room and clotheslined the first person in uniform that he saw, a 120-pound female officer. Her male partner, John Dillan, was obviously pissed and immediately struck Patera. Saito jumped the male and the tag team match was on. It didn't take long for Patera and

Saito to take control of the match, however, and accounts say that they double-teamed the male cop for twenty minutes or so, stretching the hell out of him, putting him in every submission hold known to man.

The female officer, Jacalyn Hibbard, in the meantime crawled out of the brawl and called for reinforcements. Eventually, she stumbled back into the room waiting on backup and was immediately clotheslined again for her troubles. When two more officers made it to the scene, the wrestlers made easy work of the first pair, the next pair after that, and two more pairs after that!

I don't know why the cops decided to go for "the test of strength" approach with the two professional wrestlers rather than to just draw their guns. Maybe they looked at it as a challenge? Anyhow, they say Saito and Patera took down eleven cops before peace was restored. The way it finally ended was the female officer just said, "Screw it," and drew her gun on Patera for the finish.

The police press relations guy was quoted as saying, "The Japanese guy's wrists were too big for the handcuffs and it required two sets to cuff him." He also said, "He was maced and hit with the baton, but it only just seemed to annoy him!"

Saito and Patera faced a bunch of charges in a trial that was also a "who's who of professional wrestling." Character witnesses for Patera and Saito included world heavyweight wrestling champion Nick Bockwinkel, Verne Gagne, and Mean Gene Okerlund.

In the end, both Saito and Patera were found guilty of battery and given two year prison sentences and six years of probation. Both of them did prison time, Patera serving the entire 24 months. Saito I think was let out of jail early for good behavior. To show just how tough he is, they say he was released from jail in the morning and went and wrestled a show that night.

Saito didn't let it phase him. He reportedly went back to Japan where he continued his wrestling career.

Today, Ken Patera is living in Minneapolis and is more upset about what happened than Saito is. He was recently interviewed about this and didn't like the topic.

"What kind of trouble are you trying to start? I'm not in the mood to talk about being railroaded by a sleaze-ball judge and district attorney and a bunch of old jurors who took my professional career and turned it to dog shit. They screwed up my life. You get it? They are a bunch of scumbags."

The WWF eventually brought Patera back to the company in the spring of 1987 after he had spent the previous year in prison. They aired vignettes on WWF TV and released *The Ken Patera Story* on video, which chronicled his career and his return. To ensure the fans would accept him as a babyface, they said former manager Bobby Heenan had abandoned him and "sold him down the river" while he was in prison and he began feuding with the Heenan Family. In his first match back at Madison Square Garden, he defeated the Honky Tonk Man, via submission with a bearhug, to a huge ovation.

Shortly after his return, however, there was more bad luck for Patera who ruptured the bicep tendon in his right arm. This injury led him to miss some time and re-emerge afterward with a stiff and bulky full-length brace for protection.

Within six months, Patera was being defeated by newer, younger talent. In his final televised WWF matches in late 1988, Gorilla Monsoon and Lord Alfred Hayes remarked on-air that Patera's skills were in decline and that he should consider retirement.

His final appearance in the WWE would be at the *1988 Survivor Series*.

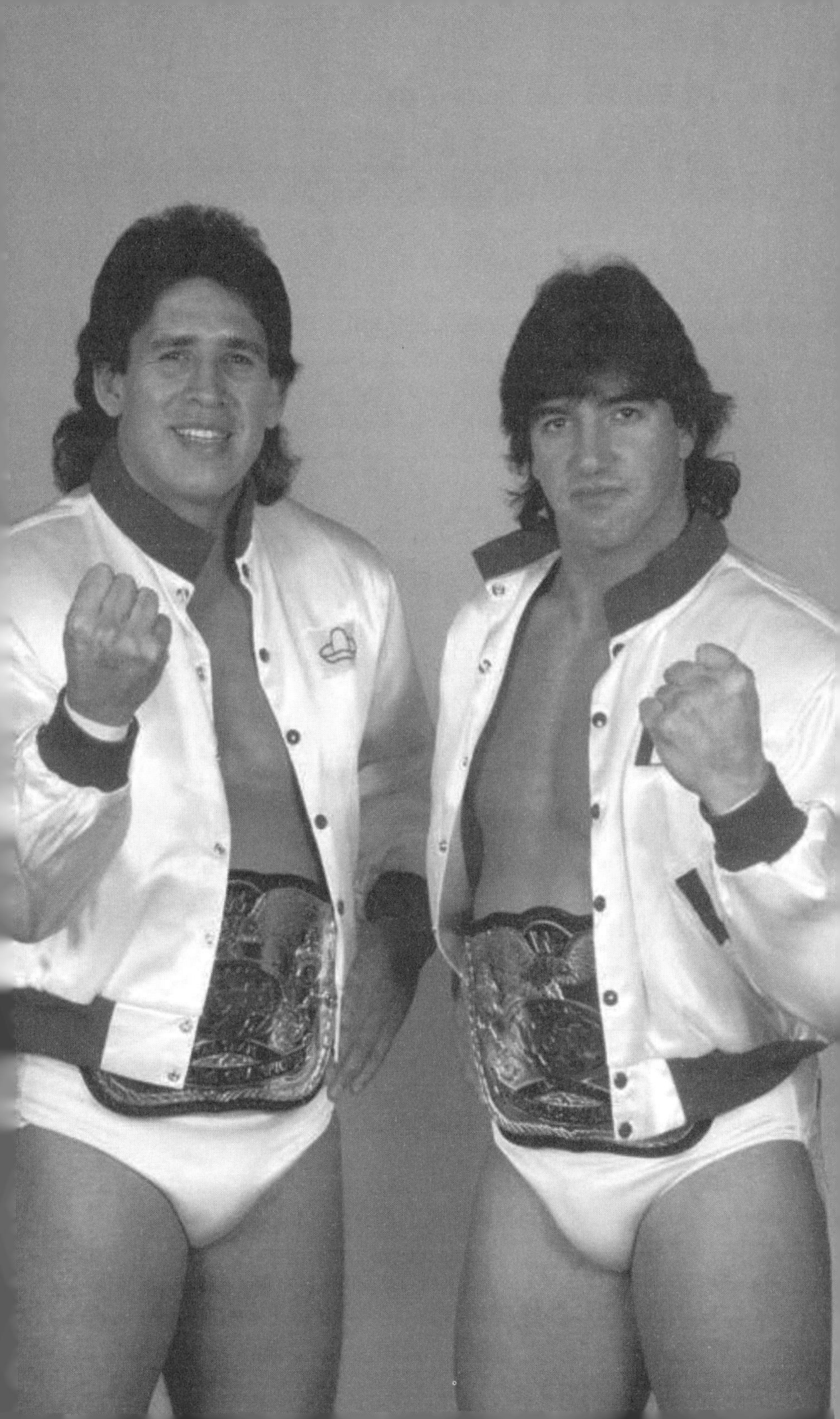

CHAPTER 18 - STRIKE FORCE

In Japan, they have a term that is translated as being "Western Dualism." This term means that in the west (America) we tend to look at everything as either black or white or right or wrong, there is no in between. However, most great thinkers realize that there are always two sides to every story and both may actually have bits of truth to their arguments. Such is the case with a rising tag team in the WWF called The Can-Am Connection.

Rick Martel and Tom Zenk were being groomed to potentially be one of the biggest babyface teams ever. One minute they were set to be the next WWF tag team champions and the next minute, they were gone.

What happened?

The story is a little blurry, depending on who you ask.

CAN-AM DISCONNECTION

Just before Rick Martel left the AWA around 1986, Nick Bockwinkel went up to him and said, "Hey Rick, I just saw a guy practicing a little in the ring with Curt. You know what? He reminds me of a young Rick Martel."

"Who's that?" Rick asked.

"Guy by the name of Tom. Tom Zenk."

Curious, Rick hunted him down. Curt Henning and Tom Zenk were old high school buddies from Minneapolis, and Curt was bringing him in to practice and eventually tag team with him. When Rick Martel saw Tom in the ring working some moves with Curt, he was shocked because it was like he was looking in a mirror! Tom Zenk was so similar in appearance and how he moved in the ring that they could have been brothers. It was uncanny. Because of this, Rick went down to the ring and asked Tom if he wanted to try tagging with him at some point. Tom agreed.

After Rick officially finished with the AWA, he went to work for Lutte Internationale aka "International Wrestling" in Montreal Canada. This promotion was closer to his home so he could spend more time near his family. This particular professional wrestling promotion operated out of Montreal by

Canadian promoters/owners Frank Valois, André the Giant and Gino Brito. Rick knew, however, that Vince was soon to take over the company's area and put the territory out of business, so he thought he would push for the tag team to happen as a test.

It was common knowledge among the wrestling community that Rick couldn't give great interviews because he had a hard time with English. Tagging with Tom could have been beneficial to both, he thought, as he could also be a mentor to him and help get him ready for bigger things.

Tom was just starting out and wasn't that good of a worker yet back then. Rick gave him a lot of good insight. He critiqued his work and gave constructive criticism.

Martel taking him on as a tag team partner was beneficial to both of them. It helped Tom get polished and also lighten the work load for Martel. The idea of working tag teams again was inviting to him because it would give him a little opportunity to work lighter and let his body heal up a little from his big singles run in the AWA. As a tag team, things went pretty well for both of them in Canada.

Eventually, they got along so well that Tom was welcomed in almost as part of Rick's family. Because of this, he became the boyfriend and eventually fiancée of Martel's sister-in-law.

In 1986, Rick Martel was contacted about a return to the WWF. At this point, Vince McMahon was grabbing up all the names he could from different territories so that when he ran syndicated television there, people would make the switch. Rick hadn't worked for the WWF since back in 1982, but he recently finished a great AWA title run and his stock was looking pretty valuable.

"I am interested, Vince," Rick said, "but more interested if you would consider booking me in a tag team with Tom Zenk."

It made sense.

Back in 1982 before he left the WWF the first time to go to the AWA, Martel and Tony Garea held the WWWF tag team championship on two different occasions. Vince knew that Rick was a great tag team competitor, so he thought it over and finally agreed.

The Can-Am Connection in the WWF was born.

Vince's idea was that the Can-Am Connection would work their way up the ranks and eventually defeat The Hart Foundation for the tag team titles.

The new duo came in. They started working house shows and dark matches and got even more polished as a team. Official WWF merchandise was being created to inevitably push this new faction, and everyone knew that they were going to be the next big thing in the tag team division.

Once everything was ready to go, they made their debut and started getting some great exposure on television.

The ball was rolling.

Now, here is where the stories get a little different, depending on who you talked to at the time.

According to Rick Martel, Tom Zenk almost immediately "changed the moment he made it to New York." Martel says, "He pretty much became an ego maniac right from the start before my very eyes."

Martel's side of the story said Zenk didn't want to work hard. He had to constantly motivate Zenk about the big push they were getting and to push him to put the work ethnic needed so they could succeed. However, "Zenk wouldn't listen." Martel says that he showed up late. He was lazy with his training and in the ring. He said that Zenk constantly complained about horrible pay, the number of work dates and the lack of superstar-level accommodations.

"He was bitching nonstop."

Rick said he told Tom that he really needed to save his money, but he just wouldn't listen. He was belligerent and "upgraded tickets and hotel rooms for unnecessary reasons, wasted his cash on expensive dinners and just didn't listen to any advice."

Rick also says that Tom didn't respect any kind of authority very well.

"On only the second week of being in the WWF, the office put a new dress code into effect. Tom absolutely hated it and said it wasn't part of the deal when he signed up," Martel said. "So, Tom continued to dress the way wanted because he believed that the dress code was stupid."

The office didn't like this. After a show one night, Vince approached Rick Martel about Tom Zenk's bad attitude.

"You know Rick, we brought Tom in under your good recommendation," Vince said, "so I am hoping you can get things straightened out with him. I don't know if he is having issues at home, or not, but we would like him to be more in line."

"Absolutely," Martel said. "Say no more."

Later on back at the hotel after their show in Boston, Rick pulled Tom aside to talk, but it turned into a pretty bad argument.

That night, Zenk left an envelope at the front desk for his Martel. In it was a thank you note to Martel and the keys to their rental car.

Essentially the note thanked Martel for the opportunity, but that the WWF was not for him.

He had quit the WWF with no notice.

"He left like a thief in the night," Rick said.

If you ask Rick today why Tom left, he says, "When we got to the top, we turned up the volume and went into that category where you really have to put out, day in and day out," he said. "Every day you go to that gym. Every day, even if you're injured, you've got to keep going. I think that was too much for Tom, and also the pressure of wrestling in front of big crowds and always performing to your top level. He just couldn't take the pressure."

Tom Zenk has since passed away, god rest his soul. However, whenever anyone asked him about this situation, he had a similar, yet very different story than Martel as to why he left.

Tom Zenk says that his biggest issue with the WWF at this time was over money. His overall claim was that Rick Martel made a side deal for himself with Vince to be paid more than Zenk because Martel himself was the creator and the only "name" behind their tag team. This meant that **he** really was the Can-Am Connection. This was kind of like saying Tom Zenk was hired as a contractor to fill the other spot; much like Gene Simmons is KISS but he just hires some nutsack to play the drums for $50.

Tom Zenk, even more, took umbrage to being the "hired nutsack" in the role without an equal share because he was "taking all the big bumps and doing most of the selling," while Rick was booked more to sit on the apron and chill.

"Rick used me. As the vet, he called the matches. I did all the selling, Rick made all the comebacks, and Rick did all the finishing moves," he said in an interview. "He also took advantage of me and set it up so he would get the majority of the money in form the tag team from Vince."

Zenk has stated that after taxes, food and travel expenses, there was nothing left.

"I was getting $2,500 a week as his tag partner in WWF. Vince paid for airfares but he booked us onto 6 a.m. early morning flights to save himself money. That meant we arrived into cities too early in the morning to check into hotels to get some rest," he said in an interview. "At the other end of the day, we were also often the last match. By the time we got out of the building and back to the hotel, cleaned our ring gear, there wasn't much time to sleep before you had to be up again at 5 a.m. to check out of the hotel, return the hire-car and book in for the next flight. We had to pay for all the hotels, rental cars, food and incidentals. Deduct all that from $2,500 a week and then taxes, I was paying a single guy's taxes and there was not much left."

Tom Zenk claimed that he got paid about $10,000 for *WrestleMania III*, but the other guys in matches below them got at least $20,000. He said that Rick always told him he made the same money that he did, but he no longer trusted him. He heard from the other boys that he should have received around $100,000 for that slot on the PPV.

Tom has stated that they agreed that if they weren't earning $5,000 a week after 6 months in WWF, they were going to take up an offer in Japan for $10,000 a week. But even after talking to Rick about the bad payoffs, Rick refused to get their deal re-negotiated.

"Rick would never let me look at his contract. By then, I knew he must have had a better deal," Tom said. "Japan wanted us, but he wasn't interested, so he must have had something better! If you don't want to go to Japan and work for $5,000 a week, then you must have something even better, right?"

When Tom started thinking about leaving, he said he talked to his friend who was an attorney.

"He told me to get out of there as soon as possible, otherwise, I was really going to lose money. If I stayed just a little longer and then left, my contract would have held me liable for all the costs of lost merchandising," he said. "So I had to go before getting legally caught up in merchandise agreements and royalties kicking in, and that's just what I did."

After he left, Vince had Rick wait three or four days, then flew Rick Martel and Blackjack Lanza out to Minneapolis to try to salvage the tag team.

Tom was working in his garage, refinishing his kitchen cabinets. Tom said that Rick was honest and finally gave away how much he was earning. Tom said that Martel admitted to secretly negotiating an individual contract worth three times more than his partner's contract when, traditionally, tag teams were paid roughly equal salaries.

Blackjack said that they would try to make good with the money and that the Can-Am was set to work a program with Demolition and even win the titles.

Tom Zenk refused then kicked both Martel and Blackjack out.

Jack Lanza was one of the guys in AWA who helped out Tom Zenk early on, and he asked him back for one final match. I guess they planned to '"finish his career" on TV, to write him off so to speak in a match with the Islanders.

"We will pay you well. Haku will piledrive you and break your neck, and then we will just say you're out of the business."

Tom refused.

He said they later tried to get him for breach of contract, but he threatened Linda McMahon on the phone about "calling to the news to come forward about steroids in the locker room" during that whole big lawsuit, and they just finally let it go.

Martel strongly disagrees about the whole money thing still today. In *Mad Dogs, Midgets and Screw Jobs*, he said, "Ever since I was fired by Jim Barnett, I decided not to discuss money matters with other wrestlers, again. ... I did the same thing with Tom, and he put it in his head that I made more than him. But as far as Vince was concerned, if you were in a tag team, you earned the same amount of money." He also insists that Tom was overwhelmed by it all. "Wrestling is very hard on your body. Hard on you mentally. Hard on you physically. Tom wasn't mentally or physically hard as I thought he would be."

Now, I don't know if Vince was really giving Rick a bigger piece of the pie or not. I also don't know if Tom had an ego or was difficult to work with. Like any challenging disagreement, maybe it was a little of both. What I do know is, when Tom finally left, he left something behind; a hole for me to fill. I stepped right in.

STRIKE FORCE

By late 1987, my name was dropping on the card, fast. I was no longer getting very much television time, and when I did, it was more or less filler. I felt as if my wrestling career was winding down in the WWF, and was thinking about moving on.

Then, out of nowhere, I was given another opportunity in late 1987 to be in the main events again and earn big money as the replacement member of The Can-Am Connection. Because I was available, I was going to be plugged into the storyline and continue right where things left off.

That is why you always have your gear on you, right?

Rick Martel lost his partner, and Vince decided to put me in Tom's spot.

CHAPTER 18 – Strike Force

Now, tag team competition was not quite the comeback I had hoped for. Of course, I would have preferred singles competition; more spotlight, more growth potential. But like a prostitute who needed the money, I accepted the position without hesitation.

We were told first thng on day one that we were going to get the belts. I guess Vince had confidence that we would get over.

After it was set and I was to replace Zenk in the storylines that had already been mapped out for us, Vince called us into his office. He knew that he clearly couldn't continue with the name "Can-Am" because I was from Mexico.

"What I am thinking is, we call your team Border Patrol, you get it?" he said, half smirking like he did. "One of you is from the Northern border, and the other is from the South, same as before, only different."

I know what Vince was going for. He was still paying off of the geographical mixing idea of "The Can-Am Connection," however, this choice of wording just wasn't a good one.

I wrinkled my nose like I just sniffed a shit.

"What?" Vince said laughing at my expression. "You don't like it?

I shook my head.

Earlier that year, several illegal immigrants crossing the border from Mexico had died in a boxcar along the Arizona border. It was all over the news. Many attributed the deaths at to the unnecessary action of border security.

"Well," I said. "If we use this name, we will immediately be a heel tag-team in at least some of the fans' minds. Mexicans and Mexican Americans will hate us."

Vince was not trying to be stereotypical here. He was just looking for a good gimmick to patch the pothole Zenk was leaving behind. The hatred of border patrolmen in the eyes of some Latinos was also a cultural thing that Vince probably wasn't aware of out of the possibility of using this name. Vince heard me out and agreed, and eventually, we settled on something else.

That is when Rick and I became the newest hottest babyface tag team at that time, *Strike Force*.

So, the hottest new tag team in the ranks, Strike Force, got its official start as a WWF tag team in July of 1987, But the funny thing is, that wasn't our first time together. Back on August 29, 1982, I tagged with Rick Martel in the AWA. We were wrestling against the AWA tag team champions Greg Gagne and Jim Brunzell, The High Flyers. We lost, but who knew we would find great success just half a decade later.

By the summer of 1987 on an episode of *WWF Superstars*, The Islanders attacked Rick Martel after a match with Barry Horowitz. They were still mad at him from their feud with The Can-Am Connection and decided to finish some unfinished business. In an interesting twist, I was right there ringside performing commentary at the Spanish broadcast booth. I ran to the ring to help Rick Martel and that was the storyline start of our team.

In the storyline, our name Strike Force came from a line in my promo where I said that we will "be striking with force." Immediately, Martel (being the creative genius that he is) came up with the team's name based on that sentence and that was it.

Essentially after that, it was the team of Rick Martel and Tito Santana as the good looking babyfaces. Strike Force picked right up where Can-Am left off. They just plugged us into everything they had planned out for the other team.

Around this time, another wrestling album was coming out and equally as cheesy as the last one, only without commentary. This one was called *The Wrestling Album 2: Piledriver*. As they were planning for the new record, they contacted a singer named Robbie Dupree who was to produce a song called "Girls In Cars", to be used as the new ring entrance theme for the Can-Am Connection. The track was done, but the music video was not!

CHAPTER 18 – Strike Force

That meant that Rick and I had to posse up and drive around all day in a convertible, winking at girls on the beach. Tough day at the office, I know.

I was determined to make our tag team successful. I knew Rick could carry his end, And I made sure I carried my end. We enjoyed chemistry together and were very good in the ring, so the fans backed us from the start. We rode that momentum toward the World Tag Team championship belts.

We ran a "climbing the ladder" contender type program with The Islanders in the fall of 1987. Then we finally got our title match against The Hart Foundation for the WWF Tag Team Championship.

On October 27, 1987, we won the titles with Jim "The Anvil" submitting to Rick Martel in a Boston crab finish. Then we were really off and running again, and it felt like my program with Valentine. With the titles on us, that meant more promos, more appearances, and ... more money. ¡Arriba! While still feuding with the Harts, we were also taking on the Islanders, but they kept the titles on us, with us beating both teams at house shows across the country.

Rick and I got along just fine, unlike he did with his last tag team partner.

"In a tag team, you have to feel supported, that the guy you're tagging with can get the job done. I remember the first day I teamed up with Tito. Right away, he was an instant hit," Rick said in a recent interview. "Inside the ring, outside the ring. We got along just like two peas in a pod. I could feel comfortable having him beside me. I had somebody that could get the job done. He was a great guy, a really nice guy."

On the road, we collaborated a lot and came up with different things to say in promos, and different things to do in the ring. Maybe Tom Zenk was looked at more like being a subordinate to Rick, but for me, he treated me like and equal and always with respect.

"Tito's attitude compared to the other asshole (former partner Tom Zenk) was like, man, what a dream. There was no ego involved. We were there for the match. Tito and I

WWF TAG TEAM CHAMPIONS

STRIKE FORCE
RICK MARTEL   TITO SANTANA

were just like that, man," Rick said as he clasped his fingers together.

The feeling was mutual. To team up with somebody as good as Rick Martel and the chemistry we had together, it really was an enjoyable night every time we went out there. The fans got behind us right away, we had a great following and it's always a good feeling when the fans are behind you, you never get tired of people screaming your name.

Our team took off, and we hit the ground running.

WRESTLEMANIA IV

Being back in the spotlight re-energized my passion for wrestling, which I can honestly say I had started to lose before this happened. While I preferred singles, working as a tag team wrestler was also something new and exciting, and also a welcomed change for me.

It wasn't long before they were feeding us to one of the most badass tag teams in the WWF at that time. Demolition, at this point consisted of just the originals, Ax and Smash, managed by Mr. Fuji.

Now, I've said it before, I used to ride a lot with the heels. Up until my run with Martel, they were my go-to guys to share car rentals with, but I lightened up on this a little when they were becoming my opponents. It was too much of a risky offense against kayfabe if anyone were to see us together. Before this, I had gotten to know them a whole lot, but I had never much worked against them.

After we started working some together, I started calling them "Cement-o-lition" because they were so damn stiff.

Our tag team success led to Vince booking us in a semi-main event featured match at *WrestleMania IV* in Atlantic City, New Jersey. At Trump Plaza, in March of 1988, we were the second-to-last match of the evening, and Rick and I were defending our titles against, you guessed it, Demolition.

Again, the idea of "the chase" came up, and it only made sense for us to drop the belts that night. As I explained before, in wrestling, it makes more sense and builds more excitement amongst fans for the good guys to be in pursuit of a belt held by the bad guys, rather than the other way around. Subsequently, Rick and I lost our belts at *WrestleMania IV.*

One time in a match, they were throwing around some potatoes and I remember saying to Barry, "You don't have to convince me! Convince the fans!"

To that, Smash (Barry Darsow) threw a few more my way that were even more snug just to get my goat.

"Ugggh!," I said, even though it actually was kind of funny, because those guys always took care of me. For the record, Barry Darsow loved to poke the bear, however. Barry got a hold of Nailz one night as a rib. He knew Nailz was upset about a payoff, so he riled him up so badly that when he actually confronted Vince McMahon, he physically attacked him! (More on that later!)

Anyhow, at the end of that match at *WrestleMania IV,* Rick Martel put Smash in the Boston crab. Just when you thought we had them beat, Ax hit Rick in the back of the head with Mr. Fuji's cane as the ref was distracted by Fuji picking a fight with me.

Another reason we were dropping the belts was one that we really couldn't avoid. Rick had asked for a leave of absence to help take care of his wife, who was very sick and needed him there.

MORE ON WRESTLEMANIA IV

The highlight of *WrestleMania IV* for me obviously didn't come in the ring, but outside it. Backstage that night, I met legendary middleweight boxer Sugar Ray Leonard!

The locker room was packed with celebrities and special guests again. Vanna White from *Wheel of Fortune* was there, but she was coated in make-up and too skinny for my likings. I'll just say that she looked better on TV than she did in person. (You know I like my women with a little meat on them. ¡Arriba!)

But again, Sugar Ray was really the big draw for me. I didn't know it at the time, but he was a huge professional wrestling fan. Despite the fact that he was a lot smaller than all the wrestlers, we knew he was one tough SOB and could kick a lot of the boys' asses in the locker room.

I got to know him one on one that night and enjoyed our conversation. He was very impressed with the vigourous training that wrestlers had to go through and our skill set in the ring. Coming from a champion, those words meant a lot to me.

After that, Sugar Ray started attending many of our events, and I would run into him some on occasion. He really is a class act.

NEVER A HEEL

The fans figured we were robbed from our belts, and they wanted us to win them back. That sense of moral justice rallied our fan base. Vince knew exactly what he was doing. He made his best money when good and evil feuded, and the fans sided with the good. So, for the next few months, we battled Demolition. We also had matches against The Hart Foundation, The Bolsheviks, and The Islanders. Once again, though, due to an unfortunate situation, this run came to an end.

An illness in Rick's family was taking him away from wrestling for nearly a year. I tried to talk him into working some around it, but knew that family was family. He decided it was more important for him to stay at home and tend to the sensitive situation.

Come July 1988, Rick was simply written off TV with an injury angle at the hands of Demolition, after taking their filthy finisher on the floor.

This "injury" would split up the team of Strike Force for many months and moved me back into singles competition.

Now, I had never worked heel, but really, really wanted to and heard an opportunity where that could maybe happen for me. I knew that Rick would eventually return and one of the buzzings in the locker room was that they would break us up when he did. However, what I was hearing in those whispers was that after our break up, some were saying it was Rick who would turn against me.

Like I mentioned before, quite often, I would ride with the heels. Granted, in the time of kayfabe locker rooms, we weren't supposed to be seen together, but that didn't stop me. I would just go down the block and wait in a gas station restroom for a few minutes, then meet up with guys like Muraco, or Bob Orton, or Demolition. Hearing all the fun they had heeling, I just wanted a shot to try it myself sometime in my career, and I thought I could do a really good job at it myself.

"So, I hear you may be breaking us up?" I asked Vince one day after a production meeting before a show.

"Well, I don't know just yet," he said.

"Not that I have a problem with it or anything," I said, knowing it is better to have a conversation with the boss, rather than a confrontation. "It's just that I thought maybe it would be interesting if maybe we through a twist at everyone and turned me heel."

Vince stopped and scratched his butt-chin. I could see the wheels turning, but I wasn't sure if they were creative wheels, or just the wheels he turned to give a political answer.

"I mean, I'm sure the idea is likely that Rick will go heel, but I think it might be interesting to make him the face and consider me for a heel run."

"Interesting," he said. "Maybe we will consider it. Thank you, Tito."

But as you likely may know, that never happened. They stuck with the original plan, and I missed the opportunity. However, I guess it is also a cool thing that very few people have ever been just babyface their entire career and I am in really good company. One of the only other big names they ever say this about is my fellow "blood" brother, Richard Blood a.k.a. Ricky Steamboat.

I had a bunch of singles matches while Rick Martel was away. They had me stay dressed in the tag gimmick the whole time Rick was off so people wouldn't forget, because the plan along was we would jump back into something. And that we did.

SURVIVOR SERIES 1988

On Thanksgiving night in 1988, André the Giant, Rick Rude, Curt Hennig, Dino Bravo and Harley Race defeated my team including Ken Patera, Jake Roberts, Hacksaw Jim Duggan, Scott Casey and myself.

I was eliminated by André, after he sat, yes *sat*, all of his 500 pounds of giant ass on my chest.

I thought I was literally going to be smooshed to death!

Almost twenty years after scraping me off the mat with a spatula, I see four of the five wrestlers in that match who I fought against have passed away. André died of natural causes. Dino was murdered by the mafia, and both Rick and Curt died from substance abuse.

As a side note here, the fast life and problems in wrestling really caught up with a number of the boys. The abuse of steroids, painkillers, alcohol and other drugs damaged wrestlers' bodies, ended careers; and even sometimes ended lives. It is often sad to look back, today at what some of them once had.

WRESTLEMANIA V

The two of us would reunite again soon when Rick made is return to the Royal Rumble in 1989. When Rick returned to the WWF, we reformed Strike Force and just continued where we left off. The wrestling world was our oyster.

We quickly regained momentum and won a tag team title shot against the Brain Busters at *WrestleMania V*. Tully Blanchard and Arn Anderson were a talented team being managed by one of my all-time favorites, Bobby "The Brain" Heenan.

This one took place on April 2, 1989, at the Boardwalk Hall in Atlantic City, New Jersey. The special celebrities included Donald Trump, Morton Downey, Jr. and Run-DMC who performed a WrestleMania Rap that was especially fresh.

Mania that year was the setting for the breakup that I had heard was coming. So when I saw the finish written on the posted card that read, "Santana accidentally hits Martel with a flying forearm," I was not surprised.

Around 15 minutes into the match, I "accidentally bumped into Rick." Rick played off his reaction perfectly and was very condescending, like I had hit him on purpose. When it played out in the ring and Martel came to, he walked out of the match leaving me alone in the ring to fend for myself.

I took a pretty good beating before they finally decided they had enough fun with me. After the Brain Busters delivered a spike-piledriver, they took the belts and that was it. Rick was gone. What I didn't know at the time was he actually was not planned to return as a heel. He was actually not planned to return at all. He was walking out of the company altogether after putting in his notice!

What I learned later was Rick wanted the heel turn even more than I did and is the one who actually created the buzz I heard of our "possible breakup" in the first place.

See, sometime before that match, Martel had a secret meeting with Vince. He wanted to break off of me and become a heel character so badly that he actually gave his own boss an ultimatum. As for his strategy, I guess he went in there and acted like he was completely tired of tag team matches and ready to just hand in his notice! Vince McMahon thought he was bluffing and tried to talk him out of it using his Jedi mind tricks as usual, but Rick stayed firm.

It supposedly looked something like this…

"I want to go back as a single competitor," Rick said. "I am tired of tag team matches, and I want to change my style a little bit, too," (meaning turn heel.)

"No, no, you guys have a great thing going," Vince said. "People like you the way you are."

Vince didn't want us to change and thought there was still more money in us as a team. He wanted Rick to stay with Strike Force and wasn't listening.

"Well, I'm sorry Vince," Rick said, "But if you don't want it this way, maybe somebody else will," he threatened. Then, Rick went back to the hotel, called the office and formally put in his notice, because his contract was about to expire after the PPV.

So when Rick walked out on me in the storyline at *WrestleMania V*, he was actually also walking out on the company. Not one to be threatened, Vince was going to let him go. He said something to Rick along the lines of, "I'm sorry you feel this way, but the WWF doesn't need Rick Martel."

However, his holding out strategy worked. Two weeks after the walkout and refusing to sign a new contract, Vince gave Rick a call.

"Okay, Rick. Come back and let's talk," he said.

I guess what had happened was the fans' reaction to the break up was much bigger than Vince thought it would be. He didn't anticipate Rick's leaving would have the impact that it did and realized that there could actually be money in his idea now. Therefore, he went with it.

The promos began. In the days and weeks to come, the answer as to why Rick Martel waked away was answered. He explained that I was "riding his coattails" and was "sick and tired of carrying me.

The fans hated his selfish words, and we feuded for the next year. During that time, he turned into Rick "The Model" Martel.

Rick was like me. He worked mostly babyface his whole career. So when he came back and people started booing him, he was not used to it. It was the first time he had ever heard that. I was a little jealous that he got to experience it instead of me, but I was also happy for him. His career took off from there in a different way. We still got to work together which was cool, just with him on the other side of the ring now, so it was hard to be so jealous as to not like the guy.

Both of us would chalk up victories over each other in a 50/50 booking-type scenario. I got a pretty good win over Martel in the final of the *1989 King of the Ring Tournament*, and it served that bastard right for turning against me! ¡Arriba! But then Martel beat me later that year at the

Survivor Series via pinfall in the first elimination of the opening match of the night.

People have asked why I kept very similar tights/gear as to what I wore long after we broke up. Well, the spandex was fresher and cleaner looking than the old polyester jobbers that I wore in the 70s & 80s. I felt like it also made me look younger so I stuck with it. Being a babyface for the majority of my career, wearing white only made sense.

Our feud was decent, but it eventually died down after Survivor Series. After that, we would occasionally get booked against each other in matches on house shows here and there until it just fizzled out. Any time we would cross paths somehow on a card say in a battle royal or something, for fun, we would always rekindle the feud and not let the fans forget.

Around this time, Vince decided that while I didn't have a whole lot of character push, maybe he could use me to help other guys get over. He considered me to have a wealth of knowledge so he encouraged me to pass the torch a little as a mentor. That is when I got an assignment to start training the Warlord. He had an awesome look but was still relatively green. Vince really saw something in him so I started driving around with him to shows and coaching him.

WRESTLEMANIA VI

In a match that had no real build up or storyline, I lost to The Warlord's partner The Barbarian at *WrestleMania VI* in front of 67,000-plus fans at the SkyDome in Toronto.

The Barbarian, whose real name was Sione Havea Vailahi, was a nice guy from the South Pacific island of Tonga (King Tonga was also from the same island.) I thought he was one of the strongest guys in the territory. He had an awesome look and along with his partner, the Warlord, they had a good tag team gimmick called The Powers of Pain. They never won the tag-team title, but The Barbarian had a long career in both the WWF and WCW.

The highlight of the evening for the fans, of course, was The Ultimate Warrior defeating Hulk Hogan for the heavyweight belt. But for me, one of the more memorable matches of that evening was Dusty Rhodes and his manager, Sapphire, against Randy Savage and Sensational Sherri. The mixed tag-team match was won by Dusty and Sapphire, with a little help from Miss Elizabeth. I always enjoyed watching Dusty and Sapphire dance in the ring after their matches. Dusty was just horrible, but in a great way! It was a train wreck that you just had to look at because it was so awesome.

Unlike "The Macho Man," Dusty came unto the WWF with an impressive track record. He was a booker and main event talent with the Crocket promotion in the South, where he was incredibly popular in the state of Florida. His feud with Kevin Sullivan in the Sunshine State was the stuff of legend. Dusty had lots of charisma and drawing power, and Vince had no problem bringing him to the larger stage in New York.

But Dusty's transition to the WWF wasn't a smooth one. When he signed on, Vince stacked the deck against him with making him wear huge the ugliest gear he could imagine. Some saw it as a rib, others as an act of humiliation, and yet others saw it as a challenge.

There had been plenty of banter between the WWF and Dusty's promotion on the South when Dusty was the booker there. So when Dusty, a former-competitor to the

WWF finally showed up looking for a job, I think Vince intended to show Dusty who had the power, and that WWF was the premier wrestling company in the world.

Dusty, a huge recognized name all over the world with an already defined look, debuted in a polka-dotted costume. Vince aligned him with an overweight African American woman manager, Sapphire, who had no real experience.

In my opinion, Dusty turned a negative into a positive. He did what he had to do to work for the number-one wrestling company, and because of his talent, he got the gimmick to work in his favor. He was a great character, and he really understood how to work the crowd. Since he was another West Texas State graduate, I was very proud of him for being able to make chicken salad out of chicken shit, as they say in wrestling.

I enjoyed my time working with him, despite the fact that he often roamed the locker room butt-naked. As much as I liked Dusty, his bare ass in your face when you are trying to lace up your boots was not a pretty sight.

He was a comical guy though, for sure, and he was a credit to the professional wrestling industry.

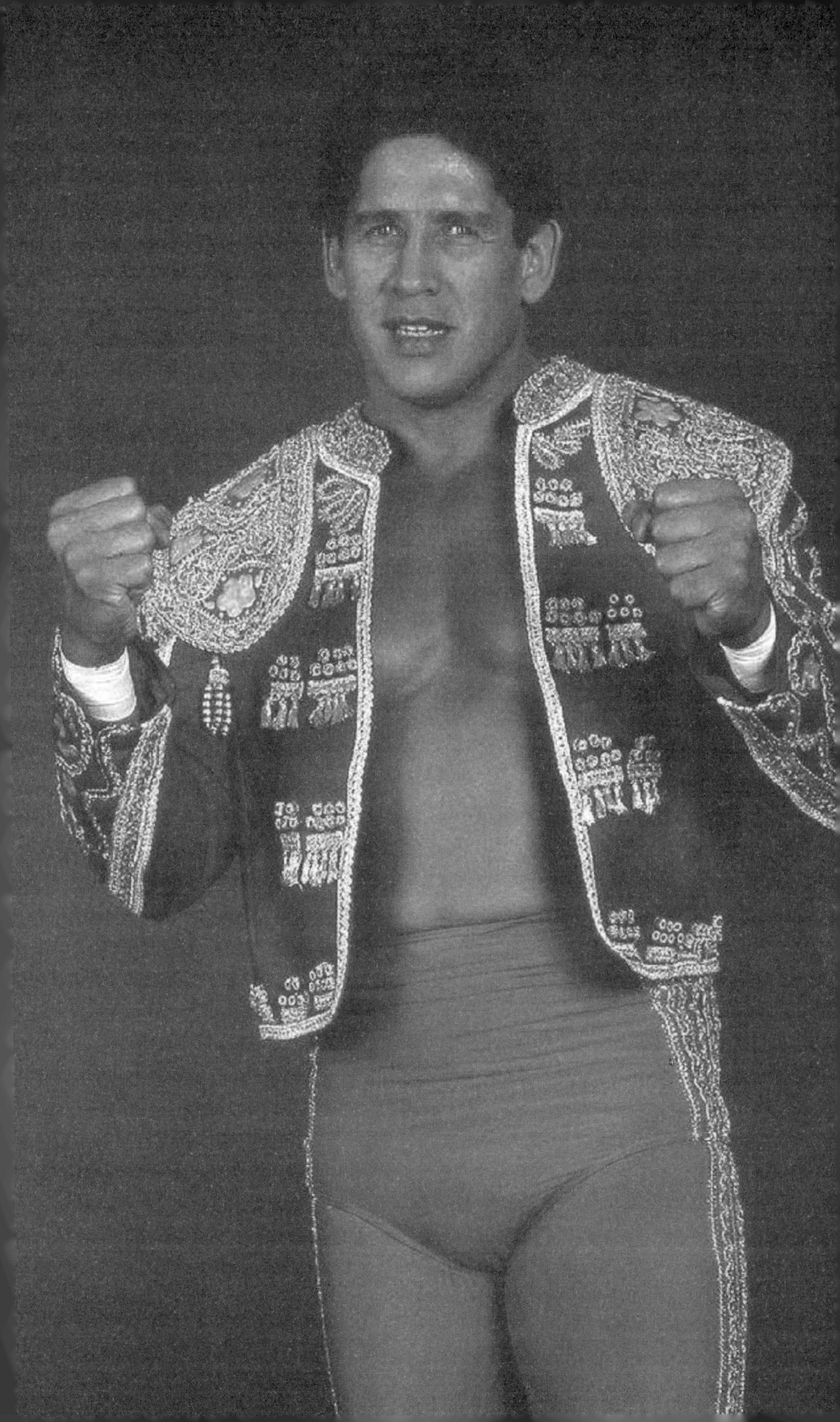

CHAPTER 19 - EL MATADOR

After 'Mania in 1990, things slowed down. I felt left out in the cold again. I was not getting used much at all. I was basically only making appearences as an afterthought, or a substitute maybe on cards.

The look that Vince was searching for continued to evolve. Vince still wanted everything larger than life, but not just size. He wanted all of his wrestlers to be jacked now, too. The days of just being tall or big in general were over. To be successful in WWF, you had to have a more muscular look, which was something I didn't quite I have. Don't get me wrong, I was in great shape, but I think at this time, Vince felt my look was no longer sufficient.

Because I wasn't jacked body guy, it felt like maybe I was getting pushed to the sideline.

Now, I had worked many years for the company, and always gave it my all. That rejection hurt me but forced me to finally accept the fact that in the wrestling business there was no such thing as loyalty.

I worked out hard and lifted weights, stayed away from drugs, and didn't get into any trouble. I did what the company told me and never disrespected anyone. Yet all of this meant very little in the end. When it came right down to it, Vince was all about making money and looking to the future, not the past. He had a vision for the WWF, and that vision apparently didn't include me.

Toward the end 1990, I was getting more and more bummed. My pay had dwindled down to half what I was making, and I was barely ever featured on WWF programming. I was again ready to give it all up and retire.

One day I had had enough waiting. At a TV taping in Toledo, Ohio, I told Vince that I really needed to talk to him. He took me into a quiet room, and we sat down.

"Vince, I appreciate all you have done for me, but I think I am ready to finish up my career and leave the company."

CHAPTER 19 – El Matador

After exchanging pleasantries and thanking him for the good times, I let him know that I was just simply unhappy and had discussed everything with my wife.

He nodded and listened.

"My mind is made up. I think it is time for me to leave the company and move on to the next chapter of my life."

After listening to my reasons, Vince had something to say. I don't think he really had anything for me in mind, but he also didn't really want to see me go.

"Tito, you have always been a great employee for us and of great value," he said unexpectedly. "So we are not finished with you yet."

Using an imaginary sliding scale to explain my value to the WWF, he held his hands up in the air and explained to me that my career had always found me in the top half of the scale. He had never brought me below the halfway mark. That was not his intention.

"I have actually been throwing some ideas around for you," he explained. "And I had this new idea to create a fresh character for you which I want to call … The Matador."

He went on to explain that the new character would continue to play up my ethnic roots and appeal to the Hispanic demographic while giving me a chance to rise to stardom in a new role.

The idea sounded like a good opportunity for me.

As far as the actual idea of this new character, it wasn't just something Vince pulled out of his ass last second to try to salvage me and stop me from leaving.

"The Matador" concept actually originated in the creative but twisted mind of Dick Ebersol, who used to produce the *Saturday Night Main Event* show for the WWF. Well before my meeting with Vince, Dick had told me that he had pitched this gimmick to Vince. However, Vince never bit on it.

If Vince had acted on Dick's suggestion at the time, it wouldn't have been "Vince's great idea." He liked to be the creator and take credit for the stuff you would see on his programs day in and day out. This stroked his ego, I think.

So if he had used "The Matador" idea when it was first pitched, he wouldn't get the credit. However, by the time Vince suggested this so-called "new" idea to me, Dick was no longer with the company. That made "The Matador" idea all his.

I was no dummy. There was no way I was going to tell him I knew that Dick came up with the idea for the gimmick.

"This idea sounds great, Vince!" I said.

Vince told me to learn as much as I could about real life matadors, but to keep the idea between the both of us for the time being.

I did as I was told.

I remember going to the public library in my free time to research matadors and prepare for my rebirth in the WWF.

THE WAITING

Now, I don't know if Vince was serious about the gimmick or just trying to keep me around because he felt bad for me, or what? But the gimmick didn't happen right away. It didn't happen right away at all. While I was studying to become El Matador, I just continued to wrestle in my normal gimmick, Tito Santana.

Not to nag the boss, but every three weeks or so, I would hunt him down at the TV tapings.

"So Vince?" I would ask. "Do you think it would be a good time soon to launch the character?"

Vince always had a good excuse to put the debut of "The Matador" off. He would cite some storyline that was going on or some new angle that was already in the works. Whatever it was, it was something that had to happen first, before the new character could happen and have time to breathe.

Clearly, the idea of "The Matador" was not the very top of his priority list.

I kept waiting. I kept wrestling for the company and waiting for my new spot, but was demoted to the very bottom of the pecking order!

CHAPTER 19 – El Matador

Every time I asked him, Vince made it very clear that when I came in as "El Matador," I would be a brand new character that he would build into a superstar.

But after six months had passed, I was still wrestling solely as Tito, and I started having my doubts.

Why would he do this to me? Why is he stringing me along? If he is not going to go with the new character, why not just let me go?

Finally, my waiting paid off. One day, I went up to Vince at a taping to see what was happening as I often did. As I approached him, he was nodding yes at me even before I got to him.

"Good to see you, Tito," he said. "Or should I say, *El Matador?*"

After that, I nodded. "Yes, yes!" I said shaking his hand. I was then informed in October 1990 that the upcoming Survivor Series would be my last match as Tito Santana.

1990 SURVIVOR SERIES

Now, the pay-per-view franchise itself, Survivor Series, was originally created as an alternative for cable companies who were planning on booking with Jim Crockett promotion's Starrcade. When Vince's biggest threat decided to throw his hat into the PPV market a few years before this one, Vince gave the cable providers an ultimatum.

"If you book Starrcade on Thanksgiving night, we will not make WrestleMania available to you."

No Mania if we book Starrcade?! You got it.

Cable companies knew where the money was and that was in New York. So they were ready to oblige, however, they asked Vince for a WWF PPV option they could buy instead.

Now, Vince's favorite holiday was Thanksgiving. He loved to throw parties with massive feasts the day before that holiday and have everyone pigging out. Therefore, he didn't really want to offer a big event on a holiday, but he had backed himself into a wall so he felt he had to.

In the same vein as Pat Patterson coming up with the very popular gimmick match, *The Royal Rumble*, Vince wanted to create a cool gimmick that the yearly Thanksgiving PPV could revolve around. That is when he came up with the whole idea of "Teams of five work to survive" elimination gimmick match.

For the *1990 Survivor Series*, this would be the first one with "an all stars match" at the end, meaning all the survivors of each match would battle at the end in one giant match with one final survivor. That was about all the commentators said on television. It was all very vague. Many thought it would have been a battle royal, but it was a big tag match with heels and faces, and it ended up with Hogan and Warrior winning so it was a bit of a letdown. What they really should have done was to have their partner take it all! More on that soon... ¡Arriba!

This particular edition of the Survivor Series opened with a dark match for the fan before it officially aired nationally on television. It was Buddy Rose vs Shane Douglas. Now, I have talked about Buddy being funny in a gross way in the past. It was not long before this that he was spraying diarrhea in a locker room in Japan all over the walls, and dragging in wrestlers to see his masterpiece. The reason my *WrestleMania One* opponent was back was he recently pitched something called a "Blow Away Diet" to Vince after a show at a Denny's. Vince thought it was so funny he would give it a shot. (The idea was to air a commercial for a fake product that allows you to eat whatever you want and just put a powder on your body and the fat blows away.) Playboy loved making fun of his weight. He used to carry around a scale to show he weighed 217 when he actually was around 300.

There were a lot of memorable things at this event. First, I might as well start with the elephant in the room, *er*, should I say *turkey*?

The Gobbledy Gooker was actually one of the most anticipated and hyped part of that evening. For those of you who don't know what I am talking about, this year's Survivor Series started by showing a giant egg, hyped heavily on

CHAPTER 19 – El Matador

WWF programming in the weeks leading up to the big PPV. Commentator's promised that the world would find out what's in the egg at big pay-per-view event on Thanksgiving. For weeks, people wondered who was in the egg. One of the biggest predictions was that it was Ric Flair!

When Survivor Series finally aired, all was revealed. "Mean" Gene Okerlund, the voice of the WWF in the 1980s was there for the hatching to call play-by-play. When the egg finally did break open, nobody in the crowd at Connecticut's Hartford Civic Center could believe what they saw inside; someone dressed in a giant turkey costume!

Earlier in the day when I got to the arena, I saw Hector Guerrero. It was great to see him because he was a great guy, but I can't say that I was a little nervous. My role as the link to the Hispanic audience had been dwindling, and I have to be honest when I say I was a little worried for a second when I saw Hector. He had taken up gymnastics and was able to do all these flips and all, and I was worried that he was maybe there to take my spot. However, when I saw him backstage putting on a Turkey costume, I knew my spot was just fine!

It was a massive flop. The idea was to have Hector as The Gobbledy Gooker become a mascot for the WWF, not unlike The San Diego Chicken in baseball. The Gooker was going to go up in the stands and dance with the kids and all. However, the hatching debut didn't translate well on TV. Hector couldn't see well enough in the costume covered in feathers to do the moonsaults and flips that would get him over, so he and Mean Gene just danced around the ring. It was the shits and everyone shit on it.

Besides that mess, this marked the last of Demolition as fans would remember them. In their promos, they started to wear black masks and they were becoming a threesome. (Crush would be added to the mix.) What happened was Bill Eddie, Ax, had health issues and a heart condition. Many state commissions wouldn't license him to wrestle, so Vince wanted him to manage. This insulted Bill who was a proud man to some degree, and he would soon leave the promotion because of this after this event.

Another tag team was also on the outs. It was the swan song for The Hart Foundation because, after this, Bret was going to be ushered into singles competition.

Another change showed Dusty Rhodes somehow convincing Vince by this point to allow him to wear smaller red polka dots down the side of his tights and a top hat with an eagle claw. But in the same match that Dusty was in, it is more worth of note to mention that there was an empty WILD CARD slot on the opposite side because Bad News Brown suddenly left the company.

To fill in for Bad News was a new comer they called "Kane The Undertaker". The name "Kane" lasted two weeks after the PPV but The Undertaker himself has lasted even until this very day with the company.

Brother Love a.k.a. Bruce Prichard managed The Undertaker that night in his debut and was very instrumental in Taker's look. The idea was Taker was to be Brother Love's henchman and look like a polar opposite of him. Soon after this, Prichard was offered to either become the full time manager of The Undertaker or take an office job. He took the office job allowing Percy Pringle to debut as Paul Bearer and the rest is history.

Even though The Undertaker was an instant hit, there was at least one person who didn't like his debut. I remember seeing Koko backstage complaining after he took the tombstone, bitched him out backstage and saying to anyone who would listen that he "dropped me on my head."

For my match with The Mercenaries, this was one of the last times I would be seen in my old gear. It seemed like someone actually put a little thought into how the classic Tito Santana character that I did for so many years go out.

It was always great when they would book a guy leaving and give subtle nods to a wrestler's past history. Sometimes they would do this by having us work with former opponents of past feuds/promotions that were no longer or never mentioned on WWF programming. It was great when

CHAPTER 19 – El Matador

they did little things that only real fans would notice, and that is just what they did with this match. I was booked to work with Sarge, DiBiase, Martel and even Warlord when the night was all said and done. (The only real guy missing was Greg Valentine who had just dyed his hair to team with Honky and didn't look the same, anyhow.)

First, I teamed with my friend Nikolai Volkoff and the Bushwackers versus a newly heel "Iraqi Supporter" Sgt. Slaughter with the Orient Express & Volkoff's former Bolsheviks partner, Boris Zhukov.

I eliminated Zhukov and Tanaka using my flying burrito forearms and became the sole survivor of our match when Sarge was disqualified.

I then moved forward into the "all stars" main event final match. I was set to wrestler against Hercules, Paul Roma, Rick Martel, Ted DiBiase and The Warlord with my teammates Hulk Hogan and The Ultimate Warrior!

The reason for this sudden push back to the top of the card was to keep me looking strong for the El Matador repackaging I was about to endure.

In that final "Sole Survivor" match, I eliminated The Warlord (the same guy I was actually helping to mentor) before being eliminated myself by my old buddy, Ted DiBiase.

In the end, Hulk and Warrior were the last ones left after the smoke lifted and the dust settled, but being booked in the main event did boost my spirits.

Maybe they really will do something with me!

On the night of the PPV taping, I also found out from the office that the final phase of my training for "The Matador" gimmick would be held in Spain.

Excited about the news, I remember telling Koko B Ware after hearing him complain about his stiff piledriver.

"Get this, the WWF is sending me to an actual school for matadors, which means I think I will end up in a real bullfight!"

"Holy shit," he said, still selling the first ever and not perfected-yet Tombstone piledriver.

"If they are willing to pay to have me do all that, maybe this is finally going to be a big break for me that I really need."

Koko was rubbing his head and I scratching mine.

Is my time almost here?

CHAPTER 19 – El Matador

Unlike The Honkytonk Man, a wrestler who was supposed to be a musician who couldn't sing or play the guitar, Vince wanted me to be authentic. He wanted me to know everything there was about bull fighting.

Unfortunately, things didn't work out for my trip to Spain, so instead, I was scheduled to train for bullfighting at an organization in Mexico City.

In the meantime, I was back to wrestling as my regular Tito Santana character.

WRESTLEMANIA VII

My match against The Mountie at *WrestleMania VII* ended in a disappointing fashion for me but built a lot of heat nonetheless. In less than two minutes, he pinned me after shocking me with his cattle prod taser. I would have liked to have worked the match longer, but I thought the finish made sense to the buildup of the night's story.

I have known The Mountie, French-Canadian wrestler Jacques Rougeau since he and his brother Ray signed with the WWF in the mid-1980s. I thought the pair of babyfaces made a very good tag team combination. When his brother retired, Jacques took on the gimmick of The Royal Canadian Mounted Police. I never expected The Mountie to be a good gimmick as a singles wrestler, but Jacques was persistent and it worked. He played the role perfectly and drew major heat wherever he went. For him to successfully turn into a hated heel with tons of heat, it was a total surprise.

Our match that evening was small potatoes compared to the main event between Hulk Hogan and Sgt. Slaughter. *WrestleMania VII* was held in March 1991, when the United States was waging war against Saddam Hussein and Iraq. Vince parlayed reality into a wrestling angle. Despite some negative mainstream press, fan-favorite Sgt. Slaughter turned heel and simultaneously betrayed his country. He spoke poorly of his country and talked of becoming an Iraqi sympathizer. Vince even gave him a manager, General Adnan (Sheik Adnan Al-Kaissy), whose appearance and mannerisms were meant to resemble Saddam Hussein.

I remember Sarge calling me one time during the buildup of this whole thing that started back around the end of 1990 when we had some much appreciated time off for the holidays.

"Tito, the fans hate me," he said.

"That's great, Sarge," I said. "Right?"

"No, well, I don't know. Yes and no," he said. "Vince just had a whole huge laundry bag of hate mail from the fans delivered to the house."

"Wow," I said. "Well, what are they saying?"

"There are actual death threats in there!"

While the original idea was to have Tugboat, Hulk Hogan's friend turn heel on him to face him as the big main event of the year, Vince shifted to capitalize off of news headlines to get heat on the event and it absolutely worked. People actually wanted to kill Sarge! Now *that* is heat!

It is important to mention that sometimes there is good heat and bad heat. *WrestleMania VII* was at first supposed to be held as an outside show at the Memorial Coliseum in Los Angeles. However, at the 11th hour, it was moved to the smaller Los Angeles Memorial Sports Arena.

The company told the media the reason for the event change was that it had received threats from people upset about Sgt. Slaughter's apparent allegiance with Iraq. Whether that reason is credible or not, I think there was another reason; *low ticket sales.* For wrestling, the Memorial Coliseum in Los Angeles had enough seating for 90,000 people. Some of the agents shared with the boys that ticket sales weren't going so well. The Sports Arena has a capacity of only 16,700 for wrestling. It turns out, *WrestleMania VII* only drew about 16,200, enough to make the smaller venue seem sold out.

To me, I think that the reason for the poor attendance had a lot to do with the overdone U.S. - Iraq angle. It was initially a good short-term program, but it quickly ran its course because people were legitimately angry with what was going on in the world, so much so that they were fed up and turned off by it.

CHAPTER 19 – El Matador

The Gulf War began in August 1990 and for intents and purposes, it was over in a matter of weeks. American forces won decisively and easily, and the actual war ended shortly before WrestleMania. But Vince didn't want to pull the plug on the angle. To his credit, Sgt. Slaughter did a great job with the angle and his character. Yet it was inevitable that the American hero, Hulk Hogan, would eventually win the belt back. Everyone knew it. So why attend the marquee match if the outcome was predetermined?

In my opinion, the company exploited the war. Sgt. Slaughter had come into the company years earlier as a heel and received instant heat because of his ability and expertise at ring psychology.

All along, Sarge told me that he was uncomfortable with the Iraqi sympathizer gimmick. Because of the negative heat he initially received from the public with the gimmick, he had to continuously watch his back. There were some crazy people out there. Fans damaged the cars he rode in, and some even made personal threats to him. Still, as a testament to his professionalism, Sgt. Slaughter stuck with the gimmick and made it all work.

MATADOR IN THE MAKING

By 1991, the WWF had begun to branch out into Europe, doing more business with those countries and organizing tours there a couple of times a year. It was a brand new market for us, one that made lots of money for Vince. The huge European arenas got WWF programming on their TVs and were starved to see a show in their area. That is why they would always sell out in a matter of hours.

I received the news that my matador training class in Mexico was postponed. I guess one of the bulls got sick, so they decided to use me overseas.

I was sent to Europe for seven days in April 1991. I performed as Tito Santana, wrestling in London, Manchester, Berlin, Brussels and Barcelona. It was a nice trip, but very unfulfilling for me as I was wrestling in preliminary matches of little consequence. I didn't get a chance to do any sightseeing, either.

The younger guys went bar hopping every night. I mean, they were in Germany so drinking was pretty much mandatory, right? They invited me to go with them, but I just couldn't keep up. I was still stressed over the whole Matador bullshit (pardon the pun) and rest was more important to me. (It was just too hard for me to have fun and relax when my future was still so uncertain.)

In early May, I went to Japan for another week of wrestling. J.J. Dillon, an ex-wrestler who had retired from the ring, was sort of acting as a foreign ambassador for the WWF. He had been around about twenty years and had also managed other wrestlers, most notably the Four Horsemen faction. Despite his experience, Dillon had the worst personality. To be blunt, it was tough for him to be nice to anyone, which made him a puzzling choice to represent the company.

On a bus travelling to a town in Japan, J.J. Dillon came over to my seat and pushed me over. I thought it was odd because he wasn't all that much of a social butterfly, but I obliged.

"I just got word from Vince," he said. "that after the tour of Japan, you are off to another one."

"Uggg," I said. "I just did Europe."

"Well, this one you will like, I think," he replied. "Next you will travel to Tijuana, Mexico."

I sat up in my seat. In less than two weeks, that meant I was off to start my matador schooling!

It was a huge relief to know that I would finally be able to complete my transformation to El Matador and begin to work the gimmick.

J.J. left. I sat back in my seat and closed my eyes. I listened to the cars out on the road outside and tried to sleep. My mind began to wander.

Deep down inside, it hit me. I was praying and praying to do this gimmick, but I actually wasn't very comfortable becoming a gimmick wrestler!

CHAPTER 19 – El Matador

It was weird. Since I had spent so much of my career wrestling as a normal guy, I really didn't know how I was going to fare playing a character.

With my eyes closed, I tried to imagine myself in the role probably for the first time. I heard the horns playing the Bullfighter's song, "The Paso Doble." I heard the roar of the audience. I pictured myself walking out into the sand of the arena and holding up a giant cape. I swung it around and around and around. I imagined the crowd going wild.

¡Olé!

I pictured bowing and then dozens of roses being thrown to my feet.

What the fuck am I getting into?!

I laughed to myself, before dozing off to sleep.

Well, if that is what the boss wants, that is what he is going to get.

¡Olé!

TRAINING

In Mexico, I learned as much as I could about the matador from a man named Maestro Jesus. He was a very small man but had been a matador nearly all of his adult life. He was a very patient instructor, which I both appreciated and needed.

We practiced at a ranch in the middle of nowhere. There, using man-made bulls as my opponents, I practiced all the techniques of a matador,

Like wrestling, I learned that positioning was a big part of it. I also learned that there were certain moves you needed to know for your own safety. I studied special bullfighting maneuvers with my cape. I also learned how to handle the *banderoles*; the two lances that a matador uses to stick into the bull's neck before using a sword for the final kill.

By my third day there, it was time for an actual bullfight. I went down to an arena where the event was being thrown. It was complete with a live crowd and an amateur matador who was ready to stand in as my stunt double.

The event that we went to for shooting footage drew a good crowd, and afterward, I went through a procession with other matadors in which we were introduced to the fans. Of course, I wanted to take a few passes at the bulls, but Vince McMahon made it clear that he did not want me to take a chance. So I did not get too close to the bulls. From what I saw, they were a scary sight.

The footage for the vignettes was to be cut and pieced together for TV in a way that made it appear as if I were the one fighting the bull by the end.

I have always admired matadors, who are greatly skilled and fearless men. I remember as a kid, my dad took our family to see two bullfights when I was very young. Back then, I remember being in awe of the bullfighters, who truly were considered to be heroes in Mexico and Spain. As ironic as it may sound, now that I'm older, I just don't see the sport in killing a tired bull. It's simply inhumane.

With my training complete and the footage ready to go, it was time to see if wrestling fans (many of whom had appreciated me as Tito Santana) would take to El Matador in the same way.

MY DEBUT & SID'S

El Matador was supposed to be introduced at the *SummerSlam 1991*, but that didn't happen. Shortly before the event, I was told that another superstar in the making by the name of Sid Justice was also to be making his debut at the event.

We agreed that it wouldn't be fair for either one of us if we were both making our debut on the same night. So I had to wait while Sid, a huge wrestler at about 6-foot-10 and 340 pounds, made his debut.

Sid had a reputation for having a bad temper that preceded him, hence his eventual nickname Sycho Sid. Vince had been warned about Sid's hostile behavior by Hulk Hogan and a few others, but Vince always felt invincible and liked a good challenge. Therefore, he thought he would have no problem trying to tame him.

CHAPTER 19 – El Matador

Sid got the royal treatment at SummerSlam. He had such a good look to him that the general idea was that Sid could have been the one to replace Hulk Hogan. Eventually, the two would go on to fight each other in *WrestleMania VIII*, but after that, things didn't pan out for him as planned. He stuck around for less than a year before getting fed up and quitting for reasons that were really unclear.

At the time, the WWF had played some damage control. They had everyone thinking that Sid had just walked out. Then, the boys found out through the grapevine that he had been suspended for testing positive for steroids. Sid's manager Harvey Wippleman confided in me that it was indeed a positive steroid test that had caused his departure.

After that, Sid went back to the WCW where he had come from, but he didn't last long there, either. Sid had just been resigned to a big WCW contract, and after a few beers, he began bragging about his money. Arn Anderson, who was more experienced than Sid but had never made that kind of money, took it hard. One of them hit the other with a chair across the head, and somehow that led to a stabbing involving a pair of scissors. He was fired after getting into a seriously bloody fight in a hotel room that night with Arn Anderson.

Sid later returned to the WWF, but he never became a star like Hogan.

AIRING OF THE VIGNETTES

About three weeks after *SummerSlam '91*, J.J. Dillon showed up on the scene.

"Your time has come," he said.

I was ecstatic, to say the least. I was happy that I would finally have the chance to introduce the matador gimmick to wrestling fans.

In the two 30-second vignettes, both produced by Vince, it was very much like my daydream in that bus in Tokyo. In the first, I talked about the origins of El Matador.

My second vignette showed me entering an empty bullfighting arena with glimpses of what could be. They dubbed in my own voice overs reading from a script that Vince put together explaining my journey.

"In order to excel to the heights I wish to achieve in the World Wrestling Federation, I know there is something I must do. I must return to my native land. I must stand before my peers. I must look into the eye of the bull. I must come as close as possible to the menacing wreck of horror. I must know the thrill of the charge of a 2,000 pound beast. I must hear the adulation of my fans. I will become the very best that I can be in the World Wrestling Federation! I will become, El Matador!"

It was perfect. I had no more worries about playing some ridiculous cartoon-like character and not being able to pull it off. My transition to El Matador was an easy transition for fans to accept because of one primary reason; I remained Tito Santana. I didn't transform into some weird character. Instead, we were just adding the El Matador tag to my name; *Tito Santana, El Matador.*

In the third vignette, they used footage of an actual bull walking into the arena. I remember when we shot that, that my trainer Jesus explained the danger of the horns and the bull's ability to inflict severe harm.

"Tito," he said at the time. "You see, the more danger that is involved, the more that bullfighting fans will appreciate The Matador."

After hearing that bloodthirsty detail, it seemed that wrestling and bullfighting were not that far off.

The following week, Vince released another vignette that focused on the advanced training that I had gone through to become a matador. Wrestling fans witnessed my mounting confidence as I practiced on a mechanical bull that charged me. As I eluded the bull, I stuck him with a pair of *banderoles* on the back of the neck. My trainer drove home the point that "one simple mistake could be my last." He also praised my agility, noting that most matadors were small men; that I was so talented at my size and "it was quite an accomplishment."

We put a lot of time and effort into the fifth vignette. In this particular one, I was shown completing my training and

CHAPTER 19 – El Matador

returning to my fictional hometown in Tijuana, Mexico, where I would perform in front of my own people. A fiesta was held to celebrate the event.

In the sixth and final vignette, I was shown fighting an actual bull. Of course, the piece was edited to make it appear as if I were battling the beast, but I was not. It was my double.

All in all, the vignettes worked out much better than I had ever expected. Fan mail was coming in from around the world and it was clear that the fans, after following my extensive training footage clips on TV, they were all ready to get behind me.

November 1, 1991, was established as the new debut date for El Matador. For the first match, I wrestled Hercules Hernandez. We were pitted against each other several times during my initial tour. Hercules was an old veteran and people liked him, so it was tough for him to play the role of heel. The fans also wondered if I was going to remain a babyface or turn heel. I remained a good guy, a trait that I maintained through my entire career, a rarity for a wrestler.

My first few matches in Pittsburgh, Milwaukee and Moline, Illinois, were tough. Not until my fourth night in Denver did I get a good response from the crowd. I had been putting a lot of effort into this character but had yet to receive the big push that Vince had promised me. There was no way El Matador was going anywhere with that push.

The positive reception from fans continued while touring in California. The reaction from the predominantly Hispanic crowd in both Oakland and San Diego reassured me I was on track for success. But I was still not getting much play on TV yet, and after some investigation, I learned there was nothing really planned for Matador merchandise.

No shirts. No dolls. Nothing was designed. That let me know where I stood with Vince for the moment.

I was upset. I thought about pushing the issue with Vince but knew fighting him on the issue of merchandise wasn't going to do me any good. Because around this time, someone else was doing the same thing and getting nowhere.

Around this time, I was summoned to a court case for a deposition by Bill Eadie (Ax of Demolition,) who was suing Vince.

Demolition split up around 1990, and Bill became just one of many wrestlers who had been more or less forced to quit the WWF. He moved on to the independent circuit, but he soon found a reason to bring the fight back to the WWF. Promises had been made to Bill that weren't kept, and he wanted some justice.

The WWF had stopped paying him all royalties from the merchandising of his dolls, games and video tape appearances. From my recollection, I don't think Bill recovered anything from Vince. In turn, he was buried even further from the eyes of the company.

Not wanting to fight that battle for myself, I decided not to complain about the lack of merchandise. I made up my mind to just do such a kickass job with the character that they would have to put merchandise out.

ALMOST WORLD CHAMPION

There was a rumor that late into 1991 and well into 1992, Vince McMahon was seriously considering replacing Hulk Hogan and bringing up a new champion; one who could reach and connect to an international audience and, subsequently, one who increased tours in those areas.

The Hulkster was on his way out. He had just taken a leave of absence from the WWF due to the recent steroid scandal and he also was creating more Hollywood commitments. As he was attempting a career change, he was taking up more and more acting roles.

Ric Flair was the champion around this time, but he too was on his way out, so Vince would soon not be able to use him as a crutch for the promotion. You see, Ric had given a massive notice so that he could leave the company on good terms. He was feeling homesick for the Carolinas and WCW and told them months ahead of time that he was ready to leave the company once his commitments to Vince were done.

That is was when Vince got an idea. "Why not make our new champion younger, and one who could help pull in more international ratings?" His question to the others around the booking table was two-fold, "But just who and where?"

To the north was Canada, a country that takes its wrestling seriously. That was the obvious first option. He had a relationship with promoter Stu Hart and his rigorously trained sons, and access to a whole host of others who proved tough enough to survive the legendary Hart Dungeon. Vince already had ties to Canada country anyhow. He had already absorbed Maple Leaf Wrestling and was been using that promotion's former booker, Jack Tunney, as the WWF figurehead "president" authority for years.

While north made perfect sense, the other thought was to target the south. The idea was that since the WWF already had a strong presence in Canada, maybe they could tap Central and South America. Hitting an entirely different continent would be sailing in uncharted waters.

From my driving Mil Mascaras days in Houston, I got my Lucha Libre history lessons. I knew that it was no secret that fans south of the border not only take their pro wrestling so seriously that it was almost a religion! Guys like Mil were literally treated like movie stars because they were movie starts. El Santo was actually in more movies than James Bond!

It was no secret to Vince and the office that the Latino fan base was one that revered wrestling so much that it would have been a mistake to at least not think about trying that avenue.

Both north and south were considered worthy areas for Vince's envisioned international champion idea, and expansion. But who would become the new center of attention? Who would become the new main draw?

After years as a member of the successful Hart Foundation tag team with Jim Neidhart, Bret was an obvious choice. He had been working as a singles competitor. Like myself, he had a great run with the Intercontinental championship. He had proven he could headline a major PPV, having great matches with guys like Curt Hennig, Jacques Rougeau, and his brother-in-law, Davey Boy Smith. Bret would do very well in Canada for the promotion.

For many years, Bret was a middle-card worker and he didn't make a lot of money. We often chatted in the locker room, and I always remember that every tax season he barely had enough money to pay his taxes. Yet he too was loyal to the company, and he never complained about his spot. He followed the rules, learned the ropes and waited for a good amount of time before he finally got his break.

On the other hand, I was the best choice for Vince in the event that they had decided to target the Spanish-speaking markets in Central and South America.

I remember, one day before a show, Pat Patterson came up to me on the side and told me all of what was being said in booking meetings about expanding either north or south.

"And Vince has decided, for now, it is one of two people," he said. "It is between either you, or Bret."

WHAT IN THE HELL?!

Now, at this point, I knew they were thinking about international expanding, but I had no idea I was even in the running.

When all was said in the booking committee, it came down to two contenders. *Bret The Hitman Hart and me?*

Pat told me Vince had not forgotten all my hard work for the company. Being one of Vince's main draws in the mid-'80s, he had not forgotten my big feuds with Don Muraco, Greg Valentine and Randy "Macho Man" Savage, and my run with Rick Martel with the tag team title.

The reason it was such a shock to me was simple. The past few years had not been all that great for me. I was just a few notches above enhancement talent on some nights, getting other wrestlers over at my expense.

CHAPTER 19 – El Matador

"Vince knows that returning as 'El Matador' was not your choice, but you have been making the best of it and having some really great matches."

"Thank you, Pat," I said.

"Not to mention you are a likable guy, a veteran who has the respect of the locker room. Vince believes respect you can work a good match with just about anyone."

"With a new push and some key wins here and there, Vince could very well have his new champion right under his nose!"

Sometimes when the agents come to you with promises and getting your hopes up, you can smell the bullshit from a mile away. *They want something.* However, at this point in my career, I don't really know what the endgame would have been for stroking my ego. And, immediately after my chat with Pat Patterson, things did begin to change that lead me to believe that I was, in fact, being considered for the biggest run of my life.

Vince must have decided that more money was to be made south of the border over a bigger push of the product in Canada. El Matador was winning on television more frequently, and it looked like right when my career was winding down, it was moving into a revival.

I started beating mid-carders. I beat guys like Hercules Hernandez, Kato, The Barbarian, The Mountie and even Ted DiBiase.

Whenever WWF went to a Spanish-speaking country, I was got a huge pop. That meant I was huge in Spain, and both Central and South America. So you can bet that whenever we were in Spanish speaking countries, Vince was watching the fan reaction response and listening.

The WWF went on a European tour and one of the stops was in Barcelona, Spain. At the time, I was just about to start wrestling as El Matador on TV. Since we were in Spain, my gimmick went over well with the fans. In fact, the WWF was so hot in Barcelona that I was set to headline against The Undertaker in front of a record 55,000-plus crowd in the Estadi Olimpic Luis Companies Stadium.

This was a much more fun time in wrestling when the Internet wasn't around. No Internet meant they could book totally differently for foreign crowds and test things out; nobody in the States would be any the wiser. So, on Oct 5, 1991, in Barcelona, it was Tito Santana vs The Undertaker. In the end, I kicked his zombie ass and won! All kidding aside, this was a big deal for me. The audience went wild. They couldn't believe their eyes. I was actually one of the very first guys to get a victory over The Undertaker, if not the first one to beat him by pinfall.

During this time, The Undertaker's was just starting to get a major push, too. The Undertaker became a credit to the business. He is an extremely nice guy who I can't say enough good things about. He has been in the wrestling business since 1984, had that awesome WrestleMania streak, and is still going strong to this very day!

I will say this, however. Tito Santana has an undefeated streak against The Undertaker! ¡Arriba!

For a full year after that victory, I was climbing the ladder again and really showing promise. My stock in WWF had raised.

I even had a match with Ric Flair for the WWF World title. Curt Hennig (who was out on an injury and not wrestling in the ring at the time) was actually managing Flair at the time. We used him quite a bit in that match to keep me looking strong. In case a feud was to bud out of this, I needed to look good while Vince continued to test the waters on whether the WWF was to sail north or south.

But, as you know, it just wasn't in the cards.

Vince did a complete 180 from what I believed was his original plan. After reconsidering the money he thought he could potentially make from investing in a full Mexico and South American expansion, he changed his mind.

After some figuring, he realized that south was not the answer. It was hard to get the TV production crew across the borders, flights were not as easy to handle, and the value of the peso was also the shits. Vince realized that a Canadian expansion be much easier.

CHAPTER 19 – El Matador

So one day, Pat came to me again in the locker room and said, "Vince made up his mind. I know it took a long time for us to finally make a decision. It was really close. You almost got it, but they are going with Bret."

Would be lying if I was to say I wasn't disappointed. I was crushed by the news but tried to take it in stride, telling myself that business was business. I personally felt that I had the ability and talent to carry the torch for the company just as well as Bret, if not better. Nothing at all against Bret, but I had worked a lifetime and was never offered the same opportunity.

You know the rest of the story, Bret got a rocket strapped to his back. With all this momentum, he went on to become one of the greatest WWF World Champions of all-time, having legendary feuds with Yokozuna, Steve Austin, The Undertaker, and Shawn Michaels.

As for me, I immediately went back to losing. It was like night and day. Looking back, you have to wonder how different the WWE would be today had Vince stuck to his guns and targeted the uncharted waters with me steering the boat.

How would my push have messed up Bret's career? Would the Montreal Screwjob ever have happened? Would Bret have never gone to WCW? Would "Mister McMahon" have become a TV personality? Would there be a birth of "Stone Cold" Steve Austin? And if the last two never happened, would the WWF have ever won the Monday Night Wars?

I know. I know. These questions are very fanboy. You know, like "Who would win if Spiderman fought Batman?" crap. It's the Butterfly Effect. If one event in wrestling history changed, it could have set off a radically different sequence of events, leading to a completely different future. Without Bret getting the title, there are all kinds of crazy hypotheticals that could even have led to the demise of the company.

One thing is certain. With me finally leaving the WWF for good in 1993, Vince did me a favor. Seeing how all the other WWF champions ended up, I don't regret it one bit.

He did me a favor; *I didn't get divorced.*

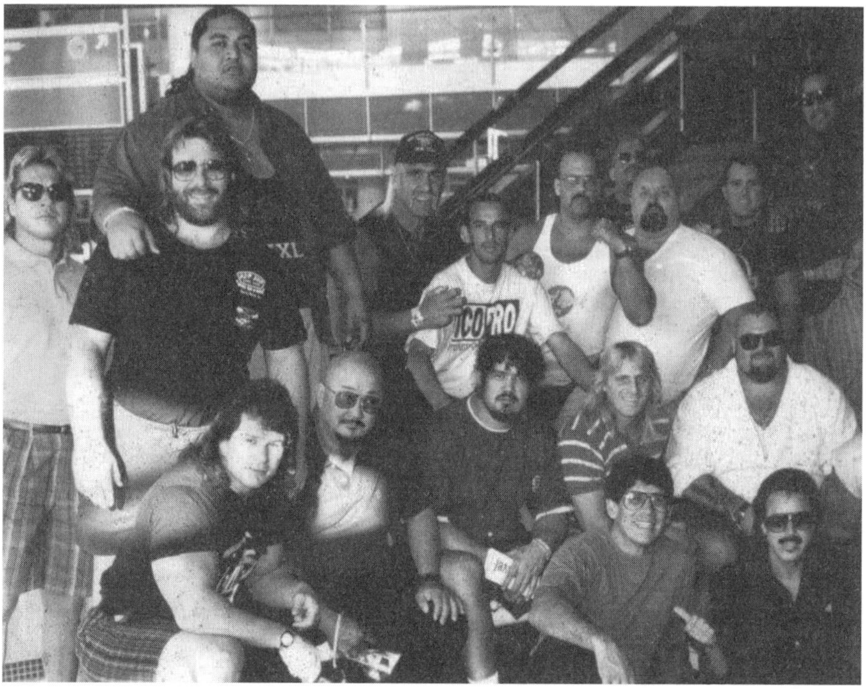

CHAPTER 20 - TAKING THE HEAT

Before I left the WWF, a bunch of crazy stuff was going down, and people worried about jail. Ironically, Nailz was an ex-con character created for the WWF by Vince around the same time. One day Nailz, whose real name was Kevin Wacholz, had a grueling argument with Vince that ended with Nailz taking down Vince and choking him. I happened to overhear the whole thing. I know a lot of people have talked about this before, but I will now tell you what I know about the topic and SMASH any rumors!

SMASHING NAILZ
My friend Barry Darsow (a.k.a Smash of Demolition) had heard that Nailz was pissed about some kind of payoff and figured he had no right being pissed because he was brand new. So what he did was he got a hold of Nailz one night as a rib, and he decided to get his goat.

"How much did you say he was paying you?" Barry asked. "Man, you are really getting ripped off. I wouldn't stand for that!"

So he riled him, riled him, and riled him up some more. He riled up Nails so bad that when he actually confronted Vince McMahon, he was going to be a mess.

Speaking of messes, on December 14, 1992, it was me and Virgil versus the Headshrikers, Samu & Fatu. I had just shown up early as I always had to The Expo Center in Green Bay for a WWF television taping when I heard some yelling down the hall, so I went to investigate.

I walked into a pretty good size dressing room, pulling my gear bag behind me. Vince McMahon was already there and sitting at a table. He was there with big Kevin Wacholz, whose skin was so steaming red, you could tell there was a problem, so rather than to hang out, I turned around and headed to another dressing room. However, I didn't go too far. I really just went around the corner so I could hear what the commotion was all about.

I look over to my right, and there is Ted DiBiase doing exactly the same thing I was doing - eavesdropping.

"*Shhhhhh,*" Ted whispered putting his finger up to his lips. He laughed like kile a schoolboy.

I nodded. We both knew that Barry was the cause of this, and we both had excellent seats to see what the outcome was going to be.

"Come on, Nailz," Vince said, always liking to use the name he came up with when talking to a wrestler.

"So, what the hell is this?" he asked, slamming his Hasbro action figure on the table.

"That is a toy," McMahon said, picking up the doll from the table where it was still sitting.

"I know what it is!" Kevin said. "A toy I never saw any money for, but I let that slide. But now, now I get my payoff for SummerSlam and it is way less than everybody else's."

"Nailz, maybe we should talk about this somewhere else," Vince said.

The Steiners were there. Kamala, Tatanka and Scott Hall were there, too. More wrestlers were starting to show up just as I had. The confrontation was in a high-traffic area and Vince didn't want Kevin losing it in front of the whole WWF roster.

"Just before you got here, he threw a chair at the lockers," Ted whispered.

"Oh shit," I said.

Tony Garea, Arnold Skaaland and Chief Jay Strongbow started to clear the locker room out after seeing how angry Kevin looked. Most of the wrestlers were leaving on their own the moment they saw what was happening. They didn't want to be any part of the action.

"And now you want me to take another drug test?" he asked. "You have them nurses look at our dicks every night. You sorry son of a bitch. Let them look at yours."

"We can talk about the drug tests later. Why don't you go get ready for the taping?"

"No. I want $100,000 more."

There was a long pause, but Vince didn't talk.

"You gonna give it to me?"

"No. We never agreed on that."

CHAPTER 20 – Taking The Heat

"Then there's nothing more to say. I'm out," Kevin said all quiet, turning slowly to walk away.

There was another long pause. Ted and I figured it was done, so we started to walk off ourselves.

The next thing I heard was commotion. Another chair went flying, and all of a sudden Nailz shouted, "He grabbed my balls! He grabbed my balls!"

Ted and I came back around the corner to see Tony Garea, Arnold Skaaland and Chief Jay Strongbow all running to Vince's defense.

Kevin was on top of Vince throwing haymakers.

The agents all meant to grab Kevin and pull him off. However, when they got there, the three older men all chickened out. They had good intentions to help but were all afraid of how angry Kevin had become and didn't know what to do. Rather than grabbing Kevin, they looked like they were grabbing each other like Scooby Doo does to Shaggy when a ghost is about to hand them their asses.

Before we got there, my man Sgt. Slaughter and The Berzerker were running in to break up the fight. It seems they were doing the same thing that we were doing, listening on the other side of a corner!

After the fight was finally done, Kevin grabbed his stuff and stormed out of the building.

After that, people say that Kevin called the police department to get his word in first, just in case Vince had decided to call the cops on him. Kevin filed a police report accusing Vince of sexually harassing him and touching him inappropriately.

Likely what happened was Kevin attacked Vince, and Vince fought back dirty and hit him below the belt in self-defense. Looking at big Nailz, I would have done exactly the same thing; nailed him right in the nuts and bolts! ¡Arriba!

A few months later, Kevin was booked to work against Sting on a WCW show. Rumor had it that Eric Bischoff marked out when he heard the story of Kevin Wacholz choking out McMahon, so much that he immediately signed him to face Sting at *Slamboree 93.* When PPV match started, the ring announcer said he hailed from Green Bay,

Wisconsin because that's where he beat up Vince. Billing him as "The Prisoner," in the end, Kevin lost. The match was so bad that they never used him again.

I never heard who was assigned to pay Kevin off for that match. Hopefully, Barry Darsow didn't talk to him first!

THE BAD GUY

Just before I left the WWF, the name "Shrug Shadow" was being tossed around behind the scenes for a new character coming in.

Shrug Shadow? What the heck does that even mean?

One thing for sure, it doesn't sound like the name of a professional wrestler.

When Scott Hall left WCW in 1992 and came to the WWF, he had been doing a Scarface impersonation to pop the boys. They would drive from town to town, and he would sometimes do his crazy impersonation at drive-thru windows, or do the voice when he checked into a hotel to make the other wrestlers laugh. It was a total lift from the Al Pacino movie, but the people he used the voice on didn't really know.

When Scott Hall finally had his meeting with Vince McMahon about what he would be doing for the company, he did the voice and won him over. He managed to convince Vince that a Scarface-type character would do well. Vince gave the gimmick the green light, and the search began for a name. The first option that Vince came up with was Shrug Shadow, of course! Fortunately, Shrug Shadow never came into fruition. Road Warrior Hawk then chimed in with 'Deadbolt', a not-as-awful name, but one that still didn't fit the character.

Scott Hall, I think, was working some house shows with us, and one night he came into the bathroom part of the locker room when I was about to go in and do my business.

"Hey, Tito," he said. "I need some help with a name."

"Just a second," I said. I knew Scott from my AWA days. He was a good guy so I was happy to help however I could.

CHAPTER 20 – Taking The Heat

"See, I think I have the first name," he said. "I'm thinking about using 'Razor' for the first name, but need a good Latino last name. Can you think of one?"

Now, I didn't want to be rude, but I really had to take a leak. "Just a second. I have to take a piss, and that will let me think about it a little."

"What do you think of the name 'Razor' for my gimmick?"

I laughed. "I really have to go! I'll be right back."

When I came back from the urinal, I washed my hands, and Scott was waiting for me.

"So?"

"How about Ramon?"

Scott smiled. "Razor… **RAMON**."

"I like it," I said.

"Me too. Thanks, chico! You are the best."

Chico?! Hey, wait just a minute!

And that was it. The name was chosen from one chance meeting at the urinals. Not too long after that, Razor Ramon was born.

SHAWN MICHAELS

As I have probably mentioned somewhere before, usually the heel controls the match unless you are a vet. In a series of matches I had with Shawn early on, I let him do it the same as I let Macho do it, even though I had some years on him. I did it, of course, because I knew he was good, but I also knew if he got lost, I could just guide him back.

Shawn, however, was really arrogant and sometimes unappreciative of anything you gave him. Other than his little posse, he really was not liked backstage. Most of the veterans and a lot of the new guys saw how selfish he was. Aside from his shitty attitude, he did "have the goods" so we all had to put up with him.

Come *WrestleMania VII* on April 5, 1992, at the Hoosier Dome in Indianapolis, Indiana, I was taking on Shawn Michaels with his manager Sensational Sherri. To open the show, country singer Reba McEntire sang a rendition of "The Star-Spangled Banner." As I entered and

Reba left, I extemporaneously kissed her on the hand. It got a big pop and Reba was a good sport. However, who I really should have kissed was Sensational Sherri! ¡Arriba!

Sensational Sherri was a very successful female wrestler and as tough as any man I have ever known. She was the only woman wrestler to work in all five of the major wrestling companies back then: WWF, NWA, AWA, WCW, and ECW. She held the WWF Women's Championship belt and would even be later inducted to the 2006 class of the WWF Hall of Fame.

Unfortunately, at one point in her life, she was married to a Puerto Rican man who physically abused her. She told me she eventually got fed up with him and beat him to a pulp with a frying pan. She literally left the guy on the floor of the house to die. Because of the experience with her ex-husband, Sherri said she developed a dislike for Hispanics, but claimed that still liked me. "I was different," she said.

Whenever I saw her, I would tease her a lot and make light of her dislike for Hispanics. Before the match at Mania, I hunted down Sherri backstage.

She was actually always fun to work with. Whenever I saw her, I basically said the same thing. I didn't compliment her on her hair or say I liked her outfit. I would hit her with the exact same line I probably did a hundred times before.

"Hey Sherri," I said. "*Oooohh* baby!"

"Never in a million years, Chico."

It was always the same response, but at least I had to try, right?

At the beginning of our big match, there was a stare down. I was supposed to make eye contact, but it was a very difficult thing to do because his nose was stealing the heat.

"There's a booger in your nose," I said over the 62,000 screaming fans in attendance.

Shawn walked away and then came back.

"Did I get it?" he asked.

"You got it."

If you don't believe me, look it up on the network and read my lips. ¡Arriba!

CHAPTER 20 – Taking The Heat

It was great to be able to bust Shawn's chops, and hopefully, knock him down a level with those in the know.

When Vince decided to push Shawn Michaels, he completely changed his boy-band looking gimmick and transformed Shawn into this "Boy Toy" heel character, "The Heart Break Kid." At Mania, I was asked by Vince to help get Michaels over with the crowd as a singles wrestler, and I had no problem acquiescing to the request because despite his bad attitude, he was really, really good in the ring.

My match against Michaels at *WrestleMania VIII* catapulted Shawn on to an Intercontinental title shot against the champion, Davey Boy Smith. In October of 1992, he beat "The Bulldog" to win the title. It was the first of many singles championships for Shawn. My only regret is that we didn't wrestle much against each other. He had great abilities in the ring and our styles complimented each other well. I think we could have made a lot of money together.

It was just too bad that he was letting the fame go to his head at the time.

One time, we had just taken off for a European tour. We were flying out to Glasgow, Scotland, and I was sitting in seat 4D of the plane. I was looking at a magazine and there was some kind of crossword puzzle. I got out of my seat a second to get something to write with from the overhead compartment. When I turned around to sit back down, I saw that Shawn Michaels had jumped in my seat.

"Shawn, you are in my seat," I said.

Shawn shrugged. He sat back and chewed his gum like a little asshole pretending not to hear me.

I wasn't going to play his games. I saw a stewardess and tapped her on the shoulder.

"I think there must be some mistake," I said to her. "But this kid seems to be in my seat."

The flight attendant asked Shawn for his ticket. When he couldn't produce it, the stewardess, asked him to move. Shawn stood up and then stormed somewhere to the back of the plane like a spoiled brat.

When I sat back down, it wasn't even five minutes later before I felt the annoying pressure of someone's knees in my back of my chair and moving. If you have flown before, I am sure you know what I mean. I ignored it for a few minutes until it was obvious that his motion was intentional.

I turned around, saw that it was Shawn and shook my head. Shawn somehow managed to trade for seat 5D directly behind me.

"Don't you ever talk to me like that again," he said.

That was it. The straw that broke the camel's back.

"Or else what?" I replied.

Shawn said nothing.

"Shawn," I said. "I hate to inform you, but I will kick your fucking ass. This is not wrestling where they will tell you who is going to win."

He laughed.

"You think it is funny, asshole?" I said. "Wait until you get off this plane. You won't be laughing then."

"Lighten up! Calm down."

I knew I had him scared. He didn't talk to anymore for mostly the rest of the trip, hopefully worried that he was going to have a "flying burrito" for lunch when we landed whether he wanted one or not.

He just snapped at the wrong guy at the wrong time that day. I'll admit it. I was cranky and tired, and not in the mood to take any crap that day. Shawn quieted down when I told him I would kick his butt. After we landed we made up, so everything was cool.

Travel could really beat on us all. We were like kids in a way, arguing and fighting with each other all the time. We usually just laughed it off in the morning, but not always.

Now you know why The Rockers eventually broke up. Once Shawn really started to get a head on his shoulders, he was intolerable. Couple that with a tough road schedule and nobody wanted to put up with him. When he started to pull that shit on his own partner, Marty wouldn't tolerate it.

Marty would just kayfabe his nonsense, then would wait until they got back to the hotel room that night and ambush him when he would least expect it for revenge.

Marty had his number. He used to beat Shawn up a lot in hotel rooms.

MARTY THE PRANKSTER

Unlike Shawn Michaels, who I was not a very big fan of, Marty Jannetty from The Rockers has a great personality and was a very likeable guy. But, man oh man, he liked to pull pranks on people.

For one, he loved to party with girls. One of his famous pranks was waiting for them to pass out, shaving their hair off and draw faces on their bodies with permanent markers.

Once on a plane flight, Marty was sitting next to three college kids. They knew he was a wrestler and were bragging about how much they could party more than a wrestler.

"Oh yeah?" he asked. "You really think you can party harder?"

Calling their bluff, Marty gave them all a drug called GHB, which then was a legal powder that bodybuilders used to burn body fat. Taking GHB on an empty stomach would knock a person right out, which is precisely what happened to these partiers.

When they came to, you would have thought they were sitting next to Brutus "The Barber" Beefcake, not Marty Jannetty. All of their eyebrows had been shaved off, and half of their heads were bald, all compliments of Marty Jannetty.

On another particular plane flight, a group of wrestlers, including me, were sitting near a loud-mouthed guy. The jerk had clearly been drinking too much and was insulting all the wrestlers. He kept challenging us, saying that he was tougher than all of us, saying that he could kick our asses. He went at it over and over, and only finally shut up when he passed out, and fell asleep.

That was a big mistake.

When the poor guy woke up, he was greeted to a horrible smell. Stealing a page out of Mr. Fuji's book, Marty had left the stranger a gift; his lunch, fully digested in this guy's lap.

Yes. There was a full brown, glistening turd chilling on this guy's leg.

The stranger was pissed!

"Who did this?!" he screamed! "Who did this?!"

We all laughed but nobody was saying shit, pardon the pun.

"Whoever did, I am going to shoot you!" he said. "You hear me? I said I am going to shoot you!!!"

Verbally threatened to shoot whichever wrestler had done him wrong was probably not the best move to do at an airport.

When we landed, security was alerted to the situation, and they were waiting for the guy right outside the door. They detained him and brought him to security.

It turned out, the crazy man had just been released from prison. Then, when security searched his luggage, lo and behold, they found a loaded gun!

When Shawn and Marty finally split as a team, it was likely because of Shawn's greed and sick of Marty beating on him behind-the-scenes. After feuding against Shawn for a while, Marty was fired shortly thereafter.

Despite the pranks, Vince saw something in Michaels. At the time, Shawn's big push was considered to be a big prank by some of the boys because of Shawn's unprofessionalism. However, deep down, I knew that he was very talented and that sooner or later he would grow up and get focused. And I was right.

In the end, the joke was on us. Shawn eventually cleaned up his act and became a legitimate superstar.

A GIANT LOSS

André the Giant passed away in January of 1993. It was a very sad day, and he is very missed. Vince had looked around a little to find a replacement for him, but how could you really do that? André was really one of a kind!

CHAPTER 20 – Taking The Heat

Vince continued to look around and, one day, he actually saw another wrestling giant on WCW television. This one was a legitimate 7-foot-6 and weighed close to 450 pounds.

Jorge González's size (particularly his height) was his original ticket to America, as the NBA's Atlanta Hawks scouted him and brought him in to see if he had any talent. He had already been playing pro basketball over in the European leagues when Ted Turner (owner of the Hawks) sent scouts to the UK looking for new players. They scooped him right up, paid him, and brought him over for preseason games. Jorge had already been playing basketball for several years by this point, so his knees were already starting to go on him.

He had talent, but his knees just didn't hold up well to the rigors of NBA basketball, and because of that, he never ended up playing season games for the Hawks. He would play hard for about three minutes, but then his legs would start to give out on him and he needed to rest. The Hawks cut Gonzalez after spending big bucks to get him in shape but proposed to shift their investment over to another Turner-owned company, WCW.

Jorge was under contract with Ted Turner, however, so someone came up with the idea of salvaging the find by shifting him to one of his other programs on his network. They decided to try to make him into a professional wrestler.

Gonzalez initially refused the proposal and flew back home to Argentina. After calling him at home and offering to pay even more to train him as a wrestler, he agreed.

After a year of training, González was introduced to WCW fans as El Gigante on May 19, 1990, at the Capital Combat pay-per-view. Wearing shorts, he competed as a fan favorite and billed as being close to eight feet tall.

Working for WCW, he had to have a personal assistant while here, and the man tapped for the job was WCW referee Bill Alfonso. Bill explained that Ted Turner always had to put him up in a really nice hotel because he was just so big. He really needed a giant bed. When a van wasn't available where a seat could be removed, the only car they could rent to fit in was a Cadillac, and even then, his knees were buckled up to his chest.

"It was just me and him traveling around the world for three years, which was pretty cool because I got paid to do it. We became terrific friends, super friends."

Over the next two years, El Gigante feuded with Ric Flair for the WCW World Heavyweight Championship, participated in a Chamber of Horrors match in 1991, and also had a scrumptious date with Missy Hyatt. He wrestled other big guys like Sid Vicious and One Man Gang who both stood at around 6'9" to determine just who the real giant of WCW was. He also participated in a cross promotional stint with New Japan Pro Wrestling. Then he got the call from the World Wrestling Federation WWF in 1993. After his stint at WCW as El Gigante, Jorge was being romanced by New York to become their new resident giant.

Jorge had some pretty giant shoes to fill taking over for André, though. Vince told him he would turn him into a superstar, and to his credit, Vince tried his best. He started by hiring his WCW helper, Bill Alfonso, as a referee and to stay on as his assistant. Bill would continue to handle his day-to-day concerns and coach him on what he needed to do to be successful in wrestling.

"Jorge was a good athlete on the court, but not much of a performer in the ring at this point. It just wasn't a natural fit for him to be into wrestling, because he had never seen it or even heard of it, before these bookings," Bill says. "He absolutely had to have an assistant with him 24 hours a day. He was a giant. He was almost eight feet tall and just couldn't go any old place he wanted to. He just didn't fit!"

Jorge grew out a beard, wore a full body suit that featured airbrushed muscles with bushy hair attached, and was managed by Harvey Wippleman. Giant González debuted at the *1993 Royal Rumble* eliminating Wippleman's nemesis The Undertaker. At *WrestleMania IX*, Gonzalez knocked out the Undertaker using chloroform, losing the match by disqualification. He lost again to The Undertaker at SummerSlam, and after the match, he turned against Wippleman and turning babyface in the process. His last appearance was on October 4th's *Monday Night Raw* in a 20-man battle royal match for the IC championship. Three days later, his contract expired and he was gone.

Giant González got all kinds of TV buildup, but it just wasn't enough. He just couldn't get it done in the squared circle anywhere near as well as André did. His bad knees just didn't allow it.

The funny thing I remember about Jorge is how much he could eat. If we went to dinner after a show, it would take three entrees to fill his stomach, so he would order three different meals. It was incredible to see him put it all down.

Bill Alfonzo also told me that Jorge's metabolism would burn through that massive meal and his stomach would come calling for more in the middle of the night. He would regularly call Bill almost every night around 3 a.m., to have him go find the nearest burger joint. There he'd get him three double cheese burgers to quench his giant appetite.

SCANDALS

The WWF overcame some unreal obstacles during my stint with the league in order to keep a lot of potential scandals from erupting. It seemed to me like every month brought with it a new scandal. If you stop to think about it, that is really not surprising.

There were at least 60 wrestlers on the road at any given time. Many of those wrestlers were on a big-time ego trip and hopped up on drugs, booze, or steroids. One can imagine the sort of havoc we could wreak. As hard as we were working in the ring, we were also often working double-time outside the ring to keep our brutal professional lives from wearing us down.

The WWF was doing well, but then there were obstacles. There were sexual allegations, drug allegations, and even office personnel accused of transporting minors across state lines. Vince was accused of a sex scandal with a female referee. A group of wrestlers appeared on TV shows with Geraldo Rivera and Phil Donahue stating that certain higher ups at the WWF demanded sexual favors for career advancement. Worst of all, Vince has been accused of distributing steroids to his wrestlers.

Some things were true, but a lot was not. There was enough though that WWF was making tabloids every day!

MEL PHILLIPS

Did you ever see any **FOOT**age old angle where Terry Funk beat up the ring announcer for putting on his hat while collecting gimmicks to bring back to the locker room? He was an African-American ring anoucer who often wore a brown suit. If you did, that guy was Mel Phillips.

Mel Phillips was on a number of early WWF shows. He was in charge of the ring crew for a time and had a number of other organizational duties. Before shows started, I would come into the arena to check out the ring. There, I often saw Mel Phillips in the ring with his collection of local "ring boys" he brought to the show to help set up chairs and the whole deal. Wherever the WWF went, Mel Phillips added to his list of teen helpers from broken homes and troubled backgrounds. In return for free tickets and sometimes free t-shirts, he had these kids help set up the ring, sell programs, and get coffee for the wrestlers.

I never really thought much of it when I saw him play wrestling with the kids. I actually thought he was just cool to hook them up. He seemed to be trying to give something back to the community.

Come 1992, a former ring boy eventually decided to step up and finally talk about his time working with Mel. Tom Cole was a boy who helped Mel set up rings, getting his start around 13 years old.

Tom Cole alleged that Mel Phillips had a fetish for young boys' feet! He said that when they finished setting up for the show, Mel would initiate quick wrestling matches with the boys to "test the ring." During these tests, Mel would eventually stop wrestling, pull off shoes, go for a "toe hold," and then "suck their toes" as his finisher.

Wait a minute. Suck their toes? What in the hell?!

Cole said Mel wasn't the typical type of predator who would just stick his hands down your pants like everyone else. He was way more inventive.

Cole said Mel would playing with your toes but try to make you believe you were still wrestling. He would pretend that the toe-sucking was a joke, however, it was obvious in hindsight that this was not the case because the punchline just never ended. The problem was, these "test matches" lasted too long, they were practically iron man matches with no time limits! He would appearently put on a "toe-hold" with his mouth for so long that it just wasn't right. Cole said he would "play with your foot for like a half hour!"

Fortunately, WWF officials didn't tread lightly on these charges. Phillips resigned in March of 1991 and nobody since has seen heads, nor tails, ...nor feet, of him, either.

STEROIDS

Early in 1992, I was out on my way to California for an eleven day tour when one of the boys told me that that Hulk Hogan was getting grilled by the media over steroids.

I guess "Superstar" Billy Graham and "Dr. D" David Schultz were both guests on a TV talk show. They were talking about steroids and its use in professional wrestling. Graham and Schultz both threw the Hulkster under the bus, pinning all the blame on him and the media took notice.

As a fellow wrestler, I felt sorry for Hulk. As successful as he had become, the man had a good heart, and he cared for other people. He had done a lot to help a lot of us earn a living in wrestling for so long. In my opinion at the time, he was the only WWF wrestler who was worth every cent he received.

After an FBI investigation, something happened. The focus shifted over to Vince because it turned out that there was a doctor on staff that he used for his shows in PA who helped some of the boys get drugs that were illegal.

On February 15, 1994, I received a call from Vince's secretary asking me to contact Vince's lawyers. The FBI had been investigating Vince for about two years in relation to steroids being distributed in the WWF, and his role in the matter. He was scheduled to go to trial in May. I had heard tons of rumors, including that Hulk was supposed to be the FBI's main witness all in a case against Vince.

In a deposition, I was asked, "Has Vince ever asked you, or anyone else, to take any steroids?" My answer was no. I went up to Vince myself and asked him if I should be doing anything else to improve my body. His answer was, "No, you look fine." I also told the lawyers that Vince had brought up steroids in one of our general meetings, telling all of us that we didn't need to use steroids, that our positions within the WWF weren't determined by appearances.

The lawyers were after the truth, period. They pressed me about steroids, and I told them over and over, "No, I never took them, and Vince never asked me to use them."

It still went to court.

During the actual trial, Vince's wife, Linda, became CEO of the WWF. This way, if Vince lost the case, he also wouldn't lose the company.

In the case against Vincent McMahon, the questionable doctor, Dr. Zahorian, was brought to the stand. There, he went into detail about how he ran a steroid operation inside the doors of the WWF. Zahorian said that, as the medic for the Pennsylvania Athletic Commission, he would take the wrestler's vitals to make sure they were fit enough to perform in the ring, but that is not all he did. The wrestlers would walk into his "safe room." He would put down the stethoscopes and hand them personalized brown paper bags filled with steroids, or even the drug of their choice, in return for cash.

They argued that Vince found out about this and allowed it to happen in his locker room. It was alleged by the prosecution that Vince preferred Zahorian's white-collar distribution over his wrestlers just getting their steroids through some other dangerous back alley drug dealers.

Some allegations stated Vince purchased a product for himself, as did his road agents Chief Jay Strongbow and Arnold Skaaland. This proved he knew. However, the doctor said that Vince and his people had nothing to do with it and that "WWF officials were never in the room."

After that, another one of the prosecutor's key witnesses was called to testify, to try to nail down Vince to the charges. It was Kevin Wacholz, a.k.a. Nailz!

He was called to testify against Vince in the steroid trial against him. Kevin wanted revenge. His full intentions were to screw Vince over by using really exaggerated incriminating testimony. When it finally went down, his testimony came off as so ridiculous that it didn't hold up in court. His harmful words actually worked to help Vince.

Many people even claim that because Kevin said stuff like "I hate Vince's guts" while on the stand, his testimony actually hurt the prosecution's overall credibility and helped Vince win. The irony is that Kevin kicks himself today for accidentally helping get Vince out of charges.

In the end, they didn't even need me. I never testified in court, and Vince was rightfully acquitted of all charges.

DRUG TESTING

As a result of all that happened, Vince had to get tougher in dealing with steroid and drug use in the 90s. He created an in-house company that started randomly testing us for illegal drugs, excluding steroids. He sent a few guys to rehab, but for some, no amount of intervention helped. I sincerely believe that this testing alone, if enforced sooner, could have helped save some of the boys' lives and maybe even their marriages, too.

Certain wrestlers will never admit it, but I do believe some owe Vince a thank you for taking extra measures to try to get the WWF's drug problems under control.

Later on, Vince also instituted testing for steroid use. Big bodies were in, so guys were doing whatever they had to do to build up their appearances. At first, steroids were not illegal, But even after they became illegal, some wrestlers say they had to use them in order to compete for the best spots. Regardless, I never heard Vince tell a wrestler to take steroids, as some have claimed. In fact, to me, Vince said you do NOT have to take steroids. "I am the one who gives you your spots, and I don't do it based on just appearance."

The company hired the number-one doctor in the drug-testing business, but their drug problems in the locker room didn't go away.

Initially, the tests were easy to beat. If a guy was concerned about failing a test, he would get a clean friend to piss in the bottle for him. As time went on, WWF got wise to these tricks. Eventually, they made us drop our pants and someone would actually watch us make pee pee from beginning to end. (This is what Nailz didn't like, incidentally.) In addition, the company began randomly testing sometimes as often as two or three times a week.

Vince took this matter seriously, as he was on a crusade to repair the promotion's public image. He did not want another scandal to ruin his big business.

If you were caught failing a test, there were consequences. For marijuana, the first offense was a $1,000 fine, followed by fines of $3,500 and $5,000. Steroid and cocaine abuse was obviously worse. Failing these tests would get a wrestler a six-week suspension. A second failed test meant a rehab program, and a third failed test meant you would get to hear Vince's catch phrase, "You're fired!!!"

I kept myself clean because it really didn't interest me, and I was a family man. *I didn't want to embarrass my family.* I couldn't see blowing money on drugs. Some guys spent up to $1,000 or more per week on enhancement drugs. I worked too hard for my money, and my family meant too much to me to blow my career just to get a perceived edge. I also felt good about being a positive role model.

Despite Vince's best efforts, there is still a drug problem in professional wrestling today (as well as our country) with pain pills. Vince is right when he says he isn't responsible for what someone does when they leave the ring. How can anyone hold the promoter responsible for what someone does in the privacy of his or her own home?
That said, it does seem like, in today's WWE, some certain big muscle-heads are still getting the big push.
It's a shame what the business has come to. Back in my day, it didn't take a brain surgeon to figure out that the guys with the better bodies were usually more aggressively promoted. But the WWF also has its share of guys who had a different look, whether they be fat, skinny, balding, hairy, you name it. I miss that.
The diversity was a reflection of society, and the fans brought into the reality of the different characters.

RUMORS
By the early 1990s, rumors of sexual misconduct ran rampant throughout the company. I heard rumors that there were several cases of guys having to sleep with officials in the main office, but I don't know how much truth there was to any of them. Some of this was certainly sour grapes.
The sex stuff I mentioned briefly above came from *The New York Post* who printed an article stating that some of the WWF's front-office personnel had been transporting minors across state lines who were hired for sexual favors. Also, there were accusations of young wrestlers being asked to participate in homosexual activities in order to advance their careers. There was even a lady referee who accused Vince of making inappropriate advances.
Allegations also fell on Vince from his former limousine driver, James Stewart, who has been fired several months before these accusations surfaced. Stewart claimed

that Vince himself went out looking for boys. To be clear, none of these rumors were ever proved to be true.

Plenty of people wanted money and have tried to catch Vince breaking the law, but no one has succeeded.

CROWN OF BROWN

In January of 1993, my days with the WWF were numbered. The Royal Rumble was held at the Arco Arena in Sacramento, California. I was a participant in the event and was eliminated by the eventual winner, Yokozuna.

Jerry "The King" Lawler was also an entrant in the Rumble. Though he would go on to be loved by all, he was despised at the time by a number of wrestlers because he was coming in from Memphis where he had been the champion of for many years. A number of the boys had to do him the favors there in the past, and he was looked at as an outsider when he finally found himself a small fish in the big WWF waters.

See, Jerry had to actually work with many guys who had heat with him. When Lawler was booking the USWA territory, he would often give the rookies horrible payoffs. There are stories of guys being paid in food stamps and having to survive by eating bags of potatoes when working for Lawler. So, when he finally ended up in WWF where a lot of his ex-rookies were, payback was a bitch, and inevitable.

During the *1993 Royal Rumble*, apparently, somebody (or a group of people) took a hot nasty steamer in Jerry Lawler's crown when he left it unguarded backstage.

When it was finally time for Jerry to be seen, he couldn't wear his trademark crown to the ring at the event, because someone had pooped in it.

When news broke out of this crappy incident, all kinds of theories hit the fan. Bobby Heenan said it was The Undertaker, while Jim Cornette and Paul Bearer blamed Steve Keirn a.k.a. Skinner. Many people said the incident just reeked of the Kliq members. This theory makes sense because X-Pac (a.k.a. The 1-2-3 Kid) once did the same thing to Sunny's suitcase.

However, nobody stepped up to take the blame.

Then, it got worse! More frequently on other shows, The King was returning again to find a crown of turds.

Raven and The Honky Tonky Man revealed during a shoot interview that the company had to actually send out a internal memo to ask people to stop pooping in King's crown.

Several guys had reasons to levy the poo, but no one ever took the credit for any of the squattings. After the incident, we all received memos with our paychecks that fines would be dumped on us if we were in on the prank.

CLASSIC OWEN HART

Everyone always asks me about ribs and who played the best pranks. Along with Fuji has to be Owen Hart.

Owen and Luger were once sharing a room, and they got up in the morning ready to fly to the next town. Before they left, Owen left the hotel room and asked a couple of women if he could borrow their underwear. Now, I don't know how he planned on getting the unmentionables back to the ladies, but let's just go with it.

While Luger was downstairs eating breakfast just before they were about to rush off and catch their flight, Owen emptied Luger's luggage and strategically added the underwear, some cutlery, and a couple of pictures of his crotch that he had taken with a polaroid camera.

The door opened right after Owen finished.

"Hey, man," Lex said. "The shuttle is about to leave!"

They grabbed their luggage and rushed down to the bus that was waiting outside, which headed for the airport.

As Luger was walking through airport security, phase one hit. The alarm went off because of the silverware.

Airport security personnel started searching his bags and to their surprise, they got an eyeful. They found his bag chock filled with women's underwear and pictures of Owen's hairy balls.

While Lex waited nervously, they called over other guards and pointed at their findings. This was classic Owen.

Everyone looked on and laughed while Luger was stood there turning red in the face.

CHAPTER 21 - MORE ROAD STORIES

Not all wrestlers get their injuries inside the ring. There were a number of guys that would live crazy lifestyles outside of the squared circle. Some of these guys were legitimate tough guys though, and injuries would more so come to the people who were around them.

HAKU

Since everybody seemed to have a pretty cool Haku story, I thought I would throw one in here, myself. They guy was a badass for sure, and the stories about how tough he was outside the ring are legendary.

One night in St. Louis, I saw Haku (going by King Tonga at the time) try to break up a bar fight. The problem with this for him was, breaking up others peoples' fights was often how he ended up in fights himself!

On this particular night, two guys were fighting and Haku jumped in there. For some reason, the bouncer at this bar was friends with one of the guys that was in the fight and didn't like the way Haku was trying to calm him down. Therefore, the bouncer hit Haku on the in the back of the head with a chair.

For someone like Haku who weighed over 300 pounds and had once studied to become a sumo wrestler, the chair shot hardly fazed him. All it did was make him mad.

Haku went nuts and bodies started flying. It looked like a scene out of an old western movie, but sped up, and maybe staring The Incredible Hulk instead of Clint Eastwood.

You don't want to see me when I'm angry. Haku smash!

To say Haku ended up hurting more than a few guys that night would be an understatement.

After some time, the police finally showed up on the scene. Haku was squirted with mace by a policeman, which made him even madder. Then, he decided to take his anger out on a couple of cops.

HAKU SMASH!!!

CHAPTER 21 – More Road Stories

Haku actually threw one police officer over the bar, before finally deciding to give up.

The police handcuffed him, but they were not nice about it. They were pissed and delivered a few blows to Haku with their nightsticks. In fact, one really big cop smacked him across the head with this nightstick.

If that were me, I would have been out cold, but Haku just shook his head and just stared at the cop. He was taken to the police department and locked up for a few hours.

I was sharing a room with Haku that night, and when he finally rolled in around 6:30 that morning he looked awful.

"You okay, brother?" I asked, squinting up at him coming in through the doorway.

His face was burned and blistered from the mace, and his ankles, wrists and shins were bruised from the handcuffs.

"I'm fine," he shrugged. "You should see the other guys."

I cleaned his face with peroxide, punctured his blisters, cleaned them up and covered his face with Neosporin He applied ice to his body in several spots to ease the swelling. He was clearly hurting.

To make matters worse, I had to wrestle him that night. He was a beat up mess. I don't know how he survived.

Bobby Heenan going over a spot with Haku as Shawn Michaels looks on.

I first met Tito Santana backstage when I was Max Moon and he was wrestling in WWE. I didn't know him that well because he didn't much go out after the shows. However, what I can say is that as a Hispanic, I related to him. There was very little Hispanic representation on American wrestling programming or TV in general at that time in history. It was refreshing to see a Latino and one that was getting a push. He really did give me a sense of pride.

I didn't go to a lot of matches growing up, but I do remember that when I moved to San Diego I went to my one and only WWE show. I remember wanting to go at the time because Mil Mascaras was on it. I also wanted to see 'Macho Man' who was my fave, and two of my fave tag teams, too; Strike Force versus The Islanders. When it was said and done, it was the tag match that really tore shit up ...

When I finally got to work with Tito, it was cool because he was always treated good while I was there. It's interesting because he was always a babyface his whole career, and still, what a career he had. Now, I never quite got why a guy that popular was turned into 'The Matador' by the silly WWE writers. That gimmick seemed very forced. I figured that he must have not liked that gimmick, and I think I was correct because, after the change, he mostly did jobs for the stars. Man, what a jojo gimmick ... But he still made it work and had a great career in the end.

Being the main Latino of the company, he wasn't threatened by me. When I went to WWE as Max Moon, he never treated me as Hispanic competition. But, instead, he was always a cool, well-spoken, and quite a humble cat.

Respect ... Konnan

MAX MOON

After being scouted by Pat Patterson, Konnan was brought in from Mexico to the World Wrestling Federation in 1992. Konnan created the character that he would be playing for the most part. It was a spaceman cyborg.

The original outfit was purchased by the WWF at around $1,300. It was blue leather with silver foam tubing stitched into it all over the place, along with a crazy mask. It also had expensive accessories featuring a pyrotechnic gun that shot sparkles as he approached the ring.

Konnan was given many different ring names as he was testing the gimmick out on dark shows. The Comet Kid, Maximillion Moves, and El Electrico were all used as character names until they eventually settled with Max Moon. His character hailed from "Outer Space" and his entrance music was a very futuristic sounding techno song to set the mood.

His first television debut was on September 1, 1992, in Hershey, Pennsylvania, where he beat Duane Gill a.k.a. Gillberg. After that, he had three more matches on WWF programming, and things looked promising. However, Konnan left the WWF after not making what he said he was promised to make by Vince McMahon.

Konnan believed that he was being discriminated against and resented McMahon's refusal to give him a guaranteed contract.

"There were also a lot of people there that were very envious of the fact I got flown in special for TV tapings, they brought in Mexican wrestlers to get me over," Konnan said. "There were a lot of people hating on the gimmick right from the start, and it didn't help that I got tired of lugging that Max Mon costume all around. I'd have to lug around eight boxes and literally take two taxis to get to the arena! It was a real pain in the ass." Konnan said he could make far more money back in his old stomping grounds. "Meanwhile, I was blowing up in Mexico, I had just done a soap opera, so I just decided to quit the WWF, and stopped showing up to work."

After that, they gave the gimmick to Paul Diamond, a former AWA tag team champion who had teamed there with

Pat Tanaka as part of Badd Company, and also with him as a masked wrestler named Kato in the WWF with The Orient Express.

The Max Moon gimmick lasted for a few years but never really got a big break. We were good friends until he crossed the line and began to have an affair with Tatanka's wife. I lost a lot of respect for him because of that.

According to rumors back then, Diamond was secretly having an affair with Tatanka's wife while on the road when they got caught. What happened was after a meeting with Max Moon that was apparently "out of this world," Tatanka's wife got into a car accident leaving Diamond's hotel. When Tatanka found out, he was furious.

The next day, Tatanka allegedly went to WWF management and gave them an ultimatum.

"If I am ever is in the same ring as Max Moon, there will be a real life homicide in the ring."

Tatanka was well respected and the threat was considered real. Paul Diamond was quickly taken off TV and efforts were made to keep the two apart.

A number of the wrestlers then made it even more difficult for Paul to stick around because they were constantly ribbing him. One time on a bus trip in Europe, The Nasty Boys started singing a song about how everyone's wives were safe back home in the States because Max Moon was on the bus with them!

It wasn't long before Paul Diamond's bookings decreased more and more until he was left with no work at all. While there were all kinds of "hookups" going on while the boys were on the road, this particular one broke the "bro code" by sleeping with one of the other boy's wives. The office didn't like this at all so they simply stopped using him.

TEXAS TORNADO

When I started in professional wrestling, I knew very little about the major players in the profession. Simply put, I wasn't a fan. In early 1977, David Von Erich and I worked together in Joe Blanchard's territory. But it wasn't until more

CHAPTER 21 – More Road Stories

years into the business that I realized how huge the Von Erich name was in wrestling.

Later on, when I was working in Atlanta, André the Giant, Kerry Von Erich and I temporarily stayed with each other in an apartment. Kerry and I became good friends. Although he was only in the Atlanta territory for a few months, when Kerry left, he told me that I was always welcome in his father's Dallas territory, World Class Championship Wrestling.

I eventually got to know all of the Von Erichs and found them all to be really nice guys. However, Kerry was always my favorite.

The story of Kerry's family is really a sad one and illustrates how the business can eat someone up if they aren't careful. It's hard to imagine, but Kerry lost four brothers; two to suicide, one by drugs, and a fourth by electrocution at a young age. As a parent, I can't imagine how Kerry's parents could have dealt with such losses.

Kerry's life was never an easy one. He got involved in drugs at a young age, and then he was involved in a serious motorcycle accident that eventually brought about the amputation of his right foot.

What happened was, on June 4, 1986, Kerry was riding his Harley in his home state of Texas without a helmet. He was driving very fast when he came around a corner and hit a police car. He ricocheted off the car and crashed into the pavement. Upon impact, he suffered several injuries including a dislocated hip and severely smashed up his right leg. While he was, in fact, lucky enough to survive the crash, he was really messed up.

In order to save his badly damaged leg, doctors needed to remove fragments of muscles from other parts of his body to replace the missing tissue.

A half of a year after the horrible motorcycle accident, Kerry was able to make an amazing return to the ring. It was tough, however. In order to do so, he had to take a lot of medications to help him get through the pain and healing process. His first match back was against another WCCW wrestler, Brian Adias.

The match wasn't all that brutal and really didn't last long, but that didn't matter. His right foot simply was not ready. With his return being too soon, his foot was instantly damaged again. The damage was so bad the second time around that his foot ended up having to be amputated.

To a common person, this certainly would have ended any sort of career in sports/athletics. However, it didn't stop Kerry Von Erich.

Kerry sucked it up. He walked the hard road to recovery, and then climbed back into the ring with a prosthetic foot.

Not wanting to be looked at as being a "freak" or some kind of circus act, Kerry asked his father to help keep the amputation a secret. Fritz Von Erich, asked the doctors and the staff involved to keep everything quiet and stick to patient confidentiality codes, which, to their credit, they did. Fritz also made his family swear not to reveal the secret to anyone.

Kerry changed his style slightly in the ring because of the missing a foot, but most people didn't realize anything was wrong. In fact, his secret remained intact to pretty much everyone until a match on November 12, 1988.

Kerry was working a bout with Colonel DeBeers when DeBeers grabbed one of his legs. In doing so, he pulled Kerry by his right foot, and his boot came right off. This accident revealed the fact that his foot was missing to all in attendance, including his opponent who easily could surmise it as being the aftermath of Kerry's motorcycle accident. Since there was no footage (no pun intended) Kerry just denied it. Rumors got out there, but there was no internet. Nothing was ever substantiated so he continued to hide it.

Around this time, Kerry got addicted to his prescription pain medication. He continued to wrestle in the ring, but the pain got increasingly worse. Thanks to that artificial foot however, he was able to keep on wrestling. He still chose to keep it all a secret.

When Kerry came to the WWF in 1990, we rekindled our friendship, often working out together.

CHAPTER 21 – More Road Stories

I will never forget Kerry Von Erich's return to New York. He had only really been there once before, and not in a wrestling capacity. At this point, he was about to perform in front of Madison Square Garden for the first time.

While I was getting ready in the dressing room, Kerry walked in to tell me about his afternoon.

"Tito, you are never going to believe this," he said excitedly. "While I was taking in the sights around 42nd street, I heard a woman scream that someone had just stolen her purse. I turned around and saw this guy running toward me with a gun in one hand and a purse in the other."

"Whoa," I said. "What happened?"

"When he got close to me, I waited until the last second and stuck out my arm," he said. "I gave him a clothesline and knocked him right to the ground! Then, I put all my weight on him and waited for the police to arrive. When they showed up, the arrested him on the spot. The lady was ecstatic."

I just laughed and told Kerry, "Welcome to New York!"

As he changed into his gear for the show, I noticed from the corner of my eye that he was grinning like a Cheshire cat. He had no concerns about whether that guy could have shot him; he was just happy to be the hero. That was Kerry being Kerry. He was just such a nice guy and he genuinely cared for others.

Come early July 1992, however, things had changed. Vince approached me about giving me a better spot in SummerSlam. The problem was, the upgrade was bittersweet.

"We would like to offer you Kerry's spot in the pay-per-view, because he is sadly, no longer with the company."

"Wait a minute? What?"

From what I remember of Kerry's time with me in the WWF, he was always under heavy medication. He told me of the constant pain he felt and the amount of morphine he needed to deal with it.

Kerry was self-admittedly prone to depressive episodes. The meds made things worse and then he found himself in darker and darker places. Because of this, Kerry also ran into some issues with the law. After his wife left him, his emotional problems escalated. He needed help even more than ever before, but he didn't ask for any and no one really stepped up to make it happen.

Sadly, Vince let me know that Kerry was fired for too many no-shows and because he wouldn't, or couldn't, stop taking pain pills. The drugs were getting the best of him.

For his family and friends, there was a moment of hope before the end. He was trying to turn his life around and give back to others who had drug addictions after a very successful rehab experience of his own. Things were looking good for his future, and we were all hoping the best.

Then, he slipped. After being caught with drugs himself yet another time, it was obvious that he fell off the wagon to everyone. That embarrassed him tremendously and the next real big news about Kerry would be his last.

Kerry committed suicide.

He ended his life at his dad's farm outside of Dallas with a single bullet in his own chest. That made Kerry the fifth of his family's six brothers to die at such a young age.

LEAVING THE ROAD BEHIND

Toward the end of my run in WWF, I began making a plan to get out of wrestling full time. I had seen what the business had done to some guys like Kerry Von Erich and their families. I had also seen how the business had beaten up on a lot of guys' bodies. Life on the road just was not all that kind to professional wrestlers. We were always on the go, and it often led to a bad ending for some.

Some guys really got addicted to pain meds. I was one of the lucky ones who never had that problem, but I can understand why it happened to many of them. Some guys were working on torn muscles and broken bones and had to figure out what they needed to do to continue to perform.

I remember seeing some guys swapping pain pills and getting pretty messed up. They were eating up pain pills like they were candy and getting addicted.

I remember seeing guys fall down face first into their soup at hotel restaurants. That is how bad things were

CHAPTER 21 – More Road Stories

getting. Some guys were so beat up that they were taking pain pills just to get out of their bed in the morning, let alone work a match. Then there were guys who will be the first to admit that they were taking way too many of them to get in the ring, but if they didn't take them, they couldn't have worked and would have lost their spots. It was horrible what it became. Some had to take them to get into the ring, to get out of the ring, and then to just get into bed and get out of bed the next morning. It was a vicious cycle that I wanted nothing to do with.

For me, the most I ever took was aspirin, and I didn't really like to even do that. But rather than to wait and see what would happen to me, I started to make an exit plan.

By this point, I was getting used less and less. I knew I was not part of the WWF's long-term plan anymore and did not want to hand around to be misused and miscast. I was slowly being phased out of the main events as the company turned to fresh faces and new talents.

It seemed inevitable that I would soon be a curtain jerker. I decided to work one more Mania and see how things were going to go.

WRESTLEMANIA IX

My last WrestleMania, the ninth annual event, took place on April 4, 1993, at Caesars Palace in Vegas. It was held outdoors with a whole Roman Gladiator theme.

The PPV featured a really crazy finish between Bret Hart, Yokozuna, and Hulk Hogan. The Hulkster came away with the championship belt after Yokozuna's manager, Mr. Fuji, unintentionally blinded his own wrestler with salt. The reason for this title change was cold feet on Bret as the face of the company and Hogan still holding some kind of power over Vince McMahon, influencing the booking of the show.

Several fans have been critical of this event citing a shitty match in The Undertaker versus Giant Gonzalez, Hulk Hogan's title win, and even the sexy Roman toga worn by Jim Ross!

Working the El Matador gimmick that night, I defeated Papa Shango in a dark match that started as a warm-up for the crowd. The office knew I was not happy, so they threw me a bone by having me go over.

Trying to keep things fresh and new, I used a new finisher that night that I called "El Paso de la Muerte," or "The Pass of Death." To get the victory on my last Mania appearance, my new finisher was a variation of my usual flying forearm smash that previous commentators Bobby Heenan and Jesse Ventura referred to as being "The Flying Burrito" or "The Flying Jalapeno." The variation in this case was it was backwards. I would hit my opponent in the back of the neck, rather than hit him in the forehead.

Although I did get the victory, most people were not watching. It was in a dark match at Mania. That was very telling for me as to how important I was to the company. I was so important that I wasn't even on the actual show.

My career was going nowhere. I was no longer one of the WWF's top competitors. I was traveling by myself and the long road trips had become exhausting. Many of the wrestlers I had socialized and traveled with in the WWF were no longer part of the league. I missed my family and I wanted to be home with my children. I was miserable.

After they didn't choose me as World champion, the writing was on the wall all along. However, I was too pro-company to give up hope and just stuck around.

By April 14, 1993, I finally decided it was time to tap out and to give Vince my notice of my resignation.

At the time, however, I was very sad. I had just given myself to the WWF for more than a decade and wasn't sure where I was going to go from there. The El Matador character teased me for so long that it was too bad that it didn't turn into any real good long term plans.

"Vince," I said, meeting up with him at a show. "I think it is time for me to go."

Vince replied bluntly, "Tito, I think you are right."

We talked for a bit. He said he thought I was making a wise decision, but he didn't really show much personal emotion about my decision. I thought he would at least express some feelings to go along with a "thanks for a long career," but he didn't really. That was just Vince.

CHAPTER 21 – More Road Stories

I will say this though, he gave me work and opportunities that many will never see in life. He helped me to provide for my family and for that, I am forever grateful.

After speaking with Vince, I began the drive to the next town where I was scheduled to wrestle. About an hour into the drive, I broke down in tears. It had finally sunk in that I was leaving the WWF.

I had no job waiting for me, and no idea how I would make a living or how I would continue to provide for my family. I had not even told my wife, Leah, about my decision.

With tears flowing down my face, I struggled to gather my composure. I turned to the one entity that had always been there for me, God. I prayed to God and asked him to do what he wished with my life. I asked him to guide me and help me take care of my family.

Although the prayer relaxed me temporarily, reality didn't take long to set in. *I would soon be unemployed.*

Right after the matches ended that evening, I went rushing back home to New Jersey. I just wanted to be home, and I arrived at the house well after midnight. My wife was asleep, but as usual, as soon as I got into bed, she quickly awakened. As we embraced, she looked into my eyes and immediately knew that something was wrong.

"Leah," I said. "I gave my notice to Vince."

She looked at me but didn't say a word. She knew it was something I had to do.

"So, my time with the WWF is up in two weeks. I'm scared, and I don't know what to do."

"It will be ok. Look, Merced," she replied. "For the past decade, Vince has controlled and owned you. You are now free. You are finally free!"

She was right. Everything I wanted to do always revolved around work. That was no longer the case.

"Don't worry. We will do what we have to do to survive. If we have to, we will sell the house and I can work extra hours. Together we are going to make it."

She was right. Her words relaxed me and I was genuinely relieved. It was crystal-clear that with my wife's support, we were, no doubt, going to make it.

My last days in the WWF were miserable. I hated going to work, but I fulfilled my commitment. When it was finally done and I had finished my last show with the WWE, I'll never forget my first night home sitting there with Leah.

I just sat there in bed with my wife staring off at the TV. My mind was racing a hundred miles a minute.

"You know, I'm scared," I said.

For the first time since we had been married, I was out of work. We had three kids to support and bills to pay. She looked at me and said, "I'm scared too, but things will work out. They always do."

"I know."

I reached over and held her for a while. She looked into my eyes and said, "But, you've got your life back now. That's got to be worth something."

I let her words sink in before replying, "You're right. We're not quitters. We'll make it one way or another."

I had some other business ventures under way to stabilize my income without full time wrestling. Just a month earlier, I had become a distributor of Quorum Alarms. I'd been reading a lot about the company and its security products for personal, home, and automobile use. I had a lot of hope of making that a good income for myself.

I also had been putting a lot of effort into opening a Gold's Gym in the New Jersey area, close to my home. My good friend Paul Alperstein and I had two locations in mind for a Gold's branch; the Rockaway and Danville area. While Paul and I negotiated with potential landlords, I talked to some very interesting representatives from a variety of gym equipment manufacturers. The whole process would cost us in the neighborhood of $150,000, so I was banking on a return from my significant investment.

Hulk Hogan gave me his word he would be at the grand opening. But in the end, the gym didn't happen because Paul and I couldn't secure a suitable building location. However, things happen for a reason, and Paul would be useful in my life somewhere else in the near future.

CHAPTER 22 - ECW

Before leaving, I had worked about 40 matches with the WWF between January and August of 1993 with a European tour being my final matches with the company. I was working a lot with Horace Hogan in my final days with the WWE who was working there in a try-out kind of status. Horace was calling himself "The Predator" (BELOW) and working there for Vince as a favor of the Hulkster.

In my final days with the WWF, I was working with (and mostly losing to) guys like Adam Bomb, Doink the Clown, Bastion Booger and Damien Demento.

After putting in my notice, I realized that Vince was keeping me those last years to give me a payday because he was very appreciative of what I did for his company. He probably would have kept me around even longer, if I had wanted it, but I wasn't really being used much as an attraction, nor was I really wanting to do so. So when I said "it is time" and Vince agreed, he just didn't want to be the one to tell me so. He wanted me to make that decision on my own.

I soon realized that I was getting older and wanted to be at home with my family, anyhow. I had some kids I wanted to spend more time with before they got too old, and I really wanted to be more selective of what dates I took. So come July and August, I wrapped up my final obligations with WWF.

This did not mean I was quitting wrestling, however. I immediately started taking bookings and found that being the big fish in a small pond could quite often mean I could get paid even more for a match than WWF had been paying me to lose. In other words, on a small promotion, they were happy to have me come in as their main draw, pay me more money, and put me over like crazy.

One of the first more regular promotions to do this was ECW.

ECW CHAMPION

People ask me about this all the time, so I thought I would put a little bit of time into it for my book. Yes, I did wrestle for ECW, and even held the ECW Heavyweight title ...*sort of*.

You might know ECW to be the land of hardcore, or maybe the most violent company to ever exist in pro wrestling. However, that isn't exactly how it was when I got there. When I first showed up, it was actually pretty tame. It wasn't even called Extreme at the beginning.

The promotion would later become ECW first started out under the name "Tri-State Wrestling Association" in 1989.

In 1992, Goodhart sold his share of the company to his partner, Tod Gordon. From what I understand, Joel didn't know a whole lot about the business and eventually sold the company to his friend Tod Gordon. Tod didn't know much either, but he at least knew that he needed to change things up.

Tri-State wasn't drawing flies and needed a major facelift. So one of the first things that Tod did was rename the company Eastern Championship Wrestling.

As ECW the promotion would, in fact, continue to use the former Tri-State heavyweight championship belt to represent its own championship, although the ECW title was

CHAPTER 22 – ECW

not considered a continuation of that title. The beginning of the new name meant a new champion was to be crowned for the first time.

The new ECW debuted in a sports bar in Philadelphia with their very first match under the new name being Jimmy Jannetty versus Stevie Richards. According to what I have heard from Stevie Richards say in the past, I guess it was pretty bad. He said that "in his own opinion" that he sucked in that match and that he wasn't in good shape at all. He looks like a million bucks today and actually has his own fitness program that he promotes, but back then, he admits that he was still green.

As for the rest of the matches on that first show, they say that those other matches were just as bad, as well. The wrestlers on it all sucked, and it was overall just a typical shitty indie show.

Eventually, Tod knew he had to get better talent. Instead of cutting back with the low ticket sales, he opened up the purse strings a little to better the quality of the shows. He started having more veterans come in to help him out. After a call to Dennis Coralluzzo, Tod made put the promotion under the NWA banner.

Immediately after this, Tod's next move was to increase the quality of the shows, so he brought in "Hot Stuff" Eddie Gilbert to book the shows to make them look better.

Some of the early Eastern Championship Wrestling shows featured the likes of Magnificent Muraco, Road Warrior Hawk, Jim Neidhart and "British Bulldog" Davey Boy Smith. This eventually led up to using "Superfly" Jimmy Snuka (who was close enough to drive into the shows) to become the first ever ECW Champion. He had hoped that this move would give the new brand credibility among the fans.

ECW had two battle royals to crown the first ever ECW champion. Then in Mount Tabor, PA on April 25, 1992, my friend "Superfly" Jimmy Snuka went on to face Salvatore Bellomo after they both won separate battle royals to become the finalists and won.

"Superfly" Jimmy Snuka
Eastern Championship Wrestling

Snuka traded the belt some with Johnny Hot Body until September 30 of 1992, when they brought in the Superfly's old nemesis, Don Muraco to take the tile off of him. Next, Don dropped the title to The Sandman, then got it back. With help from "Hot Stuff" Eddie Gilbert as lead booker, ECW managed to secure television time on SportsChannel Philadelphia in March 1993. To make the new television show look good and provide a challenger to the ECW champion that made sense, guess who they called? A former nemesis to Don Muraco, you could say, former WWF Intercontinental champion, Tito Santana! ¡Arriba!

Magnificent Muraco
ECW Heavyweight Champion

On August 8, 1993 in Philadelphia, I was booked for ECW. I wrestled three matches for a television taping, and in the end, I beat Muraco, just as I did for the IC title years before, and became the new ECW champion!

After that, however, there were many more changes to come for the promotion.

Eddie Gilbert had some great ideas and helped Tod get better connections to talent, but Eddie also had some problems of his own. From what some of the boys in the locker room said, Eddie was on some serious drugs that hurt his creative ability, and there really was nobody at the wheel. The wrestlers were all pretty much running the shows on their own with the shows and the television program drifting with no real direction. Some said that because Eddie was so focused on getting a fix he couldn't focus on fixing ECW.

Subsequently, things didn't pan out as Tod Gordon had hoped. He eventually had a major falling out with Gilbert and fired him on the spot. Gilbert was replaced in September 1993 by a 28-year-old Paul Heyman. Known on television as Paul E. Dangerously, Paul had just been fired by World Championship Wrestling (WCW) and was looking for work.

A month after winning the title, either I was not available for a big ECW card in Roanoke, VA, or I was just not booked. Either way, I didn't get to see the changing of the guards backstage. When a promotion changes leadership, the new guy makes changes. It is all very political. With Heyman came his connections and his vision for how things should go.

I didn't take not being booked for this as a slight to me personally. There were many independent promotions that had ghost title changes and all kinds of inconsistencies due to not having the money to bring back the last guy who had the title. This was actually the norm for a lot of "outlaw" promotions. I probably didn't know, nor did I care because I had no idea that ECW was about to really get a buzz on it. At this point, they hadn't exactly taken off yet.

So in September of 1993, I just wasn't there. I wasn't booked so the belt was handed off to another former WCW talent who had worked some with Heyman, Shane Douglas.

Shane Douglas won because I forfeited the title.

Changes continued to happen, and I honestly had no real desire to get booked there anyhow. It really wasn't my cup of tea. They were moving more in a hardcore direction than I was comfortable with and that just wasn't my thing.

ECW NAME CHANGE

There were more changes after they handed the belt to Shane. Heyman and Sabu were both friends with Dennis Coralluzzo who actually introduced them to Tod Gordon. In return, they pushed for ECW to join the NWA to possibly get more recognition. The National Wrestling Alliance had a rich history only years before this, and I think he thought he could maybe salvage that and put the spotlight on ECW. However, in this era, the NWA was basically dying, if not already dead.

So, ECW ran under the NWA banner for a short time before Paul Heyman recognized that the NWA was only taking money out of their promotion but putting nothing back in. There was no benefit of working under their decrepit banner, so Paul decided that he wanted to break away from the NWA. So rather than to just cancel their subpar subscription to the name, they decided to work the end of their working relationship into a storyline, and one that the NWA knew nothing about.

So Paul and Tod Gordon lobbied to have the NWA let ECW's top guy, Shane Douglas, win the NWA World title for a run with it in ECW. They agreed. The NWA scheduled Shane to win the NWA World title belt in a tournament taking place on ECW shows. After he finally won, he made this long speech recognizing everyone who held this belt before him. And then Shane told them all to "kiss his ass," because it was the beginning of a new era. The era of ECW!

That night, all the fans in the arena chanted "ECW! ECW! ECW!" for the first time ever. Immediately after denouncing the NWA affiliation, Tod and Paul broke away from NWA behind the scenes for real. Dennis Coralluzzo thought it was a work at first, but after a few days, he realized it was not.

The ECW office soon made the announcement that Eastern Championship Wrestling would be changed to *Extreme Championship Wrestling.* Magazines loved it. They picked the story up everywhere.

It worked.

The spotlight was on ECW.

So, in the end, the title I held was technically the same title and I am still recognized everywhere as being the fifth person to have ever held the ECW Heavyweight Championship, even though the company slightly changed their name right after my reign.

Tito Santana

CHAPTER 23 - AWF

Throughout my AWA days and even after my days in the WWF, Sgt. Slaughter was always there for me.

Sarge was born in Detroit, Michigan, but he was raised in Minneapolis, Minnesota which had made AWA a decent fit for a time. He attended Eden Prairie High School in Eden Prairie, where, like me, he played football. After that, however, Remus legitimately enlisted in the United States Marine Corps, and was a drill instructor at Parris Island, South Carolina, just before his professional wrestling career.

From the late 1970s to the early 1980s, Slaughter took his personality to the ring and amped it up. He became known for his dark sunglasses, his large hat, and his Vietnam War era military fatigues. He soon found success in the National Wrestling Alliance capturing the NWA United States Heavyweight Championship twice.

After seeing his success, Hasbro actually licensed a version of the Sgt. Slaughter character so they could incorporate him into their *G.I. Joe: A Real American Hero* toy line, their comic books, and even their popular animated cartoon series. This made him even larger than life.

In WWF, Sarge went on to headline *WrestleMania VII*, in 1991 and also won the WWF World Heavyweight Championship. (Because of all this, Sgt. Slaughter was inducted into the WWF Hall of Fame in the class of 2004.)

With Sarge back in the WWF, we traveled together often. He was always fun to roll with. In our travels, we eventually came across a guy named Paul Alperstein at a WWF tour stop in Chicago. He was generally a good person who was both helpful and generous because of his love of the sport. Because of that, Paul drove us to matches whenever we were in the area. When I quit WWF, Paul stepped up again. He suggested opening up a Golds Gym with me for investment purposes. When that didn't pan out, he contacted me yet again and said he wanted to start up a major promotion with me for television syndication.

Now, everybody says stuff like this all the time. Over the course of my career, I can't tell you how many TV deals I had heard were coming for me, and how many oversears tours I would be on, all that that never happened. There have always been big egos and big pipe dreams in wrestling. I didn't think much of Paul's idea at first when he told it to me, but then I heard something made this offer different.

I learned that Paul actually had the money to make things happen. Paul's family business was worth some major bucks. So Paul had his cousin buy him out of his shares of the business for somewhere to the tune of $7 million! That meant there was money to work with.

This thing could really happen!

When Paul asked me who I needed on the business side to help make things happen, I immediately said Sarge. Paul said, "say no more," and we were the AWF bookers.

When we talked about how the business should run, both Sarge and I agreed. We thought things should start out slow. If things went well, then you could throw more money into the business and let it grow.

Paul came to us one day with long-term contract booking ideas that seemed like a waste of money.

"There is no reason to go all out yet," I told him.

My real concern was that as soon as we were to get someone going as a talent, Vince would step in and sign them, and take them over. That is what he always did. So our idea was that we should build the name as a whole, and worry about going more "big time" after we were already seeing success.

Paul, on the other hand, started spending money like he had cash to burn. One of the reasons for this maybe was he had an investor who also promised to be throwing some good startup money into the promotion.

A regional wrestling manager who knew Paul went by the ring name "Rico Suave." While he would eventually turn out to be a manager on AWF television, he was also supposed to be a financial producer for the show and handle investors for the company.

Years later, some say that Rico actually had some kind of connection to the mob. He was connected to gambling boats and was supposed to be getting a percentage of casino boat revenue from their owners as an investment in the show. Because of his promises of money, Paul went all out, against our better wishes. He opened the floodgates and spared no expense on talent, as well as production behind the scenes even before the first show.

The AWF started up in 1994. The idea was to do something different than the WWF. Directly competing was not going to work, because then we would just be a poor rip-off of them. The idea was to offer the fans an alternative, something different that would lure them in to watch every week.

The AWF was going to use a round system similar to European wrestling rules. Each match would have three 4-minute rounds. If a wrestler didn't decisively win in the allotted rounds, two judges and the referee would decide who the winner was.

Also, in a very old school manner, throwing an opponent over the top rope was an automatic disqualification.

The AWF used tournaments for its titles, each wrestler would advance in the tournament by defeating the respective opponent, like in a normal match. Points scored in a card during a tournament.

Paul acted as the on-air president of the company. Jim Brunzell was hired as the on screen AWF commissioner. Why Brunzell? Because Sarge and I liked him, that's why! We also had a number of other major stars we liked like Tommy Rich, Greg Valentine, "Cowboy" Bob Orton, Mr. Hughes, Koko B. Ware, Hercules, Tony Atlas, The Warlord and even Nails. Nailz? ...*Yes, Nailz. Now that's heat!*

As you can tell by the list of names above, as a booker, I pretty much just opened my Rolodex. The AWF was certainly promising to be was a "who's-who" of 80s superstars being pushed hard in the 90s. Using guys who were recognizable to the television audience and ones who could still "go" in the ring was the key.

Paul paid big bucks do buy television time outright. For our first television taping, we planned to film six episodes at one live show and edit them later for the first batch of syndicated AWF programming. Things turned out really well on the production level and in the ring. However, it was outside of the ring we fell short and couldn't control.

The taping started with a packed house, and everything looked great on tape. The problem was we were overly ambitious in our approach to scheduling six episodes to be shot back to back. What happened was, the first few episodes were fine and the crowd was really hot. However, as the night went on, more and more people started to leave. Before we were half way through the taping, the audience was very patchy and a lot of people had left. The end result was, the episodes looked horrible. No, the AWF didn't stand for "Another Wrestling Failure." It stood for American Wrestling Federation and we were still really hoping on revolutionizing professional wrestling at the time.

To remedy this, Paul dipped into his pocket again. We decided to scrap the footage we shot and tape all over again, but this time, we were determined to make sure we had a capacity crowd for all the episodes being taped.

As part of the entertainment expense, Paul actually *booked the audience to be there.*

Yes, that is right. All of the fans were paid to be there. Paul Alperstein dipped into his $7-million dollar family business buy-out money and paid real Screen Actors Guild members to sit at ringside. He coached them to react to certain wrestlers and moments during the show. Practically every single person cheering in the arena was a plant!

To cut some costs, however, not all the fans were plants. Rumor has it that Paul offered free food to the homeless. So some of the homeless people were invited in to fill up the studios where they were taping. When the crowd wasn't loud enough, canned applause was added in the studio. Everyone seemed happy! When the homeless left, canned food was added to their shopping carts. ¡Arriba!

Timing was kind of an issue and factored into the lack of success. The TV deal that AWF setup was a full year before the Monday Night Wars took off and ECW was still gaining steam but hadn't really taken off yet. Wrestling wasn't as hot yet in the mainstream as it would eventually, later on, turn out to be.

In 1995, the company introduced its flagship program called *Warriors of Wrestling* for syndication. The initial run consisted of the footage shot from 1994 to 1995. However, he program resurfaced again late in 1996 with brand new episodes. The announce team consisted of Mick Karch on play-by-play and Terry Taylor as the color commentator. Taylor was replaced by Lord Alfred Hayes in 1996. Ken Resnick handled interview segments. Resnick was eventually replaced by Missy Hyatt in 1996.

With Paul Alperstein paying TV stations around the country to air his wrestling like an infomercial, a hell of a lot more money was going out than was coming in. Quite often, the cable companies only offered crappy time slots that you could buy outright like this. Our show as airing at like one or two in the morning meaning most fans had to video tape it.

The product itself did show promise. In one market, Orlando, I think, we were actually on at a reasonable time and actually beating the WWF in ratings! The problem was, however, nobody else in the country could ever find our show on TV and it just wasn't getting watched.

Sarge and I didn't like what we were seeing. I mean I know what Paul was trying to do. The hope was that enough fans would take to the program that it would cause a demand for house shows and eventually, touring. If this could happen, they could start running more live events and have PPVs to make up the money being invested.

Things just didn't turn out as planned. The format was choppy and before long, Paul's well was running dry.

There were some good ideas. They had a turnbuckle cam that was pretty cool. I liked the rounds system and more strict rules with referees that enforced them. Matches were booked spontaneously in a tournament by picking names out of a hat. They wanted different and were getting that, but before we could really get out there, the AWF was broke. Paul Alperstein tapped out.

As far as Rico Suave and his gambling boat investors, Suave wasn't as smooth as we had hoped. He never came through with any of the money he had promised. So when Paul had nothing left and needed to fall back on finances from the investors, we were out of luck.

In the end, the master of the gimmick table, Tom (a.k.a. WWF's Sal Sincere) Brandi bought all the left over merchandise like t-shirts and hats for pennies on the dollar. He was wrestling as The Patriot on the independents and started handing some of the AWF gimmicks out on the way to the ring.

The AWF fell apart, but the championship title did not – so I didn't let my wife throw it in garbage can. I still toted the belt around with me some to independent bookings. It was really neat gimmick to have. Do from time to time on my own, I defended the AWF Championship belt on various shows. My last AWF title defense was at a National Championship Wrestling event in York, Pennsylvania against former AWF wrestler Salvatore Sincere a.k.a Tom Brandi.

The storyline was that Sincere was claiming I had ducked him during our AWF days together and that he wanted a title match. So, I agreed to put the belt on the line against Sal Sincere, one last time.

I, of course, won the match for the last AWF title defense. ¡Arriba!

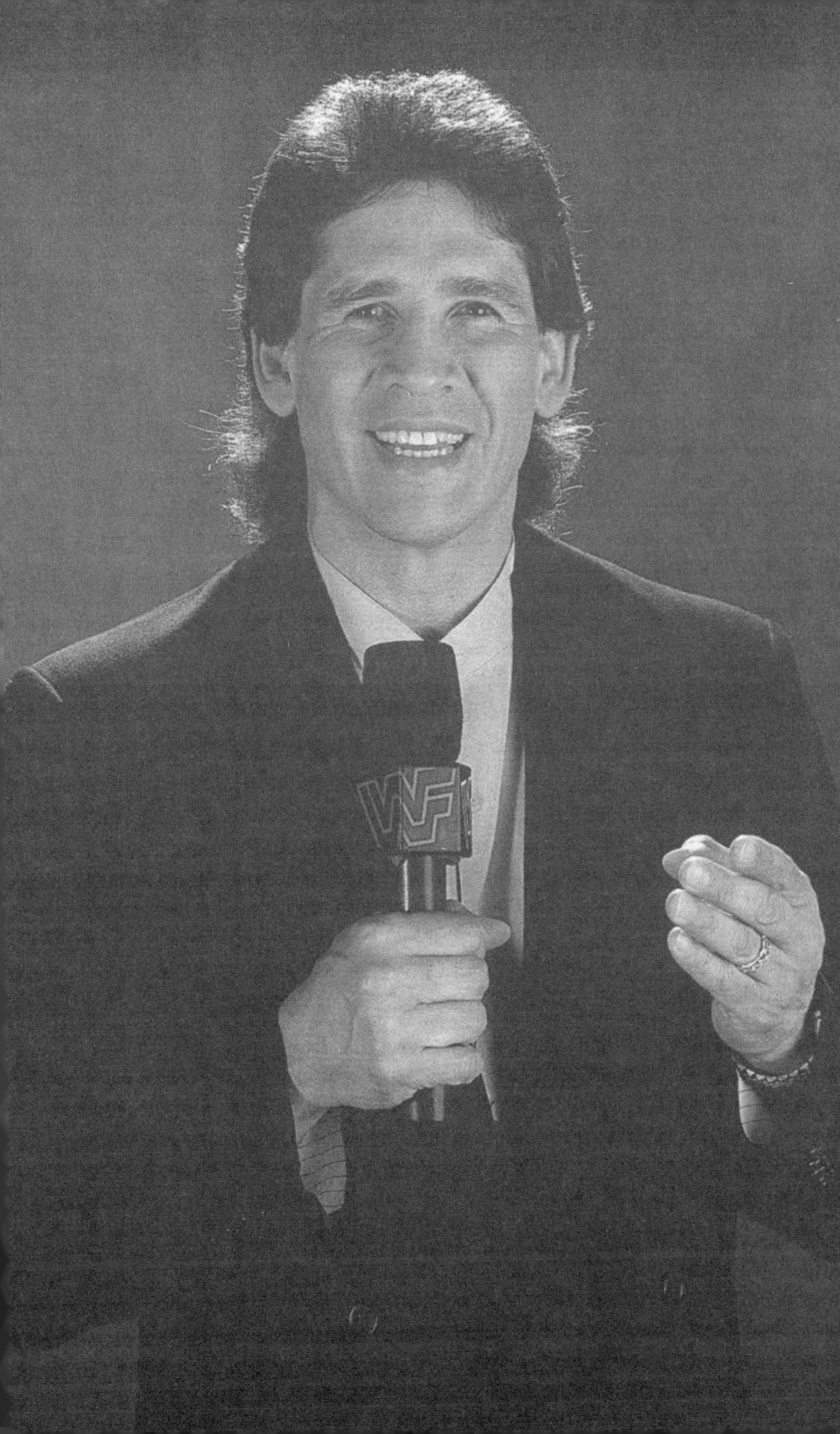
WWF

CHAPTER 24 - RETURN TO WWF

Come 1997, I started to get the itch again. The "itch" is something very hard to explain, and only a wrestler gets it. It's a weird calling back to the ring everytime you leave.

Basically, once you get into wrestling, there is no real way out. Very few ever successfully leave the business, though they have tried, without returning at some point to some capacity.

What I think happens is, you become an adrenaline junkie. There is nothing like walking down the aisle with all eyes on you waiting to see what is going to happen.

As you probably noticed a few chapters back, I was unhappy in my last few years with the WWF. I was getting older in a cosmetic sport that glorifies younger talent. There was simply nothing I could do reverse the aging process. Father Time does no jobs for anyone. (If you find a remedy for this, please contact me so we can bottle it and sell it!)

Once I had come to terms with the fact that I could no longer compete as the young fresh babyface like I had during, say, my Intercontinental run, boy did I miss it.

THE SPANISH ANNOUNCE TABLE

When wrestling on the independents, more and more wrestlers of Latino decent were approaching me to say how much they appreciated me being the hero for wrestlers of their race. They would tell me that they watched me growing up, and how I really meant the word to them. Words like these started to really mean the world to me.

Looking for another new niche for myself in the business, I had an idea and I decided to call Vince. Rather than to ask for a wrestling role, I asked Vince for a commentary job with his Spanish speaking audience.

Vince agreed that it was a great idea, and I returned to the WWF as a commentator in the Spanish Broadcast table. This was just what I needed.

I got to call matches on *Monday Night Raw*, as well as PPV events like *WrestleMania XIV*. It gave me the little bit I needed to cure the itch, and I really enjoyed doing it.

CHAPTER 24 – Return to WWF

Being with the company for about a year again, was more so for fun. It gave me an opportunity to find my smile again in the business and actually get the closure that I didn't have before when I felt the need to leave before when I was fizzling out.

Keeping things fun, Vince even found other little spots for me. In November 1997, I made an on-air appearance as El Matador one more time in something that they called the *Karate Fighters Holiday Tournament*. For this, I put on the gimmick one last time, but more tongue-in-cheek, facing Carlos Cabrera and Jerry Lawler on WWF programming.

It really was a good experience for me. In the end, my heart was more in the performing sides of things than it was in broadcasting, so eventually, I got my fill. With my contract coming up, I was happy again with the WWF, and I was happy to go and explore other business options outside of wrestling. However, there was one thing that I would be around to see before I left, first hand …

THE MONTREAL SCREWJOB

On November 9, 1997, at the Survivor Series in Montreal, Shawn Michaels became the WWF World champion for the third time, but not without controversy to say the very least! Michaels defeated Bret Hart in what is today considered the most-talked about, real-life, double-cross in the history of the business. I was ringside in Montreal that night doing the color commentary for the WWF's Spanish announcing team.

And if you ask me, I think the entire incident should have never, ever occurred.

I'm sure you all have heard of this incident, the event that single handedly ushered in the birth of the Attitude Era.

Before this PPV, as I have said before, Vince saw a lot of potential in Shawn, and he naturally wanted Shawn to be the titleholder. However, Bret was leaving the company and had unique contract stipulations written into it, one specifically giving him creative control stating he did not have to drop the title in his home country of Canada.

The two wrestlers hated each other. At one point, Shawn had said something about Bret cheating on his wife with Sunny in a promo and caused all kinds of friction at home. This eventually led to a backstage fight where Bret kicked Shawn's ass and pulled out giant clumps of his trademark lady killer locks and threw it to the locker room floor.

Because Bret refused to drop the belt to Shawn, the plan was for him to retain the title in their match and then relinquish the title the next night on RAW before leaving the company to go to WCW. However, this isn't what happened.

I was just as shocked as everyone else when referee Earl Hebner called for the bell that ended the match after Shawn put Bret in Bret's own finisher, the sharpshooter. That was not the planned finish at all and Bret never submitted. When the move was applied, Bret was supposed to roll over and then go into the actual finish, one in which he would not lose. However, Vince grabbed Earl before the match and they decided that Bret losing the title clean to Shawn was the way to go as it was, "what was best for business."

While sitting at the broadcast table, I remember thinking that something was wrong, because the ending didn't make any sense at all. I was close enough to see Bret. I could see the confusion in Bret's eyes after the bell rang.

Wait, what?! There is no way Bret would have tapped out that quickly if this was their plan!

The swerve was Vince's plan all along. He came down to ringside and ordered the bell be rung at a strategic moment to try to pull a fast one over on the fans. He wanted to make them think the match had ended with Bret losing the title to the guy the company was about to push. This would be the first strike against the company Bret was going to.

A very pissed-off Bret could not believe what had just happened. He leaned forward and spit in Vince's face at ringside, and then went crazy outside the ring, destroying television monitors and other equipment.

Triple-H and Jerry Brisco escorted Michaels back into the dressing room as the Canadian crowd roared in

CHAPTER 24 – Return to WWF

disapproval. The fans weren't stupid, they knew exactly what they had just seen. In their eyes, Vince screwed Bret.

I thought at the time that maybe this was all just part of an angle because I would have never expected Bret to conduct himself in such a way if it wasn't planned.

After the match, tensions boiled over backstage. The British Bulldog told me that Vince followed Bret to the locker room and tried to cordially explain the situation. Bret wasn't in the mood to listen and told Vince that he was taking a shower, and if Vince knew what was good for him he better not hand around.

For whatever reason, Vince stuck around, and Bret clocked him! Vince never threw a punch. The rest is history.

For all these years I never thought Shawn was in on the swerve. He said he had no idea that this was going to happen, and I believed him. I couldn't believe it when he revealed in his autobiography that he was, indeed, in on the deed along with Triple-H and Brisco. I couldn't believe it because, at the time, Michaels acted and talked like he had no idea why Vince screwed Bret.

So who do I side with on this whole thing?

All of it was shit.

From what I understand, Bret was willing to lose his belt, just not in his homeland of Canada and also not to Shawn. Nothing personal, but I think Bret was wrong and overreacted in and unprofessional manner. As a wrestler, you do what they guy is paying you.

Vince giveth and he taketh away. That's the nature of the business.

But what if it was all a work?

Now, Kenny Casanova, the guy who helped me write this book, thinks Bret was in on it and that people like me were allowed to see the aftermath so that we would truly believe and pass it on. This would push some "bigger plan" of a future return as the theory goes. There have been people who have doubted that this was a real screwjob. Earl Hebner has even himself said that it is 50/50 possible Bret was in on the deal and staged everything in front of the boys.

I don't know. It seemed very real to me, but who knows. Vince is a genius. It's possible.

There was no fallout. Everything worked out great for both Vince and Bret. Vince didn't run away from the booing fans, he gave them who they wanted. Mr. McMahon was born, one of the greatest heel characters wrestling history who would eventually pair up with Steve Austin and put WCW out of business.

Some people like Kenny "The Conspiracy Theorist" and the guys who put together *Dark Side of the Ring* on Viceland think Bret came to Vince with the huge WCW offer and they decided to have him take the money just to milk the competition, to inject a venomous cancer into their competition that would eventually take them down. Maybe they concocted the idea that Bret should go to sabotage WCW by taking the millions of dollars they were stupidly offering over the next couple of years, knowing the company wouldn't be able to afford it in the long run. Vince knew money and must have known that they couldn't continue to pay what they were paying at the rate they were going.

Others also think part of a possible "Bret and Vince master plan" was for Bret to do a lousy job in the ring in WCW. If Bret just did what they asked him to do without offering any extra help, or just allowed Hogan to play politics to bury him without stopping him, they would be paying big bucks for Bret, but reaping no benefits.

There were lots of signs that the screwjob was a written-out, insider storyline that Bret was in on. For one, a documentary was allowed to film backstage when this was unheard of. Also, Bret had a creative control clause, so Vince would have legally been in breach of contract to tell Bret he was in "X" angle but then do a "Y" angle. The cameras also continued to roll and show Bret "acting angry" and WWF left the footage on the PPV video tapes; if this were real, Vince surely would not want to include footage of being spit on. Then, there is also the fact that Owen remained working for Vince.

Others argue against the fake screwjob idea and say that Bret would have come back earlier after WCW went out of business. However, Bret was collecting off of his Lloyds of London insurance after being injured from Goldberg. He actually couldn't get in a ring or he would lose his insurance money.

Bret and Vince are both old school kayfabe like me, so I can see why people could believe that it is possible that the screwjob was all a big work.

Maybe it was a work, within a work, within a work!

What do I think? I think I saw legit confusion in Bret's eyes that night. I think it was real and Bret didn't know. It seemed very real to me, but with Vince in the mix who knows?

WORLD CHAMPIONSHIP WRESTLING

On January 10, 2000, I did the same thing Bret did and a number of the boys did who were looking for a nice little check from Ted Turner. I made a my only one-time appearance in WCW. There, I defeated Jeff Jarrett in a Dungeon match on *Nitro*.

I mean I went there because it was a good little payday, but I never had any aspirations of joining up with WCW full time. It was just a payday.

Unlike most of the aging WWF wrestlers of the 1980s that Vince had once pushed, I never joined WCW as a full-time performer. I never really gave any serious thought to joining the former Atlanta-based league after leaving the WWF in 1993.

Signing a contract with WCW, I would have had to be away from home and on the road again. Once I left the WWF, I had no desire to be on the road again, and I realized this even more so after my time back with them on the Spanish Announce Team.

I pretty much wrestled for them just to get a match and be able to say I worked for them. The bookings I was getting on the indies was always good enough for me to satisfy my itch.

2004 HALL OF FAME

One day Howard Finkel called me up. I was sitting at home, and I really wasn't expecting to hear from him. I was even more surprised to hear what he had to say.

"Vince has decided to really step up the idea of our Hall of Fame. He wants to make it a big deal, not just like a nice dinner thing for the boys like now. He wants to take it public and make an event out of it," he said.

Back then, this was the first real talk of a big legit Hall of Fame, and I didn't know what really to make of it. It was nice to be considered for the first real class. Back a number of years ago, they had done a small thing here and there just for the employees. I went to one where Pedro Morales was actually inducted, and it was very nice, but that "Hall of Fame" was more of just a company party than anything else.

So when Howard was pitching the idea to me, I wasn't saying much. I was pretty much letting him do all the talking and acting somewhat disinterested in the whole thing. Basically, I was using this means of indifference as a negotiating tactic to hold out for a better payday.

CHAPTER 24 – Return to WWF

"Well, I don't know," I said to Howard. "I've been enjoying my time at home and all. I don't really know what to make of all this. I would have to take time off here to make it happen. I don't know."

When he finally told me how much I was going to get paid, that was the only reason I agreed to go.

I know this sounds pretty cold today with tons of guys who really want to be recognized for their time and contributions to the company with this honor. However, back then, we really had no point of reference to use as this was the first real class being inducted. We had no idea that the fans were going to take to the idea and that it would become a highly-anticipated event that would go hand-in-hand with WrestleMania year after year.

It may sound funny to hear that I only agreed to be inducted because I thought I could make a little money on the appearance. But honestly, that was the truth at first.

It turned out that the idea was to make it a real class act. My family from Texas were invited. My mom, my brother, and my sister-in-law were all invited and flown in with everything covered. Vince sent two big limousines to pick me up in Jersey to bring me to New York. They got us all very nice hotel rooms.

Needless to say, I was very surprised and very impressed at what I saw!

When I saw the actual production for the Hall of Fame walking around before the ceremony, I was in shock. A number of times, the WWE had called me to see if I wanted to do a little spot on television, but I just wasn't interested. So seeing how big everything got was a real shock to me. I had retired from the WWF in 1993 and had no idea really how big the company had grown in my absence.

When I went into the locker room, some of the boys were there getting spiffed up so they would look good for television shots as part of the talent section of the audience. I was doing the same when a familiar face came up to me.

"Hey Tito!" Eddie Guerrero said.

"Hello, Eddie," I said. We had met before when he was younger, and now he was the WWF Champion!

"Look, man, I don't know if I will see you again anytime soon. But I wanted you to know that I attribute a lot of my success to you."

"Really?"

"Yes, really. You really opened up the doors of mainstream wrestling to Latinos, and man, I really want to thank you for that."

I get a little teary-eyed just writing this now thinking back about it. Eddie hugged me and it kind of shook me up.

"Thank you so much," I said. "That really means a lot to me."

That really did mean a lot to me when Eddie told me that. He was the champ at the time and defending at Mania.

He went on to tell me how I paved the way for people like him, and how I proved he had a chance to make it so he kept trying. He knew I was very humble, but he went out of his way to explain how he equated what I did and how it created an opportunity for him. I see it now, but back then I didn't know I was making a difference for Hispanics.

It was a great feeling, and still is today when I hear something like that.

The Hall of Fame event itself was a completely different program from the one I had attended earlier. There were wrestling fans from all over the world in attendance, and they were not shy about showing their appreciation for me. I was in awe by the many fans from Japan, Europe and this great nation that came up to me for photos and autographs. I really felt honored.

I was shocked when I found out that Shawn Michaels was going to induct me. Back in the day, Shawn and I had a few misunderstandings outside the ring, which never really turned into much, but still. In the end, he was one of the last guys that I would have expected to come out and say nice things about me. In the end, he was more professional and seemed like a better person all around.

In his speech, he recalled a conversation he had while traveling with Razor Ramon. The pair were riding somewhere together as usual when they both came to the realization that they were both super envious of my spot in the company. Apparently, the boys liked the longevity I had achieved with the WWF, due to my work ethic and always being a team player. I was the only WWF talent to appear in the first nine WrestleMania's, a fact that was not lost on Michaels.

Shawn's speech that night made me realize that a lot of guys had been gunning for my position; the go-to-guy that would always be there and would subsequently always have a spot, no matter how big or small. At the time, I really hadn't thought about it much. I just worked hard and kept my nose clean. That had earned me a lot of respect from the boys and also from Vince.

In the end, I am glad that I was both inducted into the Hall of Fame and that I went to the event. It made me feel very important, and I enjoyed the opportunity to give something back to the fans.

My induction into the Hall of Fame also played a major role in increasing my celebrity status among wrestling fans. That led to more independent wrestling bookings, autograph signings, photo ops and motivational speaking engagements.

For all that, *I am very thankful.*

CHAPTER 25 – SEMI-RETIREMENT

As far as my "retirement status," at the time I am writing this, I am an active 62-year-old wrestler. It is true. I have not officially retired! I still try to stay in pretty good shape, and I still enjoy getting in the ring. These two things go hand-in-hand for me, so when a promoter calls to book me for an independent show, I go!

I have never turned my back on wrestling. I am a weekend warrior of sorts now and scratch my "itch" whenever I can and perform.

As a matter of fact, my wife asks me from time to time, "How much longer do you plan on doing this?"

"As long as the fans don't start hollering 'Get out of the ring you old fart!' I'm going to keep doing it because I really enjoy it," I reply.

It doesn't get old when you step into the ring and you hear the fans let you know how much they appreciate you. This is something that never gets old.

When I aimlessly stepped away from wrestling full time in 1993, my wife said, "Well, why don't you just try teaching?" At the time, I was skeptical. I didn't know if there was really enough money to be made in it at first. Anyhow, I became a substitute teacher just to try it out. Now, believe it or not, by the time you are reading this, I am on my 23rd year of teaching! I have now spent more years as a teacher now then I have as a fulltime wrestler.

When I first started teaching full time after substituting for two years, I was assigned to be a gym teacher at Bound Brook Elementary School in Bound Brook, New Jersey. I was teaching grades 3, 4, 5, and 6. This was about a forty minute commute for me every day. On the drive, much like I did for wrestling shows, I would picture what I was going to do in the classroom on the ride.

For my first three weeks as a middle school gym teacher, everything was fine. Everything was fine, that is, until they gave me an extra class to teach. The funny story you read at the start of the book occurred when they decided

CHAPTER 25 – Semi-Retirement

to throw a curve ball at the middle school gym teacher and force me to teach pre-school.

As I mentioned, the principal just came up to me and pretty much dropped a preschool class in my lap. And in the end, it turned out exactly as I thought it would… *terrible!*

I would blow my whistle, and the kids would just keep on running.

"You can't just take off running!" I would say.

But actually, they could, and they did!

Gym teaching eventually turned into Spanish teaching for me with the older students. That has worked out very well for me and turned into another chapter of my life.

When a wrester asks me for advice today, I tell them to have a good backup plan, or exit plan after wrestling. For me, I got lucky. I fell into teaching and thankfully it turned out very well for me. However, if you don't have that backup plan, it could very easily come back to get you later on in life.

On top of my teaching career, I have another business venture that has done very well for me ever since leaving the ring behind.

For over twenty years now, I have been running Santana's Hair Salon in the Roxbury Mall in Succasunna, New Jersey.

When we first opened up Santana's Hair Salon, I had Sarge and Doink (Ray Apollo) come and do an appearance at the Salon. I never thought it would still be here today!

We must be doing something right. In fact, we have some of the very same hairstylists that have been there for almost 21 years now and have never left us.

The salon is not really wrestling-themed or anything, but there are a few pictures of my wrestling days on the wall. I work there myself every Tuesday, and I make it a point to tell my students that if they want to come talk wrestling, that is the time and the place to do it.

Now, I know they they weren't even born yet when I was on TV, but I can't tell you how many students have come up to me there and say, "You know, my mom said she used to have a crush on you when she was little!"

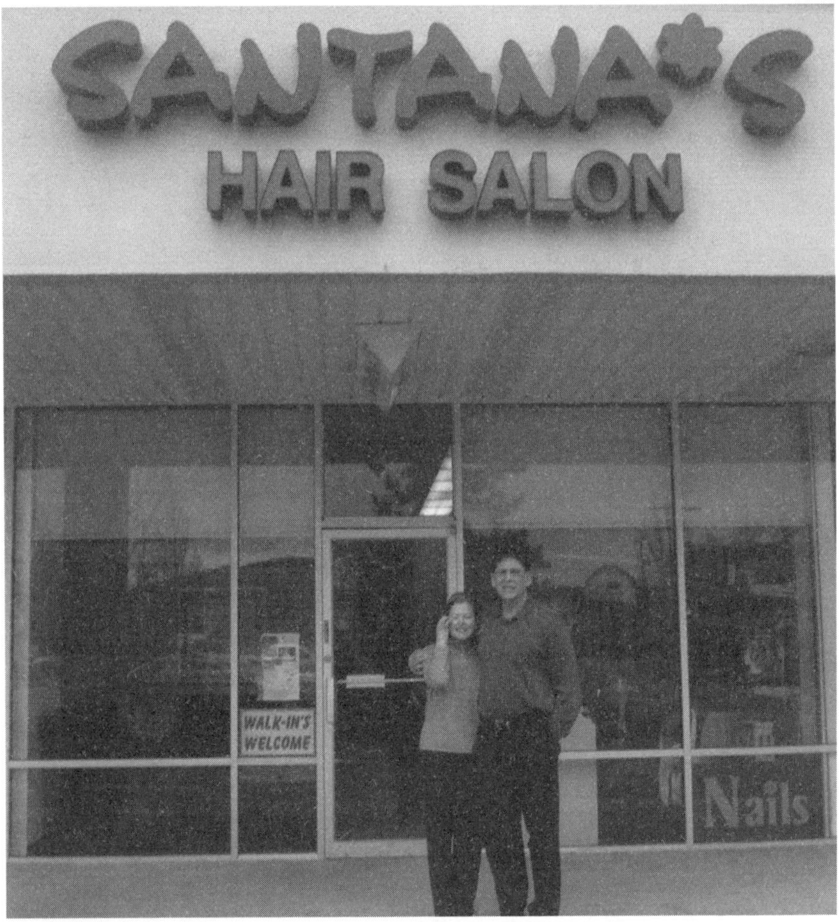
SANTANA'S
HAIR SALON
WALK-IN'S WELCOME
Nails

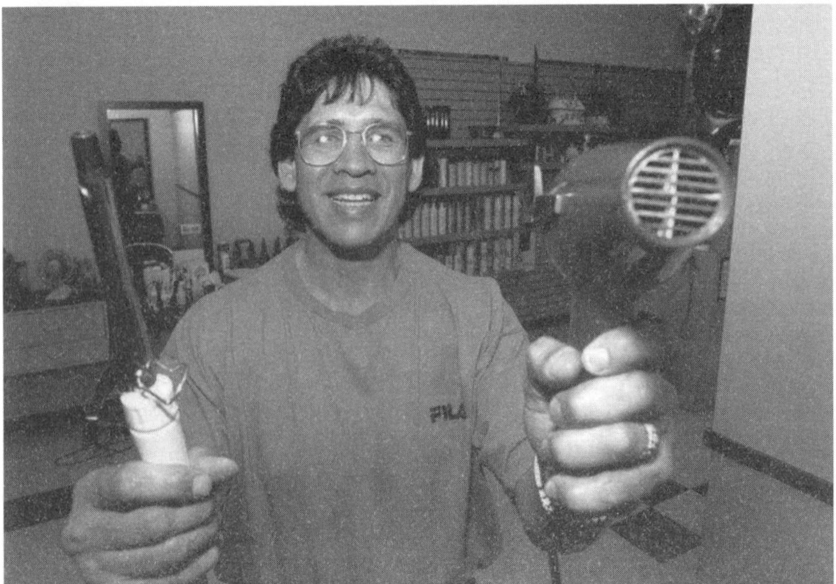
FILA

CHAPTER 25 – Semi-Retirement

See, school is school. I am usually all business there. One of my rules has always been "No autographs at school." However, I tell them that if they want a signed picture, or whatever, or if they want to talk wrestling, all they have to do is stop by the salon. If they want to come on one of my salon days, they can come to get their free autographs and talk wrestling, whatever they want. Just stop by. In school, we have fun, but I give them every opportunity to learn!

FAMILY LIFE

I am happy to have a family I love.

Any time I wrestle on the east coast, I will wrestle and drive back home. I don't go out and party. I drive home to be back with my family.

I have to brag about my wife here first. She raised our children when I was on the road. She knew I was trying to provide for our family the best that I could and did all of the stuff that I couldn't do while I was away.

I am happy to say we raised some pretty wonderful children. We kept my three sons away from stuff like drugs by raising them right and by really giving them some good fundamental values.

Matthew graduated from Rutgers and got his law degree at American University's Washington College of Law. He works for the U.S. government as a Program Analyst in the Veteran's Health Administration.

Michael graduated from Princeton with a degree in Public and International Affairs. He has lived all over the world, working for different human rights organizations. He has completed two Master's degrees, one in International Human Rights Law, and another in Gender and Development. He speaks several languages and is currently the Country Director at Trocaire in Sierra Leone, Africa. Michael is also an advanced Yoga instructor, having studied in India and Bali.

Mark double-majored at James Madison University in Finance and Accounting. He went on to get his Master's degree in Accounting at Fairleigh Dickinson University. He also studied and received his CFA (Chartered Financial Analyst). He works for Factset in New York City and holds the title of VP, Director of Performance, Attribution and Returns Product Development.

I was able to pay for each of my three sons first four years of college because of wrestling. As their parents, we are really proud of our family.

This picture has all of my beautiful family in it, except for my olderst son Michael who was in Africa at the time of the shot!

THANK YOU

    I want to thank Terry Funk for not allowing me to give up in the business before I even got started. I am forever appreciative to André The Giant and Mario Savoldi for helping me get my start in New York, and the friendship of the boys, such as Greg Valentine, Paul Orndorff, Lanny Poffo, Bobby Heenan, Rick Martel and Sgt. Slaughter.

    I also respect and thank the McMahon family for everything that they have done for my family and me.

    And once again, the biggest thanks go out to you, the fans. I want to remind every fan who reads this book that I am eternally thankful for the support. God Bless you and your family.

¡Arriba!

CREDITS

AUTHOR:
Tito Santana

CO-AUTHOR/GHOSTWRITER:
Kenny Casanova

EXECUTIVE PRODUCER & LEGAL CRAP:
Marty Carbone

EDITOR:
Brandi Mankiewicz, PWI Queen

ADDITIONAL CONTENT FROM THE FIRST BOOK:
Tom Caiazzo's *Tales From The Ring*

FINANCIAL GENIUS:
Maria Bevan

WEB SITE GURU:
Kerri LeMay

TIMELINE RESEARCH:
Jim Ruehrwein

RESEARCH/TRANSCRIPTION:
Beth Kempf

BEHIND THE SCENES HELP:
Shockwave The Robot
Mike Johnson
Joseph Feeney III
Ian Douglass
Pete Bregman

GUEST CONTENT:
Jesse Ventura
Konnan
Greg Valentine
Bobby Heenan
Paul Orndorff
Demolition Ax
Sgt. Saughter

COVER ART:
Iron Skull Productions

PHOTO COLLECTION CONTRIBUTIONS:
Tito Santanta
Peter Lederberg (Rookie Shots)
Don Freedman (Red Backdrop Shot)
Chris Swisher Collection (Early Pics)
Howard Lapes (Early Pics)
Dr. Mike Lano (AWA)
John Twomey (Title Credit Page Art)
WWE

HELPFUL RESOURCES:
WOHW.com
KennyCasanova.com
TitoSantana.com
KamalaSpeaks.com
BrutusBeefcake.com
ECWsabu.com
DangerousDannyDavis.com
ItsVaderTime.com
PWInsider.com
Slam Canoe Wrestling
ObsessedWithWrestling.com
BETwrestling.com
ProWrestlingTees.com
Steve Austin Show Podcast
Konnan's "Keepin' it 100" Podcast
Creative Control Network
Something To Wrestle With Podcast
Sean Mooney's Prime Time Podcast

A VERY SPECIAL THANKS FROM KENNY CASANOVA:
I dedicate my work to my incredible wife Maria for putting up with me and dealing with the countless hours spent on these projects! ...to my dad for bringing me to any wrestling show I wanted to go to as a kid and my sisters for "letting" me practice Tito's figure-four on them, as well. ...to Marty The Party for letting me know when something was sick but not illegal. ...and to anyone else who supports these wrestling books to keep the legend alive!

KENNY CASANOVA
CO-AUTHOR/GHOSTWRITER OF THIS BOOK

Kenny is a pro wrestling manager, ring announcer, wedding DJ, English teacher, and Fulbright Scholar. As the organizer of this project and other ones like it, his recent mission has been helping guys like Kamala, Brutus Beefcake, Sabu, Vader & Dangerous Danny Davis get their stories out there for the appreciation of future generations.

Please email questions or promotional inquiries to Kenny himself at **ken@kennycasanova.com**, or find him on all social media platforms.

Walking On Hot Waffles is at WOHW.com
for more books like this including *Kamala Speaks, Brutus Beefcake: Struttin' & Cuttin', Vader Time, Sabu: Scars, Silence, & Superglue,* and *Mr. X: Dangerous Danny Davis.*

★